Japanese/Korean Linguistics

Linguistics
Volume 25

Japanese/Korean Linguistics

Volume 25

edited by
Shin Fukuda, Mary Shin Kim,
and Mee-Jeong Park

*Published for the
Stanford Linguistics
Association by*

CSLI
PUBLICATIONS
Center for the Study of
Language and Information
Stanford, California

Copyright © 2018
CSLI Publications
Center for the Study of Language and Information
Leland Stanford Junior University
Printed in the United States
21 20 19 18   1 2 3 4 5

Library of Congress Cataloging-in-Publication Data

Conference on Japanese/Korean Linguistics (1st : 1989 :
University of Southern California)
Japanese/Korean Linguistics / edited by Hajime Hoji.

Volume 25 / edited by Shin Fukuda, Mary Shin Kim,
and Mee-Jeong Park

    p.   cm.

Includes bibliographical references and index.
ISBN-13: 978-1-68400-042-5
ISBN-13: 978-1-68400-041-8 (pbk.)
eISBN-13: 978-1-68400-043-2 (electronic)
    1. Japanese language—Congresses. 2. Korean
language—Congresses. 3. Japanese language—Grammar,
Comparative—Korean—Congresses. 4. Korean language—Grammar,
Comparative—Japanese—Congresses. 5. Linguistics—Congresses.
I. Hoji, Hajime. II. Stanford Linguistics Association. III. Center for
the Study of Language and Information (U.S.) IV. Title.
PL503.C6 1989
495.6–dc20   90-2550
                        CIP

∞ The acid-free paper used in this book meets the minimum
requirements of the American National Standard for Information
Sciences—Permanence of Paper for Printed Library Materials, ANSI
Z39.48-1984.

CSLI was founded in 1983 by researchers from Stanford University,
SRI International, and Xerox PARC to further the research and
development of integrated theories of language, information, and
computation. CSLI headquarters and CSLI Publications are located
on the campus of Stanford University.

Visit our website at
http://cslipublications.stanford.edu/
for comments on this and other titles, as well as for changes
and corrections by the author and publisher. For the

Japanese/Korean Linguistic Cumulative table of contents, please visit:
https://web.stanford.edu/group/cslipublications/cslipublications/ja-ko-
contents/jako-collective-toc.shtml/

Contents

Acknowledgments

We are delighted to present with this volume the papers delivered at the 25th Japanese/Korean Linguistics Conference (JK25), which met from October 12 to 14, 2017, at the University of Hawaiʻi at Mānoa (UHM) in Honolulu, Hawaii. Over the course of three days, JK 25 featured 28 regular oral presentations and 33 poster presentations that were chosen by double-blind review from 184 abstracts, and five presentations by invited speakers: Natsuko Tsujimura (Indiana University), Seongha Rhee (Hankuk University of Foreign Studies), Masayoshi Shibatani (Rice University), Timothy Vance (National Institute for Japanese Languages and Linguistics), and Nayoung Kwon (Konkuk University).

The papers based on the five invited presentations and 22 oral presentations are featured in this volume. They include four papers from a special session on endangered and understudied languages and dialects in Japan and Korea organized by William O'Grady (UHM) and Shoichi Iwasaki (UCLA) (with an introductory remark by the organizers), and 18 papers that represent the latest research in different sub-fields of Japanese and Korean linguistics, including syntax, semantics, psycholinguistics, phonetics, phonology, discourse analysis, and sociolinguistics. 23 papers based on the poster sessions are available on the volume's supplementary webpage at https://cslipublications.stanford.edu/ja-ko-contents/JK25/.

JK 25 celebrated the invaluable contributions of Professor Emeritus Ho-Min Sohn to Korean linguistics and JK conferences, as he recently retired from his faculty position at UHM. The conference was also held in conjunction with three satellite workshops on morpho-syntax in Japanese and Korean organized by Hiroshi Aoyagi (Nanzan University), prosody and prosody interfaces in Japanese and Korean organized by Haruo Kubozono (National Institute for Japanese Language and Linguistics), and East Asian psycholinguistics organized by Nayoung Kwon (Konkuk University) and Yuki Hirose (University of Tokyo).

We are extremely grateful to 116 reviewers for their expertise and generosity, which allowed us to put together the JK 25 program, and 23 graduate student volunteers from the Department of East Asian Languages and Literatures (EALL), the Department of Linguistics, and the Department of Second Language Studies (SLS), who played vital roles in the success of the conference. We are particularly thankful to our two graduate student assistants, Tyler Nielsen and Hye Young Smith, for their excellent assistance with the preparatin of the concerence and this volume. We would also like to thank Haruko Cook (UHM) and Shoichi Iwasaki (UCLA) for providing us with guidance as we prepared for JK25, and the faculty members in the Department of EALL, the Department of Linguistics, and the Department of SLS at UHM for their support for JK 25. Last but not least, we would like to express our gratitude to everyone who participated in the conference and made it a success.

JK 25 was supported by generous funds from the following units in UHM: Center for Korean Studies; Center for Japanese Studies (Japanese Studies Endowment); College of Languages, Linguistics, and Literature; Department of East Asian Languages and Literatures; and Japanese Language and Literature Fund.

Finally, our thanks are due to Dana Kendra Peters at CSLI, who patiently and meticulously answered every question we asked her while we prepared this volume.

Shin Fukuda,
Mary Shin Kim,
Mee-Jeong Park,
Department of East Asian Languages and Literatures
University of Hawai'i at Mānoa

Part I

Special Session

Endangered Indigenous Languages in Japan and Korea*

WILLIAM O'GRADY
University of Hawai'i at Mānoa

SHOICHI IWASAKI
Univeristy of California, Los Angeles

According to standard popular accounts, Japan and Korea are highly unusual countries in that each recognizes the existence of just one indigenous language within its borders—Japanese and Korean, respectively. [1] This absence of linguistic diversity contrasts sharply with the situation elsewhere

---

*This work was supported by the Core University Program for Korean Studies through the Ministry of Education of the Republic of Korea and the Korean Studies Promotion Service of the Academy of Korean Studies (AKS-2015-OLU-2250005).
[1] We set Ainu to the side in the case of Japan, as it appears to no longer have a community of native speakers.

Japanese/Korean Linguistics 25.
Edited by Shin Fukuda, Mary Shin Kim, and Mee-Jeong Park.

in Asia, in which almost all countries acknowledge the presence of multiple distinct languages, as summarized in Table 1.

Country	Number of indigenous languages
Bhutan	21
China	275
Indonesia	701
Mongolia	7
Myanmar (Burma)	112
Philippines	175
Taiwan	20
Thailand	50
Vietnam	93

TABLE 1 Language Diversity in a Sample of Asian Countries (data from Ethnologue.com)

There is good reason to believe that Japan and Korea also manifest significant linguistic diversity, and that a more accurate picture of their linguistic make-up would recognize at least eight indigenous languages in Japan and at least two in Korea (with Hamgyeong as a possible third).

Japan	Korea
Japanese	Korean
Amami	Jejueo
Kunigami	Hamgyeong (?)
Miyako	
Okinawan	
Yaeyama	
Yonaguni	
Hachijo	
(Ainu)	

TABLE 2 Indigenous languages in Japan and Korea

The existence of linguistic variation in Japan and Korea is widely acknowledged in both countries, but its significance has been obscured by the insistence that it consists only of 'dialectal' differences. The question of how to distinguish between a language and a dialect has long been problematic for a variety of reasons, largely because of two competing approaches to the definition of language—one political and the other linguistic.

The political definition tends to equate the notions of 'language' and 'nation'—an association that Weinreich (1945) humorously characterized with the help of the now famous aphorism 'A language is a dialect with an army and a navy.' The implausiblity of the association is reinforced by the overwhelming mismatch between the number of recognized nations (197, according to the United Nations) and the number of identified languages (over 7000, according to estimates by Ethnologue).

In contrast, the linguistic definition focuses on mutual intelligibility, a notion put forward most influentially by Hockett (1958:321), who suggested that 'people who "speak the same language" can understand each other and, conversely, that people who cannot understand each other must be speaking "different languages".' The proposal is not entirely unproblematic, as Hockett acknowledged in detail, since intelligibility is a matter of degree, and questions arise as to how it should be tested, what the cut-off point should be, whether it should involve the written language or the spoken language, and so on (for discussion, see Gooskens 2013). Nonetheless, Hockett's criterion often yields clear-cut results, and when it does—as in the case of, say, Dutch and Norwegian or Cantonese and Mandarin—there is no serious dissent among *linguists* as to whether distinct languages are in play (despite politically driven claims to the contrary in the latter case).

A vivid illustration of how the political and linguistic criteria for language-hood can clash comes from Jejueo, the traditional speech of Korea's Jeju Island. In a study involving 56 participants, Yang, O'Grady et al. (2018) demonstrated that Jejueo is largely unintelligible to people who speak only Korean. Success rates on comprehension questions designed to test understanding of a Jejueo narrative were less than 10%—an outcome roughly equivalent to the results of a similar test of the ability of Dutch speakers to understand Norwegian. Yet, the conclusion that Jejueo should be considered a language was promptly rejected by the National Institute of the Korean Language, which insists that Jejueo is simply a regional variant of Korean. In the words of one scholar who insists on dialectal status for Jejueo (Kim 2016:109-10), 'It might [be] okay to call Jejueo a language if Jeju Island had been an independent country and Jeju people had a different ethnicity. However, those two requirements are not met.' This stance reflects the long-standing belief in Korea that 'the notions of a single race/nation and single language are central to modern Korean concepts of national identity' (King 2007:229). However, it clearly runs counter to the status that Jejueo deserves: it is not a national language, but it is nonetheless a language.

The tradition of calling Japan's Ryukyuan languages 'dialects' started in the nineteenth century when the Meiji government absorbed the Ryukyu Kingdom, which had been independent from the fifteenth to the nineteenth century. A century later, the new nationalistic ideology was reflected in the then-Prime Minister Nakasone's 1986 description of Japan as a mono-ethnic nation. Although UNESCO's 2009 report on the endangered status of Ryukyuan languages prompted positive changes in the minds of Japanese people in general and some linguists in particular, the idea that Japan is a multi-ethnic and multi-lingual society needs the continuing endorsement and support of specialists.

The plight of the minority languages of Japan and Korea is dire. According to UNESCO estimates (http://www.unesco.org/languages-Atlas/), Jejueo is critically endangered, Yaeyama and Yonaguni are severely endangered, and Kunigami, Miyako, Okinawan, Amami and Hachijo are definitively endangered. These languages are all a vital part of the cultural history and fabric of their respective countries. Unless urgent and appropriate action is taken to support their preservation, they will be lost forever. The first step in that direction is to recognize their existence as languages in their own right.

In an attempt to heighten awareness of this important issue, the organizers of the 25th Japanese/Korean Linguistics Conference organized a special session on language endangerment in Japan and Korean, which included the introductory remarks on which this report is based, as well as the four presentations that follow in this volume. In addition, conference attendees were invited to endorse a statement calling for the recognition and preservation of the minority languages of Japan and Korea. That document, along with the signatures of fifty-nine linguists, has since been sent to the consulates of Japan and Korea in Honolulu as well as to the National Institute for Japanese Language and Linguistics and the National Institute of the Korean Language. We conclude our report with the statement itself.

Statement on Language Endangerment in Japan and Korea:

Since the publication in 1992 of a special issue of *Language* devoted to the problem of language endangerment,[†] there has been a general consensus that our responsibility as professional linguists extends beyond the challenges of linguistic analysis. We also have a duty to educate the public about language, especially on matters that involve social policy and communal welfare.

As linguists, we lament the ever-accelerating loss of linguistic diversity in the world, not only because of our scientific interest in the properties of language but also because we recognize that language is integral to a community's identity, as well as an essential part of the cultural history and heritage of the nation in which it is spoken.

[†]Hale, Ken, Michael Krauss, Lucille J. Watahomigie, Akira Y. Yamamoto, Colette Craig, LaVerne Masayesva Jeanne, Nora C. England. 1992. Endangered languages. *Language* 68:1-42.

As specialists in the languages of Japan and Korea, it is our professional responsibility to inform our colleagues, as well as the general public, about linguistic diversity and language endangerment in those countries, with special attention to the following vital facts:

• Varieties of speech that are not mutually intelligible are, by definition, distinct languages, regardless of their official or popular classification as dialects of the national language.

• Both Japan and Korea are linguistically diverse countries. In addition to rich and well documented dialectal variation, both are home to indigenous *languages* other than the official national language. These languages include Amami, Kunigami, Okinawan, Miyako, Yaeyama, Yonaguni, Hachijo and Ainu in the case of Japan and Jejueo in the case of Korea.

• It is possible that new research in each country will lead to the reclassification of other speech varieties as languages rather than dialects.

• The currently identified minority languages of both countries are seriously endangered. The situation has been exacerbated by stigmatization and official neglect stemming from ignorance about the status of these languages and their importance to the cultural fabric of the nations in which they are spoken. Without intervention, they will soon disappear forever.

• It is often possible to revitalize endangered languages if prompt action is taken by the appropriate agencies working in cooperation with trained linguists and with the communities where those languages are spoken.

References

Gooskens, Charlotte. 2013. Experimental methods for measuring intelligibility of closely related language varieties. *The Oxford Handbook of Sociolinguistics*, ed. R. Bayley, R. Cameron & C. Lucas, 195-213. Oxford, UK: Oxford University Press.

Hockett, Charles. 1958. *A Course in Modern Linguistics*. New York: Macmillan.

Kim, Jee-hong. 2016. Jeju Bangeonui Seoneomaleomiwa Jonggyeoleomi Chegye. [Jeju Dialect Prefix and Suffix System] *Hangeul* 313, 109-71.

King, Ross. 2007. North and South Korea. *Language and National Identity in Asia*, ed. A. Simpson, 200-34. Oxford: Oxford University Press.

Weinreich, Max. 1945. The YIVO Faces the Post-War World [in Hebrew], *YIVO Bleter: Journal of the Yiddish Scientific Institute* 25, January – June, 3-18.

Yang, C., O'Grady, W., Yang, S., Hilton, N., Kang, S. and Kim, S. 2018. Revising the Language Map of Korea. *The Changing World Language Map*, ed. S. Braun. Berlin: Springer. Available at: https://changingworldlanguagemap.weebly.com/

Dialects in Diaspora or Diaspora Dialects: Distinguishing Transplanted Varieties of Korean

SIMON BARNES-SADLER
SOAS, University of London

1 Introduction[1]

Current estimates put the population of Koreans living overseas at just over 7.4 million people (MoFA 2018). While the greater part of the migration from the Korean peninsula which led to this situation has taken place in the latter half of the twentieth century, it origins stretch back far further. Historical records attest to Koreans migrating to and settling in China and Russia in the 1860s (Piao 1990; Belikov 1991). The Korean language has spread with this global diaspora, but the formal linguistic study of transplanted varieties of Korean is a relatively recent development beginning with the work of King (1987) and Kwak (1987).

---

[1] This work was supported by Laboratory Program for Korean Studies through the Ministry of Education of the Republic of Korea and Korean Studies Promotion Service of the Academy of Korean Studies (AKS-2016-LAB-2250003)

Japanese/Korean Linguistics 25.
Edited by Shin Fukuda, Mary Shin Kim, and Mee-Jeong Park.

The current study hopes to contribute to this growing field of work on transplanted varieties of Korean by not only developing the empirical basis for their description, but also by highlighting alternative approaches to them, namely, direct comparison of transplanted varieties and quantitative analysis.

To this end, we first present an overview of tendencies in the prior research on the longest-standing, most researched transplanted varieties, upon which we also focus here: China's Vernacular Yanbian Korean (VYK) and Central Asia's Koryo Mar (KM). We then go on to outline the data upon which this study is based, then the quantitative techniques used in the analysis of this data are summarised before the results of this analysis are presented and discussed in detail. We conclude by identifying characteristic points of difference between these transplanted varieties of Korean, situating the current research within Korean dialectology, and discussing prospects for future research.

Examples of VYK and KM are presented in a broad IPA transcription and glossed using the Leipzig Glossing Rules. Contemporary Standard Korean (CSK) will be transliterated using the Yale Romanisation except in the case of personal or place names with conventionalised or preferred Romanisations.

2 Prior Approaches

Prior research into VYK and KM has largely been carried out within the framework of traditional Korean dialectology. This has, naturally, been influential in terms of the methods used in the collection and analysis of linguistic data. Strong claims about the features of these varieties (e.g. Kwak et al. 2008) and even full descriptions (e.g. Kwon 2010) have been made on the basis of consultation with only one or two speakers using data which draws heavily on explicit ellicitation and, by implication, those consultants' meta-linguistic knowledge.

A further common feature of earlier research into transplanted varieties of Korean is explicit comparison with the traditionally accepted dialects of the Korean peninusla. As a result of this it is not uncommon to conflate the language used by individual KM or VYK speakers with their specific progenitor dialects on the Korean peninsula (e.g. Pak 2005) and to characterise the transplanted varieties more broadly in terms of their similarities and differences to these varieties. Since these varieties have similar dialectological origins, it is easy to find examples of features presented as characteristic of KM which are also presented as characteristic of VYK, and vice-versa. Concrete cases of this include the phonological reduction of particles and the use of so-called 'Yukchin' formal verb endings, as in the examples drawn from prior research below:

KM: [jəgi-nɨ   musɨ   bazar-i   naga-mə]
         here-TOP   some   market-ACC go out-CONJ
         If you go out to a market here…
                                 (Kwon 2010:28)

VYK: [sənsæ-nɨ   sanbo   ai   ka-lgejo]
         teacher-TOP stroll NEG go-FUT.DECL.POL
         The teacher will not go on the trip.
                                 (Jeong 2010: 58)

KM: [ka-k'uma]
         go-PRES.DECL.POL
         (S)he goes.
                    (Yi et al. 2000: 48)

VYK: [ʃal   məg-es'-ɨk'uma]
         well   eat-PST-DECL.POL
         I ate well.
                (Kim 2013:85)

This, may lead to an impression that these varieties share a very high degree of similarity, or even to their implicit conflation. It is questionable whether the extent to which features such as these, which occur variably in the speech of Central Asian and Chinese Koreans, may be considered equally characteristic of both KM and VYK.

While we acknolwedge that there are features shared by VYK and KM as a result of their common heritage, and these features distinguish them from CSK and other peninsula varieties of Korean, the results of over 150 years of divergent development in very different transplanted contexts must not be overlooked. In contrast with the tendencies of prior research noted in the foregoing, this paper explicitly addresses the issue of linguistic (dis)similarity between these two varieties and presents a direct comparison of VYK and KM, made on the basis of more naturalistic (albeit not wholly natural) data provided by a relatively large sample of consultants. In the next section we introduce the methodology informing the collection of this data along with a characterisation of the KM and VYK speaking consultants.

3   Data Collection and Consultants

A primary goal for this research was the collection of linguistic data which differs from that of earlier research in terms of its ecological validity, and the extent to which it relied on consultants' meta-linguistic knowledge. This goal was fulfilled by using a modified version of Tagliamonte's sociolinguistic interview schedule (2006) to conduct and record semi-structured interviews with VYK and KM consultants. This method represents a compromise between gathering maximally naturalistic and maximally comparable data in that it enabled the recording of language which is more naturalistic than ellicited speech, while allowing for a more systematic comparison between speakers and varieties than simply recording observed communicative events haphazardly.

An additional goal was the consultation of a larger number of speakers than previous studies. Consultants were recruited through snowball sampling following introductions made by researchers embedded in each community. A total of 12 VYK speakers and 10 KM speakers were included in this study. The only criterion for inclusion was self-identification as a VYK or KM speaker. Further particulars on each consultant's background may be found in the tables below with columns recording their unique identifier numbers, year of birth, sex, place of birth, place of residence, and the highest level of formal education into which they had been enrolled:

ID	Year of Birth	Sex	Place of Birth	Place of Residence	Level of Education
1	1992	Male	Yanji	Yanji	Tertiary
2	Pre-1960	Female	Ryeongjeong	Ryeongjeong	Secondary
3	1991	Male	Yanji	Yanji	Tertiary
4	1951	Male	Ryeongjeong	Ryeongjeong	Secondary
5	1992	Male	Ryeongjeong	Yanji	Tertiary
6	1993	Male	Yanji	Yanji	Tertiary
7	1992	Male	Ryeongjeong	Yanji	Tertiary
8	1981	Female	Antu	Yanji	Tertiary
9	Pre-1970	Male	Hwaryeong	Yanji	Secondary
10	1991	Male	Yanji	Yanji	Tertiary
11	1961	Female	Hwaryeong	Yanji	Secondary
12	1993	Female	Yanji	Yanji	Tertiary

TABLE 1 Basic Social Information for VYK Consultants

ID	Year of Birth	Sex	Place of Birth	Place of Residence	Level of Education
13	1932	Female	Chabirovsky Kray, Russia	Almaty[1], Kazakhstan	None
14	1944	Female	Almaty, Kazakhstan	Almaty, Kazakhstan	Tertiary
15	1942	Female	Katta-Kurgan, Uzbekistan	Katta-Kurgan, Uzbekistan	None
16	1940	Male	Tashkent, Uzbekistan	Almaty, Kazakhstam	Primary
17	1933	Female	Chabirovsky Kray, Russia	Almaty Kazakhstan	None
18	Pre-1960	Female	Tashkent, Uzbekistan	Almaty, Kazakhstan	Secondary Technical
19	1941	Female	Almaty, Kazakhstan	Almaty, Kazakhstan	Secondary Technical
20	1940	Male	Almaty, Kazakhstan	Almaty, Kazakhstan	Primary
21	1940	Female	Almaty, Kazakhstan	Almaty, Kazakhstan	Tertiary
22	1923	Female	Chabirovsky Kray, Russia	Almaty[1], Kazakhstan	None

TABLE 2 Basic Social Information for KM Consultants

From the above, we can identify several points of difference between the sample of KM speaking consultants and the sample of VYK speaking consultants. Most obvious among these are the differences in sex and age. The greater age of most KM consultants and the fact that the majority were female may be attributed to the on-going shift from KM to Russian. Vanishingly few people younger than the grand-parent generation consider themselves speakers of KM, therefore our sample was drawn exclusively from that age group. This influenced the unequal representation of men and women in the KM speaking groups since women are estimated to outnumber men by almost two-to-one for that age cohort in Kazakhstan. The opposite gender imbalance may be seen in the group of VYK consultants in addition to a broader range of ages. Coincidentally, this imbalance in numbers of male and female consultants reflects general patterns of the demography of these countries and speech communities (CIA 2018a; CIA 2018b), however it is not clear if other disimilarities between the sample groups are similarly representative.

Another notable difference between the groups is a tendency for KM speakers to be more mobile and reside a considerable distance from their place of birth. Furthermore we note that at least some formal Korean-medium education was universal for members of the VYK speaking group, but a rarity for members of the KM speaking group. This may be attributed to the status of Korean as co-official language in China's Yanbian Korean Autonomous Prefecture (YKAP) (Tai 2004), in contrast to its lack of recognition in Kazakhstan.

While neither sample can be claimed to be fully representative of the VYK or KM speaking communities, we emphasise that this study still incorporates a much wider range of data than much of the prior research. Furthermore, while we emphasise the greater ecological validity of this data in comparison to more traditionally dialectological approaches, sociolingiuistic interviews cannot be regarded as entirely natural speech acts and, while attempts to mitigate it were taken, the well-known 'observer's paradox' (see Labov 1972: 113) can be assumed to have had some influence on the data provided by the consultants.

4   Methods

4.1   The Feature Catalogue

In order to run these analyses a 'top down' feature catalogue (Wolk and Szmrecsanyi 2016) was compiled on the basis of earlier work on VYK and KM and qualitative analysis of the recordings and their transcriptions. It was composed of thirty three variable features, specified in the following sub-sections.

4.1.1   Phonology

The phonological features included in the catologue cover a range of phenomena including the variable realisation of particular phonemes (realisation of /c/ as an alveolar or post-alveolar affricate, the realisation of /l/ as a trill, monophthongal realisations of traditional high front rounded vowels), the presence or absence of certain phonemes (specifically phoneme /v/ and the single phoneme resulting from the widespread merger of /ay/ and /ey/) phonotactic constraints (application of the 'head-sound rule', nasal deletion before high front vowels), and the application or not of particlar phonological processes in the consultants' speech (palatalisation of word initial /k/ before high front vowels and realisation of intervocalic /k/ as /p/). Thus, a total of nine phonological features were included.

4.1.2   Nominal Morphology

Special attention has been given to the forms of KM and VYK particles (e.g. Jeong 2010; Kim 2013). There is considerable overlap in the attested forms, however, here we concern ourselved with their distribution. The consultants' speech samples were coded for the presence or absence of the following particle forms: subject particle forms -ka and -ika, object particle forms -u, wu, or -lu, and topic particle forms -u/nu, and -unu. Also coded for was the functional rather than formal distinction of the object particle being used to mark animate beneficieries. A total of six nominal morphological features were coded for in the catalogue.

4.1.3   Verbal Morphology

The verbal morphology of KM and VYK, too, has been a particular object of interest for earlier research (e.g. Jeong 2010). The presence or absence of the following sentence final endings in consultants' speech was considered for this study: 'Yukchin' formal endings, 'North Hamgyeong' formal endings, CSK formal endings, CSK -a/eyo endings, and the plain, declarative -ci ending. Additionally the conjunctive endings –[anaj] (c.f. CSK –(u)nikka),- [gilej] (c.f. CSK -ki ttay muney), –[mjənsəɾi]/-[səɾi] (c.f. CSK -myense), and phonologically reduced forms of CSK -myen. The use of the verb final nominalizing ending -ki rather than CSK -ko in volitional constructions was also recorded. Finally, we also coded consultants' speech for pre-final endings marking subject honorification for a total of eleven verbal morphological features in the catalogue.

4.1.4   Word Order

As mentioned above, the majority of research carried out on transplanted varieties of Korean relies on data collected from direct ellicitation. The more natural speech collected for this study allows us to compare not just individual words and grammatical paradigms, but language in use. Specifically, the presence or absence of three features were included in the catalogue the long form negation (c.f. CFK haci anhta – to not do), seperable negation (e.g. [ara mo duɾo] – I do not understand c.f. CSK mos alatuleyo), and verbally post-posed oblique arguments.

4.1.5   Vocabulary

The vocabularies of both of these transplanted varieties differ starkly from that of CSK. Most notably, and naturally given their contact with the respective languages of wider communications in the areas in which they are spoken, a large number of Russian and Chinese words have been borrowed into KM and VYK, respectively. Here, though, we examine the use of words of Native Korean or Sino-Korean etymology which have been identified for these varieties and which were observed to appear in both VYK and KM primary data. Specifically, the four lexical features included in the catalogue are: non-standard kinship terms (e.g. [əʃi] – parents, [orɛbi] – elder brother of a woman, etc.), archaic demonstrative pronouns of place (e.g. [iŋgi] – here, [kəŋge] – there), k-stem nouns (e.g. [kalgi] – flour), and the productive use of the word *cil* - work.

4.2   Data Processing and Analysis

In order to proceed with statistical analysis, a feature matrix marking the presence or absence of each feature in the speech samples of each consultant was created. There are advantages and disadvantages to such binary coding, for our purposes, though, the former were found to outweigh the latter. For example, since consultants' speech data was not constrained and maximally natural, highly variable frequencies of different features could be observed in different consultants' speech. Our categorical coding gives each consultant equal weighting in the analysis despite the unequal amount of data which they provided, so a potentially outlying ideolect of single speaker would not have too great an influence on our results. Conversely, this coding does obscure each feature's absolute freqency and its context of appearance in each consultant's speech, both of which are potential areas for future investigation.

These data then underwent two quantitative analyses: agglomerative clustering and Categorical Principal Components Analysis (CATPCA). Due to the categorical coding of the data, both analyses were carried out using SPSS (IBM 2013), relying on optimal scaling as implemented in the supplementary Categories Module of that program (Meulman, Heiser and SPSS 2004).

4.3   Statistical Techniques

Following Johnson's typology for quantitative methods in linguistics (2008: 3) the statistical analyses which we carry out here have the goals of relationship discovery (clustering) and data reduction (CATPCA). In lieu of providing the full background of and reasoning behind the application of quantitative techniques in dialectology, we simply note that analyses from the same 'families' of tests are widely used in quantitative dialectology and have been characterised as the "quantitative analog to the identification of dialect regions" and the "quantitative analog to the identification of isogloss bundles in traditional dialectology", respectively (Grieve et al 2011: 20; 17). As is implicit in the quotations above, the applications of these techniques tend to be somewhat more geolinguistic than their proposed use here. Nevertheless, these techniques are appropriate for determining whether our consultant divided into groups on the basis of their status as KM or VYK speakers and, if so, which features are most strongly associated with these groups.

5   Findings

5.1   Cluster Analysis

We first discuss the findings of the cluster analysis, specifically hierarchical, agglomerative clustering using Ward's method (for discussion of the suitability of different clustering algorithms to linguistic data sat Prokić and Nerbonne 2008). A dendrogram of the clustering schedule is presented below:

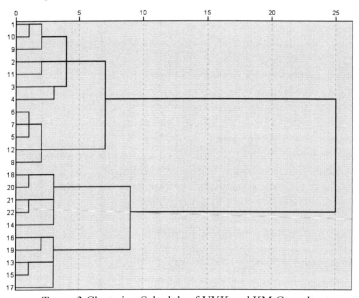

TABLE 3 Clustering Schedule of VYK and KM Consultants

Two groups of consultants can be clearly identified. Numbers 1 to12, the upper group, correspond with the VYK speakers and numbers 13 to 22, the lower group, correspond with the KM speakers. The long branches separating these groups represent a high degree of disimilarity between these groups, thus we are able to conclude that on the aggregate basis of the presence or absence of the thirty-three linguistic features identified above in our speech samples we are able to distinguish between VYK and KM.

Also of note in the above dendrogram are the smaller clusters within the KM and VYK groups. While we hesitate to draw firm conclusions from such small numbers, impressionistic examination of these sub-groups in relation to speaker age, gender, and level of education does not reveal any particular patterning. This leaves us with two possible conclusions with regard to the variety-internal heterogeneity which this analysis reveals. While it does not appear to be attributable to any major sociological indicator, it is possible that some social or other external factor for which data was not collected, for example degree of contact with CSK, may be relevant. Furthermore, we are not able to rule out the possibility that the sub-grouping is a statistical artefact caused either by the composition of the small sample group or the known tendency of Ward's clustering method to produce evenly sized groups.

5.2 Categorical Principal Components Analysis

We now turn to the CATPCA. This allows for the identification of small number of underlying linear variables (the principal components) from the larger set of originally observed variables (the feature catalogue). Just two principal components were found to account of over half of the observed variance in the data. In more detail, 41% of the variance was accounted for by the first principal comonent, and 17% of the variance was accounted for by the second. A visualisation of the consultants arranged in a scatter plot with the x and y axes representing the first and second principal components, respectively, may be seen below.

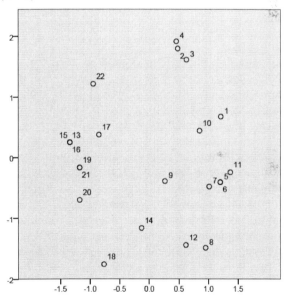

TABLE 4 Scatterplot of Consultants on First and Second Principal Components

The consultants retain the same numbering as in the dendrogram. Inspection of the scatterplot reveals similar, albeit somewhat less clear, grouping of KM and VYK speaking consultants. The KM group is loosely clustered towards the left end of the first principal component and has negative values on the x-axis. Speakers belonging to the VYK group are universally towards the right end of the first principal component and have positive values along the x-axis.

Each linguistic feature in the catalogue is assigned a score (component loading) which may be understood as representative of its association with each component. Those with larger negative loadings for the first principal component which patterned with the distribution of KM speakers in the above feature space were identified as characteristic for our sample of KM speech while those with the larger positive loadings for the first principal component which patterned with the VYK speakers were taken as representative of our sample of VYK speech.

The linguistic features which are most strongly associated with VYK are alveolar realisation of /c/, word initial /r/ and /n/ (non-application of the 'head sound rule), subject particle /ka/, used of 'North Hamgyeong' formal endings, long form negation, subject honorification, and the monopthongal realisation of /oy/ and /wi/. The linguistic features which were found to be most strongly associated with the KM sample were trilled /r/, non-etymological /v/, use of conjunctive ending –*anai*, use of archaic demonstrative pronouns of place, extended use of the ending -*ci*, and marking animate benficieries with the particle –*ru*.

We reiterate here that the above analyses represent a direct comparison between two transplanted varieties. The features associated with VYK and KM by the CATPCA only distinguish these varieties from each other and do not necessarily distinguish them from other varieties of Korean. For example, morphological subject honorification is not specific to VYK, but may be found in CSK and many other varieties of peninsula Korean, however, since our focus here is identifying points of difference between specifically KM and VYK we consider its use by VYK speakers noteworthy for its role in distinguishing these transplanted.

Although a key concern of this paper has been examining transplanted varieties of Korean in their own terms rather than with reference to CSK or other peninsula varieties of Korean, it is striking that all of the features identified above as distinguishing VYK from KM other than the alveolar realisation of /c/ may be found in other standard and non-standard varieties of Korean on the peninsula. The features most strongly associated with KM, though, are not observed in many other varieties of Korean. Possible explanations for this include greater standardisation of the language in the YKAP and the influence of more geographically proximate varieties of Korean, although further research would be required to conclusively reveal the accuracy of either theory.

6 Conclusion

The general findings of this paper, namely, that VYK and KM may be clearly differentiated on the basis of the aggregate presence or absence of various linguistic features and that certain of these features are strongly associated with just one of these varieties, is not in itself surprising.

Its main contributions, though, are twofold and particular to the field of research concerning variation in Korean. First, while the quantitative paradigm, if not the specific statistical techniques used in this paper, is cross-linguistically widely used, it is relatively uncommon in Korean dialectology. The identification of points of difference between KM and VYK using such methods adds empirical weight to the argument that new varieties of Korean are developing outside of the Korean peninsula (see Silva 2010).

Second, the empirical findings of this research open the door for investigation of of the role played by the transplanted context, both linguistic and social, in shaping diaspora varieties of Korean. That concrete points of difference between the superficially similar VYK and KM identified here may be examined within cross-lingusitically applied explanatory frameworks, for example Heine and Kuteva's contact induced grammatical replication (2005) or Trudgill's Sociolinguistic Typology (2010), and provide an additional perspective which either supports or challenges their claims.

References

CIA. 2018a *Kazakhstan* World Factbook Retrieved 12th March 2018 from https://www.cia.gov/library/publications/the-world-factbook/geos/kz.html

CIA. 2018a *China* World Factbook Retrieved 12th March 2018 from https://www.cia.gov/library/publications/the-world-factbook/geos/ch.html

Grieve, J., Speelman, D., Geeraerts, D. 2011. A Statistical Method for the Identification and Aggregation of Regional Linguistic Data. *Language Variation and Change* 23: 1-29.

Heine, B. and Kuteva, D. 2005. *Language Contact and Grammatical Change*. Cambridge: Cambridge University Press

IBM Corp. 2013. *IBM SPSS for Windows, Version 22.0*. Armonk, NY: IBM Corp.

Jeong Hyang-ran. 2010. *Yenpyen pangenuy kokyongkwa hwalyong* [Inflection and Declension in Yanbian Dialect]. Paju: Hankwuk hakswul cengpo.

Johnson, K. 2008. *Quantitative Methods in Linguistics*. Malden, MA; Osford: Blackwell Publishing.

Kim Seon-hui. 2013. Yenpyen pangen yenkwu: xosawa cwungyelemilul cwungsimulo. *Hanmincok emunhak* 64: 71-98.

King, R. 1987. An Introduction to Soviet Korean. *Language Research* 23(2): 233-277.

Kwak Chung-gu. 1987. Nohan hoyhwawa hampuk kyenghung pangen. *Cintan hakpo* 62: 79-124.

Kwak Chung-gu, Pak Jin-hyeok, and So Shin-ae. 2008. *Cwungkwuk icwu hanmincokuy enewa saynghwal: killimseng hoylyongpong* . Paju: Thayhaksa

Kwon Jae-il. 2010. *Cwungangasia kolyemaluy munpep*. Seoul: Sewultayhakkyo chwulphanmunhwawen.

Labov, W. 1972. *Sociolinguistic Patterns*. Philadelphia, PA: University of Pennsylvania Press.

Meulman, J.J., Heiser, W.J. and SPSS, 2004. *SPSS Categories 13.0*. Armonk, NY: IBM Corp.

Ministry of Foreign Affairs 2018. *Total Number of Overseas Koreans*. Retrieved from http://eng.korean.net/portal_en/information/knt.do Februrary 14th 2018.

Pak, N.S. 2005. *Koreyskiy Yazik v Kazakhstane: Problemy i Perspektivy*. Almaty: Kazakh Ministry for Science and Education.

Piao Changu. 1990. The History of Koreans in China and the Yanbian Korean Autonomous Prefecture. *Koreans in China*, eds. Suh Dae-Sook and E.J. Schultz, 44-77. Honolulu: University of Hawai'i, Center for Korean Studies.

Prokić, J. and Nerbonne, J. 2008. Recognizing Groups Among Dialects. *International Journal of Humanities and Arts Computing* 2(1-2), *Special Issue on Language Variation*: 153-172.

Silva, D. 2010. Death, Taxes, and Language Change: The Inevitable Divergence of Korean Varieties as Spoken Worldwide. *Contemporary Korean Linguistics: International Perspectives*, ed. Lee Sang-Oak, 300-319. Paju: Thayhaksa.

Tagliamonte, S. 2006. *Analysing Sociolinguistic Variation*. Cambridge: CUP.

Tai Pingwu. 2004. Language Policy and Standardization of Korean in China. *Language Policy in the People's Republic of China: Theory and Practice since 1949*, eds. Zhou Minglang and Sun Hongkai, 303-316. Boston, MA: Kluwer Academic Publishers.

Trudgill, P. 2011. *Sociolinguistic Typology: The Social Determinants of Linguistic Complexity*. New York, NY: Oxford University Press.

Wolk, C.B.S. and Szmrecsanyi, B. 2016. Top-down and Bottom-up Advances in Corpus Based Dialectometry. *The Future of Dialects*, eds. M-H. Côté, R. Knooihuizen, and J. Nerbonne, 225-244. Berlin: Language Science Press.

Yi Ki-gap, Kim Ju-won, Choi Dong-ju and Yi Heon-jong. 2000. Cwungangasia hanintuluy hankwuke yenkwu. *Hangul* 247: 5-72.

Spatial Frames of Reference in Miyako: Digging into Whorfian Linguistic Relativity*

KENAN CELIK

Kyoto University

YUKINORI TAKUBO

NINJAL

RAFAEL NÚÑEZ
University of California San Diego

1 Introduction

The Whorf-Sapir linguistic relativity hypothesis states that there are fundamental and pervasive influences of language on thought (Whorf 1956). Relatively recently, a preferred arena for investigating this hypothesis has been the study of spatial frames of reference (Levinson 2003). While speakers of some languages have been found to prefer relative frames of

* This research was supported by grants from the Japan Society for the Promotion of Science (17H02333, 25284078, 15J07204).

Japanese/Korean Linguistics 25.
Edited by Shin Fukuda, Mary Shin Kim, and Mee-Jeong Park.

reference (e.g. 'left' and 'right') to describe or think about relative positions of tabletop objects, others prefer absolute frames of reference (e.g. 'North', 'South') (Gumperz & Levinson 1996). A common interpretation of these results is that language plays a significant role in structuring fundamental domains (e.g., space) at a neurocognitive level (Majid et al. 2004). However, what are the preferences of bilingual speakers who speak languages that encode clashing absolute and relative frames of reference?

Speakers of Japanese have been reported to clearly prefer relative frames of reference (Pederson et al. 1998), while a few ethnographic descriptions have mentioned that bilingual speakers of Japanese and some endangered Ryukyuan languages often rely on absolute frames of reference (Inoue 2002, 2005; Takekuro 2007). In this study we experimentally investigate the spatial frames of reference used by speakers bilingual in Miyako and Japanese and by monolingual speakers of Standard Japanese from Tokyo.

2   Theoretical Background

The range and possibilities of the linguistic encodings of spatial configurations have been studied in a cross-linguistic perspective using various tasks, most notably the 'Men-and-tree' task, in which speakers were asked to describe photographs showing simple scenes of a man and a tree in various positions (Pederson et al. 1998). These cross-linguistic studies have yielded a three-fold typology of spatial encodings, according to which the scene of a man and a tree may be described using a relative, or egocentric, frame of reference ('Man standing right to the tree'), an absolute, or allocentric, frame of reference ('Man standing to the North of the tree'), or an intrinsic frame of reference ('Man's side next to the tree'), (Pederson et al. 1998; Levinson 2003). Speakers of languages like Dutch or Japanese have been consistently found to describe the scene using a relative frame of reference, whereas speakers of other languages like Tzeltal Mayan are found to describe the same scene using an absolute frame of reference.

Moreover, speakers of languages that are classified as absolute or relative have produced responses in non-linguistic tasks that correlate with the language they speak (Perderson 1995; Pederson et al. 1998; Levinson 2003). And this has been interpreted as language causing restructuring of cognition, the landmark of whorfian hypothesis (Levinson 2003; Majid et al. 2004). There are, however, several confounds. For instance, absolute responses tend to be found among populations that are rural, more isolated, have received little or no formal schooling, and which form smaller linguistic communities. Contrary to this, relative responses tend to be found in populations that are urban, well schooled, and which form bigger linguistic communities. Unfortunately, few studies have directly addressed the use of a particular frame of reference in the light of the opposition between rural versus urban speakers. A notable exception to this is a study that investigated subgroups of speakers of the same language —Tamil—, where rural speakers were reported to describe spatial arrays with absolute frames of reference, whereas urban speakers used relative frames of reference (Pederson 1995, correlation with modes of spatial cognition is also shown). In sum, the direction of causality between language and cognition remains problematic (Li & Gleitman 2002; Núñez & Cornejo 2012).

Japonic languages provide an interesting setting in order to disentangle some of the confounds. Japanese and Miyako for instance can be said to be structurally equivalent in terms of the possibility of spatial encodings. Both languages have precise (and sometimes cognate) words for left and right, front and back, North and South etc. (see Table 1). Moreover, Miyako speakers are all bilingual in Miyako and Japanese and they have been schooled and enculturated into the mainland Japanese culture over an extended period of time (elementary school since the end of nineteenth century, TV, Radio etc.).

FoR	Translation	Japanese	Miyako
ABS	East	higashi	agaŋ
ABS	West	nishi	iŋ
ABS	South	minami	pai
ABS	North	kita	nisŋ
REL	right	migi	ngŋ
REL	left	hidari	pŋdaŋ
REL	vertical	tate	tati
INTR/REL	side	yoko	juku
INTR/REL	front	mae, shoomen	mavkjaa
INTR/REL	front	temae	mai, tskafu
INTR/REL	before	saki	kamaa
INTR/REL	behind	ushiro	tɕibi, kusŋ
INTR/REL	straight	massugu	massŋgu
INTR	be aligned	narab-	narab-

FoR: Frame of Reference ABS: Absolute REL: Relative INTR: Intrinsic
TABLE 1 Spatial terms in Miyako and Japanese

Standard Japanese speakers have been reported to use predominantly intrinsic and relative terms, but also absolute terms in the case of large-scale spatial relationships (Pederson et al. 1998; Kita 2006). However, there have been some anecdotal reports of more extensive use of absolute terms, including tabletop objects and body parts ('eastern tooth is aching') in non-standard varieties of Japanese (Kochi dialect: Inoue 2002, 2005), or in some Ryukyuan languages (Ishigaki: Takekuro 2007).

Although Miyako has not been investigated yet and has therefore not been classified with the methodology used in previous studies, we have observed in our fieldwork that Miyako speakers spontaneously use absolute frames of reference to describe spatial configurations of tabletop objects. Given these observations, we wonder what would happen in the case of bilingual speakers of two languages structurally equivalent, but with possibly clashing frames of reference. Answering that question provides a unique opportunity to further investigate the relationships between the confounds mentioned above.

3 Background Information about Miyako Language

Miyako is an endangered language belonging to the Southern branch of the Ryukyuan languages and traditionally spoken on Miyako islands (Miyako, Ikema, Irabu, Ogami, Kurima, Tarama, Minna), situated in the prefecture of Okinawa, Japan. Most fluent speakers are above sixty of age, and the language has ceased to be transmitted to the younger generations, who are now Japanese monolinguals. All native speakers of Miyako are also bilingual in Japanese.

Miyako shares many broad morpho-syntactic properties with Japanese. It exhibits an agglutinative morphology, is dependent marking, has SV/AOV word order and a nominative/accusative case-marking system. Miyako is also characterized by systematic dialectal variations from village to village, manifested at every level of the linguistic structure (phonological, morphological, lexical etc.). Although most of the dialects are fully mutually intelligible, speakers of mainland Miyako dialects report some difficulties in understanding dialects spoken on the surrounding islands like Ikema or Tarama. Because of these dialectal variations, it is difficult to give a unified phonological account of the language, but the typical mainland dialect has four short vowels i, u, ɿ, a, one long vowel o: and seventeen consonants p, b, m, f, v, t, d, n, ts, dz, s, z, ɾ, j, k, g, h (see Pellard & Hayashi 2012 for a detailed phonetic and phonological comparison of Miyako dialects). The presence of the fricative vowel ɿ is one of the most striking phonological traits of Miyako.

Although fully aware of the dialectal differences, in this study, we consider all speakers of Miyako to belong to the same population.

4   Method

Twenty-four people (thirteen men, eleven women) participated in this study. There were three groups of speakers of eight people each who were presented with an identical task: Miyako speakers completing the task speaking in Miyako (MM), Miyako speakers completing the task speaking in Japanese (MJ) and monolingual Tokyo speakers completing the task speaking in Japanese (JJ). The participants' age ranged from 61 to 91 and the study took place in Miyako for groups MM and MJ, and in Tokyo for group JJ.

The taks proceeded as follows: participants worked in pairs facing in the same direction, either North or South. They were sitted in front of an identical table and were separated by a screen of sufficient size to hide each other's table (Figure 1). Initially, both participants were shown all the materials (figurines) used for the study and were asked to name the represented object in the relevant language.

During each trial, one participant acted as director, giving instructions, and the other as matcher. The experimenter presented the stimulus on the director's table and the director was required to give instructions to the matcher so that the matcher could recreate exactly the stimulus placed in front of the director. Director and matcher were free to interact verbally, so that the matcher could ask any questions, and were not limited in time. Once the matcher had placed the figurines on his/her table and the interactions had ended, the experimenter removed the screen and the matcher's result was compared with the director's stimulus. All the instructions were given in the relevant language (in Miyako for MM, in Japanese for the two other groups) and the participants were explicitly required to speak in the relevant language when completing the task. There were four trials per pair, and the roles of director and matcher were switched at each trial, so that each participant acted twice as director and twice as matcher. For each pair, each trial had a different stimulus given in random order.

Two identical sets of five realistic small figurines (pig, piglet, rooster, dog and corn field) were used, one to compose the stimuli on the direcotr's table, and the other for the matcher to recreate, following Copperider et al. (2017) (see Figure 2). All trials were videotaped with a camera judiciously placed in order to fully capture the interactions between director and matcher.

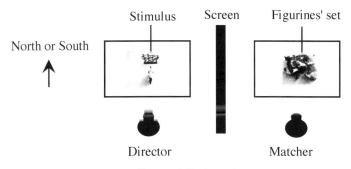

FIGURE 1 Task setting.

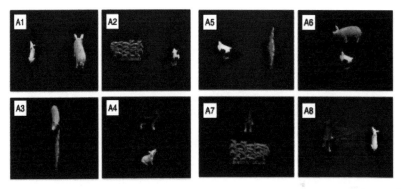

FIGURE 2 Stimuli used in the study (from Cooperrider et al. 2017), as viewed from the perspective of participant.

5   Results

All participants' utterances were transcribed, glossed and translated into English. Here, we provide two typical examples from each group when presented with stimulus A2 (examples 1-6, below) and A8 (examples 7-12) as depicted in figure 2. Spatial expressions are bracketed and marked in bold, D stands for 'director' M for 'matcher'.

Participants in the MM group exhibited a marked tendency to describe the spatial configurations of the figurines using absolute terms, such as 'West', 'East' (examples 1, 2, 7, 8). Occasionally, participants from two pairs also used relative terms, such as 'right' or 'left' (example 8). In stark contrast, participants in MJ and JJ groups almost exclusively relied on relative terms to describe the stimuli (MJ: examples 3, 4, 9, 10; JJ: examples 5, 6, 11, 12).

(1) Stimulus A2, MM pair number 3; facing North

D: hai   toomorokoshi   M: hai

ok   corn   ok

'so, the corn ...'   'yes'

D: [iŋ+agaɿ=nkai]   shii

    [east+west=DIR]   do.CVB

    'it is aligned East-West'

(2) Stimulus A2, MM pair number 4; facing North

D: tori=ne

    chicken=SFP

    'so, the chicken'

M: biki+duŋ?

    male+chicken?

    'the rooster?'

D: nn   tuz=zu   **[pai=nkai   futsɿ]**

    yes   chicken=ACC   **[south=DIR   facing]**

    'yes (place) the rooster facing South'

(3) Stimulus A2, MJ pair number 2; facing South

D: toomorokoshi=o   tate-te   **[migi+gawa=no   hoo=ni]**

    corn=ACC   erect-CVB   **[right+side=GEN   direction=DAT]**

    'place the corn standing, on the right side'

(4) Stimulus A2, MJ pair number 3; facing South

D: toomorokoshi+batake=no   ee   **[migi+te=no   hoo=ni]**

    corn+field=GEN   FIL   **[right+hand=GEN   direction=DAT]**

    'at the right of the corn field (there is the rooster)'

(5) Stimulus A2, JJ pair number 1; facing South

D: sore=de   niwatori=o   mig   **[toomorokoshi=no**

    this=INST   chicken=ACC   HES   **[corn=GEN**

    migi=no   tokoro=ni]

    right=GEN   place=DAT]

    'then, put the chicken on the right of the corn'

(6) Stimulus A2, JJ pair number 4; facing South

D: [atakushi=no   migi=no   hoo=ni=wa]   niwatori=ga

[I=GEN   right=GEN   direction=DAT=TOP]   chicken=NOM

ori-masu

be.HUM-POL

'on my right there is the rooster'

(7) Stimulus A8, MM pair number 1; facing South

D: hai   ffuu~ffu=nu   in

ok   RED~black=GEN   dog

'OK, do you see the black dog?'

M: ffuu~ffu=nu   in=nu?

RED~black=GEN   dog=ACC

'the black dog?'

D: minami=nkai   fut=tsa   shii=du=u

south=DIR   facing=INA   do.CVB=FOC=IPV

'it is facing South'

(8) Stimulus A8, MM pair number 2; facing North

D: ee   [nisɿ=nkai   fut=tsa   shii]

fil   [north=DIR   facing=INA   do.CVB]

'facing the North, [...]'

D: [pɿdaɿ+tii=n]   in=nu   ffo=o

[left+hand=DAT]   dog=GEN   child=ACC

'place the dog on the left-hand side'

(9) Stimulus A8, MJ pair number 3; facing South

D: de   buta=no   ko=ga   [migi+te=no   hoo=ni]

then   pig=GEN   child=NOM   [right+hand=GEN   direction=DAT]

[mukoo+muki=de   naran-de]

[opposite=orientation=INST   be_aligned-CVB]

'and the small pig, facing the other side, is aligned on the right side'

(10) Stimulus A8, MJ pair number 4; facing North

D: dee   buta=ga   ko+buta=ga   [migi]

then   pig=NOM   small+pig=NOM   [right]

'and the pig, the small pig is on the right'

(11) Stimulus A8, JJ pair number 1; facing South

D:	inu=ga		M.	hai
	dog=NOM			ok
	'the dog ...'			'Yes'
D:	**[shoomen**	**mui-te]**	hi	**[hidari]**
	[front_face	**face-CVB]**	HES	**[left]**
	'looking at the front, on the left'			

(12) Stimulus A8, JJ pair number 4; facing North

D:	ee	**[hidari+gawa=ga]**	inu	desu
	FIL	**[left+side=NOM]**	dog	COP.POL
	'on the left side, it is the dog'			

Interestingly, although MJ participants almost excusively used relative terms, one participant from this group produced an absolute term while speaking Japanese (example 13). No participants from the JJ group ever produced absolute terms.

(13) Stimulus A5, MJ pair number 2; facing South

D:	niwatori=ga	**[higashi=o**	**mui-te]**
	chicken=NOM	**[east=ACC**	**face-CVB]**
	'the rooster is facing east'		

6 Discussion

The linguistic relativity hypothesis makes clear predictions for cases of languages that are not structurally equivalent, where for instance a language does not have lexemes for left or right. However, it is unclear what the predictions would be when bilingual populations are concerned, especially of languages that are structurally equivalent but with reported clashing absolute and relative biases. In this case, it could be that, Japanese being the dominant language, it would impose the relative frame of reference that would spill over when speaking Miyako. It could also be, as it was found with a group of aboriginal australians (Meakins et al. 2016), that compulsory schooling in Japanese would enhance the bias towards preferred use of a relative frame of reference. Or perhaps, Miyako speakers would keep their traditional communicative pratices resulting in a bias towards the use of absolute frame of reference.

Our empirical results show that participants tend to choose markedly more often relative frame of reference terms over absolute ones when speaking in Japanese, and this, irrespective of the population. On the other hand, when Miyako speakers speak in Miyako, they tend to choose markedly more often absolute frame of reference terms over relative ones, and this despite the fact that both languages have at their disposal a full-blown lexicon and grammatical resources for absolute (e.g., 'North', 'South') and relative (e.g., 'left', 'right') encodings.

The Japanese language was classified as a relative language by means of the 'Men-and-tree' task. In this study, we used the 'Director-matcher' task, which is a modified form thereof. Although similar in many respects, these two tasks differ in some important dimensions. Whereas 'Men-and-tree' provides a good way for having participants explicitly use linguistic encodings of spatial configurations, the 'Director-matcher' task is more fundamentally goal-oriented, thus imposing a further communicative pressure on the participants. The director is indeed faced with a real-world interlocutor, with whom he must cooperate to achieve a certain goal, relying solely on linguistic resources (no access to eye gaze or gestures). Provided that they intend to complete the task in a successful manner, the participants are forced to maximize accuracy in their linguistic expression. Since both languages provide the speakers with the same linguistic resources, the stark difference observed between Miyako speakers speaking in Miyako and Miyako speakers speaking in Japanese can hardly be explained on pure linguistics grounds. Therefore, the explanation for this observed difference has to be sought among the several extra-linguistic factors that have so far been largely confounded in the litterature. Among the promising candidates that have been proposed to influence thought and cognition, we find communicative practices or cultural macro-views (Núñez & Cornejo 2012; Shapero 2016).

For instance, in traditional Miyako, as in many other Ryukyuan villages like Taketomi (Taketomi island) or Shiraho (Ishigaki island), houses are generally built on the same pattern, with the entrance primarily facing South. On the Easternmost side is found the so-called ichiban-za (litteraly 'first room'), the domain of men and where (male) guests are sitted, followed westward by the niban-za ('second room') and lastly by the kitchen, the domain of women, on the westernmost side. Furthermore, toilets and animals are kept in external structures on the western side of the property. To anyone aware of the spatial orientation built-in into the house pattern, cardinal directions are immediately available. The structure of the house can be seen as a material culture artifact that supports or even drives offloading of spatial cognition. And this, obviously, is not a linguistic factor but indeed the result of a cultural trait. The plausibility of this interpretation is supported for instance by findings about the Aymara population (Núñez & Cornejo 2012), where the linguistic use of absolute spatial terms correlates with traditional house orientation.

Our results call into question the version of the linguistic relativity hypothesis that it is the structure of language that uniquely determines or influences spatial cognition. The preference of absolute terms shown by Miyako speakers while speaking Miyako, but not when speaking Japanese, does not seem to be the result of cognitive restructuring driven by language proper, but rather seems to be due to cultural practices realized in the act of communicating in Miyako, and the use of culturally meaningful spatial resources. In order to further gain insight into these issues, more empirical research is needed.

7   Conclusion

Miyako/Japanese bilinguals tend to choose markedly more often absolute terms over relative terms when speaking Miyako than when speaking Japanese. The preference of frame of reference seems to be due, at least in part, to cultural conventions realized in the speaking of the relevant language. The use of absolute frames of reference in Miyako may be explained by broad macro-cultural factors like saliency of directions in Miyako's traditional culture and constitutes a topic for future research.

References

Cooperrider, K., Slotta, J., and Núñez, R. 2017. Uphill and Downhill in a Flat World: The Conceptual Topography of the Yupno House. *Cognitive Science* 41: 768–799.

Gumperz, J.J., and Levinson, S. (Eds.). 1996. *Rethinking linguistic relativity. Studies in the social and cultural foundations of language*, No. 17, Cambridge University Press.

Inoue, K. 2002. Soutai to fuhen no hazama de: kuukan shijiwaku ni yoru komyunikeeshon [Between relative and universal: communication by spatial reference frame]. In T. Ohori, *Ninchi gengogaku II: Kategoriika [Cognitive linguistics 2: Categorization]*:11-35. Tokyo: University of Tokyo Press.

Inoue, K. 2005. Kuukan ninchi to komyunikeeshon [Spatial cognition and communication]. In S. Ide and M. Hiraga, eds., *Kouza shakaigengokagaku 1: ibunka to komyunikeeshon [Sociolinguistic sciences 1: Different cultures and communication]*:118-128. Tokyo: Hitsuji Publishers.

Kita, S. 2006. A grammar of space in Japanese. in Levinson, S.C., Wilkins, D. (eds) *Grammars of space. Explorations in Cognitive Diversity. Language, Culture and Cognition*:437-474. Cambridge University Press.

Levinson, S. 2003. *Space in language and cognition: Explorations in cognitive diversity*. Cambridge, UK: Cambridge.

Li, P., and Gleitman, L. 2002. Turning the tables: language and spatial reasoning. *Cognition* 83:265-294.

Majid, A., Bowerman, M., Sotaro Kita, S., Haun, D., and Levinson, S. 2004. Can language restructure cognition? The case for space. *Trends in Cognitive Sciences* 8(3):108-114.

Meakins, F., Jones, C., and Algy, C. 2016. Bilingualism, language shift and the corresponding expansion of spatial cognitive systems. *Language Sciences* 54:1-13.

Núñez, E.R., and Cornejo, C. 2012. Facing the Sunrise: Cultural Worldview Underlying Intrinsic-Based Encoding of Absolute Frames of Reference in Aymara. *Cognitive Science* 36:965–991.

Pederson, E. 1995. Language as context, language as means: Spatial cognition and habitual language use. *Cognitive Linguistics* 6-1:33-32.

Pederson, E., Danziger, E., Wilkins, D., Levinson, S., C., Kita, S., and Senft, G. 1998. Semantic typology and spatial conceptualization. *Language* 74:557-589.

Pellard, T., and Hayashi, Y. 2012. Miyako hougen no onin —taikei to hikaku— [The phonology of Miyako dialect —structure and comparison—] in Kibe N. (Ed) *Shoumetsu kiki hougen no chousa hozon no tame no sougouteki kenkyuu Minami Ryukyu Miyako hougen chousa houkoku [General Study for Research and Conservation of Endangered Dialects in Japan Research Report on Miyako Ryukyuan]*:13-52. Ninjal Collaborative Research Project Reports 12-02. National Institute for Japanese Language and Linguistics.

Shapero, J.A. 2017. Does Environmental Experience Shape Spatial Cognition? Frames of Reference Among Ancash Quechua Speakers (Peru). *Cognitive Science* 41(5):1-1274-1298.

Takekuro, M. 2007. Language and Gesture on Ishigaki Island. *Berkeley Linguistics Society* 33(1).

Whorf, B. L. 1956. *Language, thought and reality: Selected writings*. Cambridge, MA: MIT Press.

Abbreviations

ACC Accusative COP Copula CVB Converb DAT Dative DIR Directional FIL Filler GEN Genitive HES Hesitation HUM Humble INA Inactive INST Instrumental IPF Imperfective NOM Nominative RED Reduplication SFP Sentence Final Particle POL Polite TOP Topic

On the Anaphoric Use of Demonstratives in Miyakoan*

TOMOHIDE KINUHATA
Fukuoka University

YUKA HAYASHI
JSPS/NINJAL

1 Introduction

The Shinzato dialect of Miyakoan has three series of demonstratives, *ku-*, *u-*, and *ka-*, which compose the demonstrative system suffixed by *-ri*, *-nu*, and *-ma* as shown in Table 1.

	ku-series	*u*-series	*ka*-series
thing/person	*ku-ri*	*u-ri*	*ka-ri*
genitive	*ku-nu*	*u-nu*	*ka-nu*
place	*ku-ma*	*u-ma*	*ka-ma*

TABLE 1 Demonstratives of Shinzato

In its deictic use, the *ku*-series refers to objects near the speaker, the *u*-series near the addressee and the *ka*-series distal from the interlocutors, which is very similar to the deictic uses of *ko-*, *so-*, and *a-* in Standard Japanese.[1]

* We would like to express our gratitude to the audience of the 25th J/K conference and especially to Wayne Lawrence for his valuable comments. This work was supported by JSPS KAKENHI Grant Numbers JP26770153, JP17J10117 and the NINJAL collaborative research project 'Endangered Languages and Dialects in Japan' (PI: Nobuko Kibe).

[1] This resemblance is not always observed in Ryukyuan dialects. See Shibata (1980) and Ogino (2009) for dialects which have three series of demonstratives but differ from Standard Japanese

Japanese/Korean Linguistics 25.
Edited by Shin Fukuda, Mary Shin Kim, and Mee-Jeong Park.
Copyright © 2018, CSLI Publications

There are, however, many dialects in Ryukyuan which only have two series of demonstratives (Uchima 1984). One of those examples is the Karimata dialect of Miyakoan, in which the *u*-series is used when the

	u-series	*ka*-series
thing/person	*u-ri*	*ka-ri*
genitive	*u-nu*	*ka-nu*
place	*u-ma*	*ka-ma*

TABLE 2 Demonstratives of Karimata

object is near the speaker or the interlocutors deictically, and the *ka*-series is used when the object is distant from the speaker or the interlocutors. The difference in the deictic center, i.e. the speaker or the interlocutors, is subject to intra-dialectal variation (Kinuhata 2017).

Extensive research on the relation between two-series and three-series demonstrative systems has not been conducted. Uchima (1984) argues that in many dialects of Ryukyuan the use of the *u*-series overlaps either with that of the *ku*-series or that of the *ka*-series.[2] But, as we will discuss in Section 5, simply identifying the function of the *u*-series with that of the *ku*- or *ka*-series cannot explain the historical process assumed to have occurred between those types of demonstrative systems. We will show in this paper that a proper account of the change of demonstratives presupposes an understanding of the anaphoric use[3] of demonstratives, which has also not been studied extensively in the literature. To this purpose, it is obligatory to investigate the anaphoric use of demonstratives, which will be discussed in Section 4 with a note on the method of our experiment in Section 3. Before going into our research, we take a brief note on previous studies in Section 2.

2 Previous Remark on Anaphoric Use

In Ryukyuan linguistics' literature, the main focus has been placed on the deictic use of demonstratives and little attention has been paid to their anaphoric use, yet important remarks has been made.

Shibata (1980), discussing the deictic use of demonstratives in Nishizato Miyakoan, notes that the anaphoric uses of *ku*-, *u*-, and *ka* can be understood analogously to their deictic uses: *Ku*- refers to an object which the speaker considers to be in his space, *u*- just outside his space and *ka*- far from his space. Although it is not uncomplicated how to interpret 'the speaker's space'

---

in their deictic uses.

[2] In North Ryukyuan, the distal demonstrative appears not as *ka*- but as *a*-: *a-ri*, *a-nu* etc. But we refer to both forms as *ka*- so long as it causes no confusion.

[3] Throughout this paper, we use the term 'anaphoric' to mean that demonstratives refer to an object introduced in the preceding text. In our survey of anaphoric use, we collected data referring to invisible objects, which behave differently from the deictic use of demonstratives. While some researchers use the term 'non-deictic' instead of 'anaphoric' (e.g. Hoji et al. 2003), we adopted the latter because some 'non-deictic' uses of demonstratives such as recollective reference and cataphora will not be discussed in this paper.

in the anaphoric use, it is at least clear from this statement that Shibata (1980) assumes some differences in the use of anaphoric *ku-*, *u-*, and *ka-*. Contrary to this, Ogino (2009) reports that in Yaeyaman *u-* is always used to refer to an object in the preceding text as well as in the speaker's memory.

This difference in observations seems to imply that there is dialectal variation in the anaphoric use of demonstratives. This is what we tried to make explicit in our experiment spelled out in the following sections.

3 Research Method

In order to investigate the anaphoric use of demonstratives, we conducted elicitation-based experiments: We requested informants to translate Japanese sentences into their dialects and particularly asked the naturalness of using *u-* and *ka-*.[4]

In constructing test sentences, we took two parameters into consideration: One is whether the object referred to by demonstratives is distant from the speaker, and the other is whether the object is known by the interlocutors.

	$K_{s\&a}$	K_s	K_a
dst	(1-a)	(1-b)	(1-c)
prx	(1-d)	(1-e)	(1-f)
nex	—	(1-g)	(1-h)

TABLE 3 Table for example (1)

The first parameter might be related to the Shibata's (1980) observation that the *ku-*, *u-*, and *ka*-series in the Nishizato dialect are properly used based on the distance from 'the speaker's space'. We divided this parameter into three situations: The first is that the object is distant from the speaker (abbreviated as dst in Table 3), the second is that the object is proximal to the speaker (prx), and the third is that the referent is nonexistent in reality (nex). The second parameter is also differentiated between the following three patterns: The first is the case where the object is known to both the speaker and the addressee ($K_{s\&a}$), in the second the object is known only to the speaker (K_s), and in the third the object is known only to the addressee (K_a). These three patterns coincide with Kuno's (1973) classification of the usage of Japanese demonstratives *a-* and *so-*:

> The *a*-series is used only when the speaker knows that the hearer, as well as the speaker himself, knows the referent of the anaphoric demonstrative. The *so*-series, on the other hand, is used either when the speaker knows the referent but thinks that the hearer does not or when the speaker does not know the referent. (p. 283)

Therefore, it is predicted that *a-* would be used in the situation $K_{s\&a}$ and *so-*

---

[4] We carefully pronounced *so-* and *a-* alternatively in one stimulus sentence and asked the informants about the naturalness using dialectal form, which we believe relieves informants from interference from Standard Japanese. In confirming the naturalness, the *ku*-series was disfavored in most sentences, so we ignore the use of the *ku*-series in the result given in the next section.

would be used in K_s and K_a if our experiment were tested against Standard Japanese speakers.

The above three-times-three pattern amounts to nine pattens of examples as in Table 3. However, we excluded one pattern , i.e. $K_{s\&a}$ & nex, since it is not easily imagined that an object is nonexistent but mutually known by the interlocutors. For each of the remaining eight patterns, we constructed four sentences, which gives a total of thirty-two sentences. We interviewed one informant twice, dividing the thirty-two sentences into sixteen with all patterns

We give the examples of all patterns in (1) (see Kinuhata 2017 for all test sentences).

(1)　a.　We ate a dish in Kyoto, didn't we? <u>Let's go eat **it** again.</u>
$$K_{s\&a}, dst$$
　　b.　There is a cafe named Uesuya in Nishizato. <u>I'll wait for you at **that** cafe.</u>
$$K_s, dst$$
　　c.　'I met a person named Shimoji yesterday.' <u>'What was **that** person like?'</u>
$$K_a, dst$$
　　d.　As you know, the store in front of this house sells tempura. <u>**It** is delicious.</u>
$$K_{s\&a}, prx$$
　　e.　I got a testimonial a long ago. <u>**It** is now set at the entrance.</u>
$$K_s, prx$$
　　f.　'I made a doll in this house yesterday.' <u>'Where do you keep **it**?'</u>
$$K_a, prx$$
　　g.　I saw an old woman in my dream yesterday. <u>**That** person was a cripple.</u>
$$K_s, nex$$
　　h.　'A boy in my dream gave me a dumpling.' <u>'Did you eat **it**?'</u>
$$K_a, nex$$

While the referent is (supposed to be) in a place far from where the conversation is taking place in (1-a), (1-b), and (1-c), the interlocutors are talking about an object around the house where they are in (1-d), (1-e), and (1-f). So the former examples are classified as *distal*, whereas the latter are *proximal*. On the other hand, the speaker refers to an object in a dream in (1-g) and (1-h), which is thus *nonexistent*. The sentences preceding the underlined ones present the contexts. The speaker confirms that the addressee knows the referent in (1-a) and (1-d), which means that the referent is shared, i.e. $K_{s\&a}$. In (1-b), (1-e), and (1-g), the speaker provides the hearer with new information to the hearer, thus K_s. The quotations in (1-c), (1-f), and (1-h) indicate that the speakers of the first and the second sentences are different. Since new information is given in the first sentence, the speaker of the second sentence does not know the object, i.e. K_a. These considerations lead us to classify the examples in (1) as in Table 3, which constitutes the foundation for showing our results, together with examples of the underlined parts, in the next section.

4 Results

4.1 Study Area

We have examined nine village communities in the Miyako Islands. We report the results of four of those areas in this article. The reason for not informing the results of other areas is that 1) we have interviewed only one person per one area in those communities and 2) their distributions of demonstrative pronouns are complex so that we found some difficulties in interpreting them, i.e. we have not decided whether the differences are the consequence of area, age, or individuals.[5]

The locations of the four communities are given in Figure 1. We will first give the results of the Karimata dialect, in which we consulted with four informants. The data presented in the next section are those of two informants, whose judgments we consider to be a typical of the two-series demonstrative system. See Kinuhata (2017) for the individual differences observed in this dialect. In Section 4.3, we turn to the data of the Shinzato dialect to show a dialectal difference mentioned in Section 2. There is, however, only one informant we have conducted our experiment with so far. We will therefore refer to a result of the Aragusuku dialect, which is also located in the south part of Miyako Island. As for the Oura dialect, we will not present the data here but will utilize it in the discussion of historical change in Section 5.

FIGURE 1 Miyako Islands

---

[5] Let us note some characteristics of the use of demonstratives in the areas we will not mention in the following. In the Nishihara (born in 1943, male) and Yonaha (1935, male) dialects, both u- and ka-series are broadly used so that it is not straightforward to find the difference between them in their anaphoric use. In the Nikadori dialect (1944, male), the use of ka- is preferred to that of u- in most cases. In the Matsubara dialect (1943, male), ka- is preferred particularly for $K_{s\&a}$, which is similar to Standard Japanese, but this dialect differs from other dialects in allowing the use of ku- in a broad range of patterns. The most interesting pattern for the subsequent discussion is the result of the Irabu dialect (1930, male), in which u- is strongly preferred in every example, a similar pattern to the Shinzato dialect. But since Irabu and Shinzato are genealogically and geographically different, we leave it for future research to explain why these two dialects resemble each other.

4.2 Karimata

As shown in Table 2, the Karimata dialect has only two series of demonstratives: *u-* and *ka-*. The former refers to a proximal object and the latter a distal object in the deictic system. The distance from the deictic center still affects the choice of demonstratives in the anaphoric use in this dialect.

Table 4 (born in 1933, female) and 5 (1934, female) are the results of our elicitation with two informants. We recorded the preference for each cell in the tables, with 'preference' meaning various cases such as; the other is impossible (marked as # in the following examples); one is more natural than the other (marked as ??); the speaker did not utter the other form despite our request to do so (marked as ?). These marked cases were eliminated from the tables and only when the informants uttered both sentences with *u-* or *ka-* and accepted them as natural, did we represent it as '*u-/ka-*'. (The order of *u-/ka-* is irrelevant.)

	$K_{s\&a}$	K_s	K_a
	u-	*ka-*	*ka-*
dst	*ka-*	*ka-*	*ka-*
	ka-	*ka-*	*ka-*
	ka-	*ka-*	*ka-*
	ka-	*u-/ka-*	*u-*
prx	*ka-*	*u-*	*u-/ka-*
	u-	*u-*	*ka-*
	u-	*u-*	*u-*
		ka-	*ka-*
nex		*ka-*	*ka-*
		ka-	*ka-*
		ka-	*ka-*

TABLE 4 KF$_{33}$

	$K_{s\&a}$	K_s	K_a
	ka-	*ka-*	*ka-*
dst	*ka-*	*ka-*	*ka-*
	ka-	*ka-*	*ka-*
	ka-	*ka-*	*ka-*
	ka-	*u-/ka-*	*u-*
prx	*ka-*	*u-*	*u-*
	u-/ka-	*u-*	—
	u-/ka-	*u-*	*u-/ka-*
		ka-	*ka-*
nex		*u-*	*u-/ka-*
		u-	*u-/ka-*
		ka-	*u-*

TABLE 5 KF$_{34}$

From the tables, it is clear that the informants use *ka-* when the object is in a distant place. The only exception to this generalization is the top left cell of KF$_{33}$, the reason for which is unclear to us; the other informants always preferred *ka-* in this example. We can learn from this instance that it is difficult to draw rigorous judgments about the use of demonstratives from the nature of them[6] and it is imperative for the study of demonstratives to observe distribution patterns in controlled contexts as illustrated here.

While there are few exceptions in the *dst* row, it is not the case that *u-* is dominant in the *prx* row, in which an object is relatively close to the conver-

---

[6] One important factor which prevents us from drawing decisive judgments is that the use of demonstratives is affected not only by the objective but also by the subjective, or psychological, distance of an object. Imagine that English *this* and *that* can alternate even if the speaker is in the same location. A Karimata speaker reported that she uses *u-* for an object intimate to her.

sation place. The reason why *ka-* is used in this context is that we were asking about invisible objects in the experiment on anaphoric use: If the speaker wants to designate those objects deictically, she has no alternative than to use *ka-*. This also implies that it is not necessarily denied that *ka-* in the *dst* row is used to refer to invisible objects deictically, but we consider it significant that the speaker always prefers to use *ka* in the context of *dst*, when compared with the result of the Shinzato dialect given in the next subsection. It is also notable in this connection that the use of *u-* in the above tables indicates the existence of the anaphoric use of *u-* in this dialect since the deictic use of *u-* refers to objects right in front of the speaker.[7]

The last remark we should make about the tables is the difference in the *nex* row between the informants. While it is clear from the exclusive use of *ka-* that KF_{33} regards nonexistent objects as remote, more complicated pragmatic factors seem to be involved in the identification of nonexistent objects by KF_{34}.[8]

The following examples are the translations of (1) with judgments of the use of demonstratives by KF_{33}.

(2)   a.   mmi putun {#uri/ kari}=u   fai mii busɨ-kan   ra.
            more once {*u-/   ka-*}=ACC *eat try* OPT-ACOP DM

    b.   {#uma/ kama}=n   ura-di=siba.
        {*u-/   ka*-}=LOC *exist*-VOL.=CSL

    c.   {#uri/ kari}=a   nooci=nu putu=du   a-taɨ?
        {*u-/   ka-*}=TOP *how*=GEN *person*=FOC COP-PST

    d.   {uma/ #kama}=nu tempura=a   ati   mma-an   ra.
        {*u-/   ka-*}=GEN   *tempura*=TOP *very delicious*-ACOP DM

    e.   {unu/ #kanu} sjoodzjoo=ju   uma=n   kadzari uɨ.
        {*u-/   ka-*}   *testimonial*=ACC *there*=LOC *set*   CONT

    f.   {unu/ #kanu} ningjoo=ja ndza=n=du   a=riba?
        {*u-/   ka-*}   *doll*=TOP   *where*=LOC=FOC *exist*=Q

---

[7] Another piece of evidence for the anaphoric use of *u-* is its bound variable use as in (i) (see Hoji et al. 2003 for bound variable anaphora resulting in 'covariant interpretation' in Japanese),

(i)   ndza=ara=n   maccja=nu a-tigaa,   {∅/ uma/ *kama}=ai paddzigi munu=u
        where=INDET=LOC *store*=NOM *exist*-COND {∅/ *u-/ ka-*}=ALL *enter*   *stuff*=ACC
        kaa.
        *by.*VOL
    'If we find a store somewhere (along this road), let's enter it and buy something.'

though the informants would rather have used a sentence without any demontratives in this context, and some informants dispreferred the sentences with them.

[8] Although it is outside the scope of this paper to make the relevant factors fully explicit, some subjective distance seemed to be involved. For example, while the informant used *u-* for a ball which she was holding in her dream, she didn't for a person showing up in her dream: She can be close to a ball by holding it, whereas it is impossible to hold a person in her arms.

g. {#uri/ kari}=a   pag<del>i</del>=nu=du   jami   u-ta<del>i</del>=djaa.
    {u-/   ka-}=TOP *leg*=NOM=FOC *be.injured* CONT-PST=EVID

h. vva=a   {#uri/ kari}=u=du   fai?
    2SG=TOP {u-/   ka-}=ACC=FOC *eat*.PST

4.3 Shinzato

The results of our survey with a speaker of the Shinzato dialect (1927, male) is given in Table 6 and that of an Aragusuku speaker (1949, male) in Table 7. The data are represented in the same way as those of the Karimata dialect.

	$K_{s\&a}$	K_s	K_a			$K_{s\&a}$	K_s	K_a
dst	u-/ka-	ka-	u-		*dst*	ka-	u-	ka-
	u-	u-	u-			ka-	u-	u-
	u-/ka-	u-	u-			ka-	ka-	u-
	u-/ka-	u-	u-/ka-			u-/ka-	u-	u-
prx	u-	u-	u-		*prx*	u-	u-	u-
	u-	u-	u-			u-	u-	u-
	u-	u-	u-			u-	u-	u-
	u-	u-	u-			u-/ka-	ka-	u-
nex		u-	u-		*nex*		u-	u-
		u-	u-				u-	u-
		u-	u-				u-	u-
		u-	u-				u-	u-

TABLE 6 SM_{27} TABLE 7 AM_{49}

Although there are some irregularities, particularly in the use of *ka-*, the difference between Table 6 and the result from Karimata is obvious: Even when an object is in a remote place, *u-* is used or preferred; a strong preference for the use of *u-* is observed when an object is not distant or is nonexistent. Since the objects referred to in our experiment are not interpreted as occupying a position close to the addressee, Table 6 indicates the development of the non-deictic use of the *u*-series compared with the Karimata dialect. The result of the Aragusuku speaker shows a similar tendency to that of the Shinzato dialect. A conspicuous difference of Table 7 from Table 6 is that *ka-* is favored to refer to mutually known distant objects in the former whereas *u-* and *ka-* are evenly used in the latter. Whether this difference is caused by a difference of community, generation, or individual preference is an unsettled question in this paper.

We give the translations and judgments of (1) by the informant of the Shinzato dialect in (3).

(3) a. {uri/ kari}=u   nkjagi=ga   mmjaa-di=na?
         {u-/ ka-}=ACC *eat*.HON=PURP *go*.HON-VOL=Q

b. {unu/ #kanu} sjokudoo=n   maci uri.
   {u-/ ka-}   *restaurant*=LOC *wait* CONT.IMP

c. {unu/ #kanu} pitu=a   naubasi=nu pitu=ga
   {u-/ ka-}   *person*=TOP *how*=GEN *person*=FOC.Q
   ya-ta=ryaa?
   COP-PST=Q

d. {#uma/ kama}=nu tempura=a   aggai mma-munu=doo.
   {u-/   ka-}=GEN *tempura*=TOP ITJ   *delicious*-NMLZ=SFP

e. {unu/ #kanu} turufii=ju=du   genkan   kadzari uki.
   {u-/ ka-}   *trophy*=ACC=FOC *entrance*.LOC *set*   PERF

f. {unu/ #kanu} ningjoo=ja ndza=n=du   uciki uki?
   {u-/ ka-}   *doll*=TOP *where*=LOC=FOC *put*   PERF

g. {unu/ #kanu} pitu=a   pagi=nu=du   yamii=nu
   {u-/ ka-}   *person*=TOP *leg*=NOM=FOC *be.injured*=GEN
   pitu   ya-tam=doori.
   person COP-PST=EVID

h. anti vva=a   {uri/ #kari}=uba   fai?
   then 2SG=TOP {u-/ ka-}=ACC.TOP *eat*.PST

4.4 Interim Conclusion

We have seen a dialectal difference between the Karimata dialect and the Shinzato(/Aragusuku) dialect in the use of demonstratives. It is characteristic of Karimata that *ka-* is exclusively used to refer to distant objects, which entails that *u-* only refers to relatively proximate objects. This distinction can be construed parallel to their deictic use, in which *u-* and *ka-* respectively refer to objects close to or far from the interlocutors in visible environments, though we have to admit particularly the growth of the anaphoric *u-* in that it can denote objects not near the interlocutors.

On the other hand, the anaphoric use of *u-* is prevalent in the Shinzato dialect: It can refer to contextually induced elements irrespective of their locations in deictic space. This prevalence of the anaphoric use of *u-* is not unrelated to the fact that this dialect has three series of demonstrative pronouns *ku-*, *u-*, and *ka-* as was summarized in Table 1: Since *u-* is used as medial in the deictic use, the proximal and distal distinction in the anaphoric use cannot be expressed by using *u-* and *ka-* as in the Karimata dialect.

5 Discussion on Historical Change

In our survey of the anaphoric use, the *u-* and *ka-*series are differentiated in the Karimata dialect according to the distance from the locus of the dialogue. We represent this usage of demonstratives as in the left diagram of Figure 2, in which *dct* and *aph* stand for the *deictic* and *anaphoric* uses respectively.

The strong preference for the *u-* series in the Shinzato dialect, on the other, can be depicted as in the right diagram of Figure 2, which implies that in the anaphoric use *u-* is used irrespective of distance. Given the above diagrams and genealogically close relations, what historical changes caused the two dialects to diverge from each other?

A simple answer would assume that the change took place from one to the other. We argue, however, that it is problematic to assume a direct derivational relationship between the two systems.

Let us first consider the possibility of a change from the Karimata type to the Shinzato type. This change involves at least the following two steps to achieve its goal: One is the appearance of the *ku*-series and the other is the development of the anaphoric *u*-series, which is schematized in Figure 2.

Karimata

	dct	aph
prx	u-	u-
dst	ka-	ka-

Intermediate

	dct	aph
prx	ku-	u-
med	u-	
dst	ka-	ka-

Shinzato

	dct	aph
prx	ku-	
med	u-	u-
dst	ka-	

FIGURE 2 Possible change from Karimata to Shinzato

While it is plausible for the anaphoric use to be integrated into the *u*-series during the change, it is highly unlikely that the *ku*-series would appear in the local change of Miyakoan because the *ku*-series is attested all over the Ryukyuan dialect area: According to Uchima (1984), forty-eight out of fifty three dialects have *ku*-series demonstratives. Moreover, since *ku*- phonologically corresponds the Japanese demonstrative *ko-*, it must trace back to the Proto-Japonic *ko.

We now turn to assess the possibility of a change from the Shinzato to the Karimata type. Two steps to be presupposed are the reverse of the above change: The disappearance of the *ku*-series and the divergence of the anaphoric use.

Shinzato

	dct	aph
prx	ku-	
med	u-	u-
dst	ka-	

Intermediate

	dct	aph
prx	u-	u-
dst	ka-	

Karimata

	dct	aph
prx	u-	u-
dst	ka-	ka-

FIGURE 3 Possible change from Shinzato to Karimata

The latter process is reasonable since it can be viewed as being triggered by analogy to the distinction in the deictic use of *u-* and *ka-*, an instance of 'analogical extension' in the sense of Bybee (2015: ch. 5). The former process, on the other, needs some justification. It seems difficult to explain the change based on the meanings of *ku-* and *u-* (and *ka-*), because in Ryukyuan dialects any combination of *ku-*, *u-*, and *ka-* can constitute a two-series demonstrative system (Uchima 1984), e.g. *ku-* vs. *u-* system in the Sonai (Iriomote) dialect of Yaeyaman, *ku-* vs. *a-* system in the Torishima dialect of Okinawan etc. Rather, the wide distribution of two-series systems, thirteen dialects out of fifty-three samples according to Uchima (1984), with arbitrary choices of forms implies the existence of a semantic basis in Ryukyuan languages to prefer two-series demonstrative systems.

The above consideration leads us to posit a system which has only two series of demonstratives to be opposed semantically, but still needs three series morphologically. Thus, we hypothesize a proto-type as in Figure 4 which derives the Shinzato type on the one hand and the Karimata type on the other.

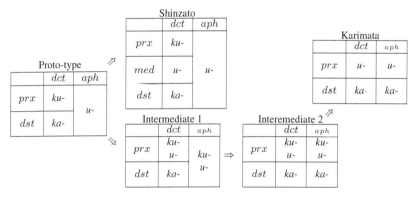

FIGURE 4 Change from Proto-type to Shinzato and Karimata

The change from the proto-type to the Shinzato type is achieved by the *u*-series acquiring a deictic use as a medial. Since the medial demonstrative *so-* in Japanese also originates in the anaphoric use (Hashimoto 1986) and first took on its deictic use in Medieval Japanese (Fujimoto 2008), it is not surprising that the *u-* series underwent the same process as *so-*.

Reconstructing the above proto-type is also attractive in having a semantic basis to prefer two-series demonstrative systems. The change from it to the Karimata type is explained based on the binary opposition of *ku-* and *ka-* in the deictic use: First, the integration of *ku-* and *u-*, second, analogical extension, and third, the loss of the *ku-* series due to redundancy. Among these changes, readers might wonder whether the integration of demonstrative forms is really actualized.

By looking at the data of the Oura dialect, located to the south of Karimata, we can conclude that the relevant integration certainly occurred. In this dialect (female, 1928), *ku-* and *u-* have precisely the same function as referring to objects close to the speaker. In the anaphoric use, as shown in Table 8, the distal demonstrative *ka-* is exclusively used to denote distant objects, whereas the use of *ku-* and *u-* becomes possible for closer objects. Therefore, the usage of demonstratives in the Oura dialect is at the stage of 'intermediate 2' in the above diagram, a stage where the analogical extension had already been completed as in the Karimata dialect. The existence of dialects such as Oura demonstrates that the integration of demonstrative pronouns is necessary in explaining the historical change of Miyakoan.

	$K_{s\&a}$	K_s	K_a
dst	ka-	ka-	ka-
	ka-	ka-	ka-
	ka-	ka-	ka-
	ka-	ka-	ka-
prn	ku,u-/ka-	ka-	ka-
	ka-	ka-	ka-
		ku,u	ku,u-
	ku,u-	ku,u-	ku,u-
NE		ka-	ka-
		ka-	ka-
		ka-	ka-
		ka-	ka-

TABLE 8 OF_{28}

6 Concluding Remark

This paper demonstrats that there is a dialectal difference in anaphoric uses in Miyakoan. While in the Karimata dialect, with a two-series demonstrative system, *u-* and *ka-* series are differentiated according to the distance from the interlocutors even in the anaphoric use, a noticeable tendency to use *u-* for the anaphoric was witnessed in the Shinzato dialect, which has three series of demonstratives. Further, we argued that in order to account for this difference it is necessary to hypothesize a system which is distinguished from both of the above types. Our proposal was that *ku-* and *ka-* were used for the deictic and *u-* was for the anaphoric use.

A remaining question is how far this hypothetical state can trace back. We think it is probable to reconstruct it not only to Proto-Miyakoan but also to Proto-Ryukyuan, because, as noted before, there are two-series demonstrative systems alongside three-series systems in Ryukyuan languages. Moreover, it is not totally impossible to reconstruct the same system in Proto-Japonic, because some researchers of Old Japanese assume *ko-* and *ka-* to be deictic and *so-* to be anaphoric (Kinsui et al. 2002) though the distal *ka-* is sometimes considered to be underdeveloped (Hashimoto 1986, Okazaki 2010). Although it falls beyond the scope of this paper to discuss the Old Japanese demonstrative system, our research undoubtedly implies that a close scrutiny of Ryukyuan demonstrative systems may throw light on the history of the Japonic family.

References

Bybee, J. 2015. *Language Change*. Cambridge: Cambridge University Press.

Fujimoto, M. 2008. Sokei shijishi niyoru kikiteryōiki no keisei [The formation of the use of *so*-series demonstratives to refer to the addressee's space]. *Gobun* 90: 40–53.

Hashimoto, S. 1986. Kodaigo no shijitaikei: Jōdai o chūshin ni [The system of Ancient Japanese demonstratives: Focusing on the Nara period]. *Hashimoto Shirō ronbunshū*, 209–227. Tokyo: Kadokawa shoten.

Hoji, H., S. Kinsui, A. Ueyama, and Y. Takubo 2003. Demonstratives in Modern Japanese. *Functional structure(s), form and interpretation: Perspectives from East Asian languages*. eds. Simpson, A. and Y. A. Li, 97–128. London: Routledge.

Kinsui, S., T. Okazaki and M. Jo 2002. Shijishi no rekishiteki taishōgengogakuteki kenkyū: Nihongo, Kankokugo, Torukogo [Historical and contrastive study of demonstratives: Japanese, Korean, and Turkish]. *Shirīzu gengokagaku 4: Taishōgengogaku*. ed. N. Ogoshi, 217–247. Tokyo: University of Tokyo Press.

Kinuhata T. 2017. Miyako Karimatahōgen niokeru shijishishiyō no kojinsa [Individual difference in the use of demonstratives in Karimata Miyakoan]. *The bulletin of central research institute Fukuoka University series A: Humanities* 17(4): 45–50.

Kuno, S. 1973. *The structure of the Japanese language*. Cambridge: The MIT Press.

Ogino, C. 2009. Ryūkyū Yaeyamachihō no shijishi nitsuite [On demonstratives of the Yaeyama dialects of Ryukyuan]. *Department bulletin paper (Nakamura University, Junior College)* 41: 17–24.

Okazaki, T. 2010. *Nihongo shijishi no rekishiteki kenkyū* [Historical study of Japanese demonstratives]. Tokyo: Hituzi syobo.

Shibata, T. 1980. Okinawa miyakogo no goitaikei 10 [The lexical system of Okinawa Miyakoan 10]. *Gekkan gengo* 9(11): 104–107. Tokyo: Taishukan Publishing.

Uchima, C. 1984. *Ryūkyū hōgen bunpō no kenkyū* [The study of the Ryukyuan grammar]. Tokyo: Kasama shoin.

Abbreviations

2SG: second person singular, ACC: accusative, ACOP: adjectival copula, CONT: continuous, COP: copula, CSL: causal, DM: discourse marker, EVID: evidential, FOC: focus, GEN: genitive, HON: honorific, INDET: Indeterminate, ITJ: interjection, LOC: locative, NOM: nominative, NMLZ: nominalizer, OPT: optative, PERF: perfect, PST: past, PURT: purposive, Q: question, SFP: sentence final particle, TOP: topic, VOL: volitive.

Integrating Analysis and Pedagogy in the Revitalization of Jejueo*

CHANGYONG YANG
Jeju National University

SEJUNG YANG
University of Hawai'i at Mānoa

WILLIAM O'GRADY
University of Hawai'i at Mānoa

* This work was supported by the Core University Program for Korean Studies through the Ministry of Education of the Republic of Korea and the Korean Studies Promotion Service of the Academy of Korean Studies (AKS-2015-OLU-2250005).

Japanese/Korean Linguistics 25.
Edited by Shin Fukuda, Mary Shin Kim, and Mee-Jeong Park.
Copyright © 2018, CSLI Publications

1 Introduction

Jejueo, the traditional language of Jeju Island, has long been misclassified as a dialect of Korean, despite important differences in its phonology, vocabulary and verbal morphology. Experimental work has shown that Jejueo is not comprehensible to people who speak only Korean (Yang, O'Grady, et al. 2018), and various international organizations (UNESCO, Ethnologue and the Endangered Language Catalogue) now recognize it as a distinct language.

The purpose of this paper is to consider how the dual challenges of linguistic analysis and language pedagogy come together as part of an ongoing attempt to save Jejueo from extinction. The next section provides a brief review of the improvised shallow orthography that is often employed to write Jejueo. As we show in Section 3, this system misrepresents the morphological structure of Jejueo words in ways that are detrimental to linguistic analysis. We then call for the adoption of a more morphophonemic orthography, similar to the one used for Korean, arguing in Section 4 that such as a system has important pedagogical advantages. We conclude with a brief discussion of parallels between Jejueo and Hawaiian with respect to the issues that lie at the heart of our paper.

2 Jejueo and Its Orthography

Jejueo has no literary tradition, but an orthography has emerged for use in pedagogical materials, in folkloric records and in linguistic work, including dictionaries, grammatical treatises, and the transcription of data from native speakers. There has been virtually unanimous agreement for some time (Hyun, Kim, et al. 2009; Ko, Song, et al. 2013) that Jejueo should be written using a version of Hangeul, the alphabetic orthography employed for Korean.

A key feature of Hangeul orthography is that letters are organized into blocks, as illustrated in (1). (We Romanize our examples with the help of the system recommended by the National Institute of the Korean language for works of linguistic analysis.)

(1)   ㄴ = /n/   ㅏ = /a/   ㅁ = /m/   ㅜ = /u/   ㅇ = /ŋ/

        나무   낭
        namu   *nang*
        'tree' (Korean)   'tree' (Jejueo)

Although these blocks are often referred to as syllables (*eumjeol*), they also tend to correspond to morphemes in Korean, as the following examples help show. (A list of abbreviations appears at the end of our paper.)

(2) 먹는다   가겠어   웃지마세요
     meog-neun-da   *ga-gess-eo*   *us-ji-ma-se-yo*
     eat-NPST-DECL   go-PROSP-DECL   laugh-COMPL-not-AH-IMP
     'S/he eats.'   'I will go.'   '(Please) don't laugh.'

Moreover, when there is a mismatch between syllable boundaries and morpheme boundaries in Korean, the latter win out. A simple example of this can be seen in the past/perfective form of 'give,' which includes the tense/aspect suffix *-eoss* (었) and the (declarative) sentence ender *-eo* (어) in the example below.

(3) 주었어
     ju-eoss-eo   [pronunciation: 'ju.eo.sseo']
     give-PFV-DECL
     'gave'

Although pronounced *ju-eo-sseo*, the word is written as *ju-eoss-eo* (주었어) in order to maintain the integrity of each of its component morphemes. Put simply, morphology takes precedence over phonology.

As illustrated by the preceding example and many others like it, the use of Hangeul presupposes an understanding of a word's morphological structure, on which its spelling depends. Herein lies the challenge for Jejueo: because its verbal morphology is substantially different from that of Korean and because the language is understudied, it is often unclear where the morpheme boundaries lie.

Because of this problem, most work on Jejueo, including efforts devoted to the preparation of pedagogical material, adopts the default assumption that each phonetic syllable after the root corresponds to a suffix. As we will see next, this opens the door to serious mis-segmentations, with negative consequences both for linguistic analysis and for language teaching.

3 Segmentation Controversies in Jejueo

As a first illustration of the problem at hand, we will consider the verb form that makes reference to a currently occurring event in a question such as 'What is s/he eating?' The verb in this pattern, pronounced *meogeomsini*, is written as follows by many linguists and teachers, dividing the word into a root and three phonetic syllables.

(4)　무신거　**먹엄시니?**
*musingeo **meog.eom.si.ni?***
'What is s/he eating?'

This spelling aligns with a popular analysis of the word's internal structure, as proposed by Hyun (1976) and Woo (1995:43), among others.

(5)　먹엄**시**니?
*meog.eom.**si**.ni*
eat-NMLZ-be-Q

This analysis has at least two compelling features: (a) the final syllable corresponds to the interrogative suffix *-ni*, which is also found in Korean, and (b) the second-to-last syllable corresponds to the copula *si*, which is independently attested in other patterns, such as (6).

(6)　할망　　집의　시어? [contracted form = 서]
*Halmang jib-ui **si**-eo?*
grandmother home-LOC be-Q
'Is grandmother at home?'

In fact, however, the analysis in (5) turns out to be entirely wrong: the interrogative marker is *-i*, not *-ni*, and there is no copula. To see this, we need to consider how Jejueo expresses ongoing events that take place in the past.

The Jejueo past/perfective marker is *-eon*, whose identity can be established straightforwardly in patterns such as the following, where it is the only suffix.

(7)　먹**언**
*meog-**eon**.*
eat-PFV
'ate'

Now consider the past/perfective continuative form of the verb *eat* (i.e., 'was eating'), which is pronounced *meogeomseoni*. As we try to make sense of this form, we know in advance that the root is *meog* and that the past/perfective marker is *-eon*. This gives us the following partial parse for the verb.

(8)　*meog-eoms-eon-**i**?*
eat　-???　-PFV-??

Two important facts now leap out.

First, the sentence-final interrogative suffix is -i, not -ni.[1] Second, there is no si to function as copula; there is just an s, which we take to be part of the preceding morpheme, as depicted in (9).

(9)   먹ㅇㅓㅄ언이?
       *meog-**eoms**-eon-i?*
       eat -CONT-PFV-Q

This segmentation is consistent with the emerging view that the continuative aspect is marked in Jejueo by the suffix *-eoms*. This conclusion has long been resisted because of the unusual coda (*ms*), for which there is no counterpart in Korean, but the analysis is starting to gain support (e.g., Jee-Hong Kim 2014b:178, 2014c:251, Yang, Yang & O'Grady 2018).

If *-eoms* is the continuative marker and *-i* is the interrogative marker, then the non-past continuative form of the verb should be analyzed and written as follows.

(10)   무신거   먹ㅇㅓㅄ**인**이?
        *musingeo meog-eoms-**in**-i?*
        what   eat -CONT-**??**-Q
        'What is [s/he] eating?'

This leaves us with the problem of identifying the *-in* that shows up between the continuative suffix and the sentence ender. There is good reason to think that it is a non-past marker, creating the following contrast with the past continuative form of the verb that we saw in (9) above.

(11)   Present continuative: Past continuative:
       먹ㅇㅓㅄ**인**이?   먹ㅇㅓㅄ언이?
       *meog-eoms-**in**-i?*   *meog-eoms-**eon**-i?*
       eat   -CONT-NPST-Q   eat -CONT-PFV-Q
       'is eating?'   'was eating?'

Independent evidence suggests that *-in* is an allomorph of the non-past suffix

---

[1] This conclusion can be confirmed by various types of independent evidence. For example, like Korean, Jejueo has a non-past marker *-(eu)neun*, as in *Geu chogi meog-**neun**-ge* '(People) eat that mushroom.' Crucially, the question marker in this case too is *-i*, not *-ni*.

(i)   *Musigeo meog-**neun**-i?* (not *meog-neun-ni)
    what   eat-NPST-Q
    'What does s/he eat?'

-eun. As the two examples below help illustrate, the default form of the non-past suffix *(-eun)* gives way to *-in* after a stem ending in *s*.

(12) 먹**은**다. 웃**인**다.
*meog-**eun**-da* *us-**in**-da*
eat-NPST-DECL smile-NPST-DECL
'[S/he] eats [something].' '[S/he] smiles.'

4 What Should Jejueo Orthography Represent?

The examples that we have been considering highlight a property of Hangeul that has long been considered to be its most valuable feature: as I. Lee & Ramsey (2000:30) note, Hangeul makes it easy to identify and recognize morphemes.

Let us now think about what this means for pedagogy. In the analysis that we propose, second language learners have to learn the following facts about the verb form used to ask about a currently occurring action.

(13) 무신거 **먹 ㅇ ㅓ ㅁㅅ 인 이?**
musingeo ***meog.eoms.in.i****?*
'What is [s/he] eating?'

a. There is a morpheme *-eoms* that gives a continuative meaning.
먹 **ㅇ ㅓ ㅁㅅ** 인 이?
*meog-**eoms**-in-i?*
eat **-CONT**

b. There's a morpheme *-in* that gives a non-past meaning (and a morpheme *-eon* that gives a past/perfective meaning).
먹 ㅇ ㅓ ㅁㅅ **인** 이?
*meog-eoms-**in**-i?*
eat -CONT-**NPST**

c. There's a morpheme *-i* that gives an interrogative meaning.
먹 ㅇ ㅓ ㅁㅅ 인 **이**?
*meog-eoms-in-**i**?*
eat -CONT-NPST-**Q**

Notice that each of the three pieces of information needed to interpret the verb is clearly and transparently represented—the very advantage for which Hangeul is known, as Lee & Ramsey note. None of this is possible when the word is spelled in a way that simply captures its syllable structure—since none of the syllables (other than the root) corresponds to a morpheme.

(14)   먹 엄 시 니?
         meog-eom-si-ni?
         eat -?? -?? -??

Indeed, as we have seen, this orthographic practice is confusing even to professional linguists.

There are countless other cases that illustrate the same point. Table 1 presents some examples from published pedagogical materials. The original 'phonetic' spelling, which obscures the word's morphological composition is in the left-hand column; the right-hand column contains the amended Hangeul spelling from Yang, Yang & O'Grady (2018), which allows a straightforward morpheme-by-morpheme analysis.

Common 'Phonetic' Spelling	Proposed Amended Spelling
어둑엄서. (Kang et al. 2009:45)	어둑ㅇㅓㅁㅅ어.
eo.dug.eom.seo.	*eo.dug-eoms-eo.*
'It's getting dark.'	dark-CONT-DECL
먹어시냐? (Hyun et al. 2009:36)	먹엇인야?
meog-eo-si-nya.	*meog-eos-in-ya.*
'Have [you] eaten?'	eat-PFV-NPST-Q
먹엄수다. (D.-Y. Kim 2017:20)	먹ㅇㅓㅁㅅ우다.
meog-eom-su-da.	*meog-eoms-u-da.*
'[S/he] is eating.'	eat-CONT-AH-DECL
가수다. (D.-Y. Kim 2017:21)	갓우다.
ga-su-da.	*ga-s-u-da.*
'[S/he] left.'	go-PFV-AH-DECL
ㅎㆍ여신가? (Kang et al. 2014:11)	ㅎㆍ엿인가?
haw-yeo-sin-ga?	*haw-yeos-in-ga?*
'Has [s/he] completed everything?'	do-PFV-NPST-Q
먹엄시라. (Lee 2014:29)	먹ㅇㅓㅁㅅ이라.
meog-eom-si-la.	*meog-eoms-ila.*
'Get started eating.'	eat-CONT-IMP

가시냐? (Song 2014:170)	갓인야?
ga-si-nya?	*ga-s-in-ya?*
'Have [you] already gone?'	go-PFV-NPST-Q
살아신디. (Chung 2017:slide 62)	살앗인디.
sal-a-si-n-di.	*sal-as-in-di*
'[S/he] has lived (there).'	live PFV NPST-DECL

TABLE 1 Comparison of two modes of spelling

As these and other examples show, there are many cases in which verbal morphology does not align with syllable structure, creating challenges both for linguistic analysis and for pedagogy. Fortunately, this problem can be addressed by combining the right morphological analysis with the spelling made possible by the standard Hangeul orthography.

More is involved here than just a decision to represent suffix boundaries rather than syllable breaks. A second, deeper issue is also at stake—with far-reaching pedagogical implications. Put simply, we need to ask whether an orthography should represent information that does not have to be learned, or information that does have to be learned.

The placement of syllable boundaries is obviously an important part of natural-sounding speech. Fortunately, a simple principle determines the location of syllable breaks. [2]

(15)   A CVCV string is pronounced CV.CV

This effect is essentially automatic. A word that is written as *ba+da* (바다) 'sea' will be pronounced the same way as a word written as *bad+a* (받아) 'receive.' No speaker of Jejueo or Korean, literate or illiterate, would ever pronounce *bada* as *bad.a*, regardless of how it is written. From the point of view of pedagogy, syllable breaks in the orthography have little to offer.

Patterns of verbal suffixation are an entirely different matter. As we have seen, the verbal morphology of Jejueo is largely opaque to Korean speakers—so much so that it is often misanalysed even by trained linguists. The particular suffixal patterns found in Jejueo verbs do not follow from any universal principle, nor can they be deduced from knowledge of Korean. They need to be learned. Fortunately, the Hangeul orthography, which Korean-speaking learners of Jejueo have already mastered in the course of learning their native language, reveals the morphological composition of

---

[2] This principle is a long-recognized universal of language (Jackobsen & Halle 1956, Hayman 2008:113ff): put simply, CV syllables are highly valued.

even the most complex verbal patterns, as illustrated in the examples that we have been considering, including those in Table 1.

In sum, thanks to the character of Hangeul orthography and its commitment to representing morphological structure, the challenges of linguistic analysis and of language pedagogy are almost perfectly aligned in the case of Jejueo. The right analysis of word structure can be transparently represented by the orthography in a manner that facilitates language teaching, allowing the objectives of linguistics and pedagogy to converge in a satisfying and productive way.

5 Concluding Remarks

Native speakers of a language are able to adjust to highly imperfect orthographies. One very good example of this comes from the traditional Hawaiian orthography, developed in the 1820s by English-speaking missionaries.

The missionaries' orthography suffered from two serious flaws. First, it treated the glottal stop as a prosodic phenomenon rather than as a consonant, spelling *makau* 'fishhook' and *makaʻu* 'fear' the same way (as *makau*). Second, it failed to make a distinction between long and short vowels (as in *lolo* 'brain, marrow' and *lolō* 'dumb, paralyzed'), thereby reducing the number of vowels in Hawaiian from 10 to 5. The end result of these two oversights was an orthography that systematically ignored a third of the language's consonant and vowel phonemes.

A reformed orthography was officially accepted by the State of Hawaiʻi in the 1990s (see Schütz 1994 for details). To this day, however, native speakers of Hawaiian still use and prefer the traditional orthography. Indeed, in response to a request from members of the Hawaiian community, the Mayor of Kauaʻi, (the county with the largest number of native Hawaiian speakers) issued a proclamation in 2016 'recognizing and supporting the traditional writing system.'

A similar attachment to tradition is evident on Jeju Island. In our experience, speakers with some degree of fluency in Jejueo, including teachers, are content with an orthography that represents phonetic syllables, without regard for morphological structure. Like speakers of Hawaiian, they are not looking to the orthography for help in learning the language. They already know the language (based on exposure to it as children) and they have a subconscious grasp of its morphological structure—without the need for orthographic cues.

If Hawaiian and Jejueo were not on the verge of extinction, there would be no need to modify the status quo. But, alas, both languages are highly endangered, and decisions need to be made about the orthography's ultimate purpose. A recent global survey of language revitalization efforts on five continents, conducted by the Smithsonian Institution and the University of Hawai'i at Mānoa, reveals that the only realistic option for critically endangered languages is to develop school-based programs. In the absence of an opportunity to learn the language at home in the traditional way, schools represent the last hope.

The first requirement of a school-based program is an orthography to support the preparation of written materials. Unfortunately, the orthography preferred by elderly native speakers may not be appropriate for second language learners. In the case of Hawaiian, for example, second language learners cannot easily fill in a missing consonant, or figure out on their own which vowels are long and which are short. Unlike native speakers, they need a writing system that provides that sort of information—which is why only the reformed orthography is used in schools and immersion programs in Hawai'i.

By the same reasoning, Korean-speaking learners of Jejueo are unlikely to thrive if words are spelled in a way that obscures their internal structure. Not only is such an orthography fundamentally different from the version of Hangeul with which they are familiar, it increases the opacity of Jejueo suffixal morphology, whose substantial differences from Korean already represent a major challenge.

There is an opportunity here that we dare not ignore. The challenges of linguistic analysis and language pedagogy converge in support of the same conclusion: Jejueo must be written in a way that makes its morphological structure as transparent as possible, in accord with the conventions of modern Hangeul. The future of Jejueo may well hang in the balance.

References

Hayman, L. 2008. Universals in Phonology. *The Linguistic Review* 25:83-137.

Jakobsen, R. & Morris, H. 1956. *Fundamental of Language*. The Hague: Mouton.

Ko, J. W., Song, S. J., Kim, J. H., Ko, D. H., Oh, C. M., Moon, S. D., and Oh, S. H. 2013. *Jejueo Orthography*. Jeju: Jeju Development Institute

Jung, S. 1999. Jeju Bangeonui Eumjowa Eumjogun [Pitch in Jeju Dialect]. *Jindanhagbo* 88:543-554.

Hyun, P. H. 1976. *Jejueo Bangeonui Jeongdongsa Eomi Yeongu* [A Study of Finite Verbal Endings in the Cheju Island Dialect]. Seoul: Asia Culture Press.

Hyun, P. H., Kim, K., Kim, Y. D., Kang, Y. B., Ko, G. M., Oh, C. M., Oh, S., and Kim, S. J. 2009. *Gaejeong Jeungbo Jejueo Sajeon* [Jejueo Dictionary]. Jeju: Jeju Special Self-Governing Province.

Kang, Y. S., Kim, S. R., Mun, D. C., Song, C. S., Yang, J. W., Jang, H., and Jeon, Y. S. 2009. *Everyday Jejueo*. Design Cheonje.

Kang, Y. B., Ko, J. W., Kim, S. J., Kim, M. J. 2014. *Jejumunwhalo Baeuneun Jejueo* [Learning Jejueo through Jeju Culture]. Center for Korean Culture, Jeju National University.

Kim, D. Y. 2017. *The Language and Literature of Jeju.* (Course reader) Jeju National University.

Kim, J. H. 2014a. Jejueo Pyogibeobui Hyeongtaebubun [Syntax in Jejueo Orthography]. *Jejueoui Ihaewa Pyohyeon* [Jejueo and Its Expressions], ed. D.-H. Ko, J.-H. Kim, C.-J. Kim, S.-D. Moon, J.-S, Moon, S.-J Song, C.-M. Oh, S.-C, Jung, H.-W. Jung & S.-S. Heo, 240-93. Jeju: Jejueo Bojeonwhoe.

Kim, J. H. 2014b. The Status Quo and the Issues of the Syntactic Studies on Jeju Dialect. *Jejubongeon Yeonguui Eojewa Naeil* [Past and Future of Jeju Dialect Studies], ed. D.-H. Ko, S.-C. Jung, S.-J. Song, Y.-J. Ko, J.-H. Kim, C. M. Oh, and S.-D. Moon,178-314. Jeju: Jeju Development Institute.

Kim, J. H. 2014c. Verbal Suffixes. *Explanations for the Jejueo Writing System*, ed. J.-W. Ko, S.-J. Song, J.-H. Kim, D.-H. Ko, C.-M. Oh, S.-D. Moon, S.- H. Oh, 115-190. Jeju: Jeju Development Institute.

Lee, U. 2014. *Sojunghan Jejueo* [Precious Jejueo]. Jeju: Jejucom.

Schütz, A. 1994. *The Voices of Eden: A History of Hawaiian Language Studies.* Honolulu: University of Hawai'i Press.

Song, S. 2014. Jeju Bangeonui Munbeob 2: Eomi [Grammar of Jeju Dialect: Verbal Suffixes]. *Jejueoui Ihaewa Pyohyeon* [Understanding Jejueo and Expressions, ed. D.-H. Ko, J.-H. Kim, C.-J. Kim, S.-D. Moon, J.-S. Moon, S.-J. Song, C.-M. Oh, S.-C. Jung, H.-W. Jung & S.-S. Heo, 144-187. Jeju: Jejueo Bojeonwhoe.

Woo, C. H. 1995. Jeju Bangeonui Sisang Seoneomal Eomie Dahayeo – 2 Inching Uimunmune Natananeun Sisang Chegyeleul Jungsimeulo [A Study on Tense and Aspectual Suffixes – On the Focus of the Tense and Aspect System in Interrogatives with a Second Person Subject]. *Seogang Eomun* 11:37-60.

Yang, C., Yang, S., and O'Grady, W. 2018. *Jejueo: The Language of Korea's Jeju Island.* Honolulu: University of Hawai'i Press.

Yang, C., O'Grady, W., Yang, S., Hilton, N., Kang, S. and Kim, S. 2018. Revising the language map of Korea. *The Changing World Language Map*, ed. S. Brunn, Berlin: Springer. Available at: https://changingworldlanguagemap.weebly.com/

Appendix: List of Abbreviations

AH	addressee honorific	NMLZ	nominalizer
COMPL	completive	NPST	non-past
CONT	continuative	PFV	perfective
DECL	declarative	PROSP	prospective
IMIT	imperative	Q	question marker
LOC	locative		

Part II

Syntax and Semantics

Nominal-based Nominalization[*]

Masayoshi Shibatani
Rice Univesity

Sung-Yeo Chung
Osaka University

1 Introduction

The current definitions of nominalization, such as the following, are based on narrow observations of nominalization phenomena and suffer from major defects in (i) the overall characterization of the process (not any noun can be derived from any verb (e.g. *laugh* > *singer*?); the process is far more constrained than any of the definitions has it, (ii) the specification of the input to the process (only verbs or members of non-nominal classes?), and (iii) the specification of the output of the process (only nouns or noun phrases?).[1]

* The work reported here was supported in part by the International Joint Research Promotion Program of Osaka University (PI: Sung-Yeo Chung) and the project "Noun modifying

Japanese/Korean Linguistics 25.
Edited by Shin Fukuda, Mary Shin Kim, and Mee-Jeong Park.

> nominalization refers to the process of forming a noun from some other word-class or, especially in classical transformational grammar, the derivation of a noun phrase from an underlying clause. (Crystal 1980: 328)

> ... operations that allow a verb to function as a noun...are called **nominali-zations**, and can be described with a simple formula: V→ N. (Payne 1997: 223)

> 'nominalization' actually conflate[s] two properties: deverbalization... and substantivization (acquisition of noun-properties). (Malchukov 2004: 6)

In this paper we shall take up the second issue, namely whether nominalization applies only to verbs or members of non-nominal categories and show first that there are actually numerous cases of nominalization applying to nouns, contrary to the definitions (section 2). We shall then make a bold claim in the rest of the paper that so-called genitive case/possessive form (e.g. *my/mine, my friend's*, *boku no* 'my/mine' in Japanese, and *emeni uy* (*kes*) 'mother's' in Korean) are actually nominal-based nominalizations by showing that their denotations/references are like ordinary nouns and verbal-based nominalizations (section 3.1), that they exhibit usage patterns paralleling those of nouns and V-based grammatical nominalizations (section 3.2), and that they are morphologically marked the same way as V-based nominalizations in numerous languages of the world, pointing out the close affinity in form between the two (section 3.3). Section 4 discusses the importance of N-based nominalizations showing that the context of "NP-use of N-based nominalizations" is a locus of innovation, where a new nominalization marker originates, which, by spreading to the modification context, eventually becomes a nominalizer. Finally, section 5 summarizes our discussions and concludes the paper, pointing out the distinction between inflection and derivation, and claiming that it is to the latter of which that genitive/possessive forms belong.

2   Nominal-based Nominalization

It is puzzling that the current definitions of nominalization restrict the inputs to the process to verbs or members of non-nominal categories, when even a familiar language like English displays numerous cases of N-based

---

expressions" (PI: Prashant Pardeshi) of the National Institute for Japanese Language and Linguistics.

[1] See Shibatani (2018, to appear) for more on these points.

nominalizations. For example, along with the verb-based agentive nominalizations (e.g. *speaker*), there are forms like *pianist* (cf. *typist*) and *grammarian*, which are clearly based on nouns. But more to the point is the productivity of the "agentive" *-er* derivation, which applies to nouns, yielding numerous new forms; e.g. *villager, New Yorker, tenner, 49ers, 18-wheeler, half-pounder, right-winger, leftfielder, knuckleballer, rear-ender, lifer, West Pointer, MLBer, no-brainer, nor'easter, spring breaker.*

Whether a derived form denotes an agent or non-agentive entity simply depends on the nature of the base form; V-based nominalizations denote an entity most closely associated with activities, namely an agent (or possibly an instrument or other), whereas N-based ones denote others metonymically evoked in close association with the denotation of the base nouns, such as people associated with specific locations, and those associated with a specific organization, philosophical orientation, quantity, time, or manner.[2]

English is by no means unique in this, and one can indeed find similar cases across a wide spectrum of languages where nouns are derived from nouns by using the same morphology for which no one would hesitate using the term nominalization. For example, Parketêjê, a Je language in northern Brazil, has a productive agentive suffix *-katê*, deriving from verb roots forms like *krere-katê* 'singer' and *jakre-katê* 'writer', but it also applies to nouns, especially animal names, productively, yielding forms like *pryre-katê* '(animal) hunter' and *rop-katê* 'jaguar hunter' (Marília Ferreira, p.c.). Central Alaskan Yup'ik has the instrumental nominalizer *-cuun* that applies to both verbs and nouns equally and whose effects Jacobson (1984:450) describes as deriving a "device for V-ing, and [a] device associated with N"; *mingqe-* 'saw' > *mingqesuun* 'sawing machine', *igar-* 'write' > *igarcuun* 'pencil, pen'; *anuqa* 'storm' (N) > *anuqessuun* 'wind generator, storm lantern', *arnassagaq* 'old woman' > *arnassagarcuun* 'old-age pension for a woman'.

The Kwa language Gã of Ghana has a suffix *(-lɔ)*, which applies to both verbs and nouns and another *(-tsɛ´)*, which applies to both adjectives and nouns; *jù* (V) 'steal' > *jù-lɔ`* 'thief', *tsɔ~`ɔ~^* 'show, teach' (V) > *tsɔ~`ɔ~´-!lɔ´* 'teacher': *ànī´háó*, 'laziness'(N) > *ànī´háó-!lɔ´* 'lazy person', *bé!í* 'quarrel' (N) > *béì-lɔ`* 'quarrelsome person', *àmálé* 'lie' (N) > *àmálé-!lɔ´* 'liar'; *àgbò* 'big' (A) > *àgbò-tsɛ`* 'big one', *bíbìóó* 'small' (A) > *bíbìóó-tsɛ`* 'small one'; *àfú* 'hump' (N) > *àfǘ-tsɛ`* 'hunchback', *shìká* 'money' (N) > *shìká-tsɛ`* 'rich person' (Campbell 2017). Similarly, Mandarin Chinese has several deverbal

----

[2] See below and Shibatani (2017, 2018, to appear) for a definition of nominalization as a metonymic process. The metonymic nature of the process would prevent a derivation like *laugh* > *singer*.

"agentive" suffixes that actually apply to nouns as well:

> -zhě (< 者 'person') jì-zhě (record (V)-SUF) 'reporter', zuò-zhě (make
> (V)-SUF) 'author'; dìguó zhǔyì-zhě (imperialism (N)-SUF) 'impe-
> rialist', bǐ-zhě (pen (N)-SUF) 'author'
> -shǒu (< 手 'hand'), zhù-shǒu (help (V)-SUF) 'assistant', hǎo-shǒu
> (good (V)-SUF) 'skilled person', qí-shǒu (flag (N)-SUF) 'standard
> bearer', pào-shǒu (gun (N)-SUF) 'gunner'
> -jiā (< 家 'house') zuò-jiā (make (V)-SUF) 'writer', huà-jiā (paint (V)-
> SUF) 'painter', yìshù-jiā (art (N)-SUF) 'artist', kēxué-jiā (science
> (N)-SUF) 'scientist'

The terms "nominalize" and "nominalization" suggest turning
something in one state to something in another state, hence changing one part
of speech to another. But that is certainly not what the phenomenon above
actually tells us. We should not let the terminology based on a narrow
perspective dictate our view of the phenomenon and close our eyes to the
pertinent facts. We can either discard the terminology that does not serve the
purpose or redefine it. Shibatani (to appear) opts for the latter, newly defining
nominalization as,

> Nominalization is a metonymy-based grammatical derivation process yielding
> constructions associated with a denotation comprised of entity (thing-like)
> concepts that are metonymically evoked by the nominalization structures such as
> events, facts, propositions, resultant products, event participants, and others that
> are recognized to be in close association with the denotion of the base form.
> Nominalizations, as grammatical structures, are similar to nouns by virtue of their
> association with an entity-concept denotation; they both denote thing-like
> concepts, which provide a basis for the referential function of an NP headed by
> these nominals.

3   Genitives/possessives as N-based Nominalizations

Having opened up the possibility for nominal-based nominalizations, we are now in a position to propose a reanalysis of the so-called genitive case or possessive form as a case of N-based nominalization. We shall motivate our analysis on the basis of various similarities between genitives/possessives and verbal-based nominalizations. Before we proceed, a brief note is in order on the distinction between lexical and grammatical nominalizations. The examples of nominalizations in section 2 above are all cases of lexical nominalizations, which are single words and are members of the noun lexicon.

Possessive forms like [*the Queen of England's*], the Japanese form *boku no* 'my/mine', and the Korean form *emeni uy (kes)* 'mother's' are not words and are not subject to a part of speech classification. Yet, they are all nominal with the property of denoting things and thing-like entities such as a hat (belonging to the Queen of England) or a book (owned by the speaker), just like ordinary nouns. Similarly V-based nominalizations like *what Mother buys* and its Japanese and Korean counterparts, [*kaasan ga kau*] (*no*) and [*emeni ka sa-nun*] (*kes*), are nominal, denoting things that Mother buys, but are not nouns. The term grammatical nominalization applies to these nominalizations that are phrasal in form and that are not part of the noun lexicon. On the other hand, pronominal-based forms like *my/mine*, *your/yours*, etc. are clearly part of the noun lexicon and are therefore lexical nominalizations. That the same nominalization process crosses over the border between the lexical and grammatical domains is not at all rare, as shown by the fact that in many languages the same nominalization morphology is used for both lexical and grammatical nominalizations (e.g. *Janet Jackson's* [*singing*]$_N$ *of the national anthem* (lexical); [*Singing the national anthem at the occasion*]$_{NMLZ}$ *irritated many people* (grammatical)).

3.1   N-based Nominalizations and Their Denotations

As adumbrated above, the very basic motivation for treating genitive or possessive forms as N-based nominalizations lies in their nominal property of denoting things and thing-like (asbtract) entities like ordinary nouns. Nominalizations, especially grammatical ones, differ from ordinary nouns in that they denote a variety of metonymically derived concepts, as opposed to relatively uniform concepts that ordinary nouns denote. For example, the noun *apple* denotes all kinds of apples but what it denotes are all classifiable as apple. On the other hand, a metonymically derived noun like *half-pounder* may denote a variety of entities intimately connected to the weight of half a pound, such a hamburger, a can of tobacco, a bag of jellybeans, a steelhead trout, or an arrow weighing half a pound.

While lexical nominalizations (e.g. *singer*, *teenager*) generally tend to be associated with more uniform denotations than forms like *half-pounder*, the genitive forms that we are concerned with, like *mine* and *my brother's*, denote a wide range of entities to which the speaker and the speaker's brother are metonymically connected, such as things that are in their possession (a hat), things over which they have temporary control (a theater seat), those that they have produced (a term paper), or things they are the subject of (a life story), etc. Ordinary metonymic expressions—those that are not grammatical derivations—are similar. Some denote a more limited range of entities than others. For example, (*I need*) *a set of new wheels* is likely used to denote a kind of automobile, but expressions like *the United States* may denote a variety of individuals, organizations, or sport teams that represent the country by this name in one capacity or another, such as the sitting US President, the US Ambassodor to the UN, the US Commerce Department, or US National Men's Hockey Team.

How is an intended denotation determined when a metonymic expression might denote such a wide range of entities? Jointly by the speech context and the Grician Cooperative Principle (in particular, the Maxim of Relevance, which prescribes discourse participants to be contextually relevant). For example, *the United States* is most likely interpreted to be denoting the sitting US president in *the United States has decided to pull out from the Paris agreement* or the US National Women's Soccer Team of the relevant year in *the United States defeated China 1-0 to advance to the semifinals of the 2015 FIFA Women's World Cup*. We shall now demonstrate that this is indeed what happens with both V-based nominalizations and genitive forms as N-based nominalizations.

No one is likely to argue against analyzing *zyukusita* (*no*) 'ripen ones' and *sukosi katamena* (*no*) 'ones that are slightly hard' below as V-based nominalizations (Shibatani 2017, 2018, to appear):

> *Yama   no   mura   no   Natanosyoo ni   tyuuzai   siteita   toki,*
> mountain GEN village GEN   LOC residence was.doing time
> *yama-gaki   ga   dekiru   to,   mura   no   ie   kara*
> mountain-persimmon NOM bear.fruit when village GEN house from
> *moratta koto wa   aru. Keredomo, **zyukusita**   no o   sonomama*
> received that TOP exist however   ripen (ones) PRT ACC as.is
> *kuu ka **sukosi katamena** no wa, kawa o   muite   hosi-gaki*
> eat Q a.little hard (ones) PRT TOP skin ACC peel.GER dried-persimmon
> *ni   suru   ka   datta.*   (MIZUKAMI Tsutomu, *Kokyō*)
> DAT do   Q   was
> "During my residency at a police substation in Natanoshō, a mountain village, when the season of mountain persimmons arrived, I indeed

received some from villagers. However, I ate ripen ones as they are, or with the slightly hard ones, I peeled them and made dried persimmons."

Clearly it is the narrative context that forces us to interpret both *zyukusita* (*no*) and *sukosi katamena* (*no*) as denoting mountain persimmons and referring specifically to the ones that the author received in the mountain village.[3] In other contexts these receive a different interpretation. For example, *sukosi katamena* (*no*) 'what is slightly hard' would likely be interpreted as referring to spaghetti if it was uttered in a pasta restaurant.

Now observe the following narrative, where we find two genitive forms, which we claim to be N-based nominalizations, *Kawabata no* 'Kawabata's' and *Konuma no* 'Konuma's' that receive interpretations in a similar manner as the V-based nominalizaions above:

> *Sono koro, bungaku syoonen no muzyakisa de, syoosetuka nizyuunin*
> that time literary boy GEN innocence at writer twenty.CLF
> *gurai no zyuusyo o Bungaku-nenkan de sirabe, nengazyoo o*
> about GEN address ACC literary-yearbook in check greeting.card ACC
> *dasita koto ga attaga tosi ga akete henzi ga kita no wa,*
> mailed that NOM was.but year NOM dawn.GER reply NOM came PRT TOP
> *Kawabata Yasunari to Konuma Tan dake data.* **Kawabata no** *wa*
> Kawabata Yasunari and Konuma Tan only was Kawabata GEN TOP
> *hondana ni kazari,* **Konuma no** *wa mune ni daite neta.*
> bookcase on decorate.GER Konuma GEN TOP bosom in hold.GEN slept
> (KUZE Mitsuhiko *Hito koishikute—yohaku no ōi jūshoroku*)
> "At that time, out of the innocence of a literary youth, (I) found out the addresses of about twenty writers in a literary yearbook and sent them New Year's greeting cards. At the New Year's start, the ones from whom replies came were only Kawabata Yasunari and Konuma Tan. **Kawabata's** was displayed on the bookshelf and **Konuma's** was held to my bosom while (I) slept."

The expression *Kawabata no* 'Kawabata's' above denotes all kinds of things that are intimately connected to the author Kawabata Yasunari, such

---

[3] Shibatani's work on nominalization distinguishes between "denotation" and "reference". The former refers to the relationship between grammatical units and concepts, while the latter, made possible by the denotations of nominals, to the relationship between grammatical units and enitites in the world. In a modification context, nouns and grammatical nominalizations (e.g. compounds and so-called relative clauses) have denotations but not references, whereas those heading an NP have references based on the match between their denotations and discourse entities.

as the books he wrote, his manuscripts, the New Year's greeting cards he wrote, and his eyeglasses. Again, the context of the narrative above leads us to understand that the expression denotes and refers to Kawabata's New Year's greeting card. The same is true of the second N-based nominalization *Konuma no* 'Konuma's'. Again, the interpretaton varies according to the context of use, such that *Konuma no* could be referring to Konuma's books under an appropriate context.

There have been proposals to handle the denotational/referential properties of both N-based and V-based nominalizations of the above type in terms of deletion of a head noun or a pronominal element (e.g., a pronominal *no* in Japanese). The problem with these proposals is that neither the deletion analysis nor the pro analysis is a complete description until they provide an account as to when the putative deletion of the posited head noun applies or how the pro head is actually distributed and interpreted. In offering a complete description, these analyses must refer to the context, similar to our analysis. Our argument is that if one has to refer to the context anyway, let the context and the Gricean Cooperative Principle handle the whole thing. Remember also that we need a context dependent interpretation for ordinary metonymies, for which neither a head deletion nor a pro head analysis is well motivated (e.g. *I need **a set of new wheels**, Move your **butt** over here*).

3.2 Two Uses of N-based Nominalizations

Ordinary nouns have two major uses in grammar. One is an NP-use, where a noun heads an NP and functions as a referential expression (e.g. $[[Cotton]_N]_{NP}$ *is a useful commodity*). The other is a modification-use, where a noun modifies another noun (e.g. $[[cotton]_N [mill]_N]_N$, $[[cotton]_N \text{ shirt}]_{NP}$). V-based nominalizations have similar usage patterns, as below:

(1) Japanese
   NP-use of V-based nominalization
   a. $[Zyukusita]_{NMLZ} no]_{NP} o$ motte kita.[4]
      ripen.ones NPM ACC carry.GER came
      '(I) brought ripen ones.'
   Modification-use of V-based nominalization
   b. $[[Zyukusita]_{NMLZ} kaki]_{NP}$ o motte kita.
      ripen.ones persimmon ACC carry.GER came
      '(I) brought ripen persimmons.'

---

[4] See next section on the nature of the particle *no* glossed as NPM (NP-use marker) in this example.

The modification structure in (1b) is what is known as a relative clause, which is in fact no more than a use of a V-based nominalization (Shibatani, 2017, 2018, to appear).

Now, N-based nominalizations also have these two uses, as below:

(2) Japanese
   NP-use of N-based nominalization
   a. [[*Konuma no*]_{NMLZ}]_{NP} *o   daite   neta.*
          Konuma GEN   ACC hold.GER slept
      '(I) slept holding Konuma's to my bosom.'
   Modification-use of N-based nominalization
   b. [[*Konuma no*]_{NMLZ} *nengazyoo*]_{NP} *o   daite   neta.*
          Konuma GEN   greeting.card ACC hold.GER slept
      '(I) slept holding Konuma's New Year's greeting card to my
      bosom.'

In western traditional grammar, pronoun-based forms like *my, your*, on the one hand, and *mine* and *yours*, on the other, are treated as two independent lexical items, with the former being classified as "possessive adjectives" (or "adjetivos posesivos" in Spanish traditional grammar) and the latter as "possessive pronouns" ("pronomes posesivos"). These characterizations confuse usage pattern and part of speech classification; i.e. what modifies is not necessarily an adjective (cf. [cotton_N shirt], [[Egyptian cotton_N] shirt]. Our analysis recognizes no such status for these pronoun-based nominalizations, as *my* and *your* are simply the **forms** used for the modification-use, and *mine* and *yours* are those of the NP-use of one and the same structure, namely a pronoun-based nominalization.

Form differentiation according to the difference in use, as in the case of *my* and *mine*, is very common in grammar, and this is exactly what we see in the usage pattern of a V-based nominalization in (1), where the NP-use marks the nominalization with the particle *no* (analogous to the *mine* form), whereas the modification-use has no such marker (analogous to *my*). This is the topic to which we turn next.

3.3 Nominalization Markers

There is ample evidence on the formal front that supports our claim that so-called genitives or possessives are nominalizations; namely, these constructions are formally marked just like verbal-based nominalizations. There are two kinds of nominalization markers that need to be kept apart. Contrary to widely held belief (Horie 2008, Serafim and Shinzato 2009,

Frellesvig 2010, Yap, Hårsta, and Wrona 2011), the Japanese particle *no*, found in e.g. (1a) above, is **not** a nominalizer. A nominalization particle of this kind appears only when a grammatical nominalization is used as an NP head. In other words, what is identified as *juntai joshi* "nominalization particle" in Japanese grammar is an NP-use marker, marking a nominalization bearing a referential function as an NP head. The difference between nominalizing morphemes (nominalizers) and the NP-use markers is easy to see if we compare the patterns of their occurrence. A true nominalizing morpheme occurs regardless of the use context, as in the case of the Mandarin Chinese nominalizer *de* below, whereas an NP-use marker occurs only in the NP-use context, as in (1) above.

(3) Mandarin Chinese
   NP-use of V-based nominalization
   a. *Ràng wǒ kàn kàn* [[*nǐ   mǎi de*]NMLZ]NP.
      let   I   see see   you buy NMLZR
      'Show me the one that you bought.'
   Modification-use of V-based nominalization
   b. *Ràng wǒ kàn kàn* [[*nǐ   mǎi de*]NMLZ *shū*]NP.
      let   I   see see   you buy NMLZR book
      'Show me the book that you bought.'

   The Korean NP-use marker *kes* patterns exactly like Japanese *juntai joshi* and unlike the Mandarin nominalizer *de*. Observe:

(4) Korean
   NP-use of V-based nominalization
   a. *na-nun* [[*sensaygnim-i ssu-n*]NMLZ   **kes**]NP-*ul ilk-ko   iss-ta.*[5]
       I-TOP   teacher-NOM write-NMLZR NPM-ACC read-CON EXIST-IND
      'I am reading the one that the teacher wrote.'
   Modification-use of V-based nominalization
   b. *na-nun* [[*sensaygnim-i ssu-n*]NMLZ   *chayk*]NP-*ul ilk-ko   iss-ta.*
       I-TOP   teacher-NOM write.NMLZR book-ACC   read-CON EXIST-IND
      'I am reading the book that the teacher wrote.'

---

[5] The particle *kes* is usually treated as a noun or a *hyengsik myengsa* (形式名詞) "formal noun" or *uycon myengsa* (依存名詞) "dependent noun" by Korean linguists. However, there is little evidence, historical or otherwise, that it is a noun. The nominal interpretation of the form marked by *kes* is due to the nominalization process involved, not this particle, which simply marks an NP-use of a nominalized form. See Lee (1975) on the nature of *kes*.

The difference between NP-use markers and nominalizers exetends to N-based nominalizations. Similarity in marking patterns between V-based and N-based nominalizations shows that the two are a unified phenomenon. There are two patterns here. In one, as in Mandarin, V-based and N-based nominalizations are marked by the identical nominalizer. Compare the marking pattern in an N-based nominalization below with that in a V-based nominalization in (3).

(5) Mandarin Chinese
NP-use of N-based nominalization
a. *Ràng wǒ kàn kàn* [[*nǐ de*]NMLZ]NP.
   let I see see you NMLZR
   'Show me yours.'
Modification-use of N-based nominalization
b. *Ràng wǒ kàn kàn* [[*nǐ de*]NMLZ shū]NP.
   let I see see you NMLZR book
   'Show me your book.'

Similarity in marking between a V-based nominalization and a genitive has long been recognized (Matisoff 1972), but there has hitherto been no answer to this puzzle.[6] As for Mandarin, Li and Thompson (1981) recognize two different *de*, one for nominalizing verbs (p. 575ff) and the other termed "associative" *de* (p. 113ff) for "possessive constructions" in a broad sense, as if we are dealing with two different particles that are accidentally similar in form. Such a treatment cannot explain why a similar "accident" happens in so many languages across the globe, where the two constructions are marked similarly in totality, as in Mandarin above, or partially as in Korean, where nominalizers are different for V-based and N-based nominalizations, but the two share the identical NP-use markers.

(6) Korean
NP-use of N-based nominalization
a. *Na-nun* [[*sensaygnim-uy*]NMLZ ***kes***]NP-*ul* *ilk-ko*   *iss-ta*.
   I-TOP   teacher-NMLZR   NPM-ACC read-CON EXIST-IND
   'I am reading the teacher's.'
Modification-use of N-based nominalization
b. *Na-nun* [[*sensaygnim-uy*]NMLZ *chayk*]NP-*ul ilk-ko*   *iss-ta*.
   I-TOP   teacher-NMLZR   book-ACC   read-CON EXIST-IND
   'I am reading the teacher's book.'

---

[6] DeLancey (1986:1), maintaining a narrow, verb-centered view of nominalization, finds it "odd that a dependent noun [of possessive constructions] would be marked as nominalized".

Compare (6) with (4), where we recognize two different nominalizers, -*uy* for an N-based and -*n* for a V-based nominalization. Yet, the structures so marked are treated alike in their NP-use, as in (6a) and (4a), where both are marked by the NP-use marker *kes*, indicating that the language treats the relevant structures as something similar. Our claim is that we are dealing with nominalization structures, one V-based and the other N-based, and that so called genitives and possessive particles (e.g. Korean *uy*, Japanese *no*) should be reanalyzed as nominalizers for N-based nominalizations, as in the glosses in (5) and (6), rather than the traditional glossing GEN used in (2) for Japanese.

Japanese dialects pattern like Korean using *juntai joshi* only for NP-use of both V-based and N-based nominalizations with a little twist in Tōkyō Japanese. Before looking at them, let us find out how widespread the Mandarin pattern of marking the two types of nominalization identically is, starting with a language situated close to and therefore possibly influenced by Sinitic and/or Tibeto-Burman languages, namely the Miao language Xong reported by Sposato (2012). This language has interchangeable morphemes *nangd* or *naond*, which Sposato glosses as ASSOC following Li and Thompson (1981), but extending the glossing to V-based nominalizations, as below:

(7) V-based nominalization in Xong

    a. [*Wud jangs* **nangd**][7] *nis ndut-lid   ndut-ghueax.* (NP-use)
       3SG plant ASSOC COP tree-plum tree-peach
       'What he planted were plum trees and peach trees.'

    b. [*Wel hauk* **naond**] *jud   jix   raut.*   (Modification-use)
       1SG drink ASSOC alcohol NEG good
       'The alcohol that I'm drinking is no good.'

(8) N-based nominalization in Xong

    a. Ob-naind nis [wel **naond**].   (NP-use)
       NOM-this COP 1SG ASSOC
       'This is mine.' (NOM = nominalizing prefix or general nominal prefix)

---

[7] This and example (8a) show that the term/gloss "associative" is quite infelicitous if what is referred to by this term "indicate[s] that two noun phrases [connected by it] are 'associated' or 'connected' in some way" (Li and Thompson 1981:113), because these examples do not involve two noun phrases connected by *nangd* or *naond*.

b. [*dab-guoud* **naond**] *zhoux.mioux*   (Modification-use)

    AN-dog   ASSOC   ear   (AN=animal prefix)

    'the dog's ear'

The next examples are from Newar, a Tibeto-Burman language.

(9) Newar V-based and N-based nominalizations in NP-use (courtesy of Kazuyuki Kiryu)

Animate denotation

    a. [*ana dan-ā   cwã:=mha*]   [*rām=yā=mha*]   *kha:.*

       there stand-CM EXIST.ND=NMLZR Ram=GEN=NMLZR COP

      'The one standing there is Ram's.' (Maybe talking about a child.)

Inanimate denotation

    b. [*ana du=gu*]   [*rām=yā=gu*]   *kha:.*

       there exist.ND=NMLZR   Ram=GEN=NMLZR COP

      'The one that is there is Ram's.' (Maybe talking about a car.)

(10) Newar V-based and N-based nominalization in modification-use

Animate denotation

    a. [*ana danā cwã: =mha*]   *maccā* [*rām=yā=mha*]   *macā kha:.*

       there stand EXIST=NMLZR child   Ram=GEN=NMLZR child   COP

      'The child standing there is Ram's child.'

Inanimate denotation

    b [*ana du=gu*]   *gāri*] [*rām=yā=gu*]   *gāri kha:.*

       there exist=NMLZR car   Ram=GEN=NMLZR car   COP

      'The car that is there is Ram's car.'

    The morpheme *yā* glossed GEN in N-based nominalizations above is likely to be an old nominalizer for N-based nominalizations. Indeed, in the modification context, as in (10), marking of N-based nominalizations by the classifier-based nominalizers *mha* and *gu* is optional.

    Nepali, an IE language in close proximity to Newar and other Tibeto-Burman languages, shows a similar marking pattern, where both V-based and N-based nominalizations are marked identically by *-ko*.

    The following data show that the Semitic language Modern Hebrew also marks V-based and N-based nominalization in the same way by *she-*:

(11) Modern Hebrew (courtesy of Anne-Marie Hartenstein)

    a. zo   [**she**   boxa] xi xavera **she**li

      this.F NMLZR cries is friend mine

      'The one (FEM) who is crying is my friend.'

b. ha sefer   ha ze   shama   hu **she**l yaakov ve ha
   the book the this there   is of Yaakov and the
   sefer ha ze po   hu **she**li
   book the this here is mine
   'That book there is Yaakov's and this book here is mine.'

Shibatani and Makhashen (2009) discuss another Semitic language Soqotri, which uses the particle *di* for both V-based and N-based nominalizations.

The Niger-Congo language Yoruba uses the particle *ti* to mark both V-based and N-based nominalizations, as below:

(12) Yoruba (Ajiboye 2005, Akua Campbell, p.c.)
   V-based nominalization
   a. Mo   ri   [tí   [Kúnle ni]]
      1SG   see   NMLZR Kunle owns
      'I saw what Kunle owns.'
   a'. ère   [tí   [Kúnle ni]]
      statue NMLZR Kunle owns
      'the statue that Kunle owns'
   N-based nominalization[8]
   b. Mo   ri   [ti   Kúnlé]
      1SG   see   NMLZR Kunle
      'I saw Kunle's.'
   b'. ère   [ti   Kúnlé]
      statue NMLZR Kunle
      'Kunle's statue'

The Kushitic language Kambaata of Ethiopia is unique in that a final accent marks both V-based and N-based nominalizations. Observe the following examples with the original glosses:

(13) Kambaata (Treis 2008)
   V-based a. [[*dagujj-ó*]   *adab-áa*]
             run-3M.PVO.REL boy-M.ACC
             '(I saw) the boy who ran'
         a'. [[*xuujj-o-sé*]   *adab-áa*]
             see-3M.PVO-3F.OBJ.REL boy-M.ACC
            '(I saw) the boy who saw her'

---

[8] *Ti* for N-based nominalizations has mid tone, while that for V-based ones has high tone.

N-based b. [*ann-í*]   *hiz-óo*
       N-M.GEN N-M.ACC
       'father's brother'
    b'. [*ann-i-sé*]   *hiz-óo*
       N-M.GEN-POSS N-M.ACC
       'her father's brother'
    b". [*ann-aakk-a-sé*]   *hiz-óo*
       N-PL-F.GEN-POSS N-M.ACC
       'her fathers' brother'

Lamaholot, an Austronesian language in eastern Indonesia, also has a suprasegmental nominalization marker that applies to both V-based and N-based nominalizations. Observe the following, where nasalization on the final vowel marks nominalization:

(14) Lamaholot (Nagaya 2011)
    V-based   a. *go   hope* [*meʔɔ̃*]   / [*topi meʔɔ̃*].
            1SG buy   red.NMLZR / hat red.NMLZR
            'I bought the red one/red hat.'
    N-based b. *gʊ gute Hugo nəʔẽ*   (*hepe*).
            1SG take Hugo 3SG.NMLZR knife
            'I will take Hugo's (knife).'

Finally, a fair number of languages use noun/numeral classifiers as nominalizers (cf. the Newar nominalizers seen earlier). This is observed in classifier languages in South America as well as in a number of Chinese dialects, including Cantonese, which uses classifiers such as *dī* and *go* as nominalizers for both V-based and N-based nominalizations, as below:

(15) Cantonese (Mathews and Yip 1994)
    V-based
      a. [[[*Ngóhdeih hái Faatgwok sihk*] *dī*]NMLZ *yéh*]NP *géi   hóu-sihk ga*.
         we   in France   eat CLF   food   quite good-eat PRT
         'The food that we ate in France was pretty good.'
      a'. [[*Gaau   léih   tàahn   kàhm*] *gó*]   ***go?***
         teach you   play   piano   that   CLF
         'the one who teaches you (to play the) piano?'
    N-based (courtesy of Haowen Jiang)
      b. *Lī dēoi hai* [*ngóh **dī**   phàngyáuh*]
        these   COP I   CLF friend

[*léih gó **dī***] *hóeng gópihn.*
you that CLF LOC   there
'These are my friends, and yours are over there.'

Languages that show partial similarity between V-based and N-based nominalizations, like the Korean marking pattern, also abound, where these nominalizations are marked identically but only in their NP-use. In the interest of saving space, we limit our discussions to Japanese dialects below, although similar examples from a diverse array of languages paralleling the Japanese pattern can be easily provided (Shibatani 2018, to appear).

Because of a slight complication seen in Tōkyō Japanese, we start with the Tosa dialect in Kōchi Prefecture, which, like the dialects in the Hokuriku region, makes use of the particle *ga* as an NP-use marker.

(16) Tosa dialect[9]

V-based in NP-use

a. [[*asoko ni   tacchuu*]NMLZ ***ga***]NP *ga* [*uchi no   musuko*] *yo.*
   there LOC standing   NPM NOM we NMLZR son   FP
   'The one who is standing there is our son.'

V-based in modification-use

a′. [*asoko ni   tacchuu*]NMLZ *kodomo*]
   there LOC standing   child
   'the child who is standing there'

N-based in NP-use

b. *Sono akai **ga**   wa* [[*kochi no*]NMLZ ***ga***]NP *ya.*
   that red NPM TOP I   NMLZR NPM COP
   'That red one is mine.'

N-based in modification-use

b′. [[*kochi no*]NMNL *kasa*]
   I   NMLZR umbrella
   'my umbrella'

Compare the above pattern with the earlier Korean forms in (4) and (6), where both V-based and N-based nominalizations receive *kes* marking only when they are in NP-use. A major difference between Korean and Japanese is that while the Korean nominalizers *-(u)n, -nun, -ul* for V-based nominalizations differ in form from the indicative conclusive verbal forms,

[9] Japanese dialect data contained in this article are mostly taken from the fireldnotes of the first author of this article.

Japanese has identical forms for V-based nominalizations (*rentaikei* 'adnominal form') and the conclusive verbal forms (*shūshikei* 'conclusive form'), though these were formally distinct in Old and Middle Japanese.

The Tosa dialect and those in Hokuriku that use *ga* as an NP-use marker (*juntai joshi*) point out an important fact, along with Tōkyō Japanese and other dialects that use *no*, that *juntai joshi* in Japanese dialects are related to the Old Japanese nominalizer (aka genitive) particles *ga* and *no*, hinting at an intimate connection between N-based and V-based nominalizations. We shall discuss this development of NP-use markers from nominalizers for N-based nominalizations in the next, final section.

Compared to the neater marking patterns in many Japanese dialects, where both V-based and N-based nominalizations in NP-use are marked identically, Tōkyō Japanese is somewhat irregular in the marking of N-based nominalizations in NP-use. Compare the following Tōkyō forms with the Tosa form (16b):

(17) Tōkyō Japanese

NP-use of V-based and N-based nominalizations

Sono [[*akai*]NMLZ ***no***]NP *wa*   [[*ore no*]NMLZ Ø]NP *da*.
that   red   NPM TOP   I   NMLZR NPM COP
'That red one is mine.'

No is missing in the NP-use of the N-based nominalization above (shown by Ø), while a more consistent marking pattern is maintained in the Tosa dialect. This peculiarity of Tōkyō Japanese is undoubtedly due to the reduction of the doubled *no-no* that the consistent use of NP-use marker would bring about. Indeed, there is some evidence that Tōkyō speech once allowed doubled *no-no* in the relevant context, as can be witnessed in the sentences of the following type found in the memoire of Natsume Sōseki by his wife, first published in 1929.

(18) *Sōseki no omoide* (Sōseki memoire)[10]

[[*anata no*]NMLZ ***no***]NP *wa osieru   yori sikaru   hoo ga   ooi.*
you   NMLZR NPM TOP teaching from scolding side NOM more
'Yours is more on the side of scolding than teaching.'

In addition, there are modern dialects that retain doubled *no-no*, as in the Toba dialect of the Nagaoka district in Mie Prefecture. E.g.,

---

[10] *Natsume Sōseki no omoide* by Kyōko Natsume (Kaizōsha, 1928).

(19) Toba dialect
  a. *Kono kuruma,* [[*sensei* **no**]$_{NMLZ}$ **no**]$_{NP}$ *ya.*[11]   (NP-use)
    his   car   teacher NMLZR NPM COP
    'This car is the teacher's.'
  b. [[*sensei* **no**]$_{NMLZ}$ *kuruma*]$_{NP}$ (Modification-use)
    teacher NMLZR car
    'the teacher's car'

4   Development of NP-use Markers (*Juntai joshi*)

The importance of N-based nominalizations for the general understanding of nominalization is that their NP-use is the locus of innovation, which subsequently spreads to the domain of V-based nominalizations, leading to the eventual development of a nominalizing morphology/nominalizer. There is ample evidence available in Japanese showing that the so-called *juntai joshi* develops out of the markers of N-based nominalizations in NP-use.

As the following sentence from Early Middle Japanese shows, older forms of Japanese did not have a marker (*juntai joshi*) for V-based nominalizations in NP-use.

(20) NP-use of V-based nominalization in EMJ (*Makura no sōshi* 60)
    [*kuriyame*   *no*   [[**kiyoge naru**]$_{NMLZ}$]]$_{NP}$ *ga*   *sasi-idete,*
    kitchen.maid NMLZR cool.looking COP.ADN NOM come-out.GER
    "*Nanigasi-dono no*   *hito ya saburapu*" *nado ipu* *mo* *wokasi.*
    so.and.so-HON NMLZR man Q exist.POL like say.ADN also fascinating
    'A cool looking one, a kitchen maid's coming out and asking like "Is there Mr. so-and-so's servant?" is also fascinating.'

The *juntai joshi* no for V-based nominalization in the NP-use context developed during the sixteenth century, and it has taken more than two hundred years for it to establish itself as an obligatory NP-use marker via a long period when the marking was optional, as the two forms below show:

(21) *Jōruri* (ballard dramas) by Chikamatsu Monzaemon (ca. 1700)
  a. [[*hito*   *o*   *noseta*]$_{NMLZ}$]]$_{NP}$ *ga*   *noserarete*
    person ACC giving.ride   NOM give.ride.PASS.GER
    'the one who gave a ride was given a ride (got tricked)...'

---

[11] Cf. the Kyōto-Ōsaka pattern, where the *no-no* sequence has been reduced to *non* (e.g. *ore non* 'mine', *yonderu non* 'one that (I am) reading'.

b. *Site darezo* [[*horeta*]$_{NMLZ}$ ***no***]$_{NP}$ *ga aruka.*
and someone fallen.in.love NPM NOM exist.Q
'And someone, the one (you) have fallen in love exists?'

The question is; where does the NP-use marker *no* above come from? Obviously, it is related to the nominalizer *no* for N-based nominalizations, aka the genitive case particle, as not only *no* but also the other Old Japanese nominalizer/genitive *ga* is used as an NP-use marker in other dialects, as we saw earlier. Our claim is that the NP-use markers *no* and *ga* for V-based nominalizations did not develop directly out of the nominalizing *no* and *ga* of the so-called possessive construction, but out of those particles used as NP-use markers of N-based nominalizations, which well antedate the marking in V-based nominalizations.

Old Japanese and Early Middle Japanese generally used N-based nominalizations as an NP head without an NP-use marker, as in the following examples:

(22) a. *kono uta…* [*Kakinomoto Hitomaro ga*]   *nari.* (*Kokinshū,*
this poem Kakinomoto Hitomaro NMLZR COP   early 10th C)
'This poem…is Kakinomoto Hitomaro's.'
    b. [*Kara no*]   *mo* [*Yamato no*] *mo kakikegasi…*
Chinese NMLZR also Japanese NMLZR also write.away
'writing away Chinese ones [poems] also, Japanese ones as well…'
                                    (*Genji monogatari,* early 11th C)

However, the earliest (optional) use of *no* as an NP use marker for N-based nominalizations is already seen in the 10th century, as below:

(23) a. *Hitozuma to* [*wa ga*]   ***no*** *hutatu omofuni hanarekosi*
man's.wife and I NMLZR NPM two think leave.behind
sode wa   awaremasereru. (*Yoshitadashū,* mid-10th C)
sleeve TOP exceedingly.sad
'As I think about both a man's wife and mine, the sleeves left behind are exceedingly sad.'
    b. *Kokin no*   *tyooka,* [*Ise ga*] ***no*** *ga   sugurete*
Kokin NMLZR long.poem Ise NMLZR NPM NOM very
omosirosi to   yuu nari. (*Jiteiki* 16th-17th C)
fascinating that say EVI
'Of the long poems of Kokin, Ise's are said to be very fascinating.'

The claim that the NP-use marker (*juntai joshi*) for V-based nominalizations developed out of that for N-based nominalization proposed above is supported by synchronic dialect data, where the presence of an NP-use marker for V-based nominalizations presupposes the establshiment of it for N-based ones. Discussed below is an ongoing spread pattern of a new NP-use marker *tu* (or possibly the change of *to* to *tu*) in the dialects of Kumamoto Prefecture in Kyūshū, where both *to* and *tu* are used depending on locality. These particles are likely related to the archaic genitive/nominalizer *tu*, seen in *ma-tu-ge* (eye GEN hair) 'eye lash', *oki tu sima* (offing GEN island) 'the island in the offing'. The following forms from Yatsushiro dialect show the overall pattern of the distribution of *to* and *tu* in the areas where the two forms are used:

(24) Yatsushiro Nisshin-chō dialect: Argument nominalizations in NP-use
    a. [*Tootyan ga mai asa yomu*] to/*tu wa sinbun tai.
        Daddy NOM every morning read.PRS NMP TOP newspaper COP
        'What Daddy reads every morning is a newspaper.'
    b. [*Tootyan ga yonda*] ?*to/tu wa sinbun tai*.
        Daddy NOM read.PST NMP TOP newspaper COP
        'What Daddy read was a newspaper.'

There appears to be a fair amount of both dialectal and idiolectal variation in how *to* and *tu* are used among speakers of different dialects within Kumamoto and among speakers of different generations, but one striking factor determining their use is the tense/aspectual split, such that only *to* is used with the present tense/imperfective form, while either *to* or *tu* may be used in the past tense/perfective form.[12] Clearly *to* is the older of the two since there are dialects, such as the Hakata dialect in Fukuoka Prefecture, that use only *to*. Thus, the general pattern for the locales where both *to* and *tu* are used is that the former was once used in all contexts, while the newer *tu* form started to replace the older *to* in the past/perfective context, giving rise to a marking pattern where only *to* is used in the present/imperfective context, while in the past/perfective environment *to* has been gradually replaced by *tu*.

---

[12] The question mark in (24b) and (26b) indicates that there are speakers who (readily) accept *to*, but the majority of speakers prefer *tu* over *to* in the relevant context. Adjectival nominalizations in NP-use are preferentially marked by *tu* in the dialects that use it.

In some areas, *tu* is coming to prevail more and more in the past/perfective context, as in the case of many speakers of the Yatsushiro dialect.

This pattern of development is correlated, we claim, with the way *tu* is used replacing the older *to* marking the NP-use of N-based nominalizations. In the Hakata dialect mentioned above, the NP-use of N-based nominalizations are marked only by *to*, as [*ore n*] *to/*tu* 'mine'. And this dialect does not use *tu* in marking V-based nominalizations in NP-use even in the past/perfective context (Takanori Hirano p.c.). Even within Kumamoto Prefecture, where *tu* is widely used, there are areas where *tu* is not used or used far less than in places like Yatsushiro and Kumamoto City. In Hitoyoshi City, *tu* is seldom used for N-based nominalizations, and the normal form is [*oga*] *to/*?tu* 'mine'. Similar to the Hakata dialect, the Hitoyoshi dialect does not use *tu* in marking the NP-use of V-based nominalizations even in the past/perfective context.

Unlike these dialects, the Kumamoto City dialect happily uses both *to* and *tu* in marking the NP-use of N-based nominalizations; accordinly both [*ore n*] *to* and [*ore n*] *tu* 'mine' are heard. Interestingly, according to Sakai (2012), both *to* and *tu* may mark the NP-use of V-based nominalizations in the past/perfective context in this dialect, as below:

(25) Kumamoto City dialect (Sakai 2012)

    a. [*Roosoku-n   kieta*] **tu**   *ba*   *mita*.
       candle-NMLZR go.out NMP ACC saw
       Lit. 'I saw a candle's what has gone out.' (a burned-out one of a
       candle stick')

    b. [*Roosoku-n   kieta*] **to**   *ba*   *mita*.
       candle-NMLZR go.out NMP ACC saw
       'I saw the candle go out.'

What is fascinating about this piece of data is that the *tu* form in (25a) marks a V-based **argument** nominalization in NP-use, such that [*roosoku-n kieta*] denotes a concrete object, a burned-out candle, with the literal meaning of "what is burned out of a candle kind". On the other hand, (25b), marked by *to*, is an **event** nominalization denoting an event of a candle going out.

The pattern of development seen in the Kumamoto City dialect is corroborated by the situation in the Yatsushiro dialect, which is at a more advanced stage in the replacement of *to* by *tu* than the Kumomoto City dialect. First, whereas Kumamoto City speakers freely allow both [*ore n*] *to* and [*ore n*] *tu*, Yatsushiro speakers prefer the *tu* form, indicating that *tu* is quickly replacing *to* in the context of NP-use of N-based nominalizations. In consonant with this, Yatsushiro speakers prefer *tu* in the NP-use of V-based nominalizations as well (see (24b)). Moreover, this dialect permits, indeed prefers, *tu* marking the NP-use of V-based **event** nominalizations, not permitted by the Kumamoto City dialect.

(26) Yatsushiro dialect event nominalization in NP-use

[*ANO KO* *ga* *naita*] '*ta waitsaa* (< *tu wa*) *hara* *ga*
that child NOM cry.PST NMP TOP/NMP.TOP stomach NOM
hetta *ken* *bai*.
decreased because COP
'(The reason) that child cried was because he was hungry.'

To summarize the above discussion, (i) NP-use marker (*juntai joshi*) starts out in the N-based domain, in the context of the NP-use of N-based nominalizations, (ii) it then spreads to V-based nominalizations, first marking the NP-use of argument nominalizations, and then (iii) to the NP-use of event nominalizations. Shibatani and Shigeno (2013) discuss a similar pattern of development in Ryūkyūan in terms of the spread of the NP-use marker *mun(u)* (< *munu* 'thing' = Japanese *mono*), replacing the older NP-use maker *si*. They also show the development of an NP-use marker as a nominalizer by the extension of it to the modification context.[13]

As the above narrative suggests, our study has important theoretical implications not only on the rise and form of nominalization markers. Specifically, it argues against a popular theory on the rise of the *juntai joshi*, namely that it was caused by the merger of the conclusive and the adnominal verbal form. Supplanting the conclusive form with the adnominal form during the Muromachi period (14ᵗʰ-16ᵗʰ C) had obliterated the formal distinction between subordinate clauses (our nominalizations), ending in the adnominal form, and main clauses, ending earlier in the conclusive form. The *juntai joshi no* arose, the popular theory claims, as a way to make a formal distinction between subordinate cluases and main clauses (Kinsui 1995). Our discussion clearly shows that the *juntai joshi* originates in the context of NP-use of N-based nominalizations, where the conclusive/adnominal merger is entirely irrelevant. Besides, Korean, which has maintained the conclusive/adnominal distinction throughout its history, has developed the *juntai joshi kes;* [*emeni uy*] **kes** 'mother's', [*emeni ka sanun*] **kes** 'the one that mother buys'.

---

[13] Cf. the Ūyama dialect of Okinawan, where *mun* now functions as a nominalizer for pronoun-based nominalizations; [*wa: mun*] *do:* '(It's) mine', [[*wa: mun*] *kutu*] 'my shoes'.

5   Summary and Conclusion

As forms like *speaker* and *Berliner* show, nominalization applies equally to both verbal and nominal bases and the results may be a word unit (lexical) or a phrasal unit (grammatical); *the [**singing**] of the national anthem* vs. [***singing the national anthem***]. These nominalizations, like ordinary nouns, may head a noun phrase (an NP-use), as in [[***Singing the national anthem***]$_{NMLZ}$]$_{NP}$ *was none other than Bill's wife*, or modify a noun (a modification-use), as in [*The woman* [***singing the national anthem***]$_{NMLZ}$]$_{NP}$ *is Bill's wife*.

Nominal-based nominalizations known as the genitive or possessive form behave exactly the same. They denote things and thing-like entities closely associated with the denotation of the base. They can be lexical (e.g. *his, mine*) or phrasal (e.g. [*the Queen of England's*], [*boku no*] 'mine', [*emeni uy*] (*kes*) 'mother's), and they also have both NP-use ([[*The Queen of England's*]$_{NMLZ}$]$_{NP}$ *is that hat*, [[*Boku no*]$_{NMLZ}$]$_{NP}$ *o totte* 'Give me mine') and modification-use [[*The Queen of England's*]$_{NMLZ}$ *hat*]$_{NP}$, [[*boku no*]$_{NMLZ}$ *boosi*]$_{NP}$ 'my hat'.

Our analysis offers a new insight into the meaning relationship between the "possessor" and the "possessum". Those various "possessive" relations (*Taro's head, Taro's father, Taro's letter, Taro's hospital*, etc.) are attributed to the metonymic inferences associated with a nominalization process creating the so-called possessive form, *Taro's*. Modification in possessive constructions means restricting the denotation of the head noun (e.g. *book*) with that of the N-based nominalization (e.g. *Taro's*), with the latter denoting things with which Taro is associated and specifying a subset of the former. The denotation of an entire possessive construction (e.g. *Taro's book*) is an intersection of the denotation of a head noun and that of an N-based nominalization, in the same way as the so-called restrictive relative clause restricts the denotation of the head noun.[14]

Traditional grammars treat the genitive case/possessive form as an inflection similar to a grammatical case such as nominative and accusative. The genitive, however, differs from grammatical case in that it either modifies another noun (*his/John's car*) or stands in NP positions where case inflected forms cannot freely stand (*His/John's/*Him is here; I saw his/John's/*he*), showing that it is different from ordinary case forms, the syntactic positions of which are fixed—a nominative form in subject

---

[14] See Shibatani (2017, 2018, to appear), who analyzes so-called restrictrive relative clauses as V-based argument nominalizations in modification-use, just as the possessor in a possessive construction is analyzed as an N-based nominalization in modification-use in this article.

position, an accusative form in object position. The genitive form, in contrast, is not bound to any particular syntactic position, and even to the modifier position in possessive constructions, as the foregoing discussions amply demonstrate. More importantly, the denotation of the nominal in different case forms remains constant, with case inflections adding only grammatical meanings. For example, the nominative *I* marks a subject function, and the accusative *me* an object function, while maintaining their denotation constant, namely the speaker. This is not so with the genitive form; *mine* does not denote the speaker but rather something metonymically related to the speaker. The same applies to languages using particles to mark case, as in Japanese forms *boku ga* (I NOM) and *boku o* (I ACC) vis-à-vis *boku no* (*o mite*) '(look at) mine'.

The nominalization analysis proposed above treats the genitive case form as derivationl, as nominal-based nominalization, similar to the derivations of *pig > piglet*, *village > villager*, which derive new nouns with new denotations, unlike the inflections such as *he/him*, *pig/pigs*, which do not change the denotations, but which differ only in grammatical meanings (subject/object, singular/plural). The same applies to Japanese, Korean and other languages that make use of particles. While Japanese particles *ga* (nominative), *o* (accusative), *ni* (dative) are case particles (*kaku joshi* 格助詞), the so-called genitive case particle (*zok-kaku joshi* 属格助詞) *no* is not. Like the English possessive clitic '*s*, it is derivational. The same goes with the Korean particle *uy*, traditionally classified as a case particle under the name of *sokkyek* (属格), *soyukyek* (所有格), or *kwanhyeng(sa)kyek* (冠形(詞)格).

References

Ajiboye, O. J. 2005. *Topics on Yoruba nominal expressions*. Doctroal dissertation, University of British Columbia.

Campbell, A. 2017. *A grammar of Gã* . Doctoral dissertation, Rice University.

Crystal. D. 1980. *A dictionary of linguistics and phonetics*. Oxford: Wiley-Blackwell.

DeLancey, S. 1986. Relativization as nominalization in Tibetan and Newari. Paper presented at the 19th International Conference on Sino-Tibetan Languages and Linguistics.

Frellesvig, B. 2010. *A history of the Japanese language*. Cambridge: Cambridge University Press.

Horie, K. 2008. The grammaticalization of nominalizers in Japanese and Korean. *Rethinking grammaticalization: New perspectives*, eds. M. J. López-Couso and E. Seoane, 169-187. Amsterdam: John Benjamins.

Jacobson, S. 1984. *Yup'ik Eskimo dictionary*. Alaska Native Language Center, University of Alaska, Fairbanks.

Kinsui, S. 1995. Nihongo no iwayuru N′ sakujo ni tsuite. *Dai 3kai Nanzan Daigaku Nihongo-kyōiku ·Nihongo-gaku kokusai shinpojūmu hōkokusho*, eds. Y. Abe, T. Sakamoto, and M. Soga. 153-176. Nagoya: Nanzan University.

Lee, S. N. 1975. A study of the word *kes* in Middle Korean. *Cintan Hakpo* 39: 105-138.

Malchukov, A. 2004. *Nominalization, verbalization: Constraining a typology of transcategorial operations*. Muenchen: Lincom Europa.

Matisoff, J. 1972. Lahu nominalization, relativization, and genitivization. *Syntax and Semantics* Vol. 1, ed. J. Kimball, 237-258. New York: Academic Press.

Matthews, S. and V. Yip. 1994. *Cantonese: A comprehensive grammar*. London and New York: Routledge.

Nagaya, N. 2011. *The Lamaholot language of eastern Indonesia*. Doctoral dissertation, Rice University.

Payne, T. 1997. *Describing morphosyntax: A guide for field linguists*. Cambridge: Cambridge University Press.

Sakai, M. 2012. Gendai Kumamoto hōgen no juntai joshi―*to* to *tsu* ni tsuite―. *Handai Shakai Gengogaku Kenkyū-nōto*. 10: 30-45.

Serafim, L. and R. Shinzato. 2009. Grammaticalization pathways for Japonic nominalizers: A view from western periphery. *Japanese/Korean Linguistics* 16: 116-130.

Shibatani, M. 2017. Nominalization. *Handbook of Japanese Syntax*, eds. M. Shibatani, S. Miyagawa, and H. Noda, 271-332. Berlin: De Gruyter Mouton.

Shibatani, M. 2018. Nominalization in crosslinguistic perspective. *Handbook of Japanese Contrastive Linguistics*, eds. P. Pardeshi and T. Kageyama, 345-410. Berlin: De Gruyter Mouton.

Shibatani, M. To appear. What is nominalization? Towards the theoretical foundations of nominalization. *Nominalization in languages of the Americas*, eds. R. Zariquiey, M. Shibatani, and D. Fleck. Amsterdam: John Benjamins.

Shibatani, M. and K. A. Makhashan. 2009. Nominalization in Soqotri, a South Arabian language of Yemen. *Linguistics of Endangered Languages: Contributions to Morphology and Syntax*, ed. W. L. Wetzels, 9-31. Leiden: Brill.

Shibatani, M. and H. Shigeno. 2013. Amami nominalizations. *International Journal of Okinawan Studies*. Vol 7: 107-139.

Sposato, A. 2012. Relative clauses in Xong (Miyao-Yao). *Journal of the Southeast Asian Linguistics Association*, Vol. 5: 49-66.

Treis, Y. 2008. Relativization in Kambaata from a typological point of view. *Interaction of morphology and syntax: Case studies in Afroasiatic*, eds. Z. Frajzyngier and E. Shay, 161-206. Amsterdam: John Benjamins.

Yap, F. H., K. Grunow-Hårsta and J. Wrona. 2011. Introduction: Nominalization strategies in Asian languages. *Nominalization in Asian languages: Diachronic and typological perspectives*, eds. F. H. Yap, K. Grunow-Hårsta, and J. Wrona, 1-58. Amsterdam: John Benjamins.

Daroo as an entertain modal: an inquisitive approach

Yurie Hara
Waseda University

1 Introduction

Many languages express question meanings morpho-syntactically and prosodically. In Japanese, the question particle *ka* marks a sentence as interrogative (1) with or without rising prosody ('↑' henceforth; L%H% in J_ToBi (Venditti 2005a)). A question-like meaning can also be expressed by a declarative sentence with rising intonation (2).

(1) John-ga kuru ka↑ / ↓   (2) John-ga   kuru↑
     John-NOM come Q   John-NOM come
     'Is John coming?'   'John is coming?'

Although all of these utterance types express some kind of question meaning, previous analyses (Büring and Gunlogson 2000; Nilsenova 2002; Gunlogson 2003; Truckenbrodt 2006; Westera 2013; Sudo 2013; Northrup 2014; Malamud and Stephenson 2015; Farkas and Roelofsen 2017) agree that they are not completely interchangeable. This study examines the interaction between the Japanese modal particle *daroo*, sentence type and intonation, which sheds new light on the influence of sentence types and intonational contours on the interpretation of sentences. I propose that *daroo* is a root-level modal which involves a deictic element pointing to the speaker's knowledge. The

Japanese/Korean Linguistics 25.
Edited by Shin Fukuda, Mary Shin Kim, and Mee-Jeong Park.

semantics of *daroo* is defined in the framework of inquisitive dynamic epistemic logic (Ciardelli and Roelofsen 2015), which provides a model in which modal operators can embed both declarative and interrogative sentences. As for the contribution of rising intonation, I propose that Final Rise is used to indicate that the speaker is uncertain about her discourse move, since her evidence is not strong enough to update the common ground. Thereby, the addressee is invited to support her discourse move. A detailed investigation of *daroo* reveals an interesting paradigm with respect to parameters such as clause type, intonation and pragmatic context.

2 Basic Paradigm

2.1 Falling Declaratives: *daroo↓*

When *daroo* is attached to the end of a plain declarative as in (3), the whole sentence indicates that the speaker has a bias toward the prejacent proposition *John-ga kuru* 'John is coming'.

(3)   John-ga   kuru daroo↓
      Jonn-NOM come DAROO
      'John is coming, I bet./Probably, John is coming.'

The conclusion that falling *daroo*-declaratives must express "the speaker's bias" is supported by the following observations:[1] 1) their co-occurrence with probability adverbs is restricted, and 2) they have an obligatory wide-scope reading under *because*-clauses.

2.2   Falling Interrogatives: *daroo ka↓*

Polar interrogatives in Japanese are marked with the sentence final particle *ka*. If *daroo* occurs within such a falling interrogative, it is interpreted as a self-addressing question, as in (4) produced with the pitch profile in Figure 1(a).

(4)   Marie-wa   wain-o   nomu daroo   ka↓
      Marie-TOP wine-ACC drink DAROO Q
      'I wonder if Marie drinks wine.'

---

[1] See Sugimura (2004) and Hara (2006) for the supporting data and arguments.

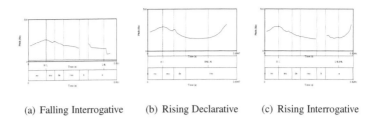

(a) Falling Interrogative   (b) Rising Declarative   (c) Rising Interrogative

FIGURE 1 Pitch Profiles of Falling Interrogative, Rising Declarative/Interrogative

Put another way, by uttering a construction like (4), the speaker is inquiring into his or her own knowledge state, i.e., entertaining an issue, namely the question of whether or not Marie drinks wine.

2.3 Rising Declaratives: *daroo*↑

Turning to the rising counterparts of the above two types, *daroo* can be used in declaratives with Final Rise intonation (L%H% in the J_ToBI system (Venditti 2005b)). Such utterances appear to function as tag/confirmation questions, as seen in (5) produced with the pitch profile in Figure 1(b).

(5)   Marie-wa wain-o   nomu daroo↑
       Marie-TOP wine-ACC drink DAROO
       'Marie drinks wine, right?'

In other words, in uttering a Final Rise *daroo*-declarative, the speaker indicates her bias toward the prejacent 'Marie drinks wine' and seeks agreement from the addressee. Thus, the rising contour seems to allow the holder of the bias to be the addressee as well as the speaker.

Note that even with rising contour, the speaker's bias does not disappear. When the context is such that the speaker is epistemically neutral, a rising *daroo*-declaratives is infelicitous:

(6)   Context: A has no idea what Marie likes. A asks B if Marie drinks wine.

       A: #Marie-wa wain-o   nomu daroo↑
            Marie-TOP wine-ACC drink DAROO
            'Marie drinks wine, doesn't she?'

2.4 Rising Interrogatives: *daroo ka*↑

Finally, *daroo* seems to be incompatible with Final Rise interrogative constructions. Native speakers judge examples like (7), with a pitch profile like that in Figure 1(c), as deviant or unacceptable.

(7) #Marie-wa wain-o nomu daroo ka↑
     Marie-TOP wine-ACC drink DAROO Q
     'I'm wondering if Marie drinks wine, right?'

3 Proposals

The investigation of the data in the previous section shows that *daroo* can express the speaker's or the addressee's bias and that it can embed either a declarative or an interrogative.[2] In order to derive the distribution and interpretations, I make the following proposals.

(8) a. Proposal 1
         Daroo is a root-level modal operator E_{SPKR}, which expresses epistemic issues associated to the speaker, SPKR.
     b. Proposal 2
         The Final Rise intonation ↑ indicates the speaker's uncertainty.

Proposal 1 further breaks down into the following two sub-proposals:

(9) Sub-proposal 1.1: Syntactically, *daroo* is a root-level operator, which moves to [Spec CP] to check off its uninterpretable feature, [uROOT].
     Sub-proposal 1.2: Semantically, *daroo* is an Entertain Modality, E_{SPKR}, in Inquisitive Epistemic Logic, henceforth IEL (Ciardelli and Roelofsen 2015).

In understanding the effects of *daroo* sentences, the current paper assumes the framework of update semantics (Stalnaker 1968; Heim 1982), in which utterances are considered as context change potentials (CCPs), i.e., functions from contexts to contexts. More specifically, an utterance of φ updates an input context associated with an attitude holder with the propositional content of φ by taking the intersection of the content of the input context and the propositional content. In IEL, as we will see below, both contexts to be updated and propositions are modelled as inquisitive states, so both declarative and interrogative updates can be uniformly defined as intersecting the input context with the propositional content. Let M be an inquisitive epistemic model, w a possible world and C a variable over contexts. Then, the interpretation of an utterance of φ can be defined as in (10). $[\![\varphi]\!]^{M,w}$ is a CCP: it acts as a function which updates the input context with the propositional content of φ.

---

[2] To confirm this observation objectively (see Schütze 1996), two rating experiments were conducted, which are not presented in the current paper for space reasons. The first experiment is briefly reported in Hara and Davis (2013a).

(10) $[\![\varphi]\!]^{M,w} = \lambda C.C \cap [\varphi]$, where $[\varphi]$ is the propositional content of φ.

In the following subsections, I motivate each sub-proposal in (9) with linguistic data and show how it is implemented.

3.1 Sub-Proposal 1.1: *Daroo* as a Root-Level Modal

First, I propose that *daroo* functions as a root-level modal operator (Zimmermann 2004; Davis 2009).[3] Under this analysis, *daroo* expresses epistemic knowledge associated with the speaker. The empirical data presented in Hara and Davis (2013b) show that *daroo* is a root-level modal which takes wider scope than the "normal" propositional modals. The agent of the knowledge must always be the speaker. Formally, *daroo* translates as an entertain modality E_{SPKR}. The root-oriented-ness of *daroo* is syntactically realized using the uninterpretable feature $[u\text{ROOT}]$, which needs to be checked off by the matching feature $[\text{ROOT}]$ at C_{root}.

(11)   [CP2 daroo$_i$/[u̶R̶O̶O̶T̶] [C2′ TP [t_i $\varnothing_{\text{DECL}}$/ka$_{\text{INTEROG}}$]]] C1/[R̶O̶O̶T̶]]

This LF configuration (11) predicts that *daroo* embeds the combination of the sentence-radical p and the sentence-type marker $\varnothing_{\text{DECL}}$/ka$_{\text{INTEROG}}$, i.e., *daroo*$(p$-$\varnothing_{\text{DECL}})$ and *daroo*$(p$-ka$_{\text{INTEROG}})$, which translate to $E_{\text{SPKR}}p$ and $E_{\text{SPKR}}?p$, respectively. As we will see below in Section 3.2, inquisitive epistemic logic indeed provides a system in which modal operators can embed both declarative and interrogative sentences.

3.2 Sub-Proposal 1.2: *Daroo* as an Entertain Modal

Next, we define the interpretation of the modal component of *daroo*, namely E_{SPKR}. An interesting feature of the syntax of *daroo* is that it can take both a declarative and interrogative as its argument. Thus, the semantics of *daroo* should be able to handle issues raised by interrogatives as well as information brought by declaratives.[4]

Inquisitive epistemic logic (IEL) (Ciardelli and Roelofsen 2015) offers a framework that can model the process of raising and resolving issues and defines an entertain modality that deals with the issues that the agents entertain. The current paper claims that *daroo* is a linguistic realization of the entertain modality the agent of which is the speaker SPKR. The following section briefly goes over the relevant technicalities of IEL.

---

[3] For the reasons of space, I omit the data and discussion to motivate this proposal. See Hara and Davis (2013b).

[4] Moreover, although *daroo* in a falling declarative indicates the speaker's bias toward the embedded proposition, the bias meaning disappears in falling interrogatives (data omitted for space reasons).

Inquisitive epistemic logic

IEL is an extension of epistemic logic where the framework is enriched with an inquisitive component. IEL models how the information is associated with a set of agents. Let W be the set of all possible worlds. As with standard epistemic logic, an information state is identified with a set of possible worlds. Inquisitive epistemic logic introduces another dimension which can characterise the issues that are entertained by the agents. An issue is defined as a set of information states:

(12)   a.   An information state s is a set of possible worlds, i.e., $s \subseteq W$.

        b.   An *issue* $I \subseteq \wp(W)$ is a non-empty, downward closed set of information states.

In inquisitive epistemic logic, there are two modal operators, a knowledge modality K and an entertain modality E. K encodes an agent's information state just like standard epistemic logic, while E encodes an agent's inquisitive state, which encapsulates the issues that the agent entertain. As discussed above, I argue that the modal particle *daroo* translates to the modality operator E with the agent SPKR:

(13)   *daroo* $\rightsquigarrow E_{\text{SPKR}}$

Semantics of the entertain modality E

An inquisitive epistemic model M is defined as in (14).

(14)   An inquisitive epistemic model for a set $\mathcal{P}$ of atomic sentences and a set Π of issues is a tuple $M = \langle W, V, \Sigma_A \rangle$ where:

        a. $\mathcal{A}$ is a finite set of agents.

        b. W is a set, whose elements are called *possible worlds*.

        c. $V : W \rightarrow \wp(\mathcal{P})$ is a *valuation map* that specifies for every world w which atomic sentences are true at w.

        d. Σ_A is a set of *state maps* $\Sigma_a : W \rightarrow \Pi$, each of which assigns to any world w an issue $\Sigma_a(w)^5$

In inquisitive epistemic logic, each agent is associated with an inquisitive state $\Sigma_a(w)$ that encodes the issues that are entertained by a at w, and the information state $\sigma_a(w)$ is obtained by taking a union of the inquisitive state:

(15) $\sigma_a(w) := \bigcup \Sigma_a(w)$.

In other words, $\Sigma_a(w)$ represents both the information and inquisitive states of the agent and we do not need $\sigma_a(w)$ as an independent notion in

---

[5] $\Sigma_a(w)$ observes factivity and introspection conditions. See Ciardelli and Roelofsen (2015).

the logical model.

The following definition (16) defines the conditions when a state s supports (notation: $\models$) a sentence:

(16) Let M be an inquisitive epistemic model, s an information state in M and g an assignment function from variables Var to agents $\mathcal{A}$.

    a. $\langle M, s \rangle \models p \iff p \in V(w)$ for all worlds $w \in s$

    b. $\langle M, s \rangle \models \neg\varphi \iff$ for all non-empty $t \subseteq s$, $\langle M, t \rangle \not\models \varphi$

    c. $\langle M, s \rangle \models \alpha \vee \beta \iff \langle M, s \rangle \models \alpha$ or $\langle M, s \rangle \models \beta$

Note that the proposition expressed by a sentence φ is defined as a set of all states that support φ:

(17) $[\varphi] := \{s \subseteq \mathcal{W} | s \models \varphi\}$

Note also that we treat $?p$ as an abbreviation of $p \vee \neg p$. Thus, the support condition for polar interrogatives is the same as that for disjunction:

(18) $\langle M, s \rangle \models ?\alpha \iff \langle M, s \rangle \models \alpha$ or $\langle M, s \rangle \models \neg\alpha$

Let us now look at the modal operators, K and E. First, when K is applied to a declarative α, $K_a\alpha$ is supported by s iff α is true everywhere in $\sigma_\alpha(w)$ for any $w \in s$. That is, α is compatible with the information available to a at any $w \in s$, which is concurrent with the knowledge modality in standard epistemic logic.

(19) $\langle M, s \rangle \models K_a\varphi \iff$ for any $w \in s$, $\langle M, \sigma_a(w) \rangle \models \varphi$

Let us look at the state depicted in Figure 2(a) as an illustration. Following Ciardelli and Roelofsen (2015), only the maximal element of each issue is represented in the diagrams. Our language only has two atomic sentences, p and q and our model consists of four worlds, $\mathcal{W} = \{w_{11}, w_{10}, w_{01}, w_{00}\}$ such that $V(w_{11}) = \{p\}$, $V(w_{10}) = \{p\}$, $V(w_{01}) = \{q\}$, and $V(w_{00}) = \{q\}$. In Figure 2(a), $\sigma_a(w_{11})$ supports p and $\sigma_a(w_{10})$ supports p. Since for any $w \in s$, $\sigma_a(w)$ supports p, s supports $\models K_a p$.

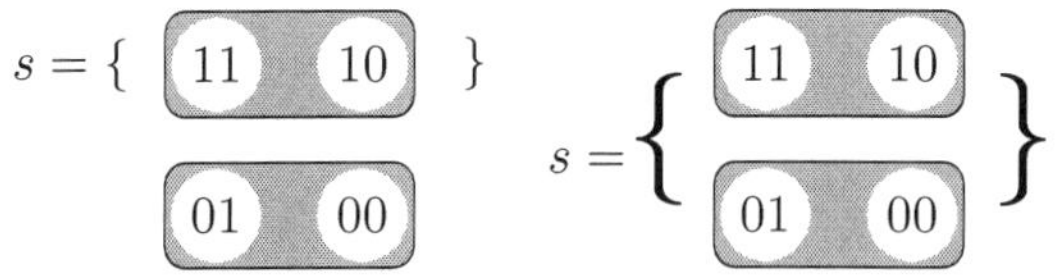

(a) $\langle M, s \rangle \models K_a p$ (b) $\langle M, s \rangle \not\models K_a ?p$, $\langle M, s \rangle \models E_a ?p$

FIGURE 2

Note that the state depicted in Figure 2(b) does not support $K_a?p$.

Finally, we are ready to define the entertain modality E. When the entertain operator E applies to φ, a state s supports $E_a\varphi$ just in case φ is supported by any $t \in \Sigma_a(w)$ for any $w \in s$. Intuitively, $E_a\varphi$ states that once the issues entertained by a are resolved, φ will be supported:

(20) $\langle M, s \rangle \models E_a\varphi \iff$ for any $w \in s$ and $t \in \Sigma_a(w)$, $\langle M, t \rangle \models \varphi$

The state depicted in Figure 2(b) supports $E_a?p$. All states support either p or $\neg p$: $\{w_{11}, w_{10}\}$ supports p, $\{w_{01}, w_{00}\}$ supports $\neg p$, $\{w_{11}\}$ supports p, $\{w_{10}\}$ supports p, $\{w_{01}\}$ supports $\neg p$, and $\{w_{00}\}$ supports $\neg p$. Thus, for any $w \in s$ and any $t \in \Sigma_a(w)$, t supports $p \vee \neg p$. Therefore, s supports $E_a?p$.

One fact about the relation between K and E is important to the current paper. If the embedded sentence is a declarative α, $E_a\alpha$ entails $K_a\alpha$.[6] Since $K_a\alpha$ entails $E_a\alpha$, $E_a\alpha$ is equivalent to $K_a\alpha$.

(21) For any declarative α and agent $a \in \mathcal{A}$, $K_a\alpha \equiv E_a\alpha$.

3.3   Proposal 2: Final Rise ↑ as an Uncertainty Marker

Section 3.1 emphasized that the holder of the knowledge expressed by *daroo* with falling intonation must be the speaker. As discussed in Sections 2.3, however, the speaker uses a *daroo*-declarative is uttered with Final Rise to seek agreement from the addressee, thus the bias appears to be attributed not only to the speaker but also to the addressee. I claim that this attribution of the bias to the addressee is pragmatically derived by the semantics of Final Rise which semantically encodes the speaker's uncertainty (Ward and Hirschberg 1985).[7]

To implement this semantically-encoded discourse effect of uncertainty, I adopt the notion of the conversational "scoreboard" model developed in the literature (Roberts 1996; Gunlogson 2003; Northrup 2014; Malamud and Stephenson 2015; Farkas and Roelofsen 2017). The idea is that the discourse context may contain multiple components each of which registers a certain type of discourse history. For the current purpose, Northrup's (2014, 39) evidential base **evidB**, which is "the set of propositions that, when taken together, serve to underwrite a commitment."

I propose that the Final Rise is a marker of minimal speaker authority.[8] A Final Rise semantically indicates that the commitment to the prejacent proposition is derived from the minimal evidential base $\text{evidB}_{\min}$. Let D be a set

---

[6] See Ciardelli and Roelofsen (2015, 1657) for the definitions of entailment and equivalence.

[7] The idea is inspired by the work by Truckenbrodt (2006) and Westera (2013).

[8] This is what Northrup (2014) proposes for the Japanese particle *ne*, thus the Final Rise is synonymous to the particle *ne*.

of discourse participants and AUTH_a be a measure function from a sentence to a numerical value that represents how much authority the discourse agent a can accumulate. Then, following Northrup's (2014, 116) notation, the side discourse effect of $\varphi \uparrow$ is defined as follows:

(22)   Side discourse effect of $\varphi \uparrow$
         Any commitment to φ is derived from a base $\mathsf{evidB}_{\min}$ such that
         $\mathsf{evidB}_{\min} = \{\psi | \forall a \in D.\mathsf{AUTH}_a \geq \mathsf{AUTH}_{\mathrm{SPKR}}\}$

Now, let us see what happens when the Final Rise is attached to a *daroo*-declarative (5). The logical form of (5) denotes the main discourse effect as $\lambda C.C \cap [K_{\mathrm{SPKR}}p]$. The Final Rise attached to the LF gives rises to a side effect that the speaker's commitment to p is derived from a minimal evidential base $\mathsf{evidB}_{\min}$. Thus, the speaker is not fully confident to add the proposition expressed by p to the common ground. Since the speaker uttered a declarative sentence, she desires to add p to the common ground. As a result, the speaker invites the addressee to be committed to p, because it is the only way to add p to the common ground.

To recapitulate, the Final Rise is a marker of uncertainty, more precisely, a marker of minimal speaker authority.

4   Deriving the Interpretations

Equipped with the interpretation function and the machinery of the IEL, we are ready to derive the intricate semantics of the Japanese modal *daroo*. The main proposals are: 1) *daroo* is an entertain modality E_{SPKR} (13), and 2) a Final Rise $\uparrow$ indicates the speaker's uncertainty (22).

4.1   Falling Declaratives

Let us see how these two proposals derive the paradigm summarized above, starting from a falling declarative like (3).

Daroo is an entertain modality E_{SPKR}, and given Fact (21) when the embedded sentence is a declarative, E_{SPKR} and K_{SPKR} are equivalent. Recall that $[\varphi]$ is the proposition expressed by a sentence φ, i.e., the set of all states that support φ.

(23)   a.   LF: $p\text{-}daroo \rightsquigarrow E_{\mathrm{SPKR}}p \equiv K_{\mathrm{SPKR}}p$
         b. $[\![K_{\mathrm{SPKR}}p]\!]^{M,w} = \lambda C.C \cap [K_{\mathrm{SPKR}}p]$

Therefore, (3) denotes a CCP $\lambda C.C \cap [K_{\mathrm{SPKR}}p]_{M,g}$, where p $=$ 'John is coming'. After the announcement, 'John is coming' is established in the speaker's information state.[9]

---

[9] $[K_{\mathrm{SPKR}}p]$ seems too strong for the intuition reported in Sections 2, that is, 'the speaker has a bias toward p'. This is analogous to a long-standing puzzle in linguistics known as the weakness

4.2 Falling Interrogatives

Let us turn to falling *daroo*-interrogative sentences like (4). Recall that the entire construction $E_a?p$ is always a declarative even if the embedded sentence is an interrogative:

(24)   a.   LF: *p-daroo ka* $\leadsto E_{\text{SPKR}}?p$
       b. $[\![E_{\text{SPKR}}?p]\!]^{M,w} = \lambda C.C \cap [E_{\text{SPKR}}?p]$

Thus, (4) denotes the CCP $\lambda C.C \cap [E_{\text{SPKR}}?p]$. After the update, for any $\iota \in \Sigma_{\text{SPKR}}(w)$, $\langle M, \iota \rangle \models ?p$. That is, 'whether or not Marie drinks wine' is supported as soon as the issues of SPKR are resolved, which can be paraphrased as: the speaker wonders whether Marie drinks wine.[10]

4.3 Rising Declaratives

Recall that a rising *daroo*-declarative seems to express a meaning similar to a tag question (5). As already discussed in Section 3.3, the semantic and pragmatic computation of (5) is as follows:

(25)   a.   LF: *p-daroo* $\leadsto E_{\text{SPKR}}p \equiv K_{\text{SPKR}}p$
       b.   Main effect
             $[\![K_{\text{SPKR}}p]\!]^{M,w} = \lambda C.C \cap [K_{\text{SPKR}}p]$
       c.   Side effect: Any commitment to p is based on $\text{evidB}_{\min}$
       d.   Pragmatic effect: the speaker invites the addressee to be committed to p, i.e., $\lambda C.C \cap [K_{\text{ADDR}}p]_M$

Thus, (5) denotes the CCP $\lambda C.C \cap [K_{\text{SPKR}}p]$ while the Final Rise indicate the speaker's commitment to p is based on the speaker's minimal evidential base. Since the speaker intends to add p to the common ground, she invites the addressee to commit himself to p, resulting in a function similar to English tag questions.

4.4 Rising Interrogatives

Finally, we address the infelicity of rising *daroo*-interrogatives (7). Again, the rising intonation $\uparrow$ indicates that the speaker's commitment to $?p$ is based on $\text{evidB}_{\min}$.

---

intuition of *must*. For the current purpose, I assume that the bare assertion p and the modalized *p-daroo* are in pragmatic competition (see Karttunen 1972; Kratzer 1991) and defer detailed discussions to the existing literature (von Fintel and Gillies 2010; Lassiter 2014, a.o.).

[10] The entertain modality E_a does not exclude the case where the agent has a bias towards a certain answer to the question. In other words, updating an inquisitive state with $E_a?p$ and K_ap consecutively does not lead the state to be absurd. That is, $\Sigma_a(w) \cap [E_a?p]_{M,g} \cap [K_ap]_{M,g} \neq \emptyset$. Indeed it is possible for $?p$-*daroo*$\downarrow$ to be felicitously followed by p-*daroo*$\downarrow$ (the data omitted for space reasons). This contrasts with Ciardelli and Roelofsen's wonder modality W_a, defined as: "$W_a\varphi := \neg K_a\varphi \wedge E_a\varphi$" (Ciardelli and Roelofsen 2015, 1659).

(26)   a.   LF: $?p$-*daroo*$\leadsto E_{\text{SPKR}}?p$
        b.   Main effect $[\![E_{\text{SPKR}}?p]\!]^{M,w} = \lambda C.C \cap [E_{\text{SPKR}}?p]_{M,g}$
        c.   Side effect: Any commitment to $?p$ is based on $\text{evidB}_{\text{min}}$
        d.   Pragmatic effect: the speaker invites the addressee to be com-
             mitted to $?p$, i.e., $\lambda C.C \cap [E_{\text{ADDR}}p]_M$

Thus, the main effect of the utterance should be the same as the falling interrogative (24). At the same time, the speaker indicates her certainty in her commitment to $?p$. The oddness of this discourse move can be explained in two ways. First, the speaker is wondering if p is true or not but she is also not sure if her evidence base is strong enough to let her entertain $?p$. In other words, (24) is paraphrased as 'I am wondering if Marie drinks wine, right?' This is odd because unlike the declarative case, the speaker does not need a strong evidential base to entertain an issue. Second, if the speaker indeed intends to invite the addressee to be committed to $?p$ since she is not sure, then she should pose a simple question $?p$, *Marie-wa wain-o nomu ka?* 'Does Marie drink wine?'. In either way, the speaker ends up making an illicit or pragmatically redundant move, thus rising *daroo*-interrogatives like (7) are perceived as infelicitous.[11]

5   Conclusion

I proposed that *daroo* is a root-level modal operator E_{SPKR}, which expresses epistemic knowledge associated to the speaker, SPKR and the Final Rise indicate the speaker's uncertainty. The first proposal is divided into two subproposals. First, *daroo* moves to [Spec CP] to check off its uninterpretable feature, [uROOT], resulting in the logical form $E_{\text{SPKR}}\varphi$, in which the modal operator E_{SPKR} embeds the declarative or interrogative sentence. Second, the semantics of *daroo* is assigned in the framework of inquisitive epistemic semantics. In particular, *daroo* translates as an entertain modality E_{SPKR} and $E_{\text{SPKR}}\varphi$ expresses that the speaker is entertaining an issue denoted by φ. When the embedded sentence is a declarative α, $E_{\text{SPKR}}\alpha$ is equivalent to $K_{\text{SPKR}}\alpha$. Thus, *daroo*-declaratives describe the epistemic state of the speaker. As can be seen, this equivalence allows us to maintain the uniform semantics for *daroo* as an entertain modality. The following table summarizes the main and side discourse effects expressed by *daroo*-sentences.

---

[11] A Final High, a variant of a rising interrogative $?p$-DAROO $\uparrow$ seems possible in a special context such as a quiz show or an instructive/Socratic questioning context (data omitted for space reasons). I speculate that with a Final High, there is a shifting of the epistemic agent from SPKR to ADDR.

	Falling	Rising
Declarative	p-*daroo*↓	p-*daroo*↑ ⤳ p-*darou*↑
	p-*darou*	Main: $K_{\mathrm{SPKR}}p$
	Main: $K_{\mathrm{SPKR}}p$	Side: p is bsed on $\mathrm{evidB_{min}}$
Interrogative	p-*daroo ka*↓	p-*daroo ka*↑ ⤳ ?p-*darou*↑
	?p-*darou*	Main: $E_{\mathrm{SPKR}}?p$
	Main: $E_{\mathrm{SPKR}}?p$	Side: ?p is bsed on $\mathrm{evidB_{min}}$

TABLE 1 The main and side dimensions meaning of darou sentences

Acknowledgments

This work was supported by JSPS KAKENHI Grant Number 17H07172.

References

Büring, D. and Gunlogson, C. (2000). Aren't positive and negative polar questions the same? USCS/UCLA.

Ciardelli, I. A. and Roelofsen, F. (2015). Inquisitive dynamic epistemic logic. *Synthese*, 192(6):1643–1687.

Davis, C. (2009). Decisions, dynamics and the Japanese particle *yo*. *Journal of Semantics*, 26:329–366.

Farkas, D. F. and Roelofsen, F. (2017). Division of labor in the interpretation of declaratives and interrogatives. *Journal of Semantics*.

Gunlogson, C. (2003). *True to Form: Rising and Falling Declaratives as Questions in English*. Routledge, New York.

Hara, Y. (2006). *Japanese Discourse Items at Interfaces*. PhD thesis, University of Delaware, Newark, DE.

Hara, Y. and Davis, C. (2013a). *Darou* as a deictic context shifter. In Yatsushiro, K. and Sauerland, U., editors, *Proceedings of Formal Approaches to Japanese Linguistics 6 (FAJL 6)*, MIT Working Papers in Linguistics 66, pages 41–56.

Hara, Y. and Davis, C. (2013b). *Darou* as a deictic context shifter. In Yatsushiro, K. and Sauerland, U., editors, *Formal Approaches to Japanese Linguistics 6*, pages 41–56. MITWPL.

Heim, I. (1982). *The Semantics of Definite and Indefinite Noun Phrases*. PhD thesis, University of Massachussets, Amherst. [Distributed by GLSA].

Karttunen, L. (1972). Possible and must. In Kimball, J., editor, *Syntax and semantics*, volume 1. Seminar Press.

Kratzer, A. (1991). Modality. In von Stechow, A. and Wunderlich, D., editors, *Semantics: An International Handbook of Contemporary Research*, pages 639–650. de Gruyter, Berlin.

Lassiter, D. (2014). The weakness of must: In defense of a mantra. In *Proceedings of SALT 24*, pages 597–618.

Malamud, S. and Stephenson, T. (2015). Three ways to avoid commitments: Declarative force modiers in the conversational scoreboard. *Journal of Semantics*, 32:275–311.

Nilsenova, M. (2002). A game-theoretical approach to the meaning of intonation in rising declarativesand negative polar questions. In Bel, B. and Marlien, I., editors, *Proceedings of Speech Prosody 2002*, Aix-en-Provence, France.

Northrup, O. (2014). *Grounds for Commitment*. PhD thesis, UCSC.

Roberts, C. (1996). Information structure in discourse: Towards an integrated formal theory of pragmatics. In Yoon, J. H. and Kathol, A., editors, *Ohio State University Working Papers in Linguistics*, volume 49, pages 91–136. The Ohio State University.

Schütze, C. (1996). *The empirical base of linguistics: Grammaticality judgments and linguistic methodology*. University of Chicago Press, Chicago.

Stalnaker, R. (1968). A theory of conditionals. In Resher, N., editor, *Studies in Logical Theory*. Blackwell, Oxford.

Sudo, Y. (2013). Biased polar questions in English and Japanese. In Gutzmann, D. and Gaertner, H.-M., editors, *Beyond Expressives: Explorations in Use-Conditional Meaning, Current Research in the Semantics/Pragmatics Interface (CRiSPI)*, volume 28. Brill.

Sugimura, Y. (2004). Gaizensei o arawasu fukushi to bunmatsu no modality keishiki 'adverbs ofprobability and sentence-final modality expressions'. *Gengo Bunka Ronshuu*, 25(2).

Truckenbrodt, H. (2006). On the semantic motivation of syntactic verb movement to c in german. *Theoretical Linguistics*, 32(3):257–306.

Venditti, J. J. (2005a). The J_ToBI model of Japanese intonation. In Jun, S.-A., editor, *Prosodic Typology: The Phonology of Intonation and Phrasing*, pages 172–200. Oxford Unviersity Press.

Venditti, J. J. (2005b). The J_ToBI model of Japanese intonation. In Jun, S.-A., editor, *Prosodic Typology: The Phonology of Intonation and Phrasing*, pages 172–200. Oxford Unviersity Press.

von Fintel, K. and Gillies, A. S. (2010). Must . . . stay . . . strong! *Natural Language Semantics*, 18(4):351–383.

Ward, G. and Hirschberg, J. (1985). Implicating uncertainty: the pragmatics of fallrise intonation. *Language*, 61(4):747–776.

Westera, M. (2013). 'attention, i'm violating a maxim!' a unifying account of the nal rise. In *Proceedings of the 17th Workshop on the Semantics and Pragmatics of Dialogue (SemDial)*.

Zimmermann, M. (2004). Discourse particles in the left periphery. In Shaer, B., Frey, W., and Maienborn, C., editors, *Proceedings of the Dislocated Elements Workshop, ZAS Berlin (ZAS Papers in Linguistics 35)*, pages 544–566, Berlin. ZAS.

Imperatives with/without Necessity[*]

SHUN IHARA
Osaka University / Japan Society for the Promotion of Science

YUYA NOGUCHI
Osaka University

1 Introduction

Japanese has a so-called imperative morpheme (i.e. *-e* or *-ro*), and when it follows a verb stem, it makes the sentence an imperative and thus allows it to be used as a directive speech act, as shown in (1a). On the other hand, some Japanese sentences can function as imperatives without including an imperative morpheme. One of such sentences is referred to as dictionary form imperatives (Noguchi 2016), where a verb stem is followed by the present tense affix -$(r)u$, as shown in (1b). Given their morphological properties, we refer to the former type of imperative as a *Morphological Imperative* (MI, henceforth) and the latter one as a *Suppletive Imperative* (SI, henceforth) in this paper.

---

[*] We would like to thank Hiroshi Mito, Masao Ochi, Sanae Tamura, Yuto Hirayama, LCCC research group at Osaka University, and the Audience at the 25th Japanese/Korean Linguistics Conference for providing valuable comment on the content of this research. I would also like to thank those who were kind enough to provide us with their felicity judgements on the examples within this paper. All errors are our own. This research has been supported by Japan Society for the Promotion of Science KAKENHI (17J03552).

Japanese/Korean Linguistics 25.
Edited by Shin Fukuda, Mary Shin Kim, and Mee-Jeong Park.
Copyright © 2018, CSLI Publications.

(1)   a. Hayaku ik-e!
           quickly go-IMP
           'Go quickly!'

       b. Hayaku ik-u!
           quickly go-PRS
           'Go quickly!'

Considering existence of these different kinds of imperatives, two of the big
questions which become might pose are (I) how they semantically differ from each
other and (II) what makes the difference between them. This paper investigates these two questions and, by proposing semantic and syntactic structures
for the two types of imperatives, argues that the difference between MIs and
SIs depends on whether or not they encode (weak) necessity modality. More
specifically, we contend that MIs encode weak necessity clause-internally
while SIs only clause-externally represent a directive operator without including any necessity modality.

   This paper is organized as follows. In Section 2, we present some key data
which indicate asymmetries between Japanese MIs and SIs. Section 3 lays out
previous semantic analyses on necessity modality. Based on the discussion in
the foregoing sections, in Section 4 we exhibit our proposal on semantic and
syntactic structures for the two types of imperatives. In Section 5, we describe
how the present proposal accounts for the puzzles shown in Section 2. Section
6 concludes the paper.

2   Key Data: Motivating the Proposal

This section presents some data which are crucial for our argument. Specifically, we indicate that the two types of imperatives behave in different man-
ners with respect to (a) weak readings, (ii) embeddability and (iii) addressee-
orientation of subjects.

2.1   Weak Readings of Imperatives

We first observe 'weak' readings in Japanese imperatives. It has been pointed
out in literature that English imperatives can pattern with both 'strong' readings (e.g. directive) and (all kinds of) 'weak' ones (e.g. advice, permission)
(See Portner 2007; Kaufmann 2012). Relevant examples are shown in (2)
and (3). Note particularly that the imperative in (3a) and (3b) is contextually forced to be construed as advice and permission, respectively, due to the
clause following it.

(2)   Strong reading:
       Go to bed! [*directive*]

(3)   Weak reading:

    a. Take the train! But you can also take the bus. [*advice*]

    b. Open the window, if you are hot! [*permission*]

Unlike imperatives, on the other hand, the strong necessity modal in English *must* can only pattern with strong readings, not with weak ones. In other words, sentences including the modal cannot be interpreted as advice or permission but can be only as directive, as exemplified in (4) and (5).

(4)   Strong reading:
    You must go to bed!

(5)   Weak reading:

    a. #$^{as\ an\ advice}$ Take the train! But you can also take the bus.

    b. #$^{as\ a\ permission}$ You must open the window, if you are hot!

Bearing these differences in mind, let us now observe how Japanese imperatives behave with respect to weak readings.[1] Japanese MIs, on one hand, can show weak readings, as do English imperatives (cf. (3)). Relevant examples are shown below:

(6) a. Densha-ni nor-e   yo. Basu-mo aru   kedo ne.
      train-to   take-IMP SFP bus-too exist-PRS but SFP
      'Take a train. But there's also a bus.'

    b. Mosi atui-no nara, mado-o   ake-ro.
      if   hot-C   then windo-ACC open-IMP
      'Open the window, if you are hot.'

On the other hand, however, Japanese SIs cannot indicate any kind of weak readings, in the same manner as English sentences including *must* (cf. (5)), as exemplified in (7).

(7) a. # Densha-ni nor-u!   Basu-mo aru   kedo ne.
      train-to   take-PRS bus-too exist-PRS but SFP
      'Take a train! But there's also a bus.'

    b. # Mosi atui-no nara, mado-o   ake-ru!
      if   hot-C   then windo-ACC open-PRS
      'Open the window, if you are hot.'

The present observation thus indicates that MIs can pattern both with weak readings and with strong ones while SIs can only be uttered in contexts of strong readings.

---

[1] Since it is self-evident that both MIs and SIs in Japanese can show strong readings (cf. (1)), we will not here deal with strong readings of them.

2.2 Embeddability

The second property of the two types of Japanese imperatives has to do with embeddability. First of all, Japanese MIs can be embedded as an indirect quotation, which is headed by the quotation marker *to* (Kuno 1988; Saito & Haraguchi 2012), as in (8).[2]

(8) Ken-ga   Aya$_i$-ni [kanojo$_i$-no haha-o   tetuda-e   to] it-ta.
     Ken-NOM Aya-to she-GEN   mother-ACC help-IMP C say-PST
     Ken told Aya to help her mother.'

(9) indicates, on the other hand, that Japanese SIs, unlike MIs, cannot be embedded as an indirect quotation (Noguchi 2016). Notice that the embedded clause can be naturally understood as a declarative, as the translation suggests; of importance here is that it cannot be interpreted as an imperative.

(9) Ken-ga   Aya$_i$-ni [kanojo$_i$-no haha-o   tetuda-u   to] it-ta.
     Ken-NOM Aya-to she-GEN   mother-ACC help-PRS C say-PST
     'Ken told Aya that he will help her mother.'

These data lead us to conclude that Japanese SIs and MIs are different in whether they can be embedded or not.

2.3 Addressee-orientation of Subjects

We finally observe properties of Japanese imperatives in terms of their subjects. Interestingly, subjects in Japanese MIs can be co-indexed not only with an addressee (i.e. the 2nd person) but also with the 3rd person, as indicated in (10) and (11).[3]

(10) (Omae[2nd]) hayaku ik-e!
      you   quickly go-IMP
      'Go quickly!'

(11) (Aitsu[3rd]) hayaku denwa-ni de-ro!
      that.man quickly phone-to take-IMP
      '[Lit.] Pick up the phone quickly!'

This property, however, cannot be found in Japanese SIs. Specifically, subjects of SIs can only refer to the 2nd person, or an addressee, as exemplified

[2] Note that the *to*-clause in (8) and (9) is interpreted as an indirect quotation, not a direct one, since the pronominal element in the embedded clause (i.e. *kanojo* 'she') is co-indexed with *Aya* in the matrix clause, construed from the viewpoint of the speaker of the quotation (i.e. *Ken*).

[3] Note that (11) is interpreted as 'desiderative' or 'complaintive,' rather than directive. We will not mention this point any longer, since it is irrelevant to the present discussion. We refer interested readers to Ihara & Noguchi (2017) for details of this property.

in (12) and (13). Thus, we can see an asymmetry in what kind of subjects MIs and SIs can take, as indicated in the current data.

(12) (Omae[2nd]) hayaku ik-u!.
     you   quickly go-PRS

     'Go quickly!'

(13) # (Aitsu[3rd]) hayaku denwa-ni de-ru!
        that.man quickly phone-to take-PRS

       '[Lit.] Pick up the phone quickly!'

2.4 Summarizing the Behavior of MIs and SIs

We have so far confirmed that there exist empirical asymmetries between the two types of Japanese imperatives, namely MIs and SIs. More specifically, MIs and SIs in Japanese are different in terms of the possibility of weak readings, embeddability and addressee-orientation of subjects. Those asymmetries are organized into TABLE 1. Considering that those asymmetries are crucial, in the following section we propose semantic and syntactic structures for the two types of Japanese imperatives.

	weak readings	embeddability	addressee-orientation
MIs	√	√	2nd/3rd
SIs	*	*	2nd/*3rd

TABLE 1

3 The Semantics of Weak Necessity

In this section we introduce the brief semantics of weak necessity for the current analysis. In this paper, we adopt the analysis of Medeiros (2013) that imperative morphology (in other words, MI) semantically represents the modal content called *weak necessity modal* '$\Box_{wn}$' (Silk 2013), which is roughly equivalent to *ought* or *should* in their interpretation, and operates independently of the directive speech-act operator.

The specific analysis of imperatives therefore depends completely upon the formal analysis of weak necessity. While Silk's (2013) formalism is not crucial for the current analysis, his formalization is convenient to make explicit the comparison between strong and weak necessity. Moreover, this formalism is more directly comparable to the semantics of imperative operator adopted by Kaufmann (2012) (that we will introduce in Section 4) as compared to the theory of weak necessity suggested by von Fintel & Iatridou (2008), since the latter introduces a third ordering source (Medeiros 2013).

Silk's model of weak necessity depends upon premise sets P, which simplify the interaction of modal base and ordering source within Kratzerian modal semantics (Kratzer 1981/1991). Premise sets P describe functions that a context supplies for the interpretation of modals. The value of P given a world of evaluation is a saturated premise set $P(w)$.[4] Within this model, strong necessity *must* is defined as follows:

(14) $[\![must(p)]\!] = 1$ iff $\cap P(w) \subseteq [\![p]\!]$ (Silk 2013)

Thus for the truth of '*must(p)*' is checked by comparing whether the conditions in the evaluation world w are s.t. the premise set $P(w)$ verifies the necessity of p. The truth of the sentence with strong necessity thus simply depends on the value of P at w.

Silk relates weak necessity to strong necessity in terms of conditional or contingent necessity; weak necessity therefore defines what is necessary if certain conditions hold. Weak necessity *ought* and *should* is defined as (15),

(15) $[\![ought/should(p)]\!] = 1$ iff $\forall w' \in \mathcal{H}(w, \chi) : \cap P(w') \subseteq [\![p]\!]$
, where $\mathcal{H}$ is a selection function which selects a set of χ-worlds that are closest to w. (Silk 2013)

$\mathcal{H}$ picks out a set of relevant worlds that are *preferred* in some contextually relevant sense i.e. most normal, expected, desirable. Given the definition above, '*ought/should(p)*' is true iff the contextually preferred worlds w' verify the necessity of p, namely iff p follows from the relevant P at every $w' \in \mathcal{H}(w, \chi)$. In other words, the weak necessity '*ought/should p*' makes a claim about the necessity of p at all closest relevant χ-worlds, for some contextually supplied condition χ. Under this model, weak necessity is contingent necessity. Medeiros (2013) therefore suggests that under the right contextual circumstances, MIs (and weak necessity modals) can pattern with weak readings (e.g. permission, advice), and can very closely approximate a strong necessity modal, as we have shown in Section 2.

4 Proposal

4.1 The Brief Semantics of Imperatives

Before moving on to illustrate our proposal, we give some brief assumptions of imperatives in Japanese. First, Japanese imperative morphology (i.e. *-e/ro*) encodes weak necessity as that of English does (Medeiros 2013). Second,

---

[4] Silk (2013, footnote 9) provides the explanation of the relationship between premise sets P and Kratzer's conversational backgrounds as follows:

> ... what follows from $P(w)$ can be understood as short for talk about what follows from all maximally consistent subsets of $f(w) \cup g(w)$, where $f(w)$ is a modal base that describes some set of relevant background facts and $g(w)$ is an ordering source that represents the content of the relevant ideal evaluation world.

clauses with a verb that bears imperative morphology do not define a proper subset of any clause type (Ihara & Noguchi 2017). In short, 'directive' (or 'command') force is represented independently of imperative morphology; instead, the directive force appears as 'directive force operator,' which requires the presupposition of imperatives as in (16), and ensures the performative effect of directive speech acts (Kaufmann 2012; Medeiros 2013). (Note that Kaufmann proposes an imperative operator with propositional *modal* and presuppositional ingredients. In this respect Kaufmann's system stands in contrast to the system we propose below, in which the propositional and presuppositional elements are separated in terms of their semantic representation.)

(16)   Directive operator 'dir' is defined iff:

  a. $\neg(t < c_T)$ $\wedge$

  b. $f, g \in \text{AUTH}'(c_S)(c)$ $\wedge$

  c. For the precontext c' of c:
      $c_S(c') \subseteq \lambda w.(\exists w' \in Bel'_{c_S}(c'_T)(w))(\exists w'' \in Bel'_{c_S}(c'_T)(w))$
      $[\neg P(t)(w') \& P(t)(w'')]$ $\wedge$

  d. Either (i) in c there is a salient decision problem $\triangle(c) \subseteq P(w)$ such that in c the imperative provides and answer to it, g is any prioritizing ordering source, and the speaker and addressee consider g the relevant criteria for resolving $\triangle(c)$;
      or else, (ii) in c there is no salient decision problem $\triangle(c)$ such that the imperative provides an answer to it in c, and g is speaker bouletic.

First, the presupposition (16a) ensures that the imperative can or will occur in the future (more formally, at or following utterance time). Second, the presupposition (16b) ensures that the speaker in c is in an 'epistemically privileged position' with respect to the conversational backgrounds f and g (Zimmermann 2000). The third presupposition in (16c), the presupposition of epistemic uncertainty, ensures that the speaker believes that fulfillment of the imperative is possible, but not a foregone conclusion. Finally, the presupposition (16d) ensures that the ordering source g must be prioritizing (Portner 2007) or speaker bouletic (See Kaufmann (2012) for some crucial data). We do not go into further details due to limitations of space, but this approach works well enough to derive the difference between MIs and SIs.

Given these assumptions, the meaning of canonical form imperatives can be divided into the two-part semantics: (i) the 'modal' meaning which shows the speaker's weak necessity modality and (ii) the speaker's (actual) directive 'speech act' meaning conveyed by the directive operator.

4.2 Imperatives with/without Weak Necessity

In this section, we propose an analysis of MIs and SIs. First, for the analysis of MIs in Japanese, we basically maintain Medeiros's (2013) analysis of canonical form imperatives, as shown in (17). Departing from Medeiros, we represent the directive operator at Speech Act Phrase (SAP; Speas & Tenny 2003, among many others). We assume that any element which occurs at the level of SAP cannot be embedded under indirect quotation (See Saito & Haraguchi 2012; Noguchi 2016). For instance, Japanese sentence final particles like *yo* or *ne*, which Saito & Haraguchi claim head SAP, cannot appear in an indirect quotation clause (See also Deng (2015) for Chinese SFP *ba*).

(17) The LF of MIs:
      $[_{\text{SAP}} \; dir \; [_{\text{TP (or ModalP)}} \; \Box_{wn} \; [\; p : \; [\dots v_{imp} \dots]]]]$

The key here is that the representation in (17) contains the two components at different positions: the presuppositional content 'dir' is located clause-externally at SAP on the one hand and weak necessity modality '$\Box_{wn}$' is located at clause-internal level (namely at TP) on the other hand.[5]

We now propose the LF of SIs in (18). The representation in (18) differs from (17) in that it does not contain the weak necessity modal; it only encodes the directive operator at SAP. In other words, while the existence of the directive operator is not the necessary condition for realization of MIs (as we will discuss in Section 5), the existence is essential for sentences with a dictionary form verb to become imperatives; SAP is responsible for determining the illocutionary force of SIs.

(18) The LF of SIs:
      $[_{\text{SAP}} \; dir \; [_{\text{TP}} \; [\; p : \; [\dots v_{prs} \dots]]]]$

In short, we argue that the differences between MIs and SIs (that we have pointed out in Section 2) can be explained by focusing on the two semantic content, namely the weak necessity operator and the directive operator.

5 Analysis

Section 5 shows how the current proposal can handle the contrast between the two types of imperatives.

5.1 Deriving the Weak Readings Property

First, we give an account for the fact that MIs and SIs are different in the propriety of weak readings. Recall that while MIs can pattern with any weak

---

[5] Note that our proposal also allows the weak necessity modal to be placed at ModalP, which is above TP. While we do not pursue a syntactic distinction between modals here, Isac (2012) shows that if a high/low distinction is to be made, the imperative modal would be high.

readings like permission and advice, SIs sound odd in such contexts(cf. (6), (7)). We argue that this simply because the existence of weak necessity modal enables sentences to pattern with weak readings. As predicted, MIs can be uttered as weak imperatives since they contain weak necessity modality. This analysis supports the common view that strong/weak readings among imperatives should be understood at the level of semantics since they all share the meaning of 'requiring' (Portner 2010; Kaufmann 2012).

On the other hand, SIs can only have strong readings, and cannot have weak readings because of the lack of weak necessity. Then why can they pattern with strong readings? We argue that the directive operator makes them possible to be a directive utterance. The task to discuss whether the directive operator in SIs is phonologically overt or not is beyond the scope of the current work and will be left to future research; it is worth noting, however, that disregarding intonation, an SI in Japanese can be interpreted either imperative or declarative. In order for the sentence to get an imperative interpretation, it has to be pronounced with a special intonation, where originally high-accented moras in the verb get a higher accent (Noguchi 2016). Although some more phonological analysis is needed, we could assume that the directive operator in SIs is marked by the special sentence final intonation.[6]

One may think that there still remains a possibility that SIs encode strong necessity which is interpreted like *must*. This possibility, however, will be eliminated once we pay attention to the data of embedded imperatives, as we will show in the next section.

5.2 Interpreting Embedded Imperatives

In section 2.2, we have shown that while Japanese MIs can be embedded as an indirect quotation, Japanese SIs cannot. We suggest that this difference can also be explained by focusing on the existence of the weak necessity. First, MIs can induce imperative meanings even when they are embedded since they contain weak necessity modal clause-internally, as the illustration in (19) shows (cf. (8)):

(19) Ken-ga   Aya-ni [$_{\text{MI}}$ $\square_{wn}$ p] to it-ta.
      Ken-NOM Aya-to   C say-PST

      $\leadsto$ [$_{\text{MI}}$ $\square_{wn}$ p]: 'it is necessary that p'

As for SIs, since they lack any modal operator, they cannot be embedded in an indirect discourse with imperative-like meanings. This analysis correctly

---

[6] Heim et al. (2014) claim that intonation can head SAP and is responsible for determining an illocutionary force of a sentence. Based on that, it can be said that the special intonation of an SI occupies the head of SAP and is responsible for the directive force.

predicts that when a dictionary form sentence is indirectly embedded, its interpretation is limited to a declarative, or an assertion, as shown in (20) (cf. (9)). Note that the directive operator operates at the level of SAP and thus cannot be embedded under indirect quotations.

(20) Ken-ga   Aya-ni [$_{\text{dic-form sentence}}$ p] to it-ta.
      Ken-NOM Aya-to   C say-PST
      $\leadsto$ [$_{\text{dic-form sentence}}$ p]: 'it is the case that p'
      ($^{\#}$[$_{\text{dic-form sentence}}$ p]: 'it is necessary that p')

Moreover, the alternative analysis that SIs encode strong necessity ends up providing a prediction that embedded sentences with a dictionary form verb convey strong necessity, contrary to fact.

5.3 Directive Performativity and the Property of Addressee-Orientation

Finally, we show that the addressee-orientation property of imperatives can be understood within the current proposal. We assume that in the model of this paper, MIs (at least in Japanese) are not inherently addressee-oriented in terms of their semantic or syntactic representation. Rather, the property of addressee-orientation is that of directive speech acts. In other words, the directive operator demands the subject to be the addressee, namely the 2nd person.

Let us handle the behavior of SIs first. As we have shown in Section 2.3, the subject in SIs can be co-indexed only with the 2nd person addressee. We explain this fact by arguing that since SIs must come with the directive operator, which enforces the presupposition of the existence of the addressee, they cannot occur with a subject other than 2nd person. It is worth noting, however, that the question of why SIs can only pattern with *true* directive speech acts which requires the existence of the addressee still remains unclear. Is the addressee-orientation property of SIs the feature of the dictionary form itself, the feature of the special sentence final intonation, or the compositional feature of 'dictionary form + special intonation'? For the first step we need to investigate the semantic/pragmatic status of sentences with a dictionary form verb in Japanese, to which little attention has been paid, and will be left to future study.

In contrast to SIs, since the existence of the directive operator is not a necessary condition for realization of MIs, the subject in MIs can be co-indexed not only with the addressee (namely the 2nd person) but also with the 3rd person; while in directive contexts, the directive presupposition requires that subjects of MIs be the 2nd person, in non-directive contexts (such as 'desiderative' or 'complaintive', see Ihara & Noguchi 2017), where the 'addressee-orientation' presupposition does not have to be fulfilled, subjects of MIs are not limited to the 2nd person but can also be the 3rd person.

Under the current analysis, differences with respect to person-orientation of imperative subjects are pushed into *language-specific* morphological systems. The fact that Japanese morphological imperatives, namely MIs, allow both 2nd and 3rd subjects is a property of Japanese, not imperatives. At the same time, the fact that English imperatives take only 2nd person subjects is a property English, not imperatives.

6 Conclusion and Outlook

Little work has been devoted to the semantic/pragmatic difference between MIs and SIs. In this study, we have proposed a new analysis for imperatives that certain types of imperatives can lack a necessity modality, even if they are typologically rare. In Japanese, MIs and SIs in directive contexts share the same presuppositional content; they have identical performative properties. However, these forms can differ with respect to modal contents, as the availability of weak readings and embedding suggests.

Our analysis supports the view that imperatives *do* contain an operator which is interpreted like the necessity modal (Kaufmann 2012), and the propositional and presuppositional element, namely the weak necessity modal and the directive operator, are separated in terms of their semantic representation (Medeiros 2013). Primary goals for future development of this account are to unify the account of SIs more fully with some non-canonical form imperatives in other languages (e.g. German, Hebrew, Greek), which share similar properties to SIs in Japanese. Cross-linguistically, some non-canonical form imperatives can only be used as strong directives, not allowing the weak readings (von Fintel & Iatridou 2017). Moreover, examining how the contrast between MIs and SIs could be accounted for from the viewpoints of 'minimal' analysis of imperatives (Portner 2004, 2007) will be implemented in the future.

References

Condoravdi, C. and S. Lauer. 2012. Imperatives: Meaning and Illocutionary Force, *Empirical Issues in Syntax and Semantics* 9: 37–58. http://www.cssp.cnrs.fr/eiss9/eiss9_condoravdi-and-lauer.pdf.

Deng, D. 2015. The Syntacticization of Illocutionary Forces and the Root vs. Non-root Distinction: Evidence from the Sentence-final Particle Ba in Mandarin. *Lingua: An International Review of General Linguistics* 162: 32–55. Amsterdam: Elsevier.

von Fintel, K. and S. Iatridou. 2008. How to Say Ought in Foreign: The Composition of Weak Necessity Modals. *Time and Modality*, 115–141 ed. J. Gueron and J. Lecarme. Dordrecht: Springer.

von Fintel, K. and S. Iatridou. 2017. A Modest Proposal for the Meaning of Imperatives. *Modality across Syntactic Categories. First edition.* ed. A. Arregui et al. 288–319. Oxford: Oxford University Press.

Haida, A. and S. Repp. 2012. 'Only' in Imperatives. *Proceedings of Sinn und Bedeutung 16.* ed. A. Guevara, A. Chernilovskaya, and R. Nouwen. 307–320. Cambridge, MA: MITWPL.

Heim, J., H. Keupdijo, Z. W. Lam, A. Osa-Gómez and M. Wiltschko. 2014. How to Do Things with Particles. *Proceedings of the 2014 Annual Conference of the Canadian Linguistic Association*: 1–15. http://cla-acl.ca/wp-content/uploads/Heim_ Keupdjio Lam Osa Gomez Wiltschko 2014 pdf

Ihara, S. and Y. Noguchi. 2017. Meireikeishikibun no Tōgokōzo: Tōgo Keitai Imi no Intāfēsu kara (The Syntactic Structure of the Imperative Form Sentence in Japanese: At the Syntax, Morphology and Semantics Interface). *Proceedings of the 41st Annual Meeting of the Kansai Linguistic Society*: 25–36. Kansai Linguistic Society.

Isac, D. 2012. Decomposing Force. *Towards a Biolinguistic Understanding of Grammar: Essays on Interfaces.* ed. A. Di Sciullo. 87–116. Amsterdam: John Benjamins.

Kaufmann, M. 2012. *Interpreting Imperatives.* London: Springer.

Kratzer, A. 1981. The Notional Category of Modality. *Words, Worlds, and Contexts: New Approaches in Word Semantics.* ed. Eikmeyer, H-J. and H. Riéser. 38–74. Berlin: de Gruyter.

Kratzer, A. 1991. Modality. *Semantics: An International Handbook of Contemporary Research.* ed. A. von Stechow and D. Wunderlich. 639–650. Berlin: de Gruyter.

Kuno, S. 1988. Blended Quasi-direct Discourse in Japanese. *Papers from the Second International Workshop on Japanese Syntax.* ed. W. Poser. 75-102. Stanford: CSLI Publications.

Medeiros, D. J. 2013. *Formal Approaches to the Syntax and Semantics of Imperatives.* Doctoral Dissertation, the University of Michigan.

Noguchi, Y. 2016. Does ForceP Determine All the Illocutionary Forces?: A Case Study of Dictionary Form Imperatives in Japanese. *Proceedings of FAJL* 8. ed. A. Sugawara, S. Hayashi and S. Ito. 43–62. Cambridge, MA: MITWPL.

Portner, P. 2004. The Semantics of Imperatives within a Theory of Clause Types. *Proceedings of SALT 14.* ed. Watanabe, K. and Robert B. Y. 235–252. Ithaca, NY: CLC Publications.

Portner, P. 2007. Imperatives and Modals. *Natural Language Semantics 15*: 351–383. London: Springer.

Portner, P. 2010. Permission and Choice. *Discourse and Grammar: From Sentence Types to Lexical Categories.* ed. T. Zimmermann and G. Grewendorf. 43–68. New York: Mouton de Gruyter.

Saito, M. and T. Haraguchi. 2012. Dering the Cartography of the Japanese Right Periphery: The Case of Sentence-final Discourse Particles. *IBERIA: An International Journal of Theoretical Linguistics* 4: 104–123. University of Seville.

Silk, A. 2013. Ought and Must: Some Philosophical Therapy. Expanded version of SALT 22 paper.

Silk, A. 2016. Weak and Strong Necessity Modals: On Linguistic Means of Expressing "a Primitive Concept OUGHT". *Meaning, Decision, and Norms: Themes from the Work of Allan Gibbard* (to appear). ed. B. Dunaway and D. Plunkett. http://www-personal.umich.edu/~asilk/Alex_Silk/home_files/silk%20ought%20must.pdf.

Speas, P. and C. Tenny. 2003. Configurational Properties of Point of View Roles. *Asymmetry in Grammar*, 315–344. ed. A. Maria. Amsterdam: John Benjamins.

Zimmermann, T. 2000. Free Choice Disjunctions and Epistemic Possibility. *Natural Language Semantics* 8: 255–290. London: Springer.

Frame Setters in Verbal *Unagi*-sentences in Japanese and Korean

Ante Kärrman
Lund University

1 Introduction

Unagi-sentences have been a hotly debated topic in Japanese linguistics for over half a century (e.g. Okutsu 1978; Kitahara 1984; Obana 2001). Although not as well-studied, the same kind of construction can also be found in Korean (Yang 1996; Nam 2004). (1) is the eponymous example in Japanese, together with its Korean counterpart.

(1) ja: *boku wa   unagi da*
         I   TOP   eel   COP
      ko: *na nun   cang.e ta*
         I   TOP   eel   COP
      'As for me, eel.' (lit. 'I am an eel.')

While previous interpretations of *unagi*-sentences have so far been perceived as relating to the copula (Okutsu 1978; Kitahara 1989; Nam 2004), or to nominal predicates (Obana 2001), similar 'illogical' utterances, where

Japanese/Korean Linguistics 25.
Edited by Shin Fukuda, Mary Shin Kim, and Mee-Jeong Park.

the relation between the topic-marked constituent and the predicate cannot be retrieved from sentence structure alone, can be seen with verbal predicates as well, e.g. (2).

(2) ja: *konnyaku wa   futora-nai*
          konjac   TOP   get.fat-NEG
     ko: *kon.yak un   an   ccinta*
          konjac   TOP   NEG   get fat
          'Konjac doesn't make you fat.' (lit. 'Konjac doesn't get fat.')

If we define *unagi*-sentences more broadly along the lines of (3), (2) can also be classified as an *unagi*-sentence since it cannot be interpreted literally, due to the topic-marked entity violating the selectional restriction of the predicate, just like in (1).

(3) An *unagi*-sentence U is any utterance involving a predicate P and at least one other constituent C that appears to be the subject of P but cannot literally be interpreted as such. The literal interpretation of U is always different from the meaning of U in context. In an *unagi*-sentence, C often, but not necessarily, appears to violate the selectional restriction of P.

This paper focuses on sentences that fall under the definition in (3) with verbal (i.e. noncopular and nonnominative) predicates in Japanese and Korean, henceforth dubbed verbal *unagi*-sentences. Specifically, an attempt at explaining a difference with regard to the acceptability of verbal *unagi*-sentences between the two languages is made using the concept of frame setters (Jacobs 2001; Krifka & Musan 2012). This difference was found during a larger empirical survey regarding various *unagi*-sentences in Japanese and Korean.

The structure of this paper is as follows. After looking at the survey where this difference between Japanese and Korean with regard to verbal *unagi*-sentences was found, a distinction is made between verbal *unagi*-sentences where the topic-marked constituent is an aboutness topic, and those with frame setters. A definition of experiencer frame setters is also made. As it turns out, it is the Korean topic marker's ability to mark experiencer frame setters that sets the two languages apart when it comes to verbal *unagi*-sentences. Then, nominativization is proposed as a test to differentiate between aboutness topics and frame setters. Finally, an explanation of why the Japanese and Korean topic markers differ in their ability to mark experiencer frame setters is suggested.

2   The Survey

The difference between Japanese and Korean with regard to acceptability of verbal *unagi*-sentences was found through a survey consisting of two acceptability questionnaires targeted at a total of 100 native Japanese and Korean speakers. In these questionnaires, a total of 28 items, seven different types of *unagi*-sentences with four items each, were tested for acceptability, with equally many filler items, 14 grammatical and 14 ungrammatical. The items were presented together with a context defining preutterance and were direct translations of each other in Japanese and Korean for each respective language questionnaire. The items with verbal predicates are presented in (4), and the results of the survey with regard to these are presented in table 1.

(4) a. ja: *([denwa de]   koko   wa   ame   ga   futte   iru.)*
            phone   LOC   here   TOP   rain   NOM   rain   be
            sō?   watashi wa   futte   i-nai.
            really   I   TOP   rain   be-NEG

     ko: *([cenhwa eyse]   yeki   nun   pi   ka   oko iss.e.)*
            phone   LOC   here   TOP   rain   NOM   rain   be
            kulay? na nun   an   o-nuntey.
            really   I   TOP   NEG   rain-MOD
            '([On the phone] It's raining here.) Really? It's not raining where I am.'

   b. ja: *(watashi   no   inu   wa   totemo   sizuka da.)*
            I   GEN   dog   TOP   very   quiet   COP
            sō?   ore   wa   itsumo   hoeru   noni.
            really   I   TOP   always   bark   MOD

     ko: *(wuli   kay   nun   acwu   coyonghay.)*
            I   dog   TOP   very   quiet
            kulay? wuli nun   maynnal   cic-nuntey."
            really   I   TOP   always   bark-MOD
            '(My dog is very quiet.) Really? My dog always barks.'

   c. ja: *(ano   hito   tte   kakkoyoku nai   ne.)*
            that   person   QT   handsome   NEG   MOD
            watashi   wa   kakkoii   yo.
            I   TOP   handsome MOD

     ko: *(ku   salam, mos   sayngkyess-ney.)*
            that   person NEG   handsome-MOD
            na nun   cal   sayngkyess-nuntey.
            I   TOP   well   handsome-MOD
            '(That person isn't very handsome, is he?) I think he is handsome.'

d. ja: *(sakki no   hito, nani o   shite ta   ndarō?)*
          earlier GEN   person what ACC   do   (be-)PST MOD
          un, watashi mo ayashii.
          yes I   also suspicious

   ko: *(akka ku   salam, mwe l   hay-ss-ci?)*
          earlier that person what ACC do-PST-MOD?
          ung, na to   swusanghay.
          yes I   also suspicious
          '(What was that person just now doing?) Yes, I find it suspicious
          as well.'

	Japanese		Korean		Difference
	z-score	SD	z-score	SD	z-score
Item 1 (4a)	-1.09	0.49	-0.30	0.85	0.79
Item 2 (4b)	-0.75	0.74	0.09	0.82	0.84
Item 3 (4c)	-0.60	0.77	0.22	0.78	0.82
Item 4 (4d)	-1.08	0.50	-0.55	0.83	0.53
Mean	-0.88	0.62	-0.13	0.82	0.75
Grm. filler mean	0.69	0.52	0.71	0.53	0.02
Ungrm. filler mean	-1.08	0.49	-1.01	0.55	0.07

TABLE 1 Acceptability of verbal unagi-sentences

The difference in the data between Japanese and Korean with regard to *unagi*-sentences with verbal predicates is taken to clearly indicate a considerable difference in acceptability between the two languages with regard to this sentence type ($p < 0.001$, Wilcoxon rank sum test). The *unagi*-sentences with verbal predicates that were tested for acceptability in the survey were judged almost as badly as the ungrammatical fillers in Japanese, while they were judged only slightly below average in Korean. The difference in judged acceptability between the two languages is consistent across each individual item. None of the items received a particularly bad judgment compared to the others in only one language, indicating that the judgment data is representative of the underlying construction represented by the sentence type for both languages.

3 Frame-setting *Unagi*-sentences

Although not investigated in the survey, as we saw earlier, there are *unagi*-sentences with verbal predicates that are equally natural in both languages, e.g. (5)–(7). The relation between the topic-marked constituent and predicate in these sentences is 'illogical,' i.e. cannot be retrieved from sentence structure alone, just like in a copular *unagi*-sentence.

(5) ja: *konnyaku wa   futora-nai*
          konjac   TOP get.fat-NEG
     ko: *kon.yak un   an   ccinta*
          konjac   TOP   NEG   get.fat
          'Konjac doesn't make you fat.'
(6) ja: *ano kantoku no   eiga wa   itsumo   naku*
          that director GEN film TOP always   cry
     ko: *ku   kamtok uy   yenghwa nun hangsang wulkey   tway*
          that director GEN film   TOP always   cry   become
          'That director's films always make me cry.'
(7) ja: *ano hito   wa   haratatsu*
          that person TOP   get.angry
     ko: *ku   salam   un   ccacungna*
          that person TOP   get.angry
          'That person makes me angry.'

Why are the *unagi*-sentences with verbal predicates in (5)–(7) possible in both languages while the items with verbal predicates tested in the survey are acceptable in Korean only? The only logical explanation is that the sentences in (5)–(7) and those in (4) represent different constructions, both being possible in Korean while only the former is possible in Japanese.

The main difference between (5)–(7) and (4) is the function of the topic-marked constituent. In (5)–(7) the topic-marked entity is what the sentence is about, i.e., it is a topic in the aboutness sense. The predicates in these sentences are therefore interpreted as describing an attribute of the topic, in other words, these sentences have a topic-comment structure. In (5) the predicate 'does not get fat' is described as a property of the topic 'konjac.' Likewise, in (6) 'always cry' is a property of 'that director's films.' The same thing goes for 'that person' and 'get angry' in (7). Who actually gets fat, who does the crying, and who gets angry is retrieved from context.

In the Korean versions of (4), on the other hand, the topic-marked entities are not what the sentences are about, but rather delimiters that set the frame within which the predicates should be interpreted. Here, the predicates are not interpreted as describing an attribute of the topic-marked entities. There is therefore no surface topic-comment structure. 'Handsome,' for example, is not an attribute of 'I' in (4c), but an attribute of a salient entity in the common ground, 'he' in this case. 'I' merely sets the frame where the predication '(he) is handsome' is to be interpreted, best translated into English along the lines of 'I think that he is handsome.' As a result, the topic-marked constituents in (4) are not topics in the aboutness topic sense, but frame setters, as described by Krifka & Musan (2012: 31–2). We can therefore call these *unagi*-sentences that have frame setting topic marked constituents 'frame setting *unagi* sentences.'

Since all of the *unagi*-sentences with verbal predicates judged for acceptability in the survey presented in this paper were frame-setting *unagi*-sentences, and all of them received unfavorable judgment scores in Japanese, one might be tempted to conclude that frame-setting *unagi*-sentences are impossible in Japanese, only being possible in Korean. This depends on which definition of *unagi*-sentences one chooses to employ. However, as they are defined in (3), sentences such as (8)–(10) definitely qualify as frame-setting *unagi*-sentences, and are completely natural in both languages.

(8) ja: *koko   wa   saite   iru*
         here   TOP   bloom be
    ko: *yeki nun phie   issta*
         here TOP   bloom be
         'Flowers are in bloom here[1].'

(9) ja: *kinō   wa   sōjishi-ta*
         yesterday TOP   clean-PST
    ko: *ecey   nun   chengsohay-ss.e*
         yesterday TOP   clean-PST
         'I cleaned yesterday.'

(10) ja: *kin'yōbi   wa   yasumu*
         Friday   TOP   have.off
    ko: *kum.yoil   un   swinta*
         Friday   TOP   have.off
         'I have Fridays off.'

It is clear that the topic-marked constituents in (8)–(10) are not topics in the aboutness sense, but frame setters that set the frame in which the

---

[1]This sentence also has the topic-comment reading available, where 'here' is interpreted as the subject of the predicate, giving the translation 'this place is in bloom.' When this reading is taken, the nominative case particle can, of course, replace the topic particle to create an exhaustive listing reading, as described below. This is however not possible with the frame setter reading.

predicates are interpreted. Naturally, 'here' is not the actor of the predicate 'bloom' in (8), just as the entity denoted by 'yesterday' is not what did the cleaning in (9), and it is not 'Friday' that has time off in (10). But since there are no further constituents present in these constructions, and the relation between the frame setter and the predicate is 'illogical' and cannot be retrieved from sentence structure alone, i.e., there are no postpositional particles explicitly marking temporal or locative readings[2], they qualify as *unagi*-sentences according to our definition. The difference between the frame-setters in (8)–(10) compared to those in the Korean versions of (4) is their semantic content. The frame setters in (8)–(10) denote time and place, while those in (4) are personal pronouns, denoting animate entities. We can safely conclude that, using the topic particle alone, frame setters are most easily formed with entities denoting time and place, as they do in (8)–(10). They are not so easily formed with expressions denoting animate entities. For an animate entity to be able to act as a frame setter while only being marked with a topic particle, it has to be clear that it represents a frame in which a predication can be interpreted[3]. Namely, the frame-setting entity must be able to be classified as an experiencer, and the frame it represents must be along the lines of the *place* where the entity is (and can therefore be experienced by the frame-setting animate entity), as in (4a), the *things* possessed by or located in the vicinity of the entity, as in (4b), or the *opinion* of the entity, as in (4c) and (4d). The predicates of (4), 'rain,' 'bark,' 'handsome,' and 'suspicious,' are interpreted within the frames represented by the topic-marked first person pronouns.

---

[2]An interpretation of (8)–(10) involving some sort of ellipsis of temporal or locative postpositional particles (*ni/de* in Japanese; *ey/eyse* in Korean) might be tempting, but this approach proves unsatisfactory, at least in (9'), since the temporal markers *ni/ey* do not bind with *kinō/ecey* in a purely temporal reading.

(9')   ja: * *kinō*   *ni*   *wa*   *sōjishi-ta*
                yesterday   TMP   TOP   clean-PST
         ko: * *ecey*   *ey*   *nun*   *chengsohay-ss.e*
                yesterday   TMP   TOP   clean-PST
                'I cleaned yesterday.'

[3]Experiencer frame setters can be marked explicitly using expressions such as *nitotte* in Japanese and *hanthey* in Korean, as in (i).

(i)   ja: *watashi nitotte*   *wa*   *kakkoii*   *yo*
            I   for   TOP   handsome   MOD
      ko: *na hantey*   *nun*   *cal*   *sayngkyess-nuntey*
            I   for   TOP   well   handsome-MOD
            'He is handsome for me.'

What decides whether a topic-marked entity can function as a frame setter or not is a combination of the lexical content of the topic-marked entity and the degree of the topic particle's ability to mark frame setters. To explain the difference between Japanese and Korean with regard to what type of frame setters are possible, we can propose the simple hierarchy of an entity's lexical content in (11), to rank the felicitousness of a topic-marked entity to function as a frame setter. The topic particles in Japanese and Korean differ in such a way that the Japanese topic particle can only easily mark frame setters with semantic content on the higher end of the hierarchy, while the topic particle in Korean can mark frame setters with entities that belong to both sides of the hierarchy. It is this difference in ability for the topic particles to mark frame setters with entities other than those denoting time and place that is the difference between Japanese and Korean in terms of frame-setting *unagi*-sentences.

(11)   time, place > experiencer

The use of experiencer frame setters in Korean is not limited to *unagi*-sentences. (12)–(14) are utterances that contain experiencer frame setters. In these utterances, the predicate does not have an 'illogical' relation to an apparent subject, like it does in an *unagi*-sentence; the real subjects of the predicates are all present and marked with the nominative case particle.

(12)   'Minswu is really handsome.'
　　　　ko: *na nun chelswu   ka   cal   sayngkyess-nuntey*
　　　　　　　I   TOP Chelswu NOM   well handsome-MOD
　　　　　　　'I think Chelswu is handsome.'
(13)   'It is raining here.'
　　　　ko: *na nun nwun i   o-nuntey*
　　　　　　　I   TOP snow NOM   fall-MOD
　　　　　　　'It is snowing where I am.'
(14)   'My cat always meows.'
　　　　ko: *wuli   nun   kay ka   maynnal   cic-nuntey*
　　　　　　　I   TOP   dog NOM   always   bark-MOD
　　　　　　　'As for me, my dog always barks.

The constructions in (12)–(14) resemble topicalized multiple nominative constructions, but cannot be classified as such, since they violate the 'characteristic property' constraint, set forth by Yoon (2009). Topicalized multiple nominative contructions are exemplified in (15b), while (15a) is a nontopicalized counterpart. The sentential predicate in a multiple nominative construction must denote a characteristic property of the major subject in order to be felicitous (Yoon ibid.) (in (15), *chelswu* is the major subject, and *meli ka coh.ta* is the sentential predicate, which denotes a characteristic property of the major subject). Furthermore, contrarily to multiple nominative constructions, the topic particles in (12)–(14) cannot be switched out for nominative case particles to create an exhaustive listing reading, as indicated in (12′)–(14′). This is conclusive evidence that the utterances in (12)–(14) are not multiple nominative constructions, but rather non-*unagi*-sentences with experiencer frame setters.

(15) a. ko: *chelswu   ka   meli   ka   coh.ta*
            Chelswu NOM head NOM good
            'Chelswu is smart.'

    b. ko: *chelswu   nun meli   ka   coh.ta*
            Chelswu TOP head NOM good
            'Chelswu is smart.'

(12′) ko: **nay ka   chelswu   ka   cal   sayngkyess-nuntey*
          I   NOM Chelswu NOM well handsome-MOD
          '*I* think Chelswu is handsome.'

(13′) ko: **nay ka   nwun i   o-nuntey*
          I   NOM snow NOM fall-MOD
          'It is snowing where *I* am.'

(14′) ko: **wuli ka   kay ka   maynnal   cic-nuntey*
          I   NOM dog NOM always bark-MOD
          '*My* dog always barks.'

Naturally, experiencer frame setters only marked with the topic particle cannot appear in Japanese in non-*unagi*-sentences, just as they cannot appear in *unagi*-sentences either, as exemplified in (16).

(16) ja: * *watashi wa   yuki   ga   futte iru*
         I   TOP snow NOM fall be
         'It is snowing where I am.'

This means that the difference between Japanese and Korean presented in this paper is not a difference with regard to *unagi*-sentences per se, but rather a difference in the topic markers ability to mark experiencer frame setters.

4 Nominativization as a Test for Differentiating Between Topics and Frame Setters

Returning to the dichotomy of aboutness topic and frame setter, one way that they differ is that topic-marked constituents that are aboutness topics can be marked with the nominative particle and receive an exhaustive listing reading, while constituents that are frame setters cannot. While this is hinted at from the possibility of nominative case marking in the multiple nominative construction in (15a), compared to the infelicitousness of (12')–(14'), it is true for frame setters in general, even temporal and locative ones, as shown in (17) & (17'), and (18) & (18'). Since the topic-marked constituents in (17) and (18) are frame setters, these utterances become infelicitous when the topic particles are exchanged for nominative case particles in (17') and (18').

(17) ja: *kyō wa watashi ga gohan o tsukuru*
    today TOP I NOM food ACC cook
   ko: *enwul un nay ka pap ul mantunta*
     today TOP I NOM food ACC cook
    'I will cook today.'

(17') ja: * *kyō ga watashi ga gohan o tsukuru*
    today NOM I NOM food ACC cook
   ko: * *enwul i nay ka pap ul mantunta*
    today NOM I NOM food ACC cook
    'I will cook today.'

(18) ja: *koko wa hana ga takusan saite iru*
    here TOP flower NOM a.lot bloom be
   ko: *yeki nun kkoch i manh.i phie issta*
    here TOP flower NOM a.lot bloom be
    'There are many flowers blooming here.'

(18') ja: * *koko ga hana ga takusan saite iru*
    here NOM flower NOM a.lot bloom be
   ko: * *yeki ka kkoch i manh.i phie issta*
    here NOM flower NOM a.lot bloom be
    'There are many flowers blooming here.'

This difference between aboutness topics and frame setters holds true even for *unagi*-sentences. In (19) the topic particle is exchanged for a nominative case particle, giving an exhaustive listing reading that answers the question 'who will have the eel?' In (20) and (21), on the other hand, where the topic-marked constituents are frame setters, the topic particles cannot be exchanged for a nominative case particle to give an exhaustive listing reading that answers the questions 'when...' in (20) and 'who...' in (21). The frame-setting reading is completely lost when the topic particle is exchanged for a nominative case particle, rendering only a subject reading possible. (20) is therefore infelicitous due to a semantic mismatch between subject and predicate, and only the reading 'I am handsome' is available in (21).

(19) ja: *boku   ga   unagi da*
           I   NOM   eel   COP
      ko: *nay   ka   cange ta*
           I   NOM   eel   COP
           '*I* will have the eel.'
(20) ja: # *kin.yōbi   ga   yasumu*
             friday   NOM   have.off
      ko: # *kum.yoil   i   swinta*
             friday   NOM   have.off
           'I have *Fridays* off.'
(21) ko: # *nay   ka   cal   sayngkyess-nuntey*
             I   NOM   well   handsome-MOD
           'I think he is handsome.'

The problem for frame setters with receiving an exhaustive listing reading with a nominative case particle is not due to a frame setter's inability to be focused, but rather their inability to be subjects, which is what the nominative case particles mark in these cases. Instead, an exhaustive listing reading is possible by dropping the topic particle and prosodically marking the frame setter. This is exemplified in (9″), which can be used to answer the question 'when did you clean?'

(9″) ja: *KINŌ   sōjishi-ta*
           yesterday clean-PST
      ko: *ECEY   chengsohay-ss.e*
           yesterday clean-PST
           'I cleaned *yesterday*.'

Naturally, the nominative case particle test cannot be applied when the topic-marked constituent is a clear nonsubject. This is because, unlike the topic particles with topicalization, the nominative case particles cannot appear together with postpositional particles nor replace the accusative case particles to create an exhaustive listing reading. An exhaustive listing reading is instead made available when the topic particle is absent, as suggested by Heycock (1993, 2008) for Japanese. Therefore, use of the nominative case particle in an exhaustive listing reading cannot be used to test whether an adverbial or accusative phrase is a frame setter or not, since the nominative particle would never bind to them anyway. This test is useful, however, to test whether the topic-marked constituent in an *unagi*-sentence is a frame setter or not.

5   A Difference in the Retrievability of the Syntactic Function of Topic-marked Constituents

On a final note, the question remains as to why the Korean topic particle can mark experiencer frame setters, while the Japanese cannot. We can hypothesize that this is due to a difference in the retrievability of the syntactic function of a topic-marked constituent in the two languages. Lee & Shimojo (2016) found that the topic particles in Japanese and Korean differ in terms of the definiteness they mark, namely that the Japanese topic particle marks discourse old entities, while the Korean topic particle marks episode old entities. Lee & Shimojo arrive at their conclusion from a comparison of Bible translations, among other things, where entities salient in discourse, but newly introduced in the current episode, are often marked with *wa* in Japanese but with *ka/i* in Korean. (22) and (23) are the relevant parts of examples of this (adapted from Lee & Shimojo ibid.:13). While the disciples are discourse old entities, they are introduced for the first time in the episode from which (22) and (23) are extracted. Since the disciples are episode new, they are marked with the nominative case particle in Korean, but since they are discourse old, they are marked with the topic particle in Japanese.

(22) ja: *deshitachi wa   aruki-nagara mugi no   ho   o*
           disciples   TOP walk-while   grain GEN   head   ACC
           tsumi hajime-ta
           pick   begin-PST
           '...the disciples began to pick the heads of grain while walking'
(23) ko: *ceycatul   i   hamkkey ka-myense milisak   ul*
           disciples NOM   together go-while   grain.head ACC
           calla   mek.-essta
           cut   eat-PST
           '...his disciples walked with him, picking up and eating some heads of grain'

The Japanese topic particle can therefore be thought of as being able to 'reach further' than the Korean topic particle. We can hypothesize that an entity that is marked as topic in Korean is given more leeway in terms of its syntactic function, compared to a topic-marked entity in Japanese. A topic-marked entity in Korean is closer and more easily retrievable in the discourse, meaning that its syntactic function is also more easily accessible. In Japanese, on the other hand, the syntactic function of a topic-marked entity is more limited, since its proximity in discourse cannot be guaranteed. The Japanese topic particle can therefore not mark a frame setter without the help of typical frame-setting semantic content, i.e. time and place.

6 Conclusion

In this paper, we attempted an explanation of a difference between Japanese and Korean with regard to the acceptability of a certain type verbal *unagi*-sentence using the concept of frame setters. Only in Korean can the topic particle mark an experiencer frame setter, while the topic particles can mark temporal and locative frame setters in both languages. Furthermore, to test whether a topic-marked constituent is an aboutness topic or a frame setter, a nominativization test was proposed; only aboutness topics can be nominativized using the nominative case particle. Finally, as an explanation as to why only the Korean topic particle can mark experiencer frame setters, it was suggested to be because the syntactic role of a topic-marked entity in Korean is more easily retrieved compared to its Japanese counterpart, since the Korean topic particle only marks episode old entities, while the Japanese topic particle can mark discourse old entities.

References

Heycock, C. 1993. Focus Projection in Japanese. *Proceedings of North East Linguistic Society* 24:157–71.

Heycock, C. 2008. Japanese *-wa, -ga*, and Information Structure. *The Oxford Handbook of Japanese Linguistics*, eds. S. Miyagawa & M. Saito, 54–83. Oxford: Oxford University Press.

Jacobs, J. 2001. The Dimensions of Topic-Comment. *Linguistics* 39(4):641–81.

Kitahara, Y. 1984. *nihongo bunpō no shōten (Focus on Japanese Grammar)*. Tokyo: Kyoiku Shuppan.

Krifka M. & Musan R. 2012. Information Structure: Overview and Linguistic Issues. *The Expression of Information Structure*, eds. M. Krifka & R. Musan, 1–44. Berlin/Boston: Walter de Gruyter.

Lee, E. & Shimojo, M. 2016. Mismatch of Topic Between Japanese and Korean. *Journal of East Asian Linguistics* 25(1):81–112.

Nam, K. I. 2004. *hyentay kwuk.e 'ita' kwumun yenkwu (Research on 'Ita' Constructions in Modern Korean)*. Seoul: Hankookmunhwasa.

Obana, Y. 2001. *Unagi*-sentences in Japanese and Mutual Knowledge. *Journal of Pragmatics* 33:725–51.

Okutsu, K. 1978. *boku wa unagi da no bunpō: da to no (The Grammar of boku wa unagi da: da and no)*. Tokyo: Kuroshio Shuppan.

Yang, J. S. 1996. *'ita' kwumun uy uymi haysek* (The Semantic Interpretation of *'ita'* Constructions). *tongpang hakci* 91:99–134.

Yoon, J. H. 2009. The Distribution of Subject Properties in Multiple Subject Constructions. *Japanese-Korean Linguistics 16*, eds. Y. Takubo, T. Kinuhata, S. Grzelak, & K. Nagai, 64–83. Stanford: CSLI Publications.

Two Forms of Relative Clauses in Osaka Japanese and Their Theoretical Implications*

Hitomi Minamida
Cornell University

1 Introduction

Head-internal relative clauses (HIRCs) in Standard Japanese (SJ) (1) are potentially homophonous with other constructions (see Grosu and Hoshi 2016) due to the lexical ambiguity of the obligatory particle *no*.[1]

(1)　Taro-wa [Hanako-ga ringo-o kitta **no**]-o tabeta.
　　Taro-TOP Hanako-NOM apple-ACC cut.PST *NO*-ACC ate
　　Lit.: 'Taro ate [that Hanako cut an apple].'

The particle *no* can be a genitive Case marker (2a), a pronoun (2b), or a complementizer (2c) (Murasugi 1991).

* I express my gratitude to John Whitman for many comments and much discussion. This project would have been impossible without his vast knowledge of Japanese. I also thank John Bowers and Miloje Despić for helpful comments and suggestions. Osaka Japanese data are from Kayoko Minamida, Shinya Minamida, Hiroyuki Mori, Misako Suzuki, and the author. I thank them for discussion. This work is supported by funding from the Cornell East Asia Program. All errors are my own.

[1] Throughout this paper, relative heads are underlined and relative clauses are in square brackets.

Japanese/Korean Linguistics 25.
Edited by Shin Fukuda, Mary Shin Kim, and Mee-Jeong Park.

(2)   a.   Kore-wa Taro-**no**   hon da.
              this-TOP Taro-GEN book COP
              'This is Taro's book.'

        b.   Kore-wa Taro **no** da.
              this-TOP Taro N   COP
              'This is Taro's.'

        c.   [Taro-wa kono hon-o   katta   **no**] da.
              Taro-TOP this   book-ACC bought C   COP
              'It is [that Taro bought this book].'

In this paper, I show that Osaka Japanese[2] (OJ) phonologically distinguishes the pronoun *no* and the complementizer *no*. My data show that what has been taken to be a single HIRC construction actually involves two distinct constructions: true HIRCs and doubly-headed relative clauses (DHRCs). Section 2 shows that HIRCs are headed by the complementizer *no*, whereas DHRCs can be headed by the pronoun *no*, using the double quantifier tests in Erlewine and Gould (2016). Section 3 argues that free relatives are homophonous with what I call one-*headed relative clauses* in SJ due to the same ambiguity of the particle *no*. OJ data show that free relatives are HIRCs without an internal head (cf. Watanabe 1992). I also show that DHRCs do not involve movement unlike HIRCs and that change of state HIRCs (Tonosaki 1996) belong to the category of DHRC. Section 4 concludes this paper.

2 Two Forms of Relative Clauses in Osaka Japanese

2.1 Particle *no* in Osaka Japanese

Unlike SJ, the three functions of the particle *no* are realized in three different forms in OJ; the genitive *no* is *no* (3a), the pronoun *no* is *non* (3b), and the complementizer *no* is *n* (3c).

(3)   a.   Kore-wa Taro-**no**   hon ya.
              this-TOP Taro-GEN book COP
              'This is Taro's book.'

        b.   Kore-wa Taro **non** ya.
              this-TOP Taro N   COP
               'This is Taro's.'

        c.   [Taro-wa kono hon-o   kauta   **n**] ya.
              Taro-TOP this   book-ACC bought C COP
              'It is [that Taro bought this book].'

In fact, the pronoun *non* in OJ is a combination of two *no*'s, where the

---

[2] In this paper, "Osaka Japanese" refers to the varieties spoken in the Osaka metropolitan area or *Kei-Han-Shin* (Kyoto-Osaka-Kobe).

second *no* is contracted; in the attributive form, *non* is used after canonical adjectives (*i*-adjectives) (4a), while only *n* is used after nominal adjectives (*na*-adjectives) (4b). The first *no* in (3b) is genitive from its meaning, but I assume that the first *no* in (4a) is a copula (cf. Nishiyama 1999).[3]

(4) a. Ano akai **no-n**-ga   hosii.
         that red   COP-N-NOM want
         '(I) want that red one.'
     b. Ano kiree   **na-n**-ga   hosii.
         that beautiful COP-N-NOM want
         '(I) want that beautiful one.'

2.2 Double Quantifier Tests

Erlewine and Gould (2016) (henceforth E&G) argue that Japanese head-external relative clauses (HERCs) (5a), HIRCs (5b), and DHRCs (5c) give us the same two interpretations with respect to the double quantifier tests. The examples below are E&G's (13)–(15).

(5) a. Junya-wa [Ayaka-ga *mit-tu*   muita] <u>ringo</u>-o   *zenbu*
         Junya-TOP Ayaka-NOM three-CL peeled <u>apple</u>-ACC all
         tabeta.
         ate
         'Junya ate *all of* <u>the apples</u> [that Ayaka peeled *three of*].'
     b. Junya-wa [Ayaka-ga <u>ringo</u>-o   *mit-tu*   muita no]-o
         Junya-TOP Ayaka-NOM <u>apple</u>-ACC three-CL peeled *NO*-ACC
         zenbu tabeta.
         all   ate
         Lit.: 'Junya ate *all of* [that Ayaka peeled *three* <u>apples</u>].'
     c. Junya-wa [Ayaka-ga <u>ringo</u>-o   *mit-tu*   muita]
         Junya-TOP Ayaka-NOM <u>apple</u>-ACC three-CL peeled
         <u>sono-ringo</u>[4]-o *zenbu* tabeta.
         that-apple-ACC all   ate
         Lit.: 'Junya ate *all of* <u>those apples</u> [that Ayaka peeled *three*
         <u>apples</u>].'

---

[3] Nishiyama (1999) analyzes -*i* in canonical adjectives as a present tense marker. I assume that Japanese adjectives are tenseless in non-past forms, following Yamakido (2005), and that -*i* is part of canonical adjectives here. However, Yamakido argues that -*i* in canonical adjectives and -*na* in nominal adjectives are purely morphologically motivated and are not copulas.

[4] E&G mention that the external head of DHRCs always requires the demonstrative *sono* 'that', but the plural form *sorerano* 'those' is also fine.

In the tests[5], there is a quantifier such as *mit-tu* 'three-CL' inside the relative clause and there is a universal quantifier *zenbu* 'all' outside the relative clause. E&G give us the context (6), where there are two groups of six apples and only three apples in the first group are peeled.

(6)   = E&G's (9)

According to E&G, there are two possible readings and all the sentences in (5) give us both interpretations. The first one is that Junya ate the three peeled apples in the first group and the second one is that Junya ate all six apples in the first group that includes the three peeled apples. Following Moulton and Shimoyama (2017), I will call the two readings the *regular reading* and the *salient set reading*, respectively (7). E&G's results are summarized in (8).

(7)   a.   **Regular reading:** Junya ate the three peeled apples in the first group (three apples reading).

       b.   **Salient set reading:** Junya ate all six apples in the first group that includes the three peeled apples (six apples reading).

(8)

	regular reading	salient set reading
(5a), (5b), and (5c)	✓	✓

Notice that HIRCs in SJ (5b) could be pronoun-headed DHRCs if the particle *no* is a pronoun. In fact, OJ makes that distinction. The OJ version of (5) in (9) shows that there are two types of HIRC: *non*-headed relative clauses (*non*-headed RCs) (9b) and *n*-headed relative clauses (*n*-headed RCs) (9c).

According to OJ speakers' judgments, all the sentences in (9) yield the regular reading. However, only (9b) and (9d) give us the salient set reading as well. A summary of the judgments is given in (10).

(9)   a.   Junya-wa [Ayaka-ga *mit-tu* muita] ringo-o   *zenbu*
             Junya-TOP Ayaka-NOM three-CL peeled apple-ACC all

             tabeta.
             ate
             'Junya ate *all of* the apples [that Ayaka peeled *three of*].'

---

[5] The point of the tests is that the quantifier outside the relative clause is *zenbu* 'all'. E&G also tested *hanbun* 'half' inside the relative clause and claim that it yields only the salient set reading, but Moulton and Shimoyama (2017) and I are skeptical about their judgments. There is no difference in meanings between *mit-tu* 'three-CL' and *hanbun* 'half' with respect to the tests; they both can give us the regular reading.

b. Junya-wa [Ayaka-ga ringo-o *mit-tu* muita **no**]
    Junya-TOP Ayaka-NOM apple-ACC three-CL peeled COP
    n-o *zenbu* tabeta.
    N-ACC all ate
    Lit.: 'Junya ate *all of* the ones [that Ayaka peeled *three* apples].'

c. Junya-wa [Ayaka-ga ringo-o *mit-tu* muita **n**]-o
    Junya-TOP Ayaka-NOM apple-ACC three-CL peeled C-ACC
    zenbu tabeta.
    all ate
    Lit.: 'Junya ate *all of* [that Ayaka peeled *three* apples].'

d. Junya-wa [Ayaka-ga ringo-o *mit-tu* muita]
    Junya-TOP Ayaka-NOM apple-ACC three-CL peeled
    sorerano-ringo-o *zenbu* tabeta.
    those-apple-ACC all ate
    Lit.: 'Junya ate *all of* those apples [that Ayaka peeled *three* apples].'

(10)

	regular reading	*salient set reading*
(9a) and (9c)	✓	

	regular reading	*salient set reading*
(9b) and (9d)	✓	✓

These data show that DHRCs can be pronoun-headed (*non*-headed RCs) (9b) and that what have been analyzed as SJ HIRCs are actually ambiguous between DHRCs and true HIRCs. My data also show that true HIRCs are complementizer-headed (*n*-headed RCs) (9c). From a comparative stand-point, Kim (2017) shows that Korean also allows HIRCs with the clear pronominal head *ku kes* 'that one', and points out that this pattern behaves like a type of DHRC (11).

(11) Na-nun [Tom-i tosekwan-eyse chayk-ul taychwulha-n]
      I-TOP Tom-NOM library-from book-ACC check.out-ADN.PST
      ku-kes-ul ilk-epo-ass-ta.
      that-one-ACC read-see-PST-DEC
      Lit.: 'I tried reading that one [that Tom checked out a book from the library].'   (Kim 2017: (2) from his abstract)

The difference in interpretations in (10) comes from the fact that *non* contains a pronoun; the regular reading is obtained when the reference of *non* is the three peeled apples in the first group, while the salient set reading is obtained when the reference of *non* is the entire first group that includes the three peeled apples. The external head in the DP-headed DHRC (9d) *sorerano ringo* 'those apples' has the same two referential possibilities.[6]

It must be noted that even in the *non*-headed RC (9b) and DHRC (9d), the more dominant reading is the regular reading. In order to get the salient set reading, we must put focus on *non* in (9b).[7] In (9b) (and (9d)), the focus intonation indicates that it is the salient set, not the three peeled apples, that the speaker is talking about. This contrasts with the case where focus is put on the external head in the HERC (9a) and on the internal head in the HIRC (9v) because it would indicate that it is apples, not oranges, for example, that Junya ate.

My claim is largely consistent with the analysis by Moulton and Shimoyama (2017), who claim that the salient set reading comes from "free relatives". More precisely, they claim that "headless relatives with a gap" give us the salient set reading. However, as the translation of their example of headless relatives (12a) and the LF of the sentence (12b) show, their free relatives/headless relatives might be analyzed as having a pronominal head with an interpretation like English *one*. ((12) is from their examples (60) and (61).) In the next section, I will discuss this issue.

(12)   a.   [Ayaka-ga $<gap>$ ringo-o   mit-tu   muita no]
                Ayaka-NOM   apple-ACC three-CL peeled *NO*
                '[(that which/the one that/what) Ayaka peeled three apples in/of]'

    b.   [$_{DP}$ THE [$_{NP}$ (one) [$_{CP}$ λx [Ayaka peeled three apples in/of x]]]]

3   Japanese Relative Clauses and Movement

3.1   Free Relatives vs. *One*-headed Relative Clauses

English distinguishes free relatives (FRs) (13a), which involve a *wh*-word and are now generally considered headless (Groos and van Riemsdijk 1981, inter alia), and relative clauses headed by pronominal elements such as *one* (*one*-headed RCs), which have a gap due to extraction (13b).

(13)   a.   John eats [what Mary cut].

---

[6] My consultants report that the salient set reading is possible only when the external head in the DHRC has the demonstrative *sorerano* 'those' (compare (5c) and (9d)). I assume that this is because the reference of *sorerano* 'those' is wider than that of *sono* 'that' due to its plurality, although Japanese does not make a clear distinction between singular and plural.

[7] I am not sure if *sorerano ringo* 'those apples' in (9d) has to be focalized to get the salient set reading. There are some reasons. First, the phrase *sorerano ringo* 'those apples' is too long to receive focus. Second, E&G's DHRCs are artificial sentences in that they are marginal for some speakers due to the redundancy of the two heads *ringo* 'apple'.

b.   John eats **the one(s)**ᵢ [that Mary cut _____ᵢ].

In languages without *wh*-like elements in relative clauses, this distinction is obscured. In Korean, for example, the relative clause headed by the bound noun *kes* 'thing, one' can be interpreted either as a FR or as a *one*-headed RC (14); *kes* can be a complementizer or a pronoun.

(14)   John-un   [Mary-i   calu-n   **kes**]-ul   mek-nun-ta.
         John-TOP Mary-NOM cut-ADN.PST C/N-ACC eat-PRES-DEC
         Lit.: 'John eats [that Mary cut].'   (FR)
         'John eats **the one(s)**ᵢ [that Mary cut _____ᵢ].'   (*one*-headed RC)

The same thing applies to SJ because the particle *no*, which appears in these constructions, is lexically ambiguous; it can be a pronoun or a complementizer as we saw in Section 2.1. (15) is a FR if *no* is a complementizer and is a *one*-headed RC if *no* is a pronoun.

(15)   Taro-wa   [Hanako-ga   kitta   **no**]-o   taberu.
         Taro-TOP Hanako-NOM cut.PST C/N-ACC eat
         Lit.: 'Taro eats [that Hanako cut].'   (FR)
         'Taro eats **the one(s)**ᵢ [that Hanako cut _____ᵢ].'   (*one*-headed RC)

In contrast, OJ can distinguish FRs and *one*-headed RCs because the pronoun *no* and the complementizer *no* are realized in two different forms. (16a) shows that *n*-headed RCs are FRs while (16b) shows that *non*-headed RCs are *one*-headed RCs. (16b) also shows that *non*-headed RCs can have a gap if there is no internal head in the clause.[8] I propose that (12a) is in fact a gapless *non*-headed RC (= DHRC) because it has the internal head *ringo* 'apple'.

(16)   a.   Taro-wa   [Hanako-ga   kitta   **n**]-o   taberu.
               Taro-TOP Hanako-NOM cut.PST C-ACC eat
               Lit.: 'Taro eats [that Hanako cut].'
         b.   Taro-wa   [Hanako-ga   _____ᵢ   kitta   **no**]   **n**ᵢ-o   taberu.
               Taro-TOP Hanako-NOM   cut.PST COP N-ACC eat
               'Taro eats **the one(s)**ᵢ [that Hanako cut _____ᵢ].'

3.2 Island-(in)sensitivity

(16a) in the previous subsection suggests that FRs are a type of HIRC (see Watanabe 1992) because they are *n*-headed RCs. (17) shows that OJ HIRCs show island-sensitivity, as in SJ (Watanabe 1992), because the extraction of the internal head *sakana* 'fish' from a relative clause island is impossible. If

---

[8] Even though (16b) is a HERC, it has the particle *no* between the relative clause and the external head as has been reported for early child Japanese HERCs (Murasugi 1991).

my (and Watanabe's) assumption is correct, FRs should also exhibit island effects and this prediction is born out in the OJ example (18).[9]

(17) *?Taro-wa [Hanako-ga [_____$_i$ sakana-o sabaita] tomodati$_i$-o
Taro-TOP Hanako-NOM   fish-ACC filleted friend-ACC
hometeta n]-o   tabetemita.
praised C-ACC tried.eating
Lit.: 'Taro tried eating [that Hanako praised her friend [who filleted fish]]'

(18) *?Taro-wa [Hanako-ga [_____$_i$ e sabaita] tomodati$_i$-o hometeta
Taro-TOP Hanako-NOM   filleted friend-ACC praised
n]-o   tabetemita.
C-ACC tried.eating
Lit.: 'Taro tried eating [that Hanako praised her friend [who filleted e]].'

In contrast, the OJ *non*-headed RC with the internal head *sakana* 'fish' (= DHRC) exhibits lesser island effects (19).

(19) ??Taro-wa [Hanako-ga [_____$_i$ sakana-o sabaita] tomodati$_i$-o
Taro-TOP Hanako-NOM   fish-ACC filleted friend-ACC
hometeta no] n-o   tabetemita.
praised   COP N-ACC tried.eating
Lit.: 'Taro tried eating the one [that Hanako praised her friend [who filleted fish]].'

The DP-headed version (20) is more acceptable. (21) makes it clear that the external head is a pronoun because it is modified by an adjective and this is better than (19).[10] These data tell us that Japanese DHRCs are not generated by head extraction.

---

[9] One consultant reported that (17) and (18) are interpreted as the friend being eaten by Taro when I first asked her. When I asked her again, however, she said that Taro might have eaten the action of praising or that *n* might refer to *sakana* 'fish'. For the second possibility, it might be because it is natural to interpret what was eaten by Taro as *sakana* 'fish' to make the sentences meaningful. My claim here is that *non* is better than *n* because *non* is referential.

[10] Compare (19)–(21) with (59)–(61) in Grosu and Hoshi (2016), which show a similar level of acceptability. However, they interpret change of state HIRCs such as their example (61) as true HIRCs and thus argue that change of state HIRCs exhibit island effects, too.

(20)   Taro-wa [Hanako-ga [_____ᵢ sakana-o sabaita] tomodatiᵢ-o
        Taro-TOP Hanako-NOM   fish-ACC filleted friend-ACC
        hometeta] <u>sono-sakana/sono-otsukuri</u>-o tabetemita.
        praised   that-fish/that-otsukuri-ACC   tried.eating
        Lit.: 'Taro tried eating <u>that fish/that otsukuri</u> (= sashimi) [that Hanako
        praised her friend [who filleted <u>fish</u>]].'

(21)   Taro-wa [Hanako-ga [_____ᵢ sakana-o sabaita] tomodatiᵢ-o
        Taro-TOP Hanako-NOM   fish-ACC filleted friend-ACC
        hometeta] <u>sono-kiree-na-n</u>-o   tabetemita.
        praised   that-beautiful-COP-N-ACC tried.eating
        Lit.: 'Taro tried eating <u>that beautiful one</u> [that Hanako praised her
        friend [who filleted <u>fish</u>]].'

There is another piece of evidence that there is no head extraction in DHRCs. Tonosaki (1996) argues that there is another type of HIRC, which she calls *change of state HIRCs*. In these HIRCs, the internal head undergoes some property change. For example, the SJ example (22) describes the result of Taro's painting a wall, rather than just a wall.

(22)   Watasi-wa [Taro-ga <u>kabe</u>-o   nutta] **no**-ga sukida.
        I-TOP   Taro-NOM wall-ACC painted N-NOM like
        'I like the result of Taro's painting a wall.'
        Lit.: 'I like <u>the one</u> [that Taro painted a wall].'

Tonosaki analyzes the *no* in these HIRCs as a pronoun. In fact, this *no* is realized as *non* in OJ (23a), confirming her claim. Moreover, the external head *n(o)* can be replaced by *sono kabe* 'that wall' (23b). (20) above is also an example of change of state HIRCs because the external head *sono otsukuri* 'that otsukuri' is the result of the friend's filleting fish. These examples show that all that is required is an aboutness relation between the internal and external heads in DHRCs.

(23)   a.   Watasi-wa [Taro-ga <u>kabe</u>-o   nutta   **no**] **n**-ga   sukiya.
               I-TOP   Taro-NOM wall-ACC painted COP N-NOM like
        b.   Watasi-wa [Taro-ga <u>kabe</u>-o   nutta] <u>sono-kabe</u>-ga
               I-TOP   Taro-NOM wall-ACC painted that-wall-NOM
               sukiya.
               like
               'I like the result of Taro's painting a wall.'
               Lit.: 'I like <u>the one/that wall</u> [that Taro painted <u>a wall</u>].'

Japanese DHRCs do not involve resumptive pronouns, either. Cross-linguistically, the external head of DHRCs is a more general term than the internal head (Cinque 2011). For instance, the paraphrase of (5c) without quantifiers would be (24a), rather than (24b).[11]

(24)   a.   Junya-wa [Ayaka-ga ringo-o   muita] sono-kudamono-o
            Junya-TOP Ayaka-NOM apple-ACC peeled that-fruit-ACC
            tabeta.
            ate
            Lit.: 'Junya ate that fruit [that Ayaka peeled an apple].'
       b.   Junya-wa [Ayaka-ga kudamono-o muita] sono-ringo-o
            Junya-TOP Ayaka-NOM fruit-ACC   peeled that-apple-ACC
            tabeta.
            ate
            Lit.: 'Junya ate that apple [that Ayaka peeled a fruit].' (cf. (5c))

(25) is a HERC with the resumptive pronoun *sono hito* 'that person' inside the clause. Unlike DHRCs, the internal head noun *hito* 'person' is a more general term than the external head noun *okyakusan* 'guest'.

(25)   [watakusi-ga sono-hito-no   namae-o   wasuretesimatta]
       I-NOM   that-person-GEN name-ACC have.forgotten
       okyakusan
       guest
       Lit.: 'a guest [that I have forgotten that person's name]'
                                                    (Kuno 1973: (20.10b))

Change of state HIRCs might not seem to fit this generalization because the external head noun *otsukuri* 'otsukuri' is less general than the internal head noun *sakana* in (20). Recall that the external head of DHRCs can be replaced by a pronoun. (26) shows that the external head of (20) can be replaced by the noun *yatu* 'thing', which is a more general term than the internal head.

(26)   Taro-wa [Hanako-ga [_____ᵢ sakana-o sabaita] tomodatiᵢ-o
       Taro-TOP Hanako-NOM   fish-ACC filleted friend-ACC
       hometeta] yatu-o   tabemita.
       praised   thing-ACC tried.eating
       Lit.: 'Taro tried eating the thing [that Hanako praised her friend [who
       filleted fish]].'   (cf. (20))

On the other hand, the external head of (25) cannot be general because (27) does not make any sense (see Cinque 2011: fn. 10).

---

[11] (24b) would mean that Junya ate a specific apple from the various kinds of fruits peeled by Ayaka. In this case, *sono* 'that' refers to *kudamono* 'fruit', which means that the actual external head is *kudamono* 'fruit'.

(27)   *[watakusi-ga sono-okyakusan-no namae-o   wasuretesimatta]
        I-NOM   that-guest-GEN   name-ACC have.forgotten
        hito
        person
        Lit.: 'a person [that I have forgotten that guest's name]'   (cf. (25))

3.3 Structures of HIRCs and DHRCs

In the previous subsection, we observed that HIRCs (and FRs) are island-sensitive, whereas DHRCs are island-insensitive in Japanese. I assume that there is null operator movement in HIRCs[12] because quantifiers are interpreted where they are pronounced in Japanese relative clauses (Shimoyama 1999), which means that the internal head (quantifier) of an HIRC cannot be outside the clause at LF. As the English translations show, the quantifier *hotondo* 'almost all' is interpreted inside the HIRC in (28a), while it is interpreted outside the HERC in (28b). The null operator analysis can account for this fact.

(28)   a.   Taro-wa [Yoko-ga   reezooko-ni   kukkii-o   hotondo
              Taro-TOP Yoko-NOM refrigerator-in cookie-ACC almost.all
              ireteoita no]-o   paatii-ni motteitta.
              put   C-ACC party-to brought
              Lit.: 'Taro brought [that Yoko put almost all of the cookies in
              the refrigerator] to the party.'   (Shimoyama 1999: (4))
        b.   Taro-wa [Yoko-ga   reezooko-ni   _____$_i$ ireteoita]
              Taro-TOP Yoko-NOM refrigerator-in   put
              kukkii-o   hotondo$_i$ paatii-ni motteitta.
              cookie-ACC almost.all party-to brought
              'Taro brought almost all of the cookies$_i$ [that Yoko had put
              _____$_i$ in the refrigerator] to the party.'
                                                        (Shimoyama 1999: (5))

Note that if the external and internal heads of DHRCs were coreferent, this would violate Condition C if the external head c-commands the internal head. I propose that DHRCs are adjoined to the external head so that the external head never c-commands the internal head (29). I assume that the reason why the external head of DHRCs must take a demonstrative (see E&G) is that it is

---

[12] Erlewine and Gould (2014) adopt the null operator analysis. Their analysis is different from Watanabe's (1992) null operator analysis in that only a non-quantificational element of the internal head moves to explain the HIRC/HERC asymmetry. I follow this type of analysis.

(i)   a.   Ayaka peeled half [apples in *Op*]
       b. λX. Ayaka peeled half [apples in X]   (Erlewine and Gould 2014: (7))

anaphoric as the pronoun-headed version shows.

(29)   = (5c) and (9d)

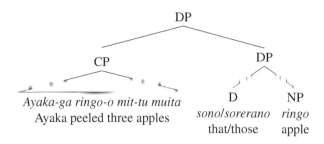

One problem with this analysis would be that it is not clear where the copula *no* comes from in OJ if the head is the pronominal *non*. Unlike English *one* (30a), the Japanese pronominal *no* (*non* in OJ) cannot stand alone (30b). This requires a tighter relation between the adjoined modifier and the head. I argue that in this environment, the copula *no* is inserted. This *no* insertion gives rise to the copula *no* + pronoun *no* sequence, which results in *non* in OJ. In SJ, the copula *no* is deleted because of an anti-haplology constraint. An example tree of pronoun-headed DHRCs in OJ is given in (31). I analyze the copula *no* as generated under Pred, following Bowers (1993), and the pronoun *n* as an NP, following Déchaine and Wiltschko (2002). I do not discuss the phrasal category of pronoun-headed DHRCs here.

(30)   a.   John bought (the red) **one**.
        b.   John-wa * (akai) **no**-o   katta.
              John-TOP   red   N-ACC bought
              'John bought (the red) one.'

(31)   = (9b)

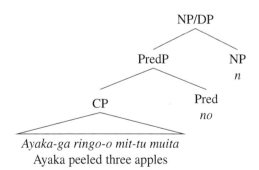

4 Conclusion

I have shown that SJ HIRCs can be ambiguous with pronoun-headed DHRCs. True HIRCs are complementizer-headed, while DHRCs can be pronoun-headed. HIRCs and FRs are structurally related and involve null operator movement. On the other hand, change of state HIRCs belong to the category of DHRC and do not involve head extraction.

References

Bowers, J. 1993. The syntax of predication. *Linguistic Inquiry*, 24(4):591-656.

Cinque, G. 2011. On double-headed relative clauses. *Revista de Estudos Linguisticos da Univerdade do Porto*, 1(6):67-91.

Déchaine, R.-M. and Wiltschko, M. 2002. Decomposing pronouns. *Linguistic Inquiry*, 33(3):409442.

Erlewine, M. Y. and Gould, I. 2014. Interpreting Japanese head-internal relative clauses. In Santana-LaBarge, R. E., editor, *Proceedings of WCCFL 31*, 160-169. Somerville, MA: Cascadilla Press.

Erlewine, M. Y. and Gould, I. 2016. Unifying Japanese relative clauses: Copy-chains and context-sensitivity. *Glossa*, 1(1):51. 1-40.

Groos, A. and van Riemsdijk, H. 1981. Matching effects in free relatives: A parameter of core grammar. In Belletti, A., Brandi, L., and Rizzi, L., editors, *Proceedings of the 1979 GLOW Conference*, 171216. Pisa: Scuola Normale Superiore.

Grosu, A. and Hoshi, K. 2016. Japanese internally headed relatives: Their distinctness from potentially homophonous constructions. *Glossa*, 1(1):32. 1-31.

Kim, H. 2017. *Syntax of internally headed relative clauses in Korean*. Paper presented at the 20th Meeting of the International Circle of Korean Linguistics.

Kuno, S. 1973. *The structure of the Japanese language*. Cambridge, MA: MIT Press.

Moulton, K. and Shimoyama, J. 2017. *On the Inverse Trace Conversion and maximal informativeness analysis of Japanese internally-headed relative clauses: A reply to Erlewine and Gould 2016*. Manuscript, Simon Fraser University and McGill University.

Murasugi, K. 1991. Noun phrases in Japanese and English: A study in syntax, learnability and acquisition. Doctoral dissertation, University of Connecticut.

Nishiyama, K. 1999. Adjectives and the copulas in Japanese. *Journal of East Asian Linguistics*, 8:183222.

Shimoyama, J. 1999. Internally headed relative clauses in Japanese and E-type anaphora. *Journal of East Asian Linguistics*, 8(2):147182.

Tonosaki, S. 1996. Change of state head-internal relative clauses in Japanese. *Studies in Language Sciences: Journal of Kanda University of International Studies*, 2:3147.

Watanabe, A. 1992. Subjacency and S-structure movement of *wh*-in-situ. *Journal of East Asian Linguistics*, 1(3):255291.

Yamakido, H. 2005. The nature of adjectival inflection in Japanese. Doctoral dissertation, Stony Brook University.

Right-Dislocation of a Wh-Phrase and its Prosodic Constraint*

YOSHO MIYATA
Meiji Gakuin University

1 Introduction

While Japanese is a strictly head-final language, it is possible for a phrase to appear after the predicate, as illustrated in (1).[1][2]

---

* I would like to thank Jun, Abe, Yoshiki Fujiwara, Kenshi Funakoshi, Shintaro Hayashi, Tes-tuya Sano, Hiroyuki Shimada, Wataru Sugiura, Satoshi Tomioka, and Shigeo Tonoike for valu-able comments and discussion. I also thank the participates of Japanese/Korean Linguistics 25 and TEAL 11 for their helpful feedback. All the remaining errors, of course, are my own.

[1] The abbreviations used in this paper are follows: ACC = accusative, C = complementizer, NEG = negation, PRT = particle, S = sentence, TOP = topic marker

[2] This paper only deals with right-dislocation of arguments, although right-dislocation of ad-juncts and gapless right-dislocation are also observed in Japanese (see footnote 4 and Kuno (1978), Soshi and Hagiwara (2004), Abe (to appear), among others).

Japanese/Korean Linguistics 25.
Edited by Shin Fukuda, Mary Shin Kim, and Mee-Jeong Park.

(1) a. Taro-wa gohan-o tabe-ta yo.
 Taro-TOP rice-ACC eat-PAST PRT
 'Taro ate some rice.'

 b. Taro-wa t_i tabe-ta yo, gohan-o$_i$.
 Taro-TOP eat-PAST PRT rice-ACC
 'Taro ate some rice.'

 (Kuno 1978; Abe 1999; Tanaka 2001; among others)

The direct object precedes the predicate in example (1a), while the former follows the latter in example (1b).[3] Examples (2) show, however, that a wh-phrase cannot be right-dislocated.[4]

(2) a. Taro-wa nani-o tabe-ta no($\nearrow$)?
 Taro-TOP what-ACC eat-PAST C
 'What did Taro eat?'

 b. *Taro-wa t_i tabe-ta no($\searrow$), nani-o($\nearrow$)?
 Taro-TOP eat-PAST C what-ACC
 'What did Taro eat?'

Given that scrambling of wh-phrases as well as non-wh-phrases is freely allowed in Japanese, syntactic constraints alone do not explain why wh-phrases are disallowed to be right-dislocated, if this is derived in the same way as

---

[3] The comma is attached to the particle *yo* or the matrix complementizer throughout this paper. It indicates a phonological break.

[4] Example (2b) becomes grammatical when this sentence is pronounced with two instances of rising intonation, but in that case, the interpretation changes, as illustrated in (i).

(i) Taro-wa *e* tabe-ta no($\nearrow$), nani-o($\nearrow$)?
 Taro-TOP eat-PAST C what-ACC
 'Did Taro eat something? What?'

Example (i) is interpreted only as a combination of a yes/no question and a wh-question. This fact clearly shows that example (i) consists of two questions, not a single wh-question, unlike example (2b).

Shigeo Tonoike (personal communication) points out that Japanese allows a single wh-phrase to be right-dislocated when right-dislocation applies to a multiple wh-question sentence, as illustrated in (ii).

(ii) Taro-wa e_i nani-o tabe-ta no($\nearrow$), doko-de$_i$($\nearrow$)?
 Tao-TOP what-ACC eat-PAST C where-at
 'What did Taro eat? Where?'

But, like example (i), example (ii) must also be pronounced with two instances of rising intonation (see also footnote 5). Thus, I will not consider this sentence to be right-dislocation sentences.

right-dislocation of non-wh-phrases. This is the main puzzle that I address in this paper.

I propose that right-dislocation of wh-phrases is prohibited due to prosodic constraints on wh-phrases. First, I discuss some empirical problems that previous analyses have and propose an alternative derivation. Second, I argue that wh-phrases have a distinguished prosodic property and that this prosody of wh-phrases can explain the ungrammaticality of right-dislocation of wh-phrases.

2   Previous Analyses

Previous studies of right-dislocation in Japanese can be classified into two groups: biclausal analyses (Kuno 1978; Abe 1999; Tanaka 2001; Takita 2011; among others) and a monoclausal analysis (Takano 2014). Biclausal analyses argue that right-dislocation consists of more than one sentence and is derived by two operations, as illustrated in schema (3).

(3) $[_{S1}...pro_i...]$ $[_{S2} XP_i \text{ [...}t_i...]]$

(Tanaka 2001)

The first operation is a leftward movement of right-dislocated elements in S2. The second operation is a deletion of repeated materials in S2.

The other analysis is a monoclausal analysis by Takano (2014). This analysis derives a right-dislocation construction from a single sentence. The monoclausal analysis posits rightward movement at PF, as illustrated in schema (4).

(4) $[...e_i...] XP_{[\text{-Focus}]i}$

(Takano 2014)

Tanaka (2001) claims that a wh-phrase is disallowed to be right-dislocated because empty proforms cannot be used for new information. I give an example to support his claim in (5).

(5)   * Hanako-ga   nani-o$_i$ kat-ta   ka boku-wa shittei-ru
      Hanako-NOM what-ACC buy-PAST C I-TOP   know-PRESENT
      kedo, Jiro-ga   *pro*$_i$ kat-ta   ka boku-wa shira-nai.
      but   Jiro-NOM   buy-PAST C I-TOP   know-NEG
      'I know what Hanako bought, but I don't know what Jiro bought.'

Now consider (6), which is the derivation of the example in (2b) under Tanaka's (2001) analysis.

(6) a. *[$_{S1}$ Taro-wa *pro*$_i$ tabe-ta   no], [$_{S2}$ nani-o$_i$ [~~Taro-wa~~ ~~t~~$_i$
         Taro-TOP   eat-PAST C   what-ACC Taro-TOP
         ~~tabe-ta   no~~]]?
         eat-PAST C
         'What did Taro eat?'   (= (2b))
    b. *[$_{S1}$ ...*pro*$_i$...] [$_{S2}$ wh-$_i$ ~~[...t$_i$...]~~]

Given that *pro* in S1 cannot refer to the wh-phrase *nani* 'what' in S2, it fol
lows that a Wh-phrase cannot be right dislocated.

  In contrast, Takano (2014) proposes that right-dislocation in Japanese is
derived by PF movement, not by syntactic movement. He claims that a [-
Focus] feature optionally triggers right-dislocation at PF. (7) is the derivation
of the example in (2b) under Takano's (2014) analysis.

(7) a. *[Taro-wa *e*$_i$ tabe-ta   no], nani-o$_i$?
         Taro-TOP   eat-PAST C   what-ACC
         'What did Taro eat?'   (= (2b))
    b. *[...*e*$_i$...] wh-$_{[+Focus]i}$

A wh-phrase, however, has a [+Focus] feature and hence, it cannot be right-
dislocated.

2.1   Some Problems of the Previous Analyses

I argue that both of the previous analyses fail to explain right-dislocation of
Negative Polarity Items (hereafter NPIs) such as *rokuna* 'no decent' and
right-dislocation of phrases with focus-sensitive particles *-dake, -nomi,* 'only'
and *-(de)sae* 'even'.

2.1.1   NPI (*Rokuna*) in Right-Dislocation and Elliptical Answers

There are two important properties to note about *rokuna* NPI in right-dislocation sentences. First, *rokuna* NPI can appear after the predicate, as shown
in example (8).

(8) kyoushitsu-ni i-nakat-ta   yo, rokuna-gakusei-ga.
    classroom-in   stay-NEG-PAST PRT NPI-students-NOM
    'No decent students stayed in the classroom.'

Note, however, that *rokuna* NPI cannot be used in an elliptical answer (see
Miyagawa et al. 2016).

(9) Q: donna-gakusei-ga   kyoushitsu-ni i-ta   no?
        what.sort.of-student-NOM   classroom-in   stay-PAST   C
        'What sort of a student stayed in the classroom?'
    A1: rokuna-gakusei-ga kyoushitsu-ni i-nakat-ta   yo.
        NPI-students-NOM   classroom-in   stay-NEG-PAST   PRT
        'No decent students stayed in the classroom.'
    A2: *rokuna-gakusei(-ga) ~~kyoushitsu-ni i-nakat-ta   yo~~.
        NPI-students-NOM   classroom-in   stay-NEG-PAST   PRT
        'No decent students.'

Example (9Q) is a question and examples (9A1) and (9A2) are its answers with *rokuna* NPI. The contrast between (9A1) and (9A2) shows that the NPI *rokuna-gakusei-ga* 'no decent student' is not allowed in the elliptical answer.

Tanaka's (2001) analysis predicts that example (8) should be ungrammatical. The derivation of (8) in the biclausal analysis is illustrated in (10).

(10) [$_{S1}$ kyoushitsu-ni *pro*$_i$ i-nakat-ta   yo],
         classroom-in   stay-NEG-PAST   PRT
      [$_{S2}$ rokuna-gakusei-ga$_i$ ~~[kyoushitsu-ni t$_i$ i-nakat-ta   yo]~~].
         NPI-students-NOM   classroom-in   stay-NEG-PAST PRT
      'No decent students stayed in the classroom.'   (= (8))

According to Tanaka's analysis, the right-dislocated phrase is derived from movement and deletion in S2. But because this derivation is exactly the same as the derivation of (9A2), the biclausal analysis cannot explain (8) and (9A2).

2.1.2 Focus-sensitive Particles in Right-Dislocation

Japanese also allows a phrase with the focus-sensitive particles to be right-dislocated, as shown in example (11).

(11) kyoushitsu-ni i-nakat-ta   yo, Taro{-dake/-nomi/-(de)sae}.
     classroom-in   stay-NEG-PAST PRT Taro{-only/-only/-even}
     'Only (even) Taro did not stay in the classroom.'

It is important to note that these focus-sensitive particles have a [+Focus] feature. Hayashishita (2008), for example, argues that particles such as *dake* 'only' and *sae* 'even' in Japanese correspond to *only* and *even* in English and refers to these words as focus-sensitive particles.

It follows, then, that a phrase with these focus-sensitive particles also has a [+Focus] feature, like a wh-phrase. But as we have seen in (11), such a phrase can be licitly right-dislocated. Example (11) has the following derivation, according to Takano's (2014) analysis.

(12) [kyoushitsu-ni e_i i-nakat-ta   yo],
     classroom-at   stay-NEG-PAST PRT
     Taro{-dake/-nomi/-(de)sae}$_{[+Focus]i}$.
     Taro{-only/-only/-even}
     'Only (even) Taro did not stay in the classroom.'

Takano (2014) predicts that right-dislocation of a phrase with a few   i-
tive particle should be ungrammatical because PF movement of a phrase with
[+Focus] feature is banned. But this is not borne out. Thus, the generalization
that a [+Focus] phrase cannot be right-dislocated is not valid.

2.1.3   Island-Sensitivity

Judgements of island effects reported in the literature are by no means uniform. According to some previous analyses (Abe 1999; Tanaka 2001; Miyata
2017; among others), right-dislocation in Japanese is clearly sensitive to islands, as illustrated in examples (13).

(13) a. John-ga [Mary-ga Bill-ni   age-ta   hon-o]   nusun-da
        John-NOM Mary-NOM Bill-DAT give-PAST book-ACC steal-PAST
        yo.
        PRT
        'John stole the book that Mary gave to Bill.'
     b. ?*John-ga [Mary-ga pro_i age-ta   hon-o]   nusun-da
        John-NOM Mary-NOM   give-PAST book-ACC steal-PAST
        yo, Bill-ni$_i$.
        PRT Bill-DAT
        'John stole the book that Mary gave to Bill.'   (Tanaka 2001, 555)

In contrast, Sells (1991) argues that the acceptability of the island example
can be improved by using a deictic verb such as *katteageru* 'buy for someone',
instead of *kau* 'buy', as illustrated in (14).

(14) ?[[Ken-ga e_i katteage-ta]   doresu-o] mi-ta   no,
     Ken-NOM buy.for.someone-PAST dress-ACC see-PAST PRT
     okusan-ni$_i$.
     wife-DAT
     'I saw the dress that Ken bought for his wife.'   (Sells 1999, 14)

Sells (1991) and Takano (2014), who cites Sells' example in (14), conclude
that right-dislocation in Japanese is not subject to island constraints. Even
though I concur with them regarding the status of example (14), I would like
to point out that island effects appear again once the example is slightly modified, keeping *katteageru* as it is (see Miyata 2017).

(15) * Hanako-wa [[Ken-ga t$_i$ katteage-ta]   doresu-o]
      Hanako-TOP   Ken-NOM   buy.for.someone-PAST dress-ACC
      korekara mi-ru   yo, okusan-ni$_i$.
      from.now see-PRESENT PRT wife-DAT
      'Hanako sees the dress that Ken bought for his wife from now.'

(Miyata 2017, 34)

In example (15), the overt subject of a matrix verb *Hanako* and the adverb *korekara* 'from now' are added and the tense of the embedded clause does not match that of the matrix clause. This example clearly shows island effects. Therefore, the example in (14) never proves that right-dislocation in Japanese is not sensitive to island effects (see also Takano (2002) and Kuno (2007), who argue that the clause-mate effect in Japanese can disappear if the embedded subject is replaced by a *pro* co-referential to the matrix subject in cleft sentences).[5]

---

[5] It has been observed that right-dislocation of DP-internal modifiers and gapless right-disloca- tion are not sensitive to island constraints, according to Takano (2014), Miyata (2017), and Abe (to appear) (cf. Tanaka 2001), as illustrated in examples (i).

(i)   a. Taro-ga [DP e$_i$ kuruma]-o kat-ta   yo, akai$_i$.
         Taro-NOM   car-ACC   buy-PAST PRT red
         'Taro bought a car. It was red.'
      b. Taro-ga [DP akai.kuruma]-o kat-ta   yo,   akai.
         Taro-NOM   red-car-ACC   buy-PAST PRT   red.
         'Taro bought a red car. It was red.'

But it is important to note that these sentences are obligatory pronounced with two instances of rising intonation if they are questions, as illustrated in (ii) (see footnote 4).

(ii) a. Taro-ga [DP e. kuruma]-o kat-ta   no?(↗) akai ?(↗)
         Taro-NOM   car-ACC buy-PAST C   red
         'Did Taro buy a car? It was red?'
      b. Taro-ga nani-o   kat-ta   no?(↗) nani-o?(↗)
         Taro-NOM what-ACC buy-PAST C   what-ACC
         'What did Taro buy? What?'

The appearance of two instances of rising intonation and the island-insensitivity show that both right-dislocation of DP-internal modifiers and gapless right-dislocation consist of more than one sentence, not a single sentence.

The following data containing the *rokuna* NPI 'no decent' appear to counter this line of rea- soning.

(iii) a. ?Taro-ga [DP e. kuruma-o] kawa-nakat-ta yo, rokuna.
         Taro-NOM   car-ACC   buy-NEG-PAST PRT NPI
         'Taro bought a car. It was not a decent one.'
      b. Taro-ga rokuna-kuruma-o kawa-nakat-ta yo, rokuna-kuruma-o.
         Taro-NOM NPI-car-ACC   buy-NEG-PAST   PRT NPI-car-ACC

3 Proposal

I propose an analysis that moves a right-dislocated phrase syntactically, as shown in schema (16) and in tree diagram (17).

(16) a. [$_{CP}$...XP...]   (Base Structure)
  b. [$_{YP}$ XP$_i$[[$_{CP}$...t$_i$...] Y]]   (Leftward XP-Movement)
  c. [$_{ZP}$ [$_{CP}$...t$_i$...]$_j$ [[$_{YP}$ XP$_i$ [t$_j$ Y]] Z]] (Remnant CP-Movement)

(17)

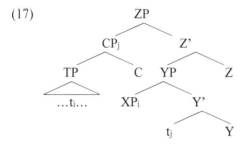

At the first step, XP is moved out of CP. At the second step, the remnant CP is moved to the sentence-initial position (see Kayne 1994). Both steps only involve leftward movement.

My proposed analysis in (16) makes two predictions. The first is that *rokuna* NPI can appear in the right-most position, because the derivation does not require ellipsis, contra Tanaka (2001). The second is that whether a right-dislocated phrase has a [+Focus] or [-Focus] feature is irrelevant, contra Takano (2014). (18) is the derivation of the example in (8).

(18) [[kyoushitsu-ni t$_i$ i-nakat-ta   yo,]$_j$ [rokuna-gakusei-ga$_i$ t$_j$.]]
       classroom-in   stay-NEG-PAST PRT   NPI-students-NOM
    'No decent students stayed in the classroom.'   (= (8))

Recall that *rokuna* NPI is allowed to be right-dislocated, but *rokuna* NPI cannot be an elliptical answer. In my analysis, both the right-dislocated phrase and the remnant are moved leftward and no ellipsis is involved. Therefore, the first prediction of my analysis that NPIs can be right-dislocated is borne out.

        'Taro bought no decent car.'

To my ears, examples in (iii) sound fine, although the *rokuna* NPI 'no decent' cannot be used in an elliptical answer, as shown in examples (9).I leave the issue open for future research.

Furthermore, the availability of right-dislocation is not affected by whether a right-dislocated phrase has a [+Focus] or [-Focus] feature. (19) is the derivation of the example in (11).

(19) [[kyoushitsu-ni t$_i$ i-nakat-ta   yo]$_j$,
       classroom-in   stay-NEG-PAST PRT
       [Taro{-dake/-nomi/-(de)sae}$_i$t$_j$].
       Taro{-only/-only/-even}
       'Only (even) Taro did not stay in the classroom.'   (= (11))

My analysis does not distinguish right-dislocation of a [+Focus] or [-Focus] phrase, which is a correct result. Therefore, the second prediction of my analysis that focus-sensitive particles can appear after the predicate is also borne out.

4   Right-Dislocation of a Wh-phrase and its Prosodic Constraints

As we have seen in Section 3, my proposed analysis can explain what previous analyses fail to explain about right-dislocation. But I have not yet explained the main puzzle: why right-dislocation of a wh-phrase is disallowed in Japanese. In this section, I will propose that syntax-prosody mapping plays a crucial role. After reviewing Ishihara (2002, 2017) briefly, I will show that a prosodic analysis can solve the main puzzle.

4.1   Ishihara (2002, 2017): Focus Prosody

Ishihara (2002) shows that Japanese has two phonological phenomena: Prosodic Focalization and Deaccenting, as in (20).

(20) Focus Prosody
    a. *Prosodic Focalization*
       Prosodic focalization assigns prosodic prominence to a focalized phrase.
    b. *Deaccenting*
       Deaccenting reduces the pitch (F0) register after the P-focalized element until the relevant functional head.

                                                                (Ishihara 2002)

Furthermore, Ishihara (2002, 2017) show that declarative sentences, wh-questions, and yes/no-questions in Japanese exhibit their own distinctive prosodic properties. His observations are summarized in table (21).

MIYATA (21)

	DIDECL	FIPy/n	FIPwh-
Prosodic focalization	No elements	Verbal complexes	Wh-phrases
Deaccenting	No	No	Until its licensing C

Table1: Ishihara's (2002, 2017) observation

In default intonation of declarative sentences (DIDECL), prosodic focalization does not assign prosodic prominence to any elements, and deaccenting does not take place. In focus intonation prosody of yes/no-questions (FIPy/n), prosodic focalization assigns prosodic prominence to verbal complexes, and deaccenting does not take place. In contrast, in focus intonation prosody of wh-questions (FIPwh-), prosodic focalization assigns prosodic prominence to wh-phrases, and deaccenting takes place and continues until its licensing complementizer.

Examples of default intonation of declarative sentences and focus intonation prosody of wh-questions are illustrated in (22).

(22) a. Naoya-ga   nanika-o   nomiya-de non-da.
        Naoya-NOM   something-ACC bar-at   drink-PAST
        'Naoya drunk something at the bar.'
    b. Naoya-ga nani-o   nomiya-de non-da   no?
        Naoya-NOM what-ACC bar-at   drink-PAST C
        'What did Naoya drink at the bar?'

(Ishihara 2002,183)

In examples (22), prosodic focalization is indicated by box. Deaccenting is indicated by underline. In (22a), neither of these operations takes place. In contrast, in the wh-question in (22b), *nani* is prosodically focused, and deaccenting is observed.

4.2   Yamashita (2010)

Yamashita (2010), adopting a biclausal analysis, argues that right-dislocation of wh-phrases is not allowed because it is incompatible with focus intonation prosody of wh-questions, as illustrated in example (23).

(23) *[CP Mari-ga   pro_i nomiya-de non-da   no]? nani-o_i?
        Mari-NOM   bar-at   drink-PAST C   what-ACC
        'What did Mari drink at the bar?'   (Yamashita 2010)

Yamashita (2010) observes that deaccenting cannot occur between the wh-phrase and the complementizer in (23), because *nani* appears in the right of its licensing complementizer. Yamashita's (2010) analysis, however, fails to explain following data.

(24) A: ano kechina Mari-ga   nomiya-de koukyuuna osake-o
        that stingy Mari-NOM bar-at   premium   sake-ACC
        non-da   yo.
        drink-PAST PRT
        'Mari, who is stingy, drunk a cup of premium sake at the bar.'

   B: [s1 Mari-ga   *pro* nomiya-de non-da   no]? [s2 $\boxed{\text{nani}}$-o
        Mari-NOM   bar-at   drink-PAST C   what-ACC
        non-da____no]?
        drink-PAST C
        'Did Mari drink it at the bar? What did she drink?'

Note that Yamashita (2010) adopts the biclausal analysis. The example in (23) consists of more than one sentence like example (24B). Therefore, Yamashita's (2010) analysis predicts that the example in (23) should behave in the same way as the example in (24B) and hence they should always be ungrammatical. But this is contrary to the fact. The example in (24B) is grammatical because deaccenting can occur between the wh-phrase and the complementizer within S2.

4.3 Prosodic Constraints on Right-Dislocation of a Wh-phrase

Now my analysis of right-dislocation, in conjunction with Ishihara's (2002, 2017) prosodic analysis, can solve the main puzzle in this paper. Under my proposed analysis, right-dislocation constructions are derived by the combination of leftward XP-movement and remnant CP-movement. (25) is the derivation of the example in (2b).[6]

(25) *[[Taro-wa t_i tabe-ta   **no**(↘)]$_j$, **nani**-o$_i$ t$_j$(↗)]?
     Taro-TOP   eat-PAST C   what-ACC
     'What did Taro eat?'   (= (2b))

---

[6] Note that a following prosody pattern is also not allowed.

  (i)   *[[Taro-wa t_i tabe-ta   **no**(↗)]$_j$, **nani**-o$_i$ t$_j$ (↘)]?
            Taro-TOP   eat-PAST C   what-ACC
            'What did Taro eat?'

As a result, a right-dislocated wh-phrase appears in the right of its licensing complementizer in the end. Hence, deaccenting from a focalized wh-phrase until its licensing complementizer cannot occur, which makes right-dislocation of wh-phrases illicit.

4.4   Interpretative Asymmetry of Wh-scope

Adopting Ishihara's (2002, 2017) prosodic analysis, my syntactic analysis can also explain an interpretative asymmetry in right-dislocation of an embedded clause containing a wh-phrase. The interpretative asymmetry is observed between examples (26) and (27).

(26) [Taro-wa [Jiro-ga   nani-o   kat-ta   ka] it-ta   no]($\nearrow$)?
     Taro-TOP Jiro-NOM what-ACC buy-PAST C   say-PAST C
    a. 'What did Taro say that Jiro bought?'
    b. 'Did Taro say what Jiro bought?'

(27) [[Taro-wa t_i it-ta   no]$_j$($\nearrow$), [Jiro-ga   nani-o   kat-ta
     Taro-TOP   say-PAST C   Jiro-NOM what-ACC buy-PAST
    ka]$_i$ t_j]($\searrow$)?
    C
    a. *'What did Taro say that Jiro bought?'
    b. 'Did Taro say what Jiro bought?'

Example (26) is ambiguous between a wh-question and a yes/no-question (see Takahashi 1993 and Saito 1994). But, if right-dislocation applies to the entire embedded clause, the sentence is unambiguously interpreted as a yes/no-question, as shown in example (27). The derivations of (27a) and (27b) under my analysis are given in (28) and (29) respectively.

(28) *[[Taro-wa t_i it-ta   no]$_j$($\nearrow$), [Jiro-ga   nani-o   kat-ta
     Taro-TOP   say-PAST C   Jiro-NOM what-ACC buy-PAST
    ka]$_i$ t_j]($\searrow$)?
    C
    'What did Taro say that Jiro bought?'

(28) cannot be interpreted as a wh-question because *nani* appears in the right of its licensing matrix complementizer *no*, and hence deaccenting is prohibited.

(29) [[Taro-wa t$_i$ **it-ta**　　no]$_j$(↗), [Jiro-ga 　**nani**-o　　kat-ta
　　　Taro-TOP　say-PAST　C　　　Jiro-NOM what-ACC buy-PAST
　ka]$_i$ t$_j$](↘)?
　C
　'Did Taro say what Jiro bought?'

On the other hand, (29) can be interpreted as a yes/no-question because, as in (21), deaccenting does not take place in a yes/no-question and nothing disrupts deaccenting from the wh-phrase to its licensing embedded complementizer.

5　Conclusion

In this paper, I proposed an alternative analysis of right-dislocation in Japanese that does not involve ellipsis or PF-movement. I have shown that my analysis, in conjunction with Ishihara's (2002, 2017) theory of prosody, explains the main puzzle: why right-dislocation of wh-phrases is prohibited.

I have left two issues open for future research. The first is the exact projections of two heads (Y and Z) under the proposed analysis in (16). The second is the exact derivation of right-dislocation of DP-internal modifiers and gapless right-dislocation (see footnote 5).

References

Abe, J. 1999. On Directionality of Movement: a Case of Japanese Right Dislocation. Ms., Nagoya University.

Abe, J. to appear. Two Types of Japanese Right Dislocation under the Bi-Clausal Analysis. In *Proceedings of the 11th Workshop on Altaic Formal Linguistics (WAFL11)*, MIT Working Papers in Linguistics. Cambridge, MA: MIT Working Papers in Linguistics.

Hayashishita, J.-R. 2008. On Adnominal 'Focus-Sensitive' Particles in Japanese. In *Japanese/Korean Linguistics 13*, eds. M. E. Hudson, P. Sells, and S. Jun. 141-151. Stanford, CA: CSLI.

Ishihara, S. 2002. Invisible but Audible Wh-Scope Marking: Wh-Constructions and Deaccenting in Japanese. In *Proceedings of the 21st West Coast Conference on Formal Linguistics*, eds. M, Line, and C. Potts,180-193. Somerville, MA: Cascadilla.

Ishihara, S. 2017. The Intonation of Wh-and Yes/No-Questions in Tokyo Japanese. In *Contrastiveness in Information Structure, Alternatives and Scalar Implicatures*, 399-415. Cham: Springer.

Kayne, R. S. 1994. *The Antisymmetry of Syntax.* Cambridge, MA.: MIT Press.

Kuno, S. 1978. *Danwa no Bunpoo (Discourse Grammar).* Tokyo: Taishuukan.

Kuno, S. 2007. Revisiting Subject Raising in Japanese. *Current Issues in the History and Structure of Japanese.* eds. F. Bjarke, M. Shibatani, J.C. Smith, 83-105. Tokyo: Kuroshio.

Miyagawa, S. N, Nishioka,. and H, Zeijlstra. 2016. Negative Sensitive Items and the Discourse-Configurational Nature of Japanese. *Glossa: a journal of general linguistics* 1: 33:1-28, DOI: 10.5334/gjgl.6.

Miyata, Y. 2017. Right-Dislocation as Leftward Movement and its Syntax-Prosody Interface. M.A. Thesis. Meiji Gakuin University.

Saito, M. 1994. Additional-Wh Effects and the Adjunction Site Theory. *Journal of East Asian Linguistics* 3: 195-240.

Sells, P. 1999. Postposing in Japanese. Ms., Stanford University.

Soshi, T. and H, Hagiwara. 2004. Asymmetry in Linguistic Dependency: Linguistic and Psychophysiological Studies of Japanese Right-Dislocation. *English Linguistics* 21: 409-453.

Takahashi, D. 1993. Movement of Wh-phrase in Japanese. *Natural Language & Linguistic Theory* 11:655-678.

Takano, Y. 2002. Surprising Constituents. *Journal of East Asian Linguistics* 11:243-301.

Takano, Y. 2014. A Comparative Approach to Japanese Postposing. *Japanese syntax in comparative perspective,* ed. M. Saito, 139-180. New York: Oxford University Press.

Takita, K. 2011. Argument Ellipsis in Japanese Right Dislocation. *Japanese/Korean Linguistics* 18, eds. W. McClure, and M. den Dikken.: 380-391. Stanford, CA: CSLI.

Tanaka, H. 2001. Right-Dislocation as Scrambling. *Journal of Linguistics* 37: 551-579.

Yamashita, H. 2010. What Makes Right Dislocation of Wh-Phrases in (Tokyo) Japanese (Im) Possible. *WCCFL 28 Online Proceedings (Prosody Poster Session).*

Particle Stranding Ellipsis in Japanese, String Deletion, and Argument Ellipsis[1]

YOSUKE SATO
National University of Singapore

MASAKO MAEDA
Kyushu Insitute of Technology

[1]This paper was presented at the 25th Japanese/Korean Linguistics Conference held at University of Hawaii, Manoa in October, 2017. Some material used here was also presented at the 19th Seoul International Conference on Generative Grammar held at Seoul National University in August, 2017 and at the Syntax/Semantics Reading Group at the Department of English Language and Literature of the National University of Singapore. We thank Jun Abe, Duk-Ho An, Kamil Deen, Yoshi Dobashi, Mitcho Yoshitaka Erlewine, Yoshiki Fujiwara, Nobu Goto, Heidi Harley, Shin-Ichi Kitada, Ted Levin, Si Kai Lee, Hiroki Nomoto, Myung-Kwan Park, Keely New Zuo Qi, Naga Selvanathan, Daiko Takahashi, Hideaki Yamashita and Masataka Yano as well as the audience members at the conference for helpful comments on the ideas presented here and discussions. This research has been supported by the Singapore Ministry of Education Academic Research Fund Tier 1 (grant #: R-103-000-124-112) awarded to Yosuke Sato as well as by the Grant-in-Aid for Young Scientists (B) (grant #: 26770170) awarded to Masako Maeda. We blame all errors on brutal humidity in Singapore. A complete version of this paper will appear as Sato and Maeda (to appear).

Japanese/Korean Linguistics 25.

1 Introduction

In this paper, we develop a new phonological analysis of the so-called Particle Stranding Ellipsis (henceforth, PSE) in Japanese as an alternative to the recent, purely structural analysis of the phenomenon espoused by Sato (2012) and Goto (2014). PSE is illustrated by Speaker B's utterance in (1), which involves the ellipsis of the topic element – *Tanaka-kun* 'Tanaka' – but leaves the overt topic particle behind.

(1) Speaker A: Tanaka-kun-wa?
        Tanaka-TITLE-TOP
        'How about Tanaka?'
    Speaker B: **wa**-ne, kaisya-o   yameta-yo.
        TOP-PRT company-ACC   quit-PRT
        'He quit his company.'   (Hattori 1960:452)

We have two goals in this paper. One goal is to demonstrate that the purely structural analysis for PSE of the sort put forth by Sato (2012) is built on a number of descriptively inadequate generalizations about PSE. More concretely, in Sections 2 and 3, we will point out that PSE applies within an embedded clause, targets a wide variety of particles and particle-like expressions beyond the topic marker –*wa*, and exhibits strict linear sensitivity for its application. We propose instead that these properties are straightforwardly captured by a phonological deletion approach to PSE along the lines of the recent claim made by Shibata (2014), according to which PSE is licensed as long as the stranded particle stands on the left edge of the first intermediate phrase which aligns with that of the utterance phrase. We implement the ellipsis approach along the lines of *String Deletion* (Mukai 2003), motivated on independent grounds. This task is undertaken in Section 3.

The other goal of this paper is to investigate possible connections between PSE and other better-studied cases of ellipsis in Japanese. In Section 4, we will present arguments on the basis of sloppy readings (Oku 1998), wide scope negation, and disjunction (Sakamoto 2016) to show that PSE may well take the form of Argument Ellipsis (AE) (Oku 1998; Saito 2007; Takahashi 2008). In doing so, we will argue against the conceivable alternative *pro*-based analysis of PSE. This result, then, lends further supporting evidence for our view that PSE involves PF-deletion, contrary to structure-oriented analyses thereof espoused by Sato (2012), Goto (2014) and others.

2   Particle Stranding Ellipsis and the Phase Theory

Sato (2012) proposes a phase-theoretic analysis of PSE, which consists of optional Spell-Out of the Top' projection containing the overt topic head *–wa* and its TP complement to PF for phonological interpretation while transferring the entire TopP to LF for semantic interpretation (see also Goto 2014).

(2)

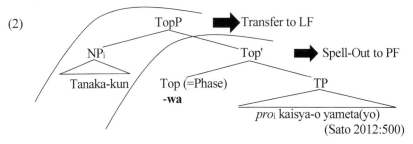

(Sato 2012:500)

Sato's (2012) phase-theoretic analysis indeed gives a plausible account for some properties of PSE, including the root-privilege of PSE, the ban on sentence-internal application of PSE, and the ban on multiple occurrence of PSE in a sentence (see Sato 2012; Yoshida 2004; Nasu 2012; Goto 2014 for the relevant data). Sato's analysis, however, is faced with both conceptual and empirical problems.

Let us start by noting that Sato's proposed derivation of PSE crucially stands on the assumption that at the root level, the intermediate Top' projection, containing the head and its TP complement, may undergo optional Spell-Out. However, it has been commonly assumed (Chomsky 2001) that Spell-Out applies to the complement of a phase head, not the combination of the head and its complement together, as required in (2). Unfortunately, the particular assumption Sato adopts for his Spell-Out domain is not motivated elsewhere on independent grounds.

More importantly, the structural analysis is faced with considerable weakness in its empirical coverage. Previous works on PSE, including Sato and Ginsburg (2007), Goto (2014), and Shibata (2014), point out that PSE can occur not only with the topic marker *–wa*, but also with a wide range of other non-topic particles. They include, but are not limited to, *–ga* (nominative case particle), *–mo* (additive particle), inherent case markers such as *–kara* 'from', complementizers, both declarative and interrogative, such as *to* 'that', and certain semi-auxiliary expressions such as *mitai* 'seem', as shown in (3–7).

(3) Speaker A: John-wa doosite naita-no?
John-TOP why cried-Q
'Why did John cry?'

Speaker B: **ga** mado-o watta kara okorareta-mitai-yo.
NOM window-ACC broke because scolded-seem-PRT
'Since John broke the window, he seems to be scolded.'

(4) Speaker A: Taroo-mo kita-no?
Taro-also came-Q
'Did Taro also come?'

Speaker B: **mo** ki-masita.
also come-POL.PAST
'Taro also came.' (Shibata 2014)

(5) Speaker A: John-kara okane-o moratta-no?
John-from money-ACC received-Q
'Did you receive money from John?'

Speaker B: **kara** moratta-yo.
from received-PRT
'I received money from John.' (Goto 2014:103)

(6) Speaker A: John-wa kita-no?
John-TOP came-Q
'Did John come?'

Speaker B: **to** omoi-masu-kedo.
COMP think-POL-though
'I think that he came.'

(7) Speaker A: Chomsky-ga sangatu-ni rainiti-suru-rasii-yo.
Chomsky-NOM March-in visit.Japan-do-hear-PRT
'It seems that Chomsky is visiting Japan in March.'

Speaker B: **mitai**-desu-ne.
seem-COP.POL-PRT
'It seems that he is visiting Japan in March.'

Since Sato's approach is specifically tailored for canonical cases of PSE, as shown in (1), which contain an overtly stranded topic marker, it is unclear how it can be extended to cover those cases, as shown in (3–7), which do not seem to involve a topic interpretation for the elided expressions followed by those non-topic particles. It would be more desirable to have an alternative analysis that provides a uniform explanation for (3–7) as well as the core cases of PSE illustrated in (1), than to have two separate explanations for the two types of PSE cases. In the next section, drawing on Shibata's (2014) insights, we submit that the problems at hand will receive a more satisfactory solution in terms of string-based deletion applying in the phonological component (Mukai 2003; An 2016).

3 Shibata's (2014) Phonological Approach to PSE and Mukai's (2003) String Deletion

Shibata observes that all the PSE cases discussed thus far involve a focused stranded particle and proposes (8) as a licensing condition on PSE, which states that PSE is possible only if the left edge of its containing Intermediate Phrase is aligned with the left edge of the Utterance and the particles undergoing PSE (can) bear focus prosody on their own.

(8) PSE is licensed in: [[X   .....]$_i$]$_u$, where X is a stranded particle
and is focused.   (from Shibata 2014, with a minor modification)

Shibata's approach to PSE does include an explicit mention of the licensing condition on this construction, but falls short of exploring what the exact derivational process involved in PSE is, such that it must meet the condition in (8).

Mukai's (2003) analysis of gapping in Japanese is suggestive in this connection. Mukai proposes that gapping examples such as (9) are derived through what she calls *String Deletion*. Mukai argues that String Deletion is a PF operation that applies to a phonetic string, regardless of its constituency, under string-based identity. The example in (9) is analyzed as in (10) under her theory.

(9)   Mike-ga   raion-ni, Tom-ga   kuma-ni osowareta   otoko-o tasuketa.
      Mike-NOM lion-DAT Tom-NOM bear-DAT was.attacked man-ACC saved
      'Mike saved the man who was being attacked by a lion, and Tom saved the
      man who was being attacked by a bear.'   (Mukai 2003:210)

(10) 1st conjunct: [$_{TP}$ Mike-ga [$_{VP}$ [$_{DP}$ [raion-ni ~~osowareta] otoko-o] tasuketa~~]]
       2nd conjunct: [$_{TP}$ Tom-ga   [$_{VP}$ [$_{DP}$ [kuma-ni osowareta otoko-o tasuketa]]

In this derivation, the underlined portion of the first conjunct is identical to the underlined portion of the second conjunct. String Deletion subsequently applies to the underlined part of the elliptical conjunct, even though the target of the operation does not form a syntactic constituent.

Extending Mukai's (2003) analysis of Japanese gapping, we now propose that the derivation of PSE involves a string-sensitive PF-deletion process, the output of which is in conformity with the licensing condition (8). Let us now illustrate how String Deletion works with the example in (1). The example has roughly the following underlying representation before PF-deletion takes place.

(11) Speaker A: Tanaka-kun-wa?
              Tanaka-TITLE-TOP
              'How about Tanaka?'

> Speaker B: [DP Tanaka-kun]-**wa**-ne, kaisya-o yameta-yo.
>   TOP-PRT company-ACC quit-PRT
>   'He quit his company.'   (Hattori 1960:452)

In this representation, the underlined portion of the DP in Speaker B's utterance is identical to the underlined portion of the DP in Speaker A's utterance, meeting the identity condition on String Deletion, as well as the licensing condition (8). The deletion subsequently applies, yielding PSE, as desired.

One of the most important theoretical implications of our analysis is that the string-based deletion at PF may ignore syntactic constituencies, though in many other cases, the PSE material happens to correspond to a syntactic constituent. One instance of non-constituent PSE comes from a tripartite coordination structure. Examples (12) and (13) illustrate the structure in question. The former involves coordination of three DPs through the conjunctive marker *to* whereas the latter involves coordination of three DPs through the disjunctive marker *ka*.

(12) Speaker A: Ano omoi piano-o Taroo-to Hanako-de motiageta-no?
                that heavy piano-ACC Taro-and Hanako-with lifted-Q
                'Taro and Hanako lifted that heavy piano?'
    Speaker B: **to** Ziroo-no san-nin-de (issyoni) motiageta-nda-yo.
                and Jiro-GEN three-CL-with together lifted-COP-PRT
                'Intended: Taro, Hanako and Jiro lifted the piano together.'

(13) [Context: Speakers A and B wonder where they might want to go for a date this Saturday.]
    Speaker A: Kon-shyuu-no doyoobi deeto doko ik-oo-ka?
                this-week-GEN Saturday date where go-shall-Q
                Omotesando ka Sinzyuku?
                Omotesando or Shinjuku
                'Where shall we go for a date this Saturday? Omotesando or Shinjuku?'
    Speaker B: **ka** Asakusa-wa?
                or Asakusa-TOP
                'Intended: Omotesando, Shinjuku or Asakusa?'

What is particularly telling about these examples for our purposes is that under no known previous analysis of coordination –simple coordination or structured coordination – would the to-be-elided expressions, marked by underlining in (12–13), not form a syntactic constituent. To illustrate this point more closely, consider the two possible syntactic structures shown in (14a) and (14b) for the relevant part of the subject portion in the pre-ellipsis sentence in (12).

(14) a. Simple Coordination Analysis b. Structured Coordination Analysis

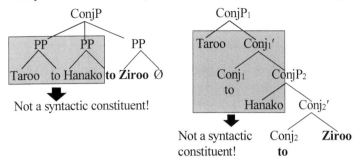

In (14a), the set of elements to be elided – *Taroo-to Hanako* 'Taro and Hanako' – do not form a syntactic constituent. Our string-based theory, on the other hand, correctly predicts this attested pattern of PSE: *Taroo-to Hanako* undergo String Deletion regardless of their syntactic constituenthood. A similar analysis holds true for the disjunctive-based PSE example in (13). The grammaticality of these two examples, therefore, provides powerful empirical support for our string-based PF-deletion theory of PSE advocated in this paper.

The present analysis also makes correct predictions regarding the (un-) availability of PSE in two contexts in a way that structural analyses such as Sato's (2012) cannot, and this provides further evidence for our PF-deletion theory. One context concerns PSE within an embedded clause. Structural approaches to PSE initiated by Sato (2012) were so designed to explain the root-privilege of PSE (Yoshida 2004). Shibata (2014) shows, however, that this observation is not adequate, showing that the embedded subject may undergo PSE, as long as it is located at the left edge of the sentence. Speaker B's utterance in (15) shows a similar point. Here, we use the subordinating conjunction marker *nagara* 'while', which requires one clause to its left as its subordinate complement and another clause to its right as its matrix complement. Again, (15) shows that PSE can occur within an embedded clause.

(15) Speaker A: Sonnani tyokoreeto katte   doo   suru-no?
                that much chocolate buy.CONJ how   do-Q
                'You bought so much chocolate. What will you do with that?'
     Speaker B: [CP1 [CP2 **o**   tabe-nagara   LGB-demo
                            ACC   eat-while   LGB-or.something
                yom-ookana-tte omotta-no]].
                read-shall-COMP thought-PRT
                'I thought about reading LGB or something while eating this much of chocolate'.

The possibility of embedded PSE is perfectly consistent with our PF-oriented approach, on the other hand, because String Deletion can apply on the basis of string identity between an antecedent and an elliptical clause; nothing prevents it from applying to an embedded context, as illustrated in (15).

The other context which distinguishes between the phonological and structural analyses of PSE has to do with the observation first made by Shibata (2014) that the target site of PSE must strictly come first: it cannot be preceded by any overt linguistic expression. Example (16) illustrates this observation.

(16) Speaker A: John-wa   kuru-no?
                John-TOP come-Q
                'Will John come?'
    Speaker B: a. *Tasika-dewa-nai-kedo,   **wa**   ki-masen-yo.
                   certain-COP.TOP-NEG-though TOP   come-POL.NEG-PRT
                   'I am not completely certain, but he won't come.'
                b. Tasika-dewa-nai-kedo,   John- **wa** ki-masen-yo.
                   certain-COP.TOP-NEG-though John-TOP come-POL.NEG-PRT
                   'I am not completely certain, but he won't come.'

The contrast between (16a) and (16b) is difficult to explain under the structural analysis because the input structure for (16a) would be (16b), which allows the topic DP to be preceded by some linguistic material without any loss of grammaticality. Our analysis, on the other hand, predicts this contrast rather straightforwardly since (16a) violates the licensing condition in (8).

4   PSE Can Involve PF-Deletion: Views from Argument Ellipsis

In this section, we investigate possible connections, if any, between PSE, analyzed here as the result of a string-based deletion, and other forms of ellipsis studied in the literature on Japanese syntax. More specifically, we will present three novel observations to show that PSE may well take the form of AE (Oku 1998; Saito 2007; Takahashi 2008). These observations, in turn, lend further indirect support to our present view that PSE involves PF-deletion, contrary to Sato's (2012) structural analysis. In doing so, we also use some of these observations to reject the conceivable non-ellipsis analysis of PSE which resorts to *pro*-drop (Kuroda 1965).

4.1   Sloppy Interpretations of Elided Arguments

Our first argument that PSE may well take the form of AE comes from the availability of sloppy interpretations of particle stranding elided arguments. To set the stage for this argument, consider (17).

(17) a. Taroo-wa   zibun-no   hahaoya-o   sonkeisiteiru.
          Taro-TOP   self-GEN   mother-ACC   respect
          'Taro respects his mother.'
      b. Hanako-mo   *e*   sonkeisiteiru.   (strict/sloppy)
          Hanako-also   respect
          'Hanako also respects (Taro's/Hanako's mother).'
      c. Hanako-mo   *kanozyo-o*   sonkeisiteiru. (strict/*sloppy)
          Hanako-also   her-ACC   respect
          'Hanako also respects her.'

Suppose that the null object argument in (17b) is understood to be somehow anaphoric to the overt object in (17a). Oku (1998) points out that, given this context, the null object argument in (17b) may exhibit either a strict interpretation (Taro's mother) or a sloppy interpretation (Hanako's mother). Now, the example in (17c) shows that an overt pronoun can only give rise to a strict interpretation. Given this restriction, Oku proposes that the null argument with the sloppy interpretation is derived not through *pro*-drop, but instead through the ellipsis of the full-fledged object *zibun-no hahaoya-o* in (17b).

Let us now consider PSE cases like (18). It is significant that PSE allows a sloppy interpretation as well as a strict interpretation for the elliptic phrase.

(18) Speaker A: Zibun-no   hahaoya-o   Hanako-wa   sonkeisitei-masu.
                 self-GEN   mother-ACC   Hanako-TOP respect-POL
                 'Hanako respects self's mother.'
     Speaker B: a. **wa,** Taroo-wa sonkeisitei-masen. (strict/sloppy)
                   TOP   Taro-TOP   respect-POL.NEG
                   'Lit. Taro does not respect self's mother.'
                b. **Kanozyo**-wa, Taroo-wa sonkeisitei-masen. (strict/
                   she-TOP   Taro-TOP respect-NEG-PRT   *sloppy)
                   'Lit. Taro does not respect her.'

In this example, the topic DP targeted by PSE – *zibun-no hahaoya-o* 'self's mother' – permits both strict and sloppy interpretations (Hanako's mother and Taro's mother, respectively), just like the null object in (44b). Note, furthermore, that when the PSE position is replaced with the overt pronoun *kanojo* 'she', the resulting sentence can only yield the strict interpretation, as indicated in (18b). The parallel behavior between AE and PSE with respect to sloppy interpretations to the exclusion of the *pro*-drop case, therefore, suggests that the derivation of PSE can take the form of AE.

4.2   Relative Scope between Universally Quantified DPs and Negation

Our second argument that PSE may take the form of AE comes from relative scope between universally quantified DPs and negation, as illustrated in (19).

(19) Speaker A: Kokoni   iru   zen'in-o   paatii-ni   syootaisita-no?
　　　　　　　　here   be   all-ACC   party-to   invited-Q
　　　　　　　　'Did you invite everyone here to the party?'
　　　Speaker B: a. **wa**   syootaisi-masen-desita,   (Neg » all)
　　　　　　　　TOP   invite POL.NEG POL.PAST
　　　　　　　　'Lit. I didn't invite *e*.'
　　　　　　　　b. **Karera**-wa   syootaisi-masen-desita. (*Neg » all)
　　　　　　　　they-TOP   invite-POL.NEG-POL.PAST
　　　　　　　　'I didn't invite them.'

The example in (19a) allows for the wide scope interpretation of negation vis-à-vis the universal quantifier, according to which Speaker B invited some, but not all, of the people present here. Significantly, however, (19b) – the variant of (19a) now with the overt third-person plural pronoun *karera* 'them' – blocks this interpretation. This interpretive contrast thus shows that the PSE case here cannot be assimilated to *pro*-drop. On the other hand, the wide scope interpretation of negation in (19a) is exactly predicted by the AE analysis, because the pre-ellipsis representation to (19a), with the quantified object fully pronounced, yields this interpretation, as shown in (20).

(20) Kokoni   iru   zen'in-wa   syootaisi-masen-desita.
　　 here   be   all-TOP   invite-POL.NEG-POL.PAST
　　 'I didn't invite everyone present here.'

4.3   Disjunctive Interpretation of Elided Arguments

Our third argument for the possibility of AE within PSE has to do with disjunctive interpretations. Sakamoto (2016) points out that in English, pronouns anaphorically linked to disjunctive antecedents accept the disjunctive E-type reading, but not the disjunctive reading. Taking (21) as an example, the pronoun *he* in (21b), which is anaphoric to the disjunctive antecedent *either John or Bill* in (21a), can only be interpreted as the person who actually visited Uconn last year (the disjunctive E-type reading); it cannot be interpreted as either John or Bill (the disjunctive reading). VP-ellipsis, on the other hand, can yield the latter interpretation, as shown in (22).

(21) a.　Last year, either John or Bill visited Uconn.
　　 b.　This year too, he visited Uconn.
　　　　 (Disjunctive E-type reading/*Disjunctive reading) (Sakamoto 2016:6)

(22) John scolded either Mary or Nancy, and Bill did [$_{VP}$ Ø], too.
(Disjunctive reading) (Sakamoto 2016:7)

The examples in (21, 22) together thus show that the availability of the disjunctive reading is contingent on the application of ellipsis. With this insight in place, Sakamoto observes that a null argument in Japanese allows the disjunctive reading, on a par with English VP-ellipsis, as shown in (23b), a result which suggests that the null argument is derived through AE.

(23) a. Kinoo   Taroo   ka   Ziroo-ga   Kanako-o   sikatta.
      yesterday Taro   or   Jiro-NOM   Kanako-ACC   scolded
      'Yesterday, either Taro or Jiro scolded Kanako.'
   b. Kyoo-wa   *e*   Ayaka-o   sikatta. (Disjunctive reading)
      today-TOP   Ayaka-ACC   scolded
      'Lit. Today, *e* scolded Ayaka.   (Sakamoto 2016:7)

Given the presence of the disjunctive reading as a useful diagnostic test for AE, our analysis predicts that PSE, analyzed here as a case of PF-deletion, should permit this reading. Example (24) shows that this prediction is indeed borne out. (24b) permits the disjunctive interpretation according to which the null argument is interpreted as representing the whole disjunctive antecedent *Taroo ka Ziroo* 'Taro or Jiro'. Note that the overt pronoun *soitu* 'that guy' cannot support the disjunctive reading, a further indication that AE is involved in the PSE case.

(24) Speaker A: Kinoo   Taroo ka Ziroo-ga   Kanako-o   sikatta-yo.
               yesterday Taro   or Jiro-NOM   Kanako-ACC scolded-PRT
               'Yesterday, either Taro or Jiro scolded Kanako.'
     Speaker B: a. **wa**, Ayaka-mo   sikatteita-yo. (Disjunctive reading)
                 TOP Ayaka-also   scolded-PRT
                 'Either Taro or Jiro also scolded Ayaka.'
              b. **Soitu**-wa   Ayaka-mo   sikatteita-yo. (*Disjunctive)
                 that guy-TOP   Ayaka-also   scolded-PRT
                 'That guy also scolded Ayaka.'

5   Conclusion

In this paper, we have argued for a PF-deletion analysis of PSE in Japanese. We started out by pointing out a number of conceptual and empirical problems with a purely structural approach to the phenomenon as represented by Sato's (2012) recent phase-theoretic analysis. We have shown that his analysis not only necessitates a special proviso concerning possible Spell-Out domains within Phase Theory but also has a serious empirical limitation, as it is designed to cover only those PSE cases with topic-marked DPs. We have further pointed out that PSE can occur within an embedded clause and exhibits strict linear sensitivity, two observations which we considered seriously undermine the purely structural approach to PSE.

On the basis of these observations, we have proposed instead, developing the insights of Shibata's (2014) recent approach, that PSE is better characterized in terms of a string-based deletion in the phonological component (Mukai 2003; An 2016) up to a focused particle so that the left edge of the first intermediate phrase aligns with the left edge of the utterance phrase. This analysis has led to the important prediction that, in certain cases, PSE could ignore syntactic constituencies, a point that we have shown to be borne out with tripartite coordination structures where the string-based deletion targets a non-syntactic constituent.

In order to further support our deletion analysis of PSE, we have also investigated possible connections, if any, between PSE and other relatively better-studied forms of ellipsis in Japanese syntax. More concretely, we have presented a wide variety of evidence concerning sloppy interpretations, negative scope readings, and disjunction to show that PSE may well take the form of AE, rejecting the alternative *pro*-based analysis of PSE (see Sato and Maeda, to appear, for further empirical support for our analysis, including parallelism on ellipsis (Fiengo and May 1994; Takahashi 2013). This result, in turn, has an important implication for contemporary debates on the mechanism of AE as follows. If PSE can take the form of AE, then it must be the case that at least some of AE cases should also involve PF-deletion. This is an important consequence in view of the latest controversies regarding the PF-deletion (Takahashi 2012; Maeda 2017) vs. LF-copy (Oku 1998; Saito 2007) theories of AE. [1]

References

An, D. 2016. Extra deletion in fragment answers and its implications. *Journal of East Asian Linguistics* 25:313–350.

Chomsky, N. 2001. Derivation by phase. *Ken Hale: A life in language*, ed. M. Kenstowicz, 1–52. Cambridge, MA: MIT Press.

Fiengo, R. and R. May. 1994. *Indices and identity*. Cambridge, MA: MIT Press.

Goto, N. 2014. A note on particle stranding ellipsis. *Proceedings of the 14th Seoul International Conference on Generative Grammar (SICOGG14)*, ed. B.-S. Park, 78–97. Seoul: Hankuk Publishing.

---

[1] Thanks to Heidi Harley (personal communication, August 2017) for suggesting this implication. See Sakamoto and Saito (2017) for suggestive evidence that PSE involves LF-copy instead of PF-deletion.

Hattori, S. 1960. *Gengogaku no Hoohoo* [Methods in linguistics]. Tokyo: Iwanami Shoten Publishers.

Kuroda, S.-Y. 1965. *Generative grammatical studies in the Japanese Language*. Doctoral dissertation, MIT.

Maeda, M. 2017. Argument ellipsis and scope economy. Ms., Kyushu Institute of Technology.

Mukai, E. 2003. On verbless conjunction in Japanese. *Proceedings of the North East Linguistic Society* 33, ed. M. Kadowaki and S. Kawahara, 205–224. Amherst, MA: GLSA.

Nasu, N. 2012. Topic particle stranding and the structure of CP. *Main clause phenomena: New horizons*, ed. L. Aelbrecht, L. Haegeman and R. Nye, 205–228. Amsterdam: John Benjamins.

Oku, S. 1998. *A theory of selection and reconstruction in the minimalist perspective*. Doctoral dissertation, University of Connecticut.

Saito, M. 2007. Notes on East Asian Argument Ellipsis. *Language Research* 43, 203-227.

Sakamoto, Y. 2016. Scope and disjunction feed an even more argument for argument ellipsis in Japanese. *Japanese/Korean Linguistics* 23, ed. M. Kenstowicz, T. Levin and R. Masuda. Stanford: CSLI Publications.

Sakamoto, Y and H. Saito. 2017. Overtly stranded but covertly not. Paper presented at the 35th Annual Meeting of the West Coast Conference on Formal Linguistics, University of Calgary, Alberta, Canada. April 28-30. [available at https://drive.google.com/file/d/0BxzV2BrxFnu0RFh1NGtuOUI4enM/view]

Sato, Y. 2012. Particle-stranding ellipsis in Japanese, phase theory, and the privilege of the root. *Linguistic Inquiry* 43:495–504.

Sato, Y and J. Ginsburg. 2007. A new type of nominal ellipsis in Japanese. *Formal Approaches to Japanese Linguistics: Proceedings of FAJL4*, ed. Y. Miyamoto and M. Ochi, 197–204. Cambridge, MA: MITWPL.

Sato, Y. and M. Maeda. to appear. Particle stranding ellipsis involves PF-deletion. *Natural Language and Linguistic Theory*.

Shibata, Y. 2014. A phonological approach to particle stranding ellipsis in Japanese. Poster presented at Formal Approaches to Japanese Linguistics (FAJL) 7, National Institute for Japanese Language and Linguistics and International Christian University, June 27–29.

Takahashi, D. 2008. Noun phrase ellipsis. *The Oxford Handbook of Japanese Linguistics*, ed. S. Miyagawa and M. Saito, 394–422. Oxford: Oxford University Press.

Takahashi, D. 2012. Looking at argument ellipsis derivationally. Talk presented at the 15th workshop of the international research project on comparative syntax and language acquisition. Nanzan University. July 28. [available at http://www.ad.cyberhome.ne.jp/~d-takahashi/DTSyntaxLab/Research.html]

Takahashi, D. 2013. A note on parallelism for elliptic arguments. In *Proceedings of FAJL6: Formal Approaches to Japanese Linguistics*, ed. K. Yatsushiro and U. Sauerland, 203–213. Cambridge, MA: MITWPL.

Yoshida, T. 2004. *Syudai no syooryaku gensho: Hikaku toogoron teki koosatu. Nihongo Kyooikugaku no Siten* [Perspectives on Japanese Language Pedagogy], ed. The Editorial Committee of Annals, 291–305. Tokyo: Tokyodo.

Light Verb Ellipsis Constructions in Korean*

CHANGGUK YIM
Chung-Ang University

1 Introduction

As a starting point of discussion, let us consider the following examples in
(1). The verb *ha-* 'do' in Korean may or may not be elided in a negative
sentence, leaving behind the italicized root.

(1)   a. Nam il-ey   *kansep*(**ha-ci**) ma-la.
        others business-at interfere.do-*ci* NEG-IMP[1]
        'Don't interfere with other people's business.'
    b. Nay mal-ey *sepsep**(**ha-ci**) anh-ass-umyen...
       my word-at dispoint.do-*ci*   NEG-PST-if

*I would like to thank Hae-Young Kim, Myung-Kwan Park, Hee-Don Ahn, Shinichiro Fukuda, and the audience for helpful suggestions and comments. All remaining errors are mine.

[1] The following abbreviations are used here: ACC = accusative; C = complementizer; DAT = dative; GEN = genitive; HON = honorific; IMP = imperative; NEG = negation; NOM = nominative; PROG = progressive; PRS = present; PST = past; TOP = topic.

Japanese/Korean Linguistics 25.
Edited by Shin Fukuda, Mary Shin Kim, and Mee-Jeong Park.

'(I wish) you would not be disappointed at me.'
c. Nemwu *sulphe*(**ha-ci**) ma-la.
   too   sad.do-*ci*   NEG-IMP
'Don't show too much sorrow.'

Drawing on this ellipsis pattern of *ha-*, I offer a syntactic analysis of *ha-* ellipsis in which *ha-* belongs to distinct verbal heads introducing their own external arguments. Specifically, the verb in question is an exponent of various verbal heads such as *v*, Appl, and Voice, as illustrated below.

(2)

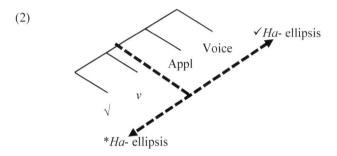

On this view, the *ha-* ellipsis behavior attributes to categorically different types of *ha-* and their corresponding syntactic structures. Appl and Voice, the two outermost verbal heads, allow the ellipsis, whereas the innermost head *v* and the root resist it. Thus, the *ha-* ellipsis follows from the fact that it is subject to syntactic hierarchy.

This article is organized as follows. Section 2 observes that the light verb *ha-* may or may not elided in negative sentences. Section 3 provides a syntactic analysis of *ha-* ellipsis in which the light verb under consideration is a functional morpheme rather than a root, and the *ha-* ellipsis is sensitive to syntactic hierarchy. Section 4 concludes the article, by stressing that the *ha-* ellipsis straightforwardly follows from the configurational theory of argument structure in which different arguments occupy different syntactic positions.

2   Light Verb Ellipsis

In Korean, there are two ways of negating a sentence: short- and long-form negation, as illustrated below. In (3b), short-form negation adds to a sentence the negator *an* 'not' immediately before the verb to be negated. In long-form negation (3c), the content verb is suffixed with the particle -*ci* and followed by light verb *ha-*.

(3) a. Celin-i   cip-e   kassta.
        Celin-NOM home-at went
        'Celin went home.'
     b. Celin-i   cip-e   **an** kassta.   *Short-form negation*
        Celin-NOM home-at NEG went
        'Celin did not go home.'
     c. Celin-i   cip-e ka-**ci** **anh**-ass-ta.   *Long-form negation*
        Celin-NOM home-at go-*ci* NEG.do-PST-C

Negative imperatives, however, do not make use of such usual short- or long-form negation, as exemplified below.

(4) a. ***An** kkomccakhay-la.   *Short-form negation*
        NEG move-imp
        'Freeze. Don't move.'
     b. *Kethmosup-ulo **an** phantanhay-la.
        appearance-by NEG judge-IMP
        'Don't judge from appearances.'
     c. *Kkomccakha-**ci an ha**-la.   *Long-form negation*
        move-*ci*   NEG do-IMP
     d. *Kethmosup-ulo phantanha-**ci an ha**-la.
        appearance-by judge-*ci*   NEG do-IMP

Instead, the negative imperatives employ a special form of negation, as shown in (5) below. In place of the negator and *ha*-, a different form is used; *mal*- 'lit., stop, cease.' Han & Lee (2007) propose that this *mal*- in the negative imperative is an exponent of the long-form negation sequence, *an ha*-, in the context of deontic modality (see Han & Lee 2007 for detail).

(5) a. Kkomccakha-ci **ma**-la.
        move-*ci*   NEG-IMP
        'Freeze. Don't move.'
     b. Kethmosup-ulo phantanha-ci **ma**-la.
        appearance-by judge-*ci*   NEG-IMP
        'Don't judge from appearances.'
     c. Nam il-ey   kansepha-*ci* **ma**-la.
        other business-at interfere-ci   NEG-IMP
        'Don't interfere with other people's business.'

Interestingly enough, in negative imperatives containing *ha*-, the light verb can undergo a (stylistically optional) ellipsis, leaving behind the Sino-Korean root. I refer to this ellipsis of *ha*- as *Light Verb Ellipsis* (hereafter, LiVE).

(6)   a. Kkomccak-∅ ma-la.   (cf. (5a))
        move-∅   NEG-IMP
        'Freeze. Don't move.'
       b. Kethmosup-ulo phantan-∅ ma-la.   (cf. (5b))
        appearance-by judge-∅   NEG-IMP
        'Don't judge from appearances.'
       c. Nam il   kansep-∅ ma-la.   (cf. (5c))
        other business in.interfere ∅ NEG-IMP
        'Don't interfere with other people's business.'

To my knowledge, Lee (1979) is the first to observe LiVE in negative contexts. As the name implies, LiVE is illicit with content verbs containing no light *ha-* (ibid. pp. 17-18). This is illustrated below.

(7)   a. **Wuski***(-**ci**) com   ma-la.
        laugh-*ci*   a.little NEG-IMP
        'Don't be kidding.'
       b. Kaeul-eyn **tteona***(-**ci**) mal-ayo.
        fall-in.TOP leave-*ci*   NEG-IMP.HON
        'In fall, don't leave me.'

The impossibility of LiVE in (7) shows that without light *ha-*, it is impossible for the *-ci* particle alone to undergo LiVE

   Based on the fact that some types of *ha-* allow LiVE whereas others resist it, I offer a syntactic analysis of LiVE in which the light verb is not (part of) a root but a functional morpheme and, in addition, different types of *ha-* belong to distinct verbal heads which introduce various external arguments such as agents, experiencers, and actional experiencers. This provides support for the configurational theory of argument structure which holds that distinct arguments (or thematic roles) are positioned syntactically differently (Baker 1988 and Hale & Keyser 1993, among others).

3   Different Types of Light Verb *Ha-* and Distinct Verbal Heads

3.1   Root *Ha-*

As a starting point, let us consider the following examples.

(8)   a. Minho-ka {tampay/meli/pap}-ul **ha**-nta.
        Minho-NOM cigarette/hair/rice-ACC do-PRS
        'Minho {smokes a cigarette/fixes hair/steams rice}.'

b. *Minho-ka   {tampay/meli/pap}-ul.
   Minho-NOM cigarette/hair/rice-ACC
   'Minho {cigarette/hair/rice}.'

This type of *ha-* is semantically "heavy" or a content verb in that it has its own lexical meaning. This is verified by the fact that without the verb, the sentence in (8b) becomes completely uninterpretable: The uninterpretability of (8b) is explained by the fact that two referential entities (the subject and object) are juxtaposed, lacking a theta-assigner. Another piece of evidence in favor of the "heaviness" of *ha-* in (8a) emerges from the fact that in (9), the verb under consideration can be replaced with semantically corresponding lexical verbs such as 'smoke', 'fix', or 'steam', depending on the object with which it co-occurs.

(9)   a. tampay-lul   {ha-/phiwu-}
          cigarette-ACC do/smoke
          'to smoke a cigarette'
       b. meli-lul {ha-/manci-}   c. pap-ul   {ha-/cis-}
          hair-ACC do/touch   rice-ACC do/make
          'to fix hair'   'to steam rice'

Given that *ha-* in (8) is a content verb, it is reasonable to suppose that it is a root $\sqrt{}$, as illustrated below.

(10)   √P
          _____
       'cigarette/hair/rice'   √*ha-*

   Bearing this in mind, let us now observe that Root *ha-* fails to undergo LiVE, as shown below.

(11)   Tampay/pap/meli-lul *(**ha**-ci) ma-la.
        cigarette/rice/hair-ACC do-ci NEG-IMP
        'Don't smoke/steam rice/fix hair.'

The LiVE of Root *ha-* can be ruled out in the same way that (8b) is ruled out: Just as (8b) is uninterpretable due to the absence of a content verb that bears all theta-roles for the arguments in the sentence, (11) also becomes uninterpretable if *ha-* is elided. Note that this type of *ha-* is a root that resists LiVE.

3.2 Agentive and Stative *Ha-*

Let us begin with Koh's (1996) analysis of the light verb *ha-*. He divides the verb into two subtypes; "verb" *ha-* and "adjective" *ha-*. The former corresponds to agentive verbs whereas the latter to stative or non-agentive state verbs. Agentive *ha-* verbs in (12a) take an agent subject, as given in (12b).

(12)   *Agentive* ha-
    a. kansepha- 'interfere', cwucangha- argue', phantanha-'judge', ...
    b. Chelswu-nun **ilpwule**   ku il-ey   kansep**ha**yssta.
       Chelswu-TOP on.purpose that business-at interfere.did
       'Chelswu interfered with that on purpose.'

In (12b), *kansepha-* allows agent-oriented adverbial modification. As is usually assumed, the possibility of 'on purpose' diagnoses the presence of a verbal head introducing an agentive external argument; hence, Voice.
In contrast, Stative *ha-* in (13a) takes an experiencer, as shown in (13b).

(13)   *Stative* ha-
    a. pwulan**ha**- 'uneasy', cilwu**ha**- 'boring', changphi**ha**- 'ashamed'
    b. Chelswu-nun (***ilpwule**) sihem kyelkwa-ka changphi**ha**yssta.
       Chelswu-TOP on.purpose exam result-NOM ashamed.did
       'Chelswu was ashamed of his exam result (*on purpose).'

Chelswu in (13b) is a typical experiencer. This is confirmed by the fact that agent-oriented adverbial modification is impossible with *changphiha-* in (13b). This leads to the conclusion that Stative *ha-* lacks an agent argument-introducing a Voice head. Note that Agentive light verb *ha-* takes an agent whereas Stative light verb *ha-* an experiencer.

    Based on the discussion so far, let us suppose that Agentive and Stative *ha-* have the structures given in (14). In (14a), Agentive *ha-* is a spell-out of Voice which introduces a full-fledged agent argument (Marantz 1997 and Kratzer 1996). Whereas in (14b), Stative *ha-* lacking Voice is an exponent of *v*, with the assumption that experiencers occur in Spec*v*P.

(14)   a. *Agentive* ha-

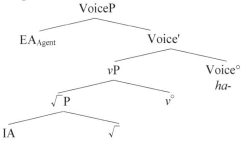

         b. *Stative* ha-

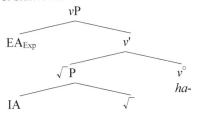

(EA = external argument, IA = internal argument)

With this in mind, let us now see whether Agentive and Stative *ha-* are compatible with LiVE. Agentive *ha-* can undergo LiVE, as shown below.

(15)   a. Ceypal nam il-ey   kansep(**ha**-ci) ma-la.
            please others business-at interfere.do-*ci* NEG-IMP
            'Please don't interfere with other people's business.'
         b. Hyencil-ul waykokhayse phantan(**ha**-ci) ma-la.
            reality-ACC distortedly   judge.do-*ci*   NEG-IMP
            'Don't judge the reality distortedly.'

In contrast, LiVE is illicit with Stative *ha-*, as illustrated below.

(16)   a. ?Ni-ka   nay mal-ey sepsep*(**ha**-ci) {mal-/anh-aya} haltheynte.
            you-NOM my word-at dispoint.do-*ci* NEG-should   wish
            'I wish you would not be disappointed at me.'
         b. Nwukwueykeyto yenghwa-ka cilwu*(**ha**-ci) {mal-/anh-}ass-
            anybody.DAT   film-NOM   bore.do-*ci*   NEG-PST-
            umyen cohkeysse.
            if wished
            'I wish the film would not be boring to anybody.'

We have seen so far that Root *ha-* and Stative *ha-* can resist LiVE whereas Agentive allows it, as illustrated in (17) below. Note that structure-wise, the outermost verbal head Voice allows LiVE, whereas the two innermost √ and *v* do not.

(17)

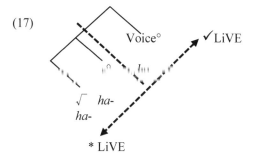

3.3 Actional Experiential *Ha-*

The next type of light verb *ha-* to be investigated in this subsection differs from the two types examined in the previous subsection. This type of *ha-* combines with (native Korean) psychological state verbs, as in (18a), unlike Agentive and Stative *ha-* taking as their stem Sino-Korean nouns (see (12a) and (13a)).

(18)   a. sulphe**ha**- 'show sorrow', kippe**ha**- 'show pleasure', miweha-
        'show dislike', …
        b. Salamtul-i   tokcayca-ui ttal-ul   cengmal miwe**ha**nta.
        people-NOM dictator-GEN daughter-ACC really   dislike.do
        'People show real dislike about the dictator's daughter.'

It is important to notice that the subject of this type of *ha-* in (18b) is not agentive although they are sentient. This is confirmed by the fact that the subject in (19) below is incompatible with agent-oriented adverbial modification.

(19)   Chelswu-ka (***ilpwule**) sewelho   chamsa-lul sulphe**ha**yssta.
        Chelswu-NOM on.purpose Sewol.Ferry disaster-ACC sad.did
        'Chelswu showed much sorrow about the Sewol Ferry disaster (*on purpose).'

The ungrammaticality of (19) indicates that *Chelswu* is not an full-fledged agent because it is not the case that Chelswu intentionally does something in order to get a result denoted by the verb. Accordingly, this *ha-* lacks Voice. A significant question to ask at this juncture is: Is there any difference between (experiencers of) Stative *ha-* and (those of) *ha-* of the type in question?

Among the most important differences is that Stative *ha-* does not allow the progressive *-ko issta* as in (20a). In contrast, this particle is compatible with the *ha-* at stake, as in (20b).

(20)   a. *Chelswu-nun sihem kyelkwa-ka changphi**ha-ko issta**.
           Chelswu-TOP exam result-NOM ashamed.do-PROG
           'Chelswu is being ashamed of his exam result.'
        b. Salamtul-i sewelho chamsa-lul sulphe**ha-ko issta**.
           people-NOM Sewol.Ferry disaster-ACC sad.do-PROG
           'The people are showing sorrow about the Sewol Ferry disaster.'

As is usually assumed, the progressive is only compatible with an actional event verb but not with a psychological state verb (see, e.g., Kim 1990:67). This sharp contrast suggests that (20a) denotes a stative event whereas (20b) an actional event. In other words, the experiencers of both types of *ha-* have to be distinctive somehow. This can follow from Choy (1973) and Kim (2007), among others. Choy (1973:218) claims that semantics-wise, *ha-* in (18a) adds to the resulting form "actionality" (*hayngtongseng*, translation mine) (ibid., p. 221). In other words, *ha-* turns non-actional into actional or dynamic verbs. Kim (2007) also makes a similar claim: that a subject of *ha-* at stake behaves like an "actor without volition." He provides a semantic feature-based analysis in which typical agents bear [+volition] and [+action] and experiencers of *ha-* in question carry [-volition] and [+action] (see also Jeong 2010:315 for a similar proposal). This means that there occurs a three-way contrast, as shown below.

(21)   a. typical agents: [+volition] [+action] ← Voice
        b. typical experiencers: [-volition] [-action] ← *v*
        c. actional experiencers: [-volition] [+action] ← ???

I refer to this new type of *ha-* as *Actional Experiential ha-* (AE *ha-*) and experiencers it takes as *actional experiencers*, as opposed to typical experiencers. Given that agents are introduced by Voice and typical experiencers by *v*, an important theoretical question to ask at this juncture is: What kind of verbal head would introduce actional experiencers?

An answer to this question comes from Kim (2011b). She argues that there are two different external argument-introducing heads in Korean, Voice and Appl. The former, but not the latter, introduces a volitional agentive argument. In contrast, an argument in SpecApplP, for instance, is not a full-fledged agent, unlike agents in VoiceP. Accordingly, agentivity is specific to

Voice. Given this, let us suppose that Appl is exponed as AE *ha-* and that its Spec position is filled by actional experiencers, as illustrated below.

(22)

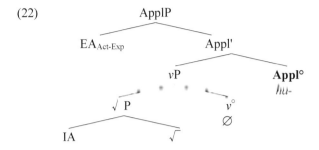

With this in mind, let us observe that AE *ha-* allows LiVE, as exemplified below.

(23)   a. Silphayhayto sulphe(**ha**-ci) ma-la.
         fail.if   sad.do-*ci*   NEG-IMP
         'Don't show sorrow if you fail.'
       b. Nam-uy chingchan-ey nemwu kippe(ha-ci) ma-la.
         other-GEN praise-at   much   pleased.do-*ci* NEG-IMP
         'Don't show too much pleasure about other people's praise.'

Note that AE *ha-* is an exponent of Appl and that SpecApplP is filled by actional experiencers. And AE *ha-* can undergo LiVE.

3.4   *Ha-*Stacking

It is of interest to notice that it is possible to stack *ha-* of one type on top of another. Specifically, Stative *ha-* can stack up onto AE *ha-*, as illustrated below.

(24)   a. Mina-nun caki milay-ka   pwulanhayssta. ← Stative *ha-*
         Mina-TOP self future-NOM uneasy.did
         'Mina was worried about her future.'
       b. Mina-nun caki milay-lul   pwulan**hayha**yssta.
                                          ← Stative *ha-* + AE *ha-*
         Mina-TOP self future-ACC uneasy.do.did
         'Mina showed concern about her future.'

As illustrated in (25) below, stacking of *ha-* can be straightforwardly explained by the current analysis that different types of light *ha-* are exponents of structurally distinct verbal heads.

(25)

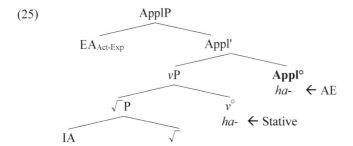

Recall that LiVE is licit with AE *ha-*, as observed in subsection 3.3, whereas it is illicit with Stative *ha-*, as shown in subsection 3.2. A prediction to make here is that the outer *ha-* can undergo LiVE whereas the inner *ha-* cannot. This prediction has been borne out, as illustrated below.

(26)   a. Pwulhapkyek-ul nemwu changphi**hay**(ha-ci) ma-la.
            failure-ACC   too   ashamed.do.do-*ci*   NEG-IMP
            'Don't show too much shame on your failure.'
        b. Pwulhapkyek-ul nemwu changphi*(**hayha**-ci) ma-la.

Note that stacking of the light verb and the (un)availability of LiVE are straightforwardly explained by the present analysis in which LiVE is subject to syntactic hierarchy. That is, as shown in Table 1, LiVE is licit with the outermost verbal heads Appl and Voice and it is illicit with the innermost √ and *v* (the shaded column).

Type	Root	Stative	Actional Experiential	Agentive
Head	√	*v*	Appl	Voice
LiVE	*	*	✓	✓

Table 1

3.5   Discussion

So far we have seen that distinct verbal heads such as *v*, Appl, and Voice can be exposed as different types of light verb *ha-* in Korean. They may or may not be elided in negative sentences, as shown in Table 1 above. LiVE is impossible with Root *ha-* and Stative *ha-* on *v*, whereas it is possible with *ha-* on Appl and Voice. This fact is straightforwardly explained if it is assumed that the light verb is not (part of) a root but a functional morpheme. Thus, the LiVE behavior of *ha-* is ascribed to syntactic hierarchy, as illustrated in (27) below. The hierarchically lower √ and *v* pattern differently from the two hierarchically higher heads Appl and Voice. Given that each verbal head introduces its own external argument within its projection, this supports the configurational theory of argument structure which identifies theta-roles with syntactic configurations in a concrete way fashion (Hale & Keyser 1993, Baker 1988, Marantz 1997, Kratzer 1996, Pylkkänen 2008, Harley 2013 and references therein).

(27)

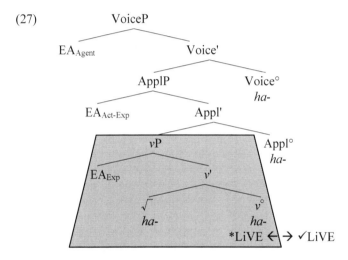

Note that the LiVE fact supports the view of a prolific inventory of syntactic verbal heads such as *v*, Appl, and Voice.

4 Concluding Remarks

The configurational analysis put forth here is compared with a non-configurational, single head analysis by others (e.g., Folli & Harley (2005, 2007) and Kallulli (2006, 2007)). Under this approach, there is one single type of *v* that consists of distinct feature bundles such as [+act], [+cause], and [+intent] for various interpretations of external arguments like agents, actors, and (unintentional) causers. Structure-wise, thus, the position that external arguments occupy is one and the same one, Spec*v*P. Accordingly, diverse flavors of *v* are not distinctive in terms of syntactic hierarchy. Specifically, Agentive and Stative *ha-* would have been assigned structures given in

(28a,b), respectively. It is important to notice that there is no difference in hierarchy between Agentive *ha-* in (28a) and Stative *ha-* in (28b).

(28)   a.

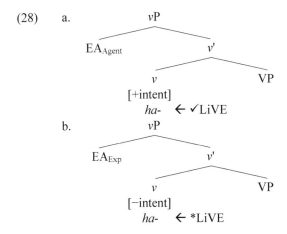

This featural approach should attribute the LiVE behavior solely to feature matrices in *v* since they are not distinguished structurally or hierarchically. Since there is no implicational relationship between those feature bundles in *v* and LiVE, there seems to be no non-ad-hoc way to offer a principled and structural explanation for the LiVE fact observed above. Specifically, it should be explained why Agentive *ha-* with [+intent] allows LiVE and Stative *ha-* with [−intent] resists it. An implication difficulty that the analysis under discussion faces is that there seems no plausible reason why LiVE is sensitive to this [intent] feature. There is a more serious problem with the featural analysis under discussion. Recall that Agentive and AE *ha-* both allow LiVE. However, what do they have in common in terms of featural matrices? It is obvious that they do not form a natural class. They are diagonally opposite in terms of the [intent] feature. But they do not behave alike with respect to agentivity or intentionality. Hence, Agentive *ha-* has [+intent] while AE *ha-* has [−intent]. In a nutshell, the featural single head approach seems to be very unlikely to accommodate the systematic range of the LiVE behavior of light verb *ha-*.

    Alternatively, I have offered a fully structural explanation for LiVE in Korean. Given that the light verb is a functional morpheme rather than (part of) a root, the LiVE fact is ascribed to structural hierarchy of distinct verbal heads. Thus, the LiVE behavior is due to structural relations rather than to interaction between structure and other components that the single head analysis would capitalize upon. This constitutes substantive evidence in favor of the configurational theory of argument structure in which semantically different external arguments and their verbal heads are distinct and treated in a different way in syntax (see also Kim 2011 and Schäfer 2012).

References

Alexiadou, A. & G. Iordăchioaia. 2014. The psych causative alternation. *Lingua* 148:53-79.

Baker, M. C. 1988. *Incorporation: A Theory of Grammatical Function Changing.* Chicago: The University of Chicago Press.

Chung, I. W. 1970. *-E hata-uy pemcwu (The category of -e hata)* [in Korean]. *Hankwukenemwunhak* 10:217-230.

Cuervo, M. C. 2003. *Datives at large.* Doctoral dissertation, MIT.

Embick, D. & A. Marantz. 2008. Architecture and Blocking. *Linguistic Inquiry* 39:1-53.

Folli, R. & H. Harley. 2005. Consuming results in Italian and English: Flavors of *v*. In *Aspectual Inquiries*, ed. R. Slabakova and P. M. Kempchinsky, 95-120. Dordrecht: Springer.

Folli, R. & H. Harley. 2007. Causation, obligation and argument structure: on the nature of little *v*. *Linguistic Inquiry* 38:197-238.

Grimshaw, J. & A. Mester. 1988. Light verbs and θ-marking. *Linguistic Inquiry* 19:205-232.

Hale, K. & S. J. Keyser. 1993. On the argument structure and the lexical expression of syntactic relations. In *The View from Building 20*, ed. K. Hale and S. J. Keyser, 53-109. Cambridge: MIT Press.

Halle, M. & A. Marantz. 1993. Distributed morphology and the piece of inflection. In *The View from Building 20*, ed. K. Hale and S. J. Keyser, 111-176. Cambridge: MIT Press.

Han, C.-h. & C. Lee. 2007. On negative imperatives in Korean. *Linguistic Inquiry* 373-393.

Harley, H. 2013. External arguments and the Mirror Principle: On the distinctness of Voice and *v*. *Lingua* 125:34-57.

Jeong, Y.-j. 2010. '-*E ha-*'wa thonghaphanun kaykkwanhyengyongsauy uymi thukseng (Semantic characteristics of objective adjectives which are combined with -*eo ha-*). *Hankwuke Uymihak* 33:297-319.

Jung, H. K. 2016. On the verbalizing suffixes in Korean and their implications for syntax and semantics. *Lingua* 179: 97-123.

Kallulli, D. 2006. Unaccusatives with dative causers and experiencers: A unified account. In *Datives and Other Cases*, ed. by D. Hole, A. Meinunger, and W. Abraham, 271-300. Amsterdam: John Benjamins.

Kang, M.-Y. 1988. *Topics in Korean Syntax: Phrase Structure, Variable Binding and Movement.* Doctoral dissertation, MIT.

Kim, I. 2007. What makes negative imperatives so natural for Korean [psych-adjective + -*e ha-*] constructions? In *Proceedings of the 21th Pacific Asia*

Conference on Language. Seoul National University. Available on http://kangwon.academia.edu/IlkyuKim

Kim, K. 2011. High applicatives in Korean causatives and passives. *Lingua* 121:487-510.

Kim, Y-J. 1990. *The syntax and semantics of Korean Case: The interaction between lexical and syntactic levels of representation*. Doctoral dissertation, Harvard University.

Koh, J.-s. 1996. Tongsa '*ha-*'wa hyengyongsa '*ha-*' (The verb *ha-* and the adjective *ha-*). *Journal of Korea Linguistics* 33:145-175.

Kratzer, A. 1996. Severing the external argument from its verb. In *Phrase Structure and the Lexicon*, ed. by Johan Rooryck and Laurie Zaring, 109-137. Springer: Dordrecht.

Lee, S. 1979. Tongsa '*malta*'ey tayhaye (On the verb *malta*). *Yenseyemwunhak* 12:13-38.

Marantz, A. 1993. Implications of asymmetries in double object constructions. In S. A. Mchombo, ed., *Theoretical aspects of Bantu grammar* 1, 113–151. Stanford, Calif.: CSLI Publications.

Marantz, A. 1997. No escape from syntax: don't try morphological analysis in the privacy of your own lexicon. In *University of Pennsylvania Working Papers in Linguistics 4*, A. Dimitriadis, H. Lee, L. Siegel, C. Surek-Clark, and A. Williams, 201-225.

Pylkkänen, L. 2008. *Introducing Arguments*. Cambridge: MIT Press.

Part III

Phonetics and Phonology

Korean Aspiration, Japanese Voicing, and Emergent Features

National Institute for Japanese Language and Linguistics
Komatsu University

1 Introduction

Mielke (2008) argues that phonological features are EMERGENT rather than innate. Thus, 'Because features are abstract, there need not always be a connection between phonetics and phonological patterns, and features do not necessarily always refer to phonetically natural classes' (Mielke 2008: 9).

According to Saussure (1916: 164), 'Linguistic signals are not in essence phonetic. They are not physical in any way. They are constituted solely by differences which distinguish one sound pattern from another.' But surely the phonetic substance that manifests spoken language has a profound influence on the formal patterns we find. Saussure's characterization contrasts sharply with what Postal (1968: 55–77) calls the NATURALNESS CONDITION, according to which classes of segments that behave together phonologically must be definable in phonetic terms. The naturalness condition is weaker than the claim that features are drawn from an innate,

Japanese/Korean Linguistics 25.
Edited by Shin Fukuda, Mary Shin Kim, and Mee-Jeong Park.

phonetically grounded set. A phonetically definable class is not necessarily 'featurally' natural (unless there is a feature for every conceivable phonetic property). As Anderson (1981: 504) puts it, 'Even if it is indeed the case that sounds which behave similarly have something in common phonetically, we must still ask whether a system of features which is appropriate for phonological analysis can serve directly as a system for phonetic description as well.' Ladd (2014: 1–28) argues that even the weaker naturalness condition cannot be maintained, and both Ladd (2014: 17) and Mielke (2008: 10) quote relevant statements by Ladefoged (1984: 85, 1990: 404).

This paper will look at two phenomena that are difficult to reconcile with universal innate features but are compatible with the notion of emergent features.

2 Korean Aspiration

As has been documented in many studies (e.g. Kim, Beddor and Horrocks 2002), the laryngeal features of word-initial lax and aspirated stops in Seoul Korean have been shifting rather dramatically in recent decades. A contrast between unaspirated and aspirated has, for some speakers, become a contrast between relatively weakly aspirated and relatively strongly aspirated. Low f0 in the immediately following vowel serves as an increasingly important cue for the lax (now weakly aspirated) stops.[1]

In the wake of the pioneering work by Lisker and Abramson (1964), it was widely accepted that there were three universally available VOT categories: lead (voiced), short lag (voiceless unaspirated), and long lag (voiceless aspirated). However, subsequent research in the half century since (e.g. Raphael et al. 1995; Riney et al. 2007) indicates that Seoul Korean is just one many cases that do not fit comfortably into these putatively universal categories.

On the other hand, as shown in (1), the difference between Korean lax and aspirated stops is represented consistently with a horizontal stroke in Hangeul orthography.[2]

(1) /p/ /pʰ/   /t/ /tʰ/   /k/ /kʰ/
    ㅂ ㅍ   ㄷ ㅌ   ㄱ ㅋ

In addition, there are colloquial labels for the two sound types: *yesa*

---

[1] In 2009, the psycholinguist Jessica Maye gave a talk at the Cross-Language Speech Perception Workshop, held at the Acoustical Society of America meeting in Portland, Oregon. After playing a recorded token of Korean word with an initial lax stop, she asked the audience members to raise their hands if they thought that stop was aspirated. Except for the Korean speakers, everyone's hand went up.

[2] The affricate phonemes follow the same pattern: /č/ ㅈ vs. /čʰ/ ㅊ.

sori 예사소리 'basic sound' (for lax) and *geosen sori* 거센소리 'strong/fierce sound' (for aspirated). These labels presumably denote psychologically real categories for native speakers.[3]

If features are emergent, ongoing changes in phonetic realization need not disrupt the system and make it problematic for future generations of speakers. The two Korean phonological classes can, of course, be characterized in phonetic terms throughout the progress of the change, although not with innate features. Korean 'aspiration' is therefore not a problem for the naturalness condition.

3 Japanese Voicing

Japanese *rendaku* is almost always described as a voicing process.[4] Because of well-understood diachronic changes, however, *rendaku* actually pairs voiced and voiceless consonants that, in most cases, differ in more than just the presence vs. absence of vocal-fold vibration (Vance 2016: 1–4). These pairings are shown in (2).

(2) VOICELESS   VOICED
    /f/   [ɸ] → [b]   /b/
    /h/ [h]~[ç] → [b]   /b/
    /t/   [t] → [d]   /d/
    /c/   [ts] → [dz]~[z] /z/
    /s/   [s] → [dz]~[z] /z/
    /č/   [tɕ] → [dʑ]   /ǰ/
    /š/   [ɕ] → [dʑ]   /ǰ/
    /k/   [k] → [g]   /g/ (or [ŋ]/ŋ/)

On the other hand, the orthographic representation of *rendaku* in *kana* is straightforward and consistent. For example, as shown in (3), the difference between the /h/[h] in /hana/ 'nose' and the /b/[b] in /aka+bana/ 'red nose' is represented in exactly the same way as the difference between /t/[t] in /tana/ 'shelf' and /d/[d] in /hoN+dana/ 'bookshelf'. In general, the *dakuten* 濁点

---

[3] I am grateful to Hyun Kyung Hwang for consulting with some of her native Korean speaking colleagues about these labels during the JK25 conference in Honolulu. Sino-Korean *pyeong-eum* 평음 平音 'ordinary sound' and *gyeok-eum* 격음 激音 'intense sound' are technical terms and are taught in school, but some of the linguists at the conference did not remember learning them. In contrast, the colloquial labels cited in the text are transparent, that is, it is obvious to Korean speakers which consonants they denote even if the labels themselves are not already familiar.

[4] Because few morphophonemic phenomena in any language have been investigated more intensively than *rendaku*, almost every phonologist in the world today has at least a passing acquaintance with it. Vance (2017) is one of many recent introductions to the details of *rendaku* research.

diacritic is added to represent a syllable/mora that begins with one of the voiced consonants in (2).

(3)   /hana/ 'nose'   はな   /tana/ 'shelf'   たな
         /aka+bana/ 'red nose' あかばな   /hoN+dana/ 'bookshelf' ほんだな

The traditional term *seion* 清音 denotes moras beginning with a voiceless obstruent other than [p].[5] The contrasting term *dakuon* 濁音 denotes moras beginning with a voiced obstruent or, for speakers who have syllable-initial velar nasals, [ŋ].[6] There is little doubt that the *seion* and *dakuon* categories are psychologically real for native speakers, but it is not clear how to separate phonology from orthography in a case like this. When my daughter was in first grade at a Tokyo elementary school, she and her friends played a language game that involved substituting a *dakuon* for every *seion* as they spoke otherwise normal Japanese. The example in (4) illustrates.

(4)   Watashi mo kudamono tabeta
      'I too ate fruit'
                PHONOLOGY   KANA ORTHOGRAPHY
      /wataši mo kudamono tabeta/   わたしもくだものたべた
      /wadaǰi mo gudamono dabeda/   わだじもぐだものだべだ

Described phonologically, the game involves replacing every consonant phoneme that appears on the left side in (2) with its partner on the right side in (2). Described orthographically, the game involves adding the *dakuten* diacritic to every *kana* letter that could carry the diacritic but in normal Japanese does not.[7]

Kawahara (2018) makes the case that it might be better simply to view *rendaku* as an orthographic phenomenon rather than as a phonological one. In what follows, however, I will assume that *rendaku* is phonological, at

---

[5] A series of historical changes have led to the exclusion of [p]-initial moras from the *seion* class. Frellesvig (2010: 201–205, 311–316) provides details and references.

[6] It is well-known that only a shrinking minority of Tokyo speakers still have syllable-initial [ŋ] (Hibiya 1999). For the even smaller minority who consistently follow the traditional pattern, the rendaku partner of [k] is always [ŋ]. Although native speakers of Tokyo Japan who do not have [ŋ] routinely assume that [ŋ] and [g] are allophones of the same phoneme, it is not at all clear that this assumption is warranted (Vance 2008: 222). In his presidential address to the Phonetic Society of Japan, Uwano (2010) argued forcefully that speakers who do have [ŋ] have two separate phonemes, as indicated by the parenthesized portion in the last line of (2).

[7] During the question-and-answer period following the oral presentation of this paper on October 14, 2017, Yuki Hirose reported playing the same game as a child. I had nearly given up on the possibility of ever investigating the details of the game, because my daughter has no memory of it and because I had never met anyone else who knew about it. I am now cautiously optimistic that there are still children who play it and can clear up some of the uncertainties about the rules.

least in part. Given this assumption, the class of all voiceless obstruents (i.e. /p f t s c š č k h/) and the class of all voiceless obstruents except /p/ (i.e. /f t s c š č k h/) are both phonologically active in Japanese, as Mielke (2008: 51–4) points out. The phonetically natural class, which includes /p/, is the complete set of consonants that ordinarily trigger vowel devoicing.[8] The phonetically unnatural class, which excludes /p/, is the set of consonants that can undergo *rendaku*.

Some of the consonant pairings in Sino-Japanese doublets have been affected by the same diachronic changes that have disrupted the phonetic parallelism of the consonants paired by *rendaku*. Ordinary speakers understand Sino-Japanese doublets as alternative 'readings' of *kanji*. In a typical case, the same character is used to write two synonymous Sino-Japanese morphemes that were borrowed at different times and from geographically different varieties of Chinese (Vance 1987: 167–8). The examples in (5) illustrate.

(5)		VOICELESS INITIAL CONSONANT		VOICED INITIAL CONSONANT	
分	/fuN/	ふん	/buN/	ぶん	
貧	/hiN/	ひん	/biN/	びん	
土	/to/	と	/do/	ど	
	/c.../		/z.../		
財	/sai/	さい	/zai/	ざい	
地	/či/	ち	/ji/	じ	
神	/šiN/	しん	/jiN/	じん	
街	/kai/	かい	/gai/	がい	

The initial consonant phoneme pairings in (5) are almost the same as the *rendaku* pairings in (2).[9] However, there do not happen to be any doublets that pair /c/ with /z/.

There is also an orthographic difference involving the /č/–/j/ pair in *rendaku* and in Sino-Japanese doublets, as shown in (6).

(6)	/či/ 'blood'	ち	/či/ 'earth, ground' ち
	/hana+ji/ 'nosebleed'	はなぢ	/ji/ 'earth, ground' じ

---

[8] Recent work by Takada (2011) indicates that the phonetic realization of the voiced and voiceless categories has been shifting in recent years, but I leave this complication aside here. Strictly speaking, the [h] allophone of /h/ is actually not as reliable a devoicer as the other phones that realize the phonemes in the phonetically natural class (Fujimoto 2015: 176).

[9] For speakers who have syllable-initial [ŋ], Sino-Japanese morphemes like /gai/ 'road' in the last line of (5) sometimes have [g] and sometimes have [ŋ]. Word-initial instances have [g] (e.g. 街灯 'streetlight' [gaito:]), and word-medial instances have [ŋ] (e.g. 市街 [ɕiŋɑi] 'city streets').

As noted above, the representation of *rendaku* in *kana* is consistent. Consequently, the native Japanese morpheme meaning 'blood' is written with *hiragana* ⟨ち⟩ when it is realized as /či/ and with *hiragana* ⟨ぢ⟩ (the letter for /či/ plus the *dakuten* diacritic) when it is realized as /ji/ due to *rendaku*. Sino-Japanese /či/ 'earth, land' is also written with *hiragana* ⟨ち⟩, but Sino-Japanese /ji/ 'earth, land' is written with *hiragana* ⟨じ⟩ (the letter for /ši/ plus the *dakuten* diacritic).

The ultimate cause of this orthographic discrepancy is the merger of [dž] and [ž], which took place about 400 years ago (Toyama 1972: 198–202; Frellesvig 2010: 384–5; Takayama 2015: 632–5). (There was also a nearly contemporaneous merger of [dz] and [z], but there are no relevant Sino-Japanese doublets, as already noted above.) The pre-merger distinction was prescriptively maintained in *kana* orthography until the modern *kana* spelling rules were adopted in 1946.[10] The new rules specify ⟨じ⟩ (the letter for /ši/ plus the *dakuten* diacritic) as the default for /ji/ but require ⟨ぢ⟩ (the letter for /či/ plus the *dakuten* diacritic) for /ji/ when /j/ alternates with /č/ by *rendaku*.[11] Thus, even though the pre-reform spelling of Sino-Japanese /ji/ 'earth, ground' was ⟨ぢ⟩, the modern spelling is ⟨じ⟩, as shown in (6), because this /j/ is not an instance of *rendaku*. The modern spelling of /ji/ in /hana+ji/, on the other hand, remains ⟨ぢ⟩, because this /j/ is an instance of *rendaku*.

The point of this rather tedious excursus into modern Japanese orthography is just that *kana* spellings of the paired *seion* and *dakuon* consonants shown in (2) are not always quite as consistent as they are in clear cases of *rendaku*. The examples in (7) summarize the situation.

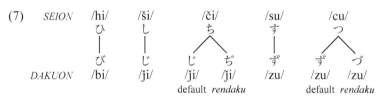

The Sino-Japanese doublet pairings in (5) are not ordinary morphophonological alternations, of course, but the paired forms in each case are 'related' in an ordinary adult speaker's mind in the sense that both are 'readings' of the same *kanji*. Furthermore, the morpheme-initial consonant pairings are mnemonic. Given a *kanji* 'reading' that begins with one of the initial consonants in (5), it is a good guess that the same *kanji* has another 'reading' that

---

[10] The modern rules were formulated by the National Language Council (Kokugo Shingi-kai 国語審議会) and adopted as a cabinet proclamation. Yoshida and Inokuchi (1962: 667–84) provide the complete text.

[11] The new rules are actually a bit more complicated, but the details are not relevant here.

begins with the partner of that consonant, although such a guess will often be wrong.[12] The upshot is that the two alternative spellings for /ji/ and for /zu/ are not entirely dependent on which *seion* consonant (i.e. /š/ or /č/, /s/ or /c/) occurs in a 'related' form.[13] Thus, we have some reason to believe that the *seion–dakuon* consonant partnerships are independent of orthography, although the evidence is admittedly weak.

In any event, if features are emergent, it is not problematic to posit paired categories for which diachronic changes have disrupted the parallelism in phonetic realization. In contrast to the Korean 'aspiration' phenomenon, the Japanese *rendaku* pairings are a serious challenge for the naturalness condition. The voiceless *seion* category cannot reasonably be construed as phonetically based, nor can the voiced *dakuon* category if it includes [ŋ].

4 Conclusion

An influential American Descriptivist linguist (Joos 1958: 96) famously wrote that 'languages can differ from each other without limit and in unpredictable ways.' This statement is surely an exaggeration, but it is not as outlandish as I and most linguists of my generation once believed. Clements and Hume (1995: 245) say that '[innate] feature theory has provided strong confirmation for the view that languages do not vary without limit, but reflect a single general pattern which is rooted in the physical and cognitive capacities of the human species.' It now seems, however, that innate feature theory is too restrictive and consequently incompatible with the development of Korean 'aspiration' and Japanese 'voicing'. On the other hand, while it is not hard to understand and sympathize with the impulse behind 'substance-free' phonology (e.g. Hale and Reiss 2000), it seems to take us back to Saussure's position. I am not yet ready to abandon the idea that phonology has something to do with phonetics.

---

[12] To illustrate, as shown in the first line of (5), the *kanji* ⟨分⟩ has the 'reading' /buN/, beginning with the *dakuon* consonanat /b/, and the 'reading' /fuN/, beginning with the paired *seion* consonant /f/. The *kanji* ⟨文⟩ also has the 'reading' /buN/, but its other 'reading' is /moN/. For a survey of the common patterns in Sino-Japanese doublet pairings, see Vance (1987: 169–72).

[13] No attempt is made here to address the thorny problem of morphological analysis raised by the fact that, in many Sino-Japanese binoms (compounds of two Sino-Japanese morphemes), a medial voiced obstruent could be due historically either to original voicing in the borrowed form or to *rendaku* after borrowing (Vance 1996, 2011). For example, given the Sino-Japanese doublet /šiN/ 'god' vs. /jiN/ 'god', the word-initial voicing in the binom /jiN+ja/ 神社 'shrine' is clearly original, but the word-medial voicing in the binom /rai+jiN/ 雷神 'thunder god' might be original or might be due to *rendaku*. Only philological evidence (which is not necessarily available) can decide the question. When the modern *kana* spelling rules were adopted in 1946, binom-medial instances of voicing were not treated as instances of *rendaku* even if they were due to *rendaku* historically (Vance 1996: 27–8).

Emergent feature theory predicts that a phonetically natural class type will be cross-linguistically common. A phonetically unnatural class type is possible, but it will be relatively uncommon or even unique, depending on how unusual the confluence of factors was that led to its emergence. We see an early recognition of this problem in a famous article about 'crazy rules'. Bach and Harms (1972: 18) suggest that there are constraints on possible rules but that they are 'much weaker than those restricting rule initiation . . .' It seems plausible that there actually are limits on possible synchronic patterns, but I do not presume to know what those limits might be.

According to Mielke (2008: 87–88), 'The main point of emergent feature theory is that phonetically natural classes are the result of common sound changes or phonetically based generalizations, while phonetically unnatural classes are the result of less common generalizations or sequences of events.' As Mielke (2008: 181) notes, there is an obvious affinity between this characterization and the 'evolutionary phonology' that Blevins (2004) advocates. The cornerstone of evolutionary phonology is that synchronic phonological patterns are emergent. Blevins (2004: 55) adopts the working assumption that 'phonological features and categories constitute part of universal grammar', but she is open to the 'possibility that these aspects of linguistic structure are also emergent.'

One question that remains open is whether orthography can play a role in keeping an unnatural class phonologically active. In the case of the Korean lax and aspirated stops discussed in §2, ongoing changes have altered the phonetic realizations of the two classes but have not disrupted the parallelism of the phonetic correspondences between the consonants in each lax–aspirated pair. Thus, the classes are not at present unnatural, but it is not hard to imagine future sound changes affecting the pairs differently. My intuition is that the orthographic parallelism shown in (1) could not impede the progress of diachronic changes that would make future descendants of the lax and aspirated classes unnatural, but I have no evidence to offer for this intuition.

Diachronic changes have already rendered the Japanese *seion* and *dakuon* classes unnatural, as explained in §3, and orthographic influence seems more likely in this case. This is not to say that orthographic regularity is what keeps the *rendaku* alternations alive, but this regularity may work to persuade speakers to see those alternations as a single, unified phenomenon rather than as an assortment of isolated consonant pairings (Vance 2015: 397–9). It is not obvious that the *seion* and *dakuon* classes would remain psychologically real classes without this orthographic support.

References

Anderson, S. 1981. Why Phonology Isn't 'Natural'. *Linguistic Inquiry* 12:493–539.

Bach, E. and R. T. Harms. 1972. How Do Languages Get Crazy Rules? *Linguistic Change and Generative Theory*, ed. R. P. Stockwell and R. K. S. Macauley, 1–21. Bloomington: Indiana University Press.

Blevins, J. 2004. *Evolutionary Phonology: The Emergence of Sound Patterns*. Cambridge: Cambridge University Press.

Clements, G. N. and E. V. Hume. 1995. The Internal Organization of Speech Sounds. *The Handbook of Phonological Theory*, ed. John Goldsmith, 245–306. Oxford: Blackwell.

Frellesvig, B. 2010. *A History of the Japanese Language*. Cambridge: Cambridge University Press.

Fujimoto, M. 2015. Vowel Devoicing. *The Handbook of Japanese Phonetics and Phonology*, ed. H. Kubozono, 167–214. Berlin: De Gruyter Mouton.

Hale, M. and C. Reiss. 2000. Substance Abuse and Dysfunctionalism: Current Trends in Phonology. *Linguistic Inquiry* 31:157–169.

Hibiya, J. 1999. Variationist Sociolinguistics. *The Handbook of Japanese Linguistics*, ed. N. Tsujimura, 101–20. Oxford: Blackwell.

Joos, M. 1958. *Readings in Linguistics*, ed. Martin Joos. New York: American Council of Learned Societies.

Kawahara, S. 2018. Phonology and Orthography: The Orthographic Characterization of Rendaku and Lyman's Law. *Glossa* 3(1), 10 (DOI: http://doi.org/10.5334/gjgl.368).

Kim, M. R., P. S. Beddor and J. Horrocks. 2002. The Contribution of Consonantal and Vocalic Information to the Perception of Korean Initial Stops. *Journal of Phonetics* 30:77–100.

Ladd, D. R. 2014. *Simultaneous Structure in Phonology*. Oxford: Oxford University Press.

Ladefoged, P. 1984. "Out of Chaos Comes Order": Physical, Biological, and Structural Patterns in Phonetics. *Proceedings of ICPhS 10*, ed. M. P. R. Van den Broecke and A. Cohen, 83–95. Dordrecht: Foris.

Ladefoged, P. 1990. On Dividing Phonetics and Phonology: Comments on the Papers by Clements and by Browman and Goldstein. *Papers in Laboratory Phonology I: Between the Grammar and Physics of Speech*, ed. J. Kingston and M. E. Beckman, 398–405. Cambridge: Cambridge University Press.

Lisker, L. and A. S. Abramson. 1964. A Cross-Language Study of Voicing in Initial Stops: Acoustical Measurements. *Word* 20:384–422.

Mielke, J. 2008. *The Emergence of Distinctive Features*. Oxford: Oxford University Press.

Postal, P. 1968. *Aspects of Phonological Theory*. New York: Harper & Row.

Raphael, L. J. et al. 1995. Intermediate Values of VOT. *Producing Speech: Contemporary Issues*, ed. F. Bell-Berti and L. J. Raphael, 117–27. Woodbury: AIP Press.

Riney, T. J., N. Takagi, K. Ota and Y. Uchida. 2007. The Intermediate Degree of VOT in Japanese Initial Voiceless Stops. *Journal of Phonetics* 35:439–43.

Saussure, F. de. 1916. *Cours de linguistique générale* (ed. C. Bailly, A. Séchehaye, and A. Riedlinger). Lausanne: Librairie Payot & Cie.

Takada, M. 2011. *Nihongo no gotō heisaon no kenkyū: VOT no kyōjiteki bunpu to tsūjiteki henka.* Tokyo: Kurosio.

Takayama, T. 2015. Historical Phonology. *The Handbook of Japanese Phonetics and Phonology*, ed. H. Kubozono, 621–50. Berlin: De Gruyter Mouton.

Toyama, E. 1972. Kindai no On'in. *Kōza Nihongoshi 2: On'inshi, mojishi*, ed. N. Nakata, 173–268). Tokyo: Taishūkan.

Iwano, Y. 2010. Ri-dakuon kō. Paper presented at the 24th General Meeting of the Phonetic Society of Japan, 9 October, Tokyo.

Vance, T. J. 1987. *An Introduction to Japanese Phonology.* Albany: SUNY Press.

Vance, T. J. 1996. Sequential Voicing in Sino-Japanese. *Journal of the Association of Teachers of Japanese* 30:22–43.

Vance, T. J. 2008. *The Sounds of Japanese.* Cambridge: Cambridge University Press.

Vance, T. J. 2011. *Rendaku* in Sino-Japanese: Reduplication and Coordination. *Japanese/Korean Linguistics 19*, ed. H.-M. Sohn et al., 465–482. Stanford: CSLI.

Vance, T. J. 2015. Rendaku. *The Handbook of Japanese Phonetics and Phonology*, ed. H. Kubozono, 397–441. Berlin: De Gruyter Mouton.

Vance, T. J. 2016. Introduction. *Sequential Voicing in Japanese: Papers from the NINJAL Rendaku Project*, ed. T. J. Vance and M. Irwin, 1–12. Amsterdam: John Benjamins.

Vance, T. J. 2017. *Rendaku* (Sequential Voicing) in Japanese Phonology. *Oxford Research Encyclopedias: Linguistics.* Oxford University Press (http://linguistics. oxfordre.com/view/10.1093/acrefore/9780199384655.001.0001/acrefore-9780199 384655-e-280?rskey=qv63bo&result=23).

Yoshida, S. and Y. Inokuchi, ed. 1962. *Meiji ikō kokuji mondai shoan shūsei.* Tokyo: Kazama Shobō.

Inhibition of Korean Palatalization in L2 English: Electropalatographic Data*

ALEXEI KOCHETOV, KELLY-ANN BLAKE, ANDREI MUNTEANU, FIONA WILSON, JESSICA YEUNG & LUKE ZHOU
University of Toronto

1   Introduction

Korean is known to have an allophonic process of palatalization whereby alveolar consonants become alveolopalatal before a high front vowel /i/ (Kim-Renaud 1974; Ahn 1998; Lee 1999, among others). This process is illustrated in the Korean data examples overleaf, indicating that the tense sibilant fricative /s*/, the nasal /n/, and the lateral /l/ become alveolopalatal [ɕ], [ɲ], and [ʎ] respectively. In contrast, no such palatalization process

---

* We would like to thank Yoonjung Kang for assistance with the materials preparation, as well Jeff Holliday, Suyeon Yun, and audiences of JK25, the University of Toronto Phonology/Phonetics Group, and the 2018 Montreal-Ottawa-Toronto Phonetics/Phonology Workshop for valuable feedback on presentations of this paper. All errors are our own. We are also grateful to the speakers for participation in the experiment. This research was conducted as part of *LIN1211H1S Advanced Phonetics* in Winter 2017, and was partly funded by a *Social Sciences and Humanities Research of Canada Grant* to the first author.

Japanese/Korean Linguistics 25.
Edited by Shin Fukuda, Mary Shin Kim, and Mee-Jeong Park.

occurs in English, where alveolars consistently maintain their place of articulation before /i/. This is evident in the lack of allophonic variation in (1b) (compared to (1a)), albeit some gradient coarticulation of consonants before /i/ is expected (Recasens 1999).

(1) a. Korean: palatalization before /i/

/sasil/	[saɕil]	'truth'
/manil/	[maɲil]	'if'
/p*alli/	[p*aʎʎi]	'quickly'

   b. English: lack of palatalization before /i/

/sæsi/	[sæsi]	'sassy'
/mʌni/	[mʌni]	'money'
/vɑli/	[vɑli]	'volley'

Previous phonetic research on second language (L2) acquisition has shown a strong influence of first language (L1) on speakers' L2 production (Flege 1987; K.H. Kang & Guion 2006; Hacking et al. 2016, among others). A classic example from this literature is the case of Voice Onset Time (VOT) in French and English stops. French voiceless stops are characterized by short VOT (below 30 ms), while English stops have much longer VOT in stops (well above 30 ms; Lisker & Abramson 1964). In his seminal study, Flege (1987) examined the VOT production of English speakers learning French as a second language and compared them to monolingual French speakers. He found that even advanced learners of French were still unable to produce stops with the same VOT as native French speakers.

Most experimental phonetic work on L2 acquisition has focused on learning phonological contrasts or their phonetic realizations (see Colantoni et al. 2015 for a review). There is considerably less work on the acquisition or inhibition of phonological or allophonic processes (see Zampini 1994; Cebrian 2000; Oh 2008). Furthermore, hardly any articulatory work has been done on the topic. Some notable exceptions include Ko's (2013) static palatography study of the acquisition of Korean coronal stops and affricates, and Hacking et al.'s (2016) study of the acquisition of Russian word-final palatalized consonants.

In an acoustic study, Oh (2008) examined L1 and L2 differences in the coarticulation of the high back vowel /u/ to the following coronal consonant /t/. French /u/ is known to be more phonetically back than English /u/. In addition, French is less susceptible to coronal coarticulation. That is, the fronting of the vowel after /t/ tends to be relatively small in magnitude, compared to the considerable fronting in English (e.g. French *tous* [tu] vs.

English *too* [tʉ]). Oh (2008) found that advanced English learners of French could partly inhibit the L1-specific fronting of /u/; that is, they could reduce the amount of fronting in L2 (vs. L1). However, they were still far from reaching the L2 target.

The focus of this study is on the allophonic process of Korean palatalization (shown in (1a)). Our goal was to investigate whether native Korean speakers transfer or inhibit the L1-specific process of palatalization in their L2 English, in a way similar to that of English speakers acquiring French /u/ coarticulation in Oh (2008). This was done using electropalatography (EPG), a method that tracks the contact between the tongue and the palate over time (Gibbon & Nicolaidis 1999), and thus allowing for precise measurements of palatalization.

Given the previous research, one may expect one of two possible outcomes. The first outcome would involve a wholesale transfer of palatalization in English, so that /s, n, l/ would palatalize in English production just like they do in Korean. The second outcome would be complete inhibition of palatalization, so that the coronal consonants fail to palatalize in L2 English (while possibly undergoing gradient coarticulation), unlike they do in Korean. We will refer to these outcomes as Hypothesis 1 (transfer of palatalization) and Hypothesis 2 (inhibition of palatalization) respectively. Given Oh's (2008) results, however, it is more reasonable for advanced or intermediate learners to exhibit a combination of these two outcomes: If Korean learners of English inhibit palatalization in their second language, they might only do it to a limited degree, depending on their level of L2 proficiency.

It should be noted that Korean fricatives (fortis /s*/ and lenis /s/) have previously received considerable attention in the phonetic literature (e.g. Cho et al. 2002; Holliday 2010, 2012; Lee & Jongman 2012), and have been investigated using articulatory methods (e.g. EPG by Baik 1998, MRI by H. Kim et al. 2011, and static palatography by Anderson et al. 2004 and Ko 2013). Among the latter studies, only Baik (1998) studied the effect of palatalization on /s*, s/, reporting a narrower central channel and a greater overall contact for the consonants before /i/, as produced by his single speaker. To our knowledge, the articulation of Korean alveolar sonorants /n, l/ has not been studied in general, or with respect to its allophonic variation. Thus, while the focus of this paper is on L1 and L2 differences in palatalization, its secondary goal is to provide a fuller articulatory description of Korean coronal contrasts.

2　Method

2.1　Participants

Custom-made artificial palates were made for two native speakers of Korean, one female and one male. Both were in their early forties; they were originally from Seoul, South Korea, and have been living in Toronto for less than three years. They studied English from the age of twelve, but have only been speaking it regularly since moving to Canada. Based on the speakers' responses to a language background questionnaire, they were considered intermediate to advanced learners of English.

2.2　Materials

The Korean stimuli consisted of thirty six established loanwords from English, taken from the *National Academy of the Korean Language* survey (Kwuklipkwukeyenkwuwen [NAKL] 1991; cf. Y. Kang 2003). We used English loanwords to maximally control for context, so that speakers were producing nearly the same words in both languages. The target segments were /s*, n, l/ before /i/ in word-initial and medial positions. The controls were these same consonants, but before vowels other than /i/, illustrated in Table 1 (a).

The speakers' English production was recorded a week later, and the stimuli for this were the thirty six English words that corresponded to our Korean loanwords. The target segments were, again, /s, n, l/; here they occurred either before /i/ or /ɪ/. The controls were the same consonants before other vowels. A subset of the stimuli is shown in Table 1 (b).

		a. Korean condition			**b. English condition**	
/s(*)/	_i	sicun	시즌	[ɕ*idʑʌn]	season	[ˈsizən]
		kasip	가십	[kaɕ*ip]	gossip	[ˈɡɑsɪp]
	_V	saikhul	사이클	[s*aikʰɯl]	cycle	[ˈsajkəl]
		khaseythu	카세트	[kʰas*etʰɯ]	cassette	[kəˈsɛt]
/n/	_i	nikheyl	니켈	[ɲikʰel]	nickel	[ˈnɪkəl]
		lenning	러닝	[rʌɲiŋ]	running	[ˈɹʌnɪŋ]
	_V	naypkhin	냅킨	[nɛpkʰin]	napkin	[ˈnæpkɪn]
		ponesu	보너스	[ponʌsɯ]	bonus	[ˈbownəs]
/l/	_i	lithe	리터	[ʎitʰʌ]	litre	[ˈlitəɹ]
		sollitu	솔리드	[soʎʎidɯ]	solid	[ˈsɑlɪd]
	_V	laymphu	램푸	[rampʰɯ]	lamp	[læmp]
		saylletu	샐러드	[sɛllʌdɯ]	salad	[ˈsæləd]

TABLE 1 A subset of stimuli used in the experiment.

The stimuli for each condition were produced 6 times in a carrier sentence *iketto __ ita* (이게 또__이다, 'This another __') for Korean and 'I saw __ over there' for English. A total of 216 tokens per speaker were collected for each language condition.

A few comments are in order on the adaptation of English sounds in Korean (see Table 1 a). English /s/ is typically adapted in Korean as /s*/, although this is not reflected in the orthography (Tranter 2000; Y. Kang 2008). Word-initial /l/ before vowels other than /i/ is expected to be realized as a tap (Lee 1999; while palatalizing before /i/). English intervocalic /l/ is adapted as a geminate lateral. Both English /i/ and /ɪ/ are adapted as Korean /i/ (Tranter 2000; Kang 2003), and thus are expected to trigger palatalization.

2.3 Instrumentation

A WinEPG system (Wrench et al. 2002) was used to collect the data using a sampling rate of 100 Hz. The participants wore custom-made artificial acrylic palates with sixty two electrodes. A sample palate is shown in Figure 1 (left). The palate electrodes are schematically represented as a grid of eight rows and eight columns (with two electrodes missing in the first row) in Figure 1 (right).

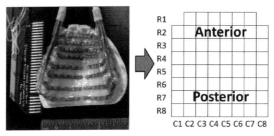

FIGURE 1 A sample EPG palate (left) and the schematic organization of electrodes by column and row (right).

2.4 Analysis

For each consonant of interest, the frame of maximum contact was annotated, and contact values (numbers of contacted electrodes) were automatically extracted using the *Articulate Assistant* software (Wrench et al. 2002). As a measure of linguopalatal contact, we used the Quotient of electrode activation in the posterior region of the palate (last four rows), Qp. Following Hacking et al. (2016), Qp was expected to be considerably higher for palatal(ized) consonants than their alveolar counterparts. Figure 2 presents sample palate profiles for [n] and [ɲ], together with the corresponding Qp values. Note that both consonants have an anterior closure, which is typical for alveolars and is also often observed for alveolopalatals (Recasens 1999). The two, however, differ in the amount of contact in the posterior region.

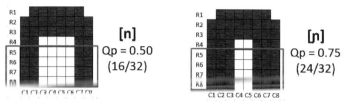

FIGURE 2 An illustration of the Quotient of electrode activation in the posterior region (Qp) measure used in the study.

The results were evaluated statistically using *Linear Mixed Effects Model (LMER)* with the nlme package (Pinheiro et al. 2016) for R (R Core Team 2014). The models were run separately by Condition (Korean, English) with fixed factors Type (target (_i), control (_V)), Variable (s, n, l), and Position (initial, medial), and random factors Speaker and Item. The intercept was set to /s/ in the control items and the α value to 0.05. Given the small sample size, statistical significance should be considered with caution.

3 Results

The results are first presented separately by the language condition, followed by a comparison across the conditions.

3.1 The Korean Condition

The LMER model for the Korean condition revealed that consonants before /i/ (the target type) had significantly higher Qp than the same consonants before other vowels (Type control: β = -0.253, SE = 0.043, DF = 59, t = -5.812, p < 0.0001; cf. Intercept = 0.696). In addition, the consonant /l/ showed significantly lower Qp than /s*/ (Variable l: β = -0.244, SE = 0.043, DF = 59, t = -5.613, p < 0.0001; cf. Intercept = 0.696); the difference between /n/ and /s*/ was not significant (p = 0.500). Further, neither Position (p = 0.305), nor any interactions of the factors were significant.

The differences between the contexts and the consonants can be seen in Figure 3. Sample palates for the speaker KM, shown in Figure 4, further indicate considerable differences in contact, particularly in the posterior region. In sum, the results clearly showed the expected palatalization of alveolars before /i/. There were also manner differences, with the lateral having the least amount of contact.

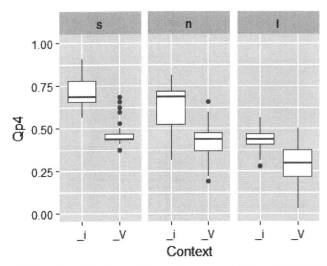

FIGURE 3 Boxplot of Qp4 by context and consonant (/s*, n, l/) in the Korean condition.

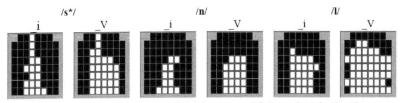

FIGURE 4 Sample palate tokens (initial context, KM speaker) in the Korean condition.

3.2 The English Condition

The LMER model for the English condition revealed no significant differences between the contexts in target and control items (Context: p = 0.201). Among the consonants, /l/ showed significantly less contact than /s/ (Variable l: β = -0.169, SE = 0.037, DF = 59, t = -4.590, p < 0.0001; cf. Intercept = 0.482), while /n/ did not differ from /s/ (p = 0.170).

These results are illustrated in the boxplot in Figure 5. Note that the consonants before /i/ showed on average higher values than the same consonants before other vowels; yet these differences were rather small, and not significant. Sample palates in Figure 6 further demonstrate the near-lack of contextual differences.

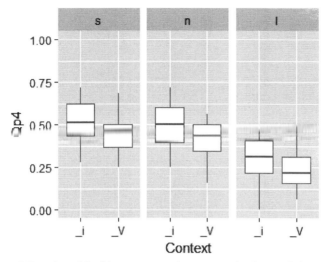

FIGURE 5 Boxplot of Qp4 by context and consonant in the English condition.

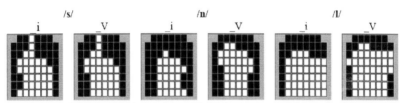

FIGURE 6 Sample palate tokens (initial context, KM speaker) in the Korean condition.

In addition to the context and consonant results, the medial position showed significantly more contact than the initial position (Position medial: $\beta = 0.088$, SE = 0.037, DF = 59, t = 2.398, p = 0.018). Yet, the factor position was also involved in significant interactions with consonant (/n/: p = 0.004; /l/: p = 0.036) and with both consonant and type (for /l/: p = 0.008). These interactions indicated that the position differences were observed for /s/ and /l/, but not /n/ (which in fact showed the opposite pattern); these differences were further affected by context, possibly reflecting some word-specific effects. It should be noted that some of these differences were speaker-specific: they were observed for KF, who showed overall greater contextual effects, but not KM. Individual differences are further explored in the next section.

The important finding obtained here was that palatalization was not clearly evident in the English data, in contrast to the Korean condition data.

Just as in the Korean condition, however, the lateral showed less contact than the other consonants.

3.3   Both Conditions

Combining the two sets of data, Figure 7 presents mean differences between the target (_i) and control (_V) contexts by condition (Korean and English), separately for each speaker. The reduction of the difference in the English condition relative to the Korean condition was substantial, particularly for the male speaker. While both speakers still showed contextual differences in the English condition, these were relatively minor. Recall that some small-scale differences were expected in English due to consonant-to-vowel coarticulation (Recasens 1999). Thus the results clearly demonstrate that the allophonic process of palatalization was present in the Korean data, but partially or fully inhibited in the English data.

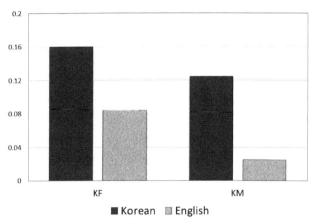

FIGURE 7 Barplot of mean differences between the contexts (_i vs. _V) by language condition, separately by speaker.

4   Discussion and Conclusion

Based on the limited findings in the previous literature on the acquisition of L2 processes (Oh 2008), two possible outcomes were predicted. The first predicted outcome was that the speakers would transfer their L1 palatalization from Korean to their English, producing similar levels of palatalization in the target context (_i). The second predicted outcome was that speakers would successfully inhibit the transfer of palatalization from Korean to English, resulting in maintenance of the alveolar place of articulation in English target contexts. Given that the speakers were intermediate to advanced learners of English, we predicted that, rather than an extreme result, the speakers might instead show a limited, but not fully native-like inhibition of palatalization.

The results described above are largely consistent with the predictions of the previous literature on the acquisition of coarticulation (Oh 2008) and phonemic contrasts (Flege 1987; K.H. Kang & Guion 2006; Hacking et al. 2016, among others). Similar to this previous work, the speakers in the current study moved towards, but did not fully achieve, native-like pronunciation of the L2 target sounds (although we cannot be fully certain of this in the absence of English controls). However, the speakers in the current study appear to be more successful at reaching their L2 targets than those of previous researchers. In particular, this was evident for the speaker KM who showed a dramatic reduction of palatalization in the English condition.

There are several possible explanations for this discrepancy. The first possibility is that the allophonic process under investigation is categorical (i.e. palatalization as a shift of alveolars to alveolopalatals), whereas the coarticulation process investigated by Oh (2008) was gradient in nature (i.e. partial fronting of the vowel). The categorical process may therefore be more salient to speakers than the gradient process, accounting for the difference in their ability to inhibit the process when learning a new contrast in their L2.

Another way in which the results of the current study differ from previous findings is in comparison with Hacking et al. (2016). In that study, English speakers of Russian largely failed to acquire Russian phonemic palatalization (/pʲ, tʲ, sʲ, nʲ, lʲ/) in word-final position. This was despite the participants being advanced learners of Russian (Hacking et al. 2016). While both this previous study and the current study investigated palatalization, the first one involved the acquisition of palatalization as a phonemic contrast, rather than an allophonic process. In addition, the learners acquiring Russian palatalization did not have such contrast in their own language. The current work, however, investigated palatalization as a process, as well as its inhibition rather than acquisition. This difference may suggest that inhibiting a process or contrast may be easier on the learner than acquiring a new process or contrast. However, this contradicts previous findings showing that inhibiting a process, such as final obstruent devoicing, can be rather difficult for learners (see Cebrian 2000 on the transfer of Catalan process to L2 English). It is possible that relative difficulty of inhibiting a process depends on the features involved (e.g. voicing vs. place), as well as on its allophonic/phonemic status. Further work is needed to investigate these questions within and across languages.

Another possible issue is the difference between Korean and English vowels in the materials. Recall that in our target items the consonants were followed by /i/ in the Korean condition and by both /i/ and /ɪ/ in the English condition. A successful acquisition of the English lax /ɪ/ by our speakers would be expected to impede the transfer of palatalization, at least to some degree. This is because this vowel is absent in Korean (Lee 1999) and is less likely to trigger palatalization or coarticulation in general, given its lower and more back quality. It is also possible that our speakers produced English /i/ differently (lower and more back) from Korean /i/, which could have also impeded the transfer of palatalization. Given this, it is necessary to extend the current analysis of the data to the following vowels.

An additional research goal of the current study was to improve the understanding of Korean palatalization and articulation in general, independent of investigating an L1 and L2 interaction. As mentioned earlier, past articulatory work on the topic has been mostly limited to obstruents (Anderson et al. 2004; H. Kim et al. 2011; Ko 2013) and has not specifically investigated palatalization (with Baik 1998 being an exception). The results of the current study do contribute to the broader understanding of Korean consonant production, by providing a new finding for Korean coronal sonorants and palatalization in general. Specifically, the L1 realization of Korean palatalization varies depending on the manner of the consonant in question. The degree of palatalization is much smaller in magnitude for /l/ than for the other two consonants, /s*/ and /n/, shown in Figure 8 (see also Figure 4). Indeed, the palatalization of the lateral is arguably better described as an /l/ with a secondary palatal articulation ([lʲ]), rather than as an actual palatal lateral ([ʎ]), which is how it is commonly described in the literature (Kim-Renaud 1974, Lee 1999, among others). While it is expected for laterals to show less side contact than for other consonants, (alveolo-)palatal laterals have been noted to be produced with a substantial amount of contact and a more retracted constriction (see Recasens et al. 1993 on palatals in Catalan and Italian). Notably, even the Russian palatalized lateral /lʲ/ in Hacking et al. (2016) showed more palatal contact than palatalized /sʲ/, which is the reverse of what we observed for Korean.

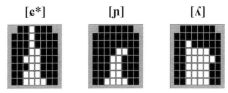

FIGURE 8 Representative palates for alveolopalatal variants of /s*, n, l/ by KF.

To conclude, the results from the current study add to the growing research on L1-L2 influences on speech production. Further work is needed to confirm our current findings. This should be done in particular using a more extensive dataset and a larger participant sample. The latter should include learners of varying proficiency levels, as well as native English speaker controls.

References

Ahn, S.-C. 1998. *An Introduction to Phonology*. Seoul: Hansin Munhwasa.

Anderson, V., Ko, I., O'Grady, W., & Choo, M. 2004. A palatographic investigation of place of articulation in Korean coronal obstruents. *Korean Linguistics* 12:1-24.

Baik, W. (1998). On tensity of Korean fricatives (Electropalatographic study), *Korean Journal of Speech Sciences* 4:135-45.

Cebrian, J. 2000. Transferability and productivity of L1 rules in Catalan-English interlanguage. *Studies in Second Language Acquisition* 22:1–26.

Colantoni, L., Steele, J., & Escudero, P. 2015. *Second Language Speech*. Cambridge University Press.

Cho, T., Jun, S., & Ladefoged, P. 2002. Acoustic and aerodynamic correlates of Korean stops and fricatives, *Journal of Phonetics* 30:193-228.

Flege, J. E. 1987. The production of "new" and "similar" phones in a foreign language: Evidence for the effect of equivalence classification. *Journal of Phonetics* 15:47-65.

Gibbon, F. & Nicolaidis, K. 1999. Palatography. In *Coarticulation: Data, theory and techniques*, eds. W. Hardcastle & N. Hewlett, 229–45. Cambridge: Cambridge University Press.

Hacking, J. F., Smith, B. L., Nissen, S. L., & Allen, H. 2016. Russian palatalized and unpalatalized coda consonants: An electropalatographic and acoustic analysis of native speaker and L2 learner productions. *Journal of Phonetics* 54:98-108.

Holliday, J. J. 2010. An acoustic study of L2 perceptual acquisition of Korean fricatives, *Harvard Studies in Korean Linguistics* 13:17-32.

Holliday, J J. 2012. The acoustic realization of the Korean sibilant fricative contrast in Seoul and Daegu. *Phonetics and Speech Sciences* 4:67-74.

Kang, Y. 2003. Perceptual similarity in loanword adaptation: English postvocalic word-final stops in Korean. *Phonology* 20:219–73.

Kang, Y. 2008. The adaptation of English /s/ in Korean. *Inquiries into Korean linguistics* 3:1-14.

Kang, K. H., & Guion, S. G. 2006. Phonological systems in bilinguals: Age of learning effects on the stop consonant systems of Korean-English bilinguals. *Journal of the Acoustical Society of America* 119:1672-83.

Kim, H. Maeda, S., & Honda, K. 2011. The laryngeal characterization of Korean fricatives: Stroboscopic cine-MRI data. *Journal of Phonetics* 39:626-41.

Kim-Renaud, Y.-K. 1974. Korean consonantal phonology. Doctoral dissertation, University of Hawai'i at Manoa.

Ko, I. 2013. The articulation of Korean coronal obstruents: Data from heritage speakers and second language learners. Doctoral dissertation, University of Hawai'i at Manoa.

Kwuklipkwukeyenkwuwen [The National Academy of the Korean Language] 1991. *Oylaye sayong silthay cosa: 1990 nyento*. [Survey of the state of loanword usage: 1990.] Seoul: Kwuklipkwukeyenkwuwen.

Lee, H. B. 1999. Korean. In *The handbook of the International Phonetic Association*, 120-3. Cambridge: Cambridge University Press.

Lee, H. & Jongman, A. 2016. A diachronic investigation of the vowels and fricatives in Korean: An acoustic comparison of the Seoul and South Kyungsang dialects. *Journal of the International Phonetic Association* 46:157-84.

Lisker, L. & Abramson, A. S., 1964. A cross-language study of voicing in initial stops: Acoustical measurements. *Word*, 20:384-422.

Oh, E. 2008. Coarticulation in non-native speakers of English and French: An acoustic study. *Journal of Phonetics* 36:361-84.

Recasens, D. 1999. Lingual coarticulation. In *Coarticulation: Theory, Data, and Techniques*, eds. W. J. Hardcastle & N. Hewlett, 80–104. Cambridge: Cambridge University Press.

Recasens, D., Farnetani, E., Fontdevila, J., & Pallarès, M. D. 1993. An electropalatographic study of alveolar and palatal consonants in Catalan and Italian. *Language & Speech* 36: 213-34.

Tranter, N. 2000. The phonology of English loan-words in Korean. *Word* 51:377-404.

Wrench, A. A., Gibbon, F. E., McNeill, A. M., & Wood, S. E. 2002. An EPG therapy protocol for remediation and assessment of articulation disorders. In *Proceedings of ICSLP-2002*, eds. J. H. L. Hansen & B. Pellom, pp. 965–8. Denver, CO.

Zampini, M. L. 1994. The role of native language transfer and task formality in the acquisition of Spanish spirantization. *Hispania* 77:470-81.

Perception of Tonal Clash: Final Accent vs. No Accent in Interrogative Melodies of Tokyo Japanese

MAYUKI MATSUI

National Institute for Japanese Language and Linguistics/ Japan Society for the Promotion of Science

HYUN KYUNG HWANG

RIKEN Center for Brain Science

1   Introduction*

1.1   Rationale

The phonetic implementation of prosodic contrast is constrained by time. Pitch contours can be modified in the contexts (i) where the duration of tone bearing units (such as syllables or moras) are too short to implement a certain tonal event as a result of a fast speech rate (see, e.g., Cho and Flemming 2015 for Seoul Korean), and (ii) where tonal events are too dense to manifest themselves (see, e.g., Odé 2005 for Russian). The present study

*This study is a part of the NINJAL collaborative research project (project name: Word Prosody and Sentence Prosody), and partially supported by KAKENHI grants (#17J08493 to the first author; #26244022 to the second author). We would like to thank Carlos Gussenhoven and the audience at the JK25 conference for valuable input during the course of this project. All remaining errors are of course our own. Also, special thanks to Manami Hirayama for helping us recruit participants and to the participants themselves for taking part in the experiment.

Japanese/Korean Linguistics 25.
Edited by Shin Fukuda, Mary Shin Kim, and Mee-Jeong Park.

focuses on one of the latter cases, an instance of tonal clash resolution. Here, the term tonal clash is used to refer to the clash of multiple tonal events within a single tone-bearing unit as a result of a lack of time, as with, for example, the drop of segment(s).

It has been acknowledged that different languages resolve tonal clash in various, language-specific ways. For example, there can occur the compression of pitch contours (see, e.g., Grønnum 1991 for Danish, Caspers and van Hauven 1993 for Dutch, Ladd 1996, 2008 for overview) or truncated (see, e.g., Grice 1995 for Palermo Italian, Odé 2005 for Russian, Ladd 1996, 2008 for overview) in the context of a tonal clash. Such contour modification strategies can result in phonological neutralization or the apparent loss of contrast (see, e.g., Odé 2005 for Russian). Most prior studies have focused on contour modification strategies in what are generally called *intonation languages*, where pitch functions only to convey post-lexical information.

Unlike previous studies dealing with tonal clash in these intonation languages, this study demonstrates the involvement of lexical contrast and neutralization in tonal clash in Tokyo Japanese (TJ), where pitch functions to convey both lexical and post-lexical information (Pierrehumbert and Beckman 1988, Kubozono 1993 for review).

In TJ, it has been widely acknowledged that the lexical contrast between final-accented and non-accented words is either neutralized or reduced, unless they are followed by a particle (Sakuma 1929, Sugito 1968, 1982, Poser 1984, Vance 1995, Sugiyama 2012). Recently, however, Matsui and Hwang (forthcoming) reported that certain speakers produce distinct pitch patterns for contrast even in denser tonal contexts involving interrogative boundary tones. Here, we examine whether listeners are able to perceive such a covert lexical contrast in interrogative melodies.

In the following section, we review the background of TJ (Section 1.2). Section 2 describes the methodology, Section 3 reports on the perceptual study and Section 4 discusses our results and concludes the paper.

1.2 Final vs. No Accent and Tonal Clash in Tokyo Japanese

The prosody system of TJ consists of both lexical and post-lexical prosody, including a lexical pitch accent (H*+L) and boundary tones, which occur at the edge of a prosodic phrase.

1.2.1 Lexical Prosody

Tokyo Japanese features a falling pitch accent (H*+L; Pierrehumbert and Beckman 1988, Kubozono 1993, among others), which is contrastive in terms of the presence/absence of the accent and the location of the accent. For example, a bimoraic disyllabic lexical word, whose prosodic length is the minimum required to exhibit a contrast in accent location (initial vs. final) and accentedness (accented vs. non-accented), can show a three-way contrast such as, *ha'si* 'chopsticks' (initial-accented) vs. *hasi'* 'edge' (final-accented) vs. *hasi* 'bridge' (non-accented), where pitch accent is indicated by apostrophes.

As mentioned in Section 1.1, there remains a debate over whether final- and non-accented words are acoustically distinguishable in cases where no particle follows and/or when they are produced in isolation (see Matsui and Hwang forthcoming for review): some studies claim that final-accented words are distinguishable for some speakers (see, e.g., Sakuma 1929, Sugito 1982, Vance 1995. See also, Pierrehumbert and Beckman 1988, Warner 1997 for theoretical discussion) but not for others (see, e.g., Sugito 1968, Poser 1984, Sugiyama 2012).

Few perceptual studies deal with the controvercial status of lexical contrast, using the stimuli that are either natural or manipulated. Studies using natural stimuli have shown that listeners cannot reliably distinguish final-accented words from non-accent words in isolation (Neustupný 1978, Sugito 1982, Vance 1995, Sugiyama 2012); in this context, listeners were biased toward final-accented words, resulting in chance level identification accuracy. Among studies with manipulated stimuli, Yoneyama (2002) showed that final-accented and non-accented words, created by eliminating particles from the original speech, were slightly different in terms of similarity judgement. Sugiyama (2012) found that listeners' responses to final-accented words vs. non-accented words were at chance level, whether or not the stimuli were natural, produced in isolation, or manipulated by the removal of a particle.

To summarize, the results of previous production studies suggest that the contrast between final accent and no accent is covert or even lost when no particle follows the word or it is produced in isolation. Perceptural studies have also suggested that listeners show limited ability to perceive this contrast. It should be noted that all the studies reviewed above have focused on lexical prosody, without considering any interaction between lexical and post-lexical prosody.

1.2.2   Post-lexical Prosody and Tonal Clash

Recently, Matsui and Hwang (forthcoming) expanded the discussion of final and no accent from an accent-intonation interface perspective: taking the post-lexical structure into account, TJ includes boundary tones at the edge of a prosodic phrase. In a neutral utterance, such as when a word is read in isolation, it is assumed that a default low tone is linked to the final mora. As in other languages, TJ boundary tones convey a pragmatic interpretation of the utterance (Igarashi 2015 for review), including questioning (Maeda and Venditti 1998).

Matsui and Hwang (forthcoming) examined the production of final- and non-accented words in interrogative melodies, while previous studies tested neutral or decralative utterances although this was not explicitedly stated. In interrogative melodies, the final accent potentially clashes with a rising boundary tone. Matsui and Hwang's results showed that (i) both final- and non-accented words created an apparently identical rising contour; however, (ii) the phonetic details of this countor are specific to the given speaker. Some speaker were found to distinguish final accents from no accents with a higher peak fundamental frequency (F0), while other speakers did not distinguish the contrast. The results are consistent both with normally produced speech and the reiterated versions of normal speech, in which segmental variation is minimized but pitch patterns of the existing words are reiterated (Larkey 1983, Warner 1997, Matsui and Hwang 2018). This suggests that the resolution of tonal clashes can be speaker-specific, resulting in either complete lexical neutralization or partial preservation of a contrast (see Matsui and Hwang forthcoming for further theoretical discussion).

1.2.3   Research Question and Hypothesis

While Matsui and Hwang (forthcoming) found an F0 peak difference between final- and non-accented words in interrogative melodies at least for the speaker, they did not address whether the difference in the F0 plays a role in perception.

The present study thus examines whether native listeners are able to perceive covert lexical contrasts as a consequence of tonal clash resolution. Previous perceptual studies dealing with declarative utterances suggested that listeners are not able to distinguish this contrast reliably. If this is also the case for interrogative melodies involving rising tones, we would expect that listeners could not reliably distinguish final accents from no accents, even when the speaker signals the F0 difference.

2   Methods

2.1   Participants

The participants were twenty native listeners of Japanese, who grew up in Tokyo or the surrounding metropolitan area (Kanagawa, Saitama, or Chiba); of these, thirteen were female and the others were male. The mean listener age was thirty-two years old, ranging from eighteen to fifty-one. All reported no known history of hearing or speaking disorders.

2.2   Stimuli

We used *reiterant speech* (Larkey 1983, Warner 1997, Matsui and Hwang 2018) as auditory stimuli. The stimuli consisted of the sequence of non sense syllables [ma], in which segmental variation is minimized but the pitch pattern is accessible. These stimuli were taken from among the subset tokens used in the authors' previous acoustic study (Matsui and Hwang forthcoming, see also Matsui and Hwang 2018). In Matsui and Hwang (forthcoming), initial-accented words (e.g., /o'no/), final-accented words (e.g., /imo'/) and non-accented words (e.g., /ume/) were recorded with rising tones. All target words consisted of two light syllables (i.e., [ma.ma]). In addition to the target words, we also recorded (i) the same set of words followed by the nominative particle -*ga* (e.g., /ono/+/ga/), where initial-, final- and non-accented words were contrastive (e.g., Sugiyama 2012). Such tokens were produced by a female speaker (Speaker FMN), who distinguished final-accented words from non-accented words (Matsui and Hwang forthcoming). The list of the stimuli is given in Tables 1a and 1b.

Initial accent (2 words × 4 repetitions)		Final accent (2 words × 4 repetitions)		No accent (2 words × 4 repetitions)	
Orthography	Phonemic	Orthography	Phonemic	Orthography	Phonemic
春？	haru	花？	hana	鼻？	hana
斧？	ono	芋？	imo	梅？	ume

TABLE 1a Stimuli (target condition).

Initial accent (2 words × 4 repetitions)		Final accent (2 words × 4 repetitions)		No accent (2 words × 4 repetitions)	
Orthography	Phonemic	Orthography	Phonemic	Orthography	Phonemic
春が？	haru-ga	花が？	hana-ga	鼻が？	hana-ga
斧が？	ono-ga	芋が？	imo-ga	梅が？	ume-ga

TABLE 1b Stimuli (control condition).

The tokens were recorded using a portable recorder (MARANTZ PMD661) and a microphone (SHURE SM10A) at a 44.1 kHz sampling rate and a 16-bit quantification level. The intensity of the stimuli was scaled at 70dB average intensity for the perceptual experiment. The sample F0 contours of the final- and non-accented stimuli are shown in Figures 1 and 2.[1]

---

[1] It should be noted that this speaker frequently produced initial-accented words with a creaky voice both in control and target conditions, thus making it difficult to obtain F0. We nevertheless included the initial-accented items in the stimuli to test all possible contrasts.

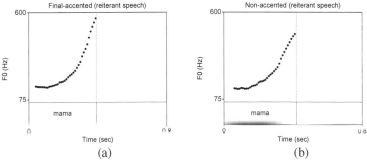

FIGURE 1 Sample F0 contours of final-accented (a) and non-accented (b) stimuli (target condition).

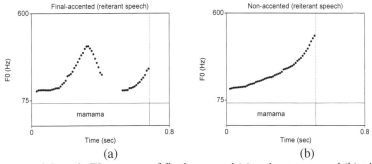

FIGURE 2 Sample F0 contours of final-accented (a) and non-accented (b) stimuli (control condition).

2.3 Procedures

Participants completed a forced-choice identification task: for each trial, only one stimulus was presented, and the participants were asked to choose what they heard from among three possible choices. For example, in one trial, listeners heard a (reiterated) *imo'* stimulus, and then three possible choices in Chinese characters were presented on the screen: '芋' (imo), '斧' (ono) or '梅' (ume). The position of the button on the screen was randomized.

The experiment consisted of two types of stimuli sets; One set (Triplet A) consisted of *ha'ru, hana'*, and *hana*. Another set (Triplet B) consisted of *o'no, imo'*, and *ume*. Triplets A and B were tested with and without particle. The experiment was thus divided into four blocks of the four conditions. A total of 5760 responses were obtained (3 accent types, 2 stimuli sets, 2 repetitions, 6 randomized button positions, 4 blocks, 20 listeners).

The experiment was implemented using Praat (Boersma and Weenink 2010). To control the possible effects of task-order, half of the participants were tested with stimuli set A first, and then the set B; the other half of the participants were tested in the opposite order. Stimuli were presented via headphones (SONY MDR-10RNC).

2.5 Statistics

To examine the effects of type of accent on the listeners' responses, binomial mixed-effects models were fitted to the data. We constructed two types of model: One model to predict listeners' response type using the Accent type of the stimuli (Model I) and the other to predict listeners' response type using the F0 value (Model II).

Both in Models I and II, listeners' responses were the dependent variables. The models were constructed per response type (i.e., three separate models for initial, final, and no responses respectively). The listeners' responses were converted to a binary format (i.e., non-initial = 0 vs. initial response = 1, non-final = 0 vs. final response = 1, and non-no = 0 vs. no response = 1). The individual listeners and items were specified as random effects. In Model I, the fixed effect was the accent type of the stimuli (initial vs. final vs. no). In Model II, the fixed effect was the F0 value of the stimuli. All three contrasts (i.c., initial vs. final, initial vs. no, no vs. final) were tested by changing intercept specifications. Statistical analyses were conducted using the lme4 package (version 1.1-7, Bates et al. 2014) in *R* 3.1.0 (R Core Team 2014).

3 Results

3.1 Overall Performance

Figure 3 shows the listeners' overall correct response rates. In the control condition, where a particle follows the word, the existing three-way contrast among initial, final, and no accent should be maintained; in the target condition, where no particle follows, the contrast between a final accent and no accent is considered to be neutralized. Figure 3 indicates that, as expected, listeners were able to identify the three-way contrast in the control condition with nearly perfect accuracy (94.2%), while they frequently misidentified contrasts in the target condition. In the following section, we will take a closer look at the target condition.

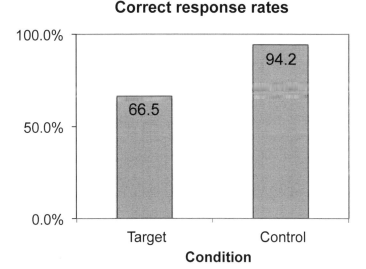

FIGURE 3 Overall correct response rates.

3.2   Effects of Accent Type on the Response

Table 2 shows the percentages for each response, broken down by stimuli type in the target condition. The given matrix shows that overall, listeners could reliably identify the initial-accented words (98.3% correct rate), while they frequently misidentified final- and non-accented words (50.6% correct rate for final accent, 51.5% correct rate for no accent).[2]

Response → Stimulus ↓	Initial	Final	No	Total
Initial	98.3	1.0	0.7	100
Final	2.3	50.6	47.1	100
No	1.0	47.5	51.5	100

TABLE 2 Response rates by accent type in the target condition (Unit: %).
Shaded cells indicate correct response rates.

---

[2] A follow-up perceptual test suggested that, interestingly, even the speaker (Speaker FMN) who produced the stimuli could not reliably distinguish final-accented words from non-accented words.

To examine the effect of the accent type on listeners' responses across individual listeners and words, binomial mixed-effects models for initial, final and no responses were fitted to the data. As stated in Section 2.5, the models were fitted separately to the data for each response type. The model summaries are provided in Tables 3, 4, and 5 respectively.[3]

The results reveal two major points. First, if we look at the contrasts between initial vs. final and initial vs. no, the results show that listeners could distinguish those contrasts at a statistically significant level. Second, in contrast, the effect of accent type on the response was not significant for the final vs. no contrast in all the models as shown in Tables 3, 4, and 5.

Contrast	Coefficient	SE	z	p	OR
Initial vs. No	**8.7513**	0.4787	18.28	< 0.001	6318.897
Initial vs. Final	**8.4971**	0.4439	19.14	< 0.001	4900.537
No vs. Final	-0.2542	0.5085	-0.50	= 0.617	N.A.

TABLE 3 Model summary for 'initial accent' response data.

Dependent variable: Response (0 for 'non-initial' response, 1 for 'initial' response); Fixed effect: accent type of the stimuli. The underlined levels of the accent type are intercepts. Statistically significant coefficients are marked in bold.

Contrast	Coefficient	SE	z	p	OR
Initial vs. No	**-3.6877**	0.2210	-16.68	< 0.001	0.025
Initial vs. Final	**-3.8347**	0.2211	-17.34	< 0.001	0.022
No vs. Final	-0.1470	0.0917	-1.60	= 0.109	N.A.

TABLE 4 Model summary for 'final accent' response data.

Dependent variable: Response (0 for 'non-final' response, 1 for 'final' response); Fixed effect: accent type of the stimuli. The underlined levels of the accent type are intercepts. Statistically significant coefficients are marked in bold.

---

[3] In the binomial mixed-effect model (a type of logistic regression), coefficients are log-odds. Therefore, the odds ratio (OR) was calculated by exponentiation of the coefficient if it was significant.

Contrast	Coefficient	SE	z	p	OR
Initial vs. No	**4.6795**	0.3413	13.71	< 0.001	107.716
Initial vs. Final	**4.5238**	0.3414	13.25	< 0.001	92.185
No vs. Final	-0.1556	0.0918	-1.70	= 0.0899	N.A.

TABLE 5 Model summary for 'no accent' response data.

Dependent variable: Response (0 for 'non-no' response, 1 for 'no' response); Fixed effect: accent type of the stimuli. The underlined levels of the accent type are intercepts. Statistically significant coefficients are marked in bold.

3.3   The Effect of F0 Peak Value on the Listeners' Response

In this section, we further investigate listeners' perception of the contrast between final and no accent to determine whether F0 peaks are correlated with listeners' identification of placement. Figure 4 shows correct response rates as a function of the F0 peak of the stimuli. This peak for the final- and non-accented stimuli ranged from 370.4 Hz to 523.8 Hz. As seen in Figure 4, higher F0 peaks are found for final-accented stimuli than for non-accented stimuli, although there is a large overlap.

To examine the effects of the F0 peak value on the listeners' responses of 'final' or 'no' responses across individual listeners and words, we separated final-accented and non-accented stimuli and applied binomial mixed-effects models to the data. The results showed that the fixed effects of F0 peak were not significant for either final-accented stimuli [coefficient: -0.001811, Std. Error: $0.002118, z = -0.855, p = 0.393$] and non-accented stimuli [coefficient: -0.0001806, Std. Error: $0.0012882, z = -0.140, p = 0.889$]. This suggests that F0 peaks do not play an important role in listeners' identification of accent.

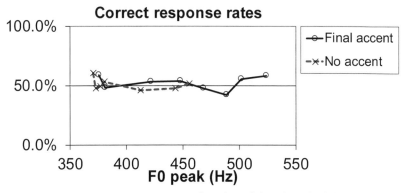

FIGURE 4 Correct response rates as a function of the F0 peak of the stimuli.

4   Discussion and Conclusions

The present study examined whether listeners were able to perceive a contrast between a final accent and no accent in interrogative melodies, where a final accent clashes with the rising boundary tone. The identification task showed that no significant differences were found in listeners' responses for final-accented and non-accented stimuli in the context of a tonal clash (target condition), although they did correctly classify them in a non-clash context (control condition). This suggests that the existance of a subtle acoustic difference in the degree of F0 peak signaled by the speaker plays no role in the identification of final-accent and non-accent in the context of a tonal clash. Such results are in line with previous perceptual studies of final accent vs. no accent (e.g., Neustupný 1978, Sugito 1982, Vance 1995, Sugiyama 2012), which have reported only a limited ability to identify contrasts.

A possible direction for future studies would be to address whether the contrasts are physically distingishable from each other. The inability to identifying a contrast does not necessarily imply the inability to hear an acoustic difference (see, e.g., Matsui 2017 for Russian voicing contrast in a neutralizing context). Acoustic discrimination is therefore worth testing in addition to identification.

In conclusion, our results support the idea that the distinctions in lexical accent are perceptually neutralized in the context where a final pitch accent clashes with a rising boundary tone. This suggests that when lexical prosody clashes with post-lexical prosody, post-lexical prosody is privileged.

References

Bates, D., M. Maechler, B. Bolker and S. Walker. 2014. Lme4: Linear mixed-effects models using Eigen and S4. R package version 1.1-7.

Caspers, J. and V. van Hauven. 1993. Effects of time pressure on the phonetic realization of the Dutch accent-lending pitch rise and fall. *Phonetica*, 50: 161–171.

Cho, H. and E. Flemming. 2015. Compression and truncation: The case of Seoul Korean accentual phrase. *Studies in Phonetics, Phonology and Morphology*, 21.2: 359–382.

Grønnum, N. 1991. Prosodic parameters in a variety of regional Danish standard languages with a view towards Swedish and German. *Phonetica*, 47: 188–214.

Grice, M. 1995. *The Intonation of Interrogation in Palermo Italian: Implications for Intonation Theory*. Tübingen: Niemeyer.

Igarashi, Y. 2015. Chapter 13, Intonation. In H. Kubozono ed., *Japanese Phonetics and Phonology*, 525–568. Berlin: Mouton de Gruyter.

Ladd, R.D. 1996. *Intonational Phonology*. New York: Cambridge University Press.

Ladd, R.D. 2008. *Intonational Phonology*. 2nd edition. New York: Cambridge University Press.

Larkey L.S. 1983. Reiterant speech: an acoustic and perceptual validation. *Journal of the Acoustical Society of America*, 73 (4): 1337–1345.

Maeda, K., and J.J. Venditti. 1998. Phonetic investigation of boundary pitch movements in Japanese. In the *Proceedings of the International Conference on Spoken Language Processing (ICSLP)*, 631–634. Sydney, Australia.

Matsui, M. 2017. Identification and discrimination of Russian incomplete word-final devoicing by native and non-native listeners: A pilot study. *Roshiago Kenkyū* [Russian Studies], 27: 9–18.

Matsui, M. and H.K. Hwang. 2018. Okikae hampuku hatsuwa ni okeru picchi patan no saigen kanōsei: Warner (1997) no tsuikentō [On the replicability of pitch patterns in "Reiterant Speech": A complementary study to Warner (1997)]. *NINJAL Research Papers*, 14: 89–97.

Matsui, M. and H.K. Hwang. Forthcoming. Final vs. no accent in interrogative melodies of Tokyo Japanese: Implications for tonal clash resolution. In J. Szpyra-Kozłowska and M. Radomski, eds., *Phonetics and Phonology in Action*. Peter Lang: Frankfurt am Mein.

Pierrehumbert, J.B. and M.E. Beckman. 1988. *Japanese Tone Structure*. Cambridge, MA: MIT press.

Poser, W.J. 1984. The phonetics and phonology of tone and intonation in Japanese. MIT doctoral dissertation.

Prieto, P. 2005. Stability effects in tonal clash contexts in Catalan. *Journal of Phonetics*, 33: 215–242.

R Core Team. 2014. R: A language and environment for statistical computing (Version 3.1.0). R Foundation for Statistical Computing, Vienna, Austria. http://www.Rproject.org/

Sakuma, K. 1929. *Nohon Onseigaku* [Japanese Phonetics]. Tokyo: Kyoobunkan.

Sugito, M. 1968. Dōtai-sokutei ni yoru Tokyo nihaku-go odaka to heiban akusento-kō [A study of final-accented and unaccented disyllabic words in Tokyo using dynamic measurement], *Onseigakkai Kaihō* [The bulletin of the phonetic society of Japan], 129: 1–4.

Sugito, M. 1982. Tokyo akusento ni okeru "hana" to "hana" no seisei to chikaku [The production and perception of "hana" and "hana" with Tokyo accent]. In *Nihongo Akusento no Kenkyū* [Studies on Japanese accent], 182–201. Tokyo: Sanseidō.

Sugiyama, Y. 2012. *The Production and Perception of Japanese Pitch Accent*. UK: Cambridge Scholars Publishing.

Vance, T.J. 1987. *An Introduction to Japanese Phonology*. Albany: State University of New York Press.

Vance, T.J. 1995. Final accent vs. no accent: utterance-final neutralization in Tokyo Japanese. Letter to the editor. *Journal of Phonetics* 23: 487–499.

Venditti, J.J., K. Maekawa and M. E. Beckman. 2008. Prominence marking in the Japanese intonation system. In S. Miyagawa and M. Saito eds., *The Oxford Handbook of Japanese Linguistics*. Oxford: Oxford University Press.

Warner, N. 1997. Japanese final-accented and unaccented phrases. *Journal of Phonetics*, 25: 43–60.

Yoneyama, K. 2002. Phonological neighborhoods and phonetic similarity in Japanese word recognition. Doctoral disseration, Ohio State University.

Denasalization of Moraic Nasals in Sino-Japanese[*]

KOHEI NISHIMURA
Iwaki Meisei University

1 Introduction

This study elucidates the morphophonological structure of Sino-Japanese bimorphemic words (SJ; Tateishi 1990, Ito and Mester 1996, etc.) on the basis of an analysis of optional denasalization in moraic nasals. A Japanese moraic nasal is usually phonetically realized as a nasalized semivowel in an intervocalic position (Vance 2008:97). Furthermore, the nasality of such a segment is very unstable and often pronounced as the latter half of a long vowel in some SJ bimorphemic words. For example, *ten-in* /teN-iN/ 'clerk' is often pronounced as [te:.iN], which is phonologically very close or identical to *tee-in* 'capacity,' a word that does not originally contain a moraic nasal in the first morpheme. It will be revealed that this phonological alter-

---

[*]This study is sponsored by the JSPS Grant-in-Aid for Scientific Research (Project Number: 16H03427).

Japanese/Korean Linguistics 25.
Edited by Shin Fukuda, Mary Shin Kim, and Mee-Jeong Park.

nation is allowed only under a very limited context. The analysis provides significant evidence of SJ phonology and morphology and their interface.

2 Data

Although denasalization in SJ moraic nasals is not an exceptional phenomenon in colloquial Japanese, little attention has been given to it in phonological studies of Japanese. The reason for this is probably that SJ denasalization is an optional alternation, which is not faithful to the canonical pronunciation of Chinese characters, and denasalized counterparts of SJ words are considered to be products of mispronunciation or lazy utterances. However, as we will see later, this phonological alternation is considerably systematic and intentional. Therefore, I want to begin this article with a descriptive generalization of this phonological alternation. To clarify several important points in the generalization, this study depends on a statistical survey of the Corpus of Spontaneous Japanese (CSJ; National Institute for Japanese Linguistics and Language 2008), which provides plenty of data on the inquiry of Japanese colloquial speech.

2.1 General Facts

A Japanese moraic nasal is a syllable-final nasal segment, which is conventionally described with /N/ as a phoneme, and it is phonologically distinct from syllable initial nasal segments /m/ and /n/ in Japanese phonology. Its place of articulation assimilates to a following consonant if the consonant has a closure. When a moraic nasal is followed by a vowel or a consonant without closure, it is generally realized as a nasalized dorso-velar (high back unrounded) semivowel [ɰ̃] (Vance 2008). Additionally, a vowel before a nasal segment is always nasalized, and the vowel nasality yields no phonological distinction in this language.

It is well known that the Japanese lexicon consists of several word classes, which are basically based on their etymological origins (McCawley 1968, Vance 1987, Ito and Mester 1995ab, etc.), and the SJ class consists of Chinese borrowings with very few exceptions. Being influenced by the phonological structure of Chinese morphemes, SJ phonology has strict restrictions on the prosodic structure of morphemes, which are often called SJ stems because of their morphological uniformity, and a moraic nasal is only found in stems with CVN structure (Tateishi 1990).

Following the general Japanese phonology argued above, the phonetic realization of a moraic nasal in this position depends on the following consonant, which is always the first segment of the following morpheme, and in intervocalic position a moraic nasal is generally realized as a nasalized dorso-velar semivowel. However, the place and nasality of this alternating segment is very unstable in some SJ bimorphemic words with CVN.VN structure, and it is often pronounced as the latter part of a long vowel. In particular, when the first vowel is /e/ and the second vowel is /i/, this happens quite often. Typical examples are illustrated in (1):

(1) a. /geN-iN/ [gẽw̃.ĩN~ge:.ĩN] 'cause'
    b. /teN-iN/ [tẽw̃.ĩN~te:.ĩN] 'clerk'

In both cases, a moraic nasal in the first stem, which is an independent nasal phoneme at the underlying level, can be realized at the surface level as either a nasalized dorso-velar semivowel or the latter part of a long vowel, which was derived from coalescence of the underlying vowel and moraic nasal. In the latter case, the nasality of the underlying moraic nasal can be lost. Interestingly, the phonetic difference between the two variants does not yield any semantic difference even though a vowel and a nasal segment are distinctive in Japanese phonology (see Nishimura 2018 for similar cases from the Loanword vocabulary of Japanese).

From a phonetical point of view, the degree of the nasality in the derived long vowel is not stable; in some pronunciations, the latter part of the long vowel still contains some nasality. In other words, the moraic nasal in this context can be phonetically realized as a nasalized vowel. Further, the fact that the moraic nasal in the second morpheme can affect the nasality of the first one makes the situation more complex. However, I want to analyze this phonological alternation as "denasalization" because this study focuses on the fact that the consonantal place of the moraic nasal can be completely lost at the surface level, and Japanese phonology does not distinguish a normal vowel from its nasalized counterpart. That is, this alternation causes a phonologically remarkable change and therefore provides significant evidence for phonological inquiry, as we will see later.

2.2 Morphological Locality

Another interesting fact about SJ denasalization is its morphological locality. Denasalization is only possible inside a word that consists of two SJ morphemes, as shown in (1). In other words, this phonological alternation may take place at the stem-level morphology, which is specific and is the most fundamental morphological operation in SJ (for details, see Tateishi 1990, Ito and Mester 1996), but not at the level of other general morphological operations such as word-level compounding. Consider the following morphologically complex words for example:

(2) a. /ʃu/+/geN-iN/   [ʃu.gẽw̃.ĩN~ʃu.ge:.ĩN]   'main cause'
    b. /ʃoo-geN/+/iN/   [ʃo:.gẽw̃.ĩN], *[ʃo:.ge:.ĩN] 'witness'
    c. /geN/+/iN-ʃi/   [gẽw̃.ĩN.ʃi], *[ge:.ĩN.ʃi]   'original factor'

d. /koN-geN/+/iN-ʃi/ [koŋ.gẽũ̯.ĩ N̩.ʃi], *[koŋ.ge:.ĩ N̩.ʃi]

'fundamental factor'

Every word in (2) contains /…geNiN…./ sequence, but denasalization is only possible in (2a), in which the whole SJ bimorphemic word is included as a constituent of compounding. In other cases in which the /…geNiN…/ sequence does not form a morphological constituent, denasalization is impossible.

This morphological locality of denasalization provides strong support to Ito and Mester's (1996) proposal on SJ morphology. The condition of denasalization is quite similar to that of SJ stem contraction. As these authors illustrated, SJ contraction is only possible at the boundary of bimorphemic conjunction, not at more complex morphological contexts. See the following examples:

(3) a. /betsu-seki/   [bes̲.s̲e.ki], *[be.tsu.se.ki] 'different seat'
    b. /toku-betsu/+/seki/ [to.ku.be.tsu.se.ki], *[to.ku.bes̲.s̲e.ki]

'special seat'

Contraction between the two morphemes, /betsu/ and /seki/ is possible in (3a), but not in (3b) even though they are linearly adjacent. They explained this situation distinguishing two word-internal morphological constituents, stems and words as argued in McCawley (1968) and Selkirk (1982), and SJ contraction is only active at the boundary between two stems. The condition of SJ denasalization illustrated in (2) can be explained similarly.

More evidence of the morphological locality is that denasalization is found only in "pure" SJ words and not in word formation with members of the other Japanese word classes. In particular, some words in the Loanword class, which mainly consists of borrowings from English and other European languages, may have a /…CeNiN…/ sequence, but denasalization is impossible in this case. Consider the following examples:

(4) a. /teN+iNtʃi/ [tẽũ̯.ĩn.tʃi], *[te:.ĩn.tʃi] 'ten inches'
    b. /peN+iNku/ [pẽũ̯.ĩŋ.ku], *[pe:.ĩŋ.ku] 'pen ink'

The phonetic contexts of these words are very similar to those in the examples in (1), but denasalization is not possible in this case. A more striking fact is found in the hybrid compound that consists of an SJ stem and a loanword morpheme. Examples are shown below:

(5) a. /geN+iNku/ [gẽũ̯.ĩŋku], *[ge:.ĩŋku] 'undiluted ink'
    b. /zeN+iNdo/ [zẽũ̯.ĩndo], *[ze:.ĩndo] 'pan-India'

In these compounds, the first morpheme is an SJ stem, and the segmental context is very similar to that in SJ words in (1), in which denasalization may happen. However, the phonological alternation is ungrammatical in these cases. This difference must be caused by the morphological structure of words but not by the phonological structure because denasalization does not involve any phonetic change in Loanword morphemes. The facts illustrated in (4) and (5) above also provide strong evidence for Ito and Mester's hypothesis; different from SJ stems, Loanword morphemes are always words in morphological operations, and therefore, denasalization is not active in compounding with Loanword morphemes.

2.3 Statistical Survey

This section provides the results of a statistical survey of the CSJ (National Institute for Japanese Linguistics and Language 2008). As argued in 2.1., denasalization in SJ bimorphemic words is allowed under very limited phonological contexts in actual speech of Japanese speakers.

The phonology of SJ allows 575 phonologically distinct words with CVN.VN structure (Tateishi 1990). In CSJ, 50 phonologically distinct words with this CV structure are found in 2264 tokens, and denasalization is observed in 15 words in 683 tokens (see the Appendix below for details). Table 1 shows the research results of words pronounced more than 50 times in the corpus. "TOTAL," "DNED," and "%" indicate the number of tokens including any variant forms, the number of tokens that show denasalization, and the frequency of denasalization, respectively:

STRUCTURE	GLOSS	TOTAL	DNED	%
geN-iN	'cause'	599	383	63.9%
oN-iN	'phoneme'	459	5	1.1%
zeN-iN	'everyone'	332	211	63.6%
seN-eN	'one thousand yen'	238	4	1.7%
dʒuN-oN	'pure tone'	122	2	1.6%
teN-iN	'clerk/changing hospital'	85	43	50.6%
kiN-eN	'nonsmoking'	64	0	0.0%

TABLE 1 Denasalization in SJ CVN.VN words (pronounced more than 50 times in CSJ)

This indicates that denasalization is mainly observed in words with high vowels, especially with CeN.iN structure as pointed out in 2.1., and it is rare or impossible to find it in a word with any other structure. In particular, the great majority of this phonological alternation occurred in three morphologically different words: /geN-iN/, /zeN-iN/, and /teN-iN/.[1]

Another possible trigger for denasalization is the identity between two vowels, but this factor seems much weaker than the previous one. The following table shows the relation between a combination of high vowels in CVN.VN words and the frequency of denasalization:

STRUCTURE	EXAMPLE	TOTAL	DNED	%
CeN-iN	geN iN 'cause'	1028	637	62.0%
CeN-eN	deN-eN 'rural area'	326	20	6.1%
CiN-eN	kiN-eN 'nonsmoking'	66	0	0.0%
CiN-iN	dʒiN-iN 'workforce'	19	5	26.3%

TABLE 2 Denasalization and high vowel combinations

Denasalization actually occurs in several words with a CiN-iN or CeN-eN structure in CSJ. However, the probability of denasalization in CeN-iN words is much higher than that in either of the other two structures, and the difference among them is statistically significant (CeN-iN vs. CiN-iN: $\chi2=3.59e-06$, df=1, p<0.01).

This survey also reveals that the existence of the word-final moraic nasal is crucial in denasalization. The following table shows a comparison among CeN-iN, CeN-i, and CeN-iCV in the corpus:

STRUCTURE	EXAMPLE	TOTAL	DNED	%
CeN-iN	geN-iN 'cause'	1028	637	62.0%
CeN-i	seN-i 'texture'	574	0	0.0%
CeN-iCV	zeN-iki 'whole area'	24	0	0.0%

TABLE 3 Denasalization and the word-final moraic nasal

The result is surprisingly clear; no denasalization occurs in words without a word-final moraic nasal. This result is, of course, statistically significant (CeN-iN vs. CeN-iCV: $\chi2=1.07e-18$, df=1, p<0.01). It is suggested that SJ

---

[1]One debatable point about SJ denasalization here is its productivity; one may suspect whether denasalization is not productive because this phonological operation is mainly found in a few lexicalized, high-frequency words, and it is rare in low-frequency words. Therefore, it is reasonable to assume that their denasalized forms are also lexicalized and that both forms are possible at the surface level. However, in that case, the question why such lexicalization is possible in words with a particular CV structure but not in others must be answered.

denasalization must result in a quantitative change but not a complete deletion of the nasality.[2]

3 Analysis

As argued in the previous section, denasalization in SJ bimorphemic words takes place only in very limited morphophonological contexts. In this section, I further analyze the trigger and other controlling factors of this phonological alternation. The questions to be answered are (i) what motivates SJ denasalization, and (ii) why is denasalization possible in words with CeN.iN structure but not in many other structures. The descriptive generalization and statistical data suggest that several phonological and morphophonological factors play crucial roles in this phonological alternation. This study claims that three factors interact in this phonological phenomenon: tongue movement simplification, the SJ long vowel inventory, and the clarification of morphological boundary.

3.1 Tongue Movement Simplification

I claim that the motivating factor of SJ denasalization is a simplification of a tongue movement. The [...ẽũ̯.ĩ...] sequence, which is included in words with CeN.iN structure in the canonical (non-denasalized) pronunciation, involves a rapid back-and-forth movement of the tongue. Omitting the consonantal place of the moraic nasal, denasalization can drastically smooth the tongue movement because the denasalized sequence [...eː.ĩ...] consists only of front vowels. Additionally, the instability of intervocalic semi-vowel is also solved through denasalization because it disappears in the simplified form.

This viewpoint can also account for famous metathesis pattern in the SJ word *funiki* [fũũ̯.ĩ.ki], 'atmosphere'. Japanese speakers often pronounce this word [fu.ĩŋ.ki] with a reversal of the moraic nasal and the front vowel /i/, ignoring the morphological boundary between the first and second morphemes. The requirement for a simplified tongue movement favors the metathesis because the canonical form contains the [...ũ̯.ĩ...] sequence, which requires a complex tongue movement. Further, in the metathesis form, the moraic nasal is stable because it is realized as a dorsal nasal, whose place of articulation is provided in the following dorsal stop.

---

[2]This suggests that SJ denasalization can be understood as a fusion of the two moraic nasals at the word-final position followed by augmented vowel lengthening, as illustrated below:

    i. /geN$_1$-iN$_2$/ [geː.iN$_{1,2}$] 'cause'

It is debatable whether such an intense morphophonological operation, which overcomes the morphological boundary, is actually possible as an optional alternation. I want to leave this line of argument open to further research.

3.2 Long Vowel Inventory

While the simplification of a tongue movement can provide a motivation for SJ denasalization, it overproduces some unattested denasalized forms. This suggests that there are other factors that block this phonological alternation in particular contexts. In particular, the difference between the frequency of denasalization in CeN.iN words and that in CiN.iN words, which was statistically illustrated in Table 2, should be explained.

One possible factor is the long vowel inventory of SJ. As pointed out in Tateishi (1990), the phonological/phonetic structure of SJ morpheme is highly restricted compared to other Japanese word classes. One such restriction is found in the vowel lengthening; while all of the five Japanese vowels /i, e, a, o, u/ can be short vowels, possible long vowels are limited to /e:/, /u:/, and /o:/, and /a:/ and /i:/ are prohibited in SJ at least at the lexicon level. This can account for the statistical difference in denasalization between a CeN.iN word and CiN.iN word; denasalization in the latter word generates an ill-formed long vowel [i:] at the surface level. [3]

One noteworthy fact is that these lexically prohibited long vowels are found under some morphologically derived environments. A few examples are shown below:

(6) a. /tʃi-iki/   [tʃi:.ki]   'area'
     b. /i-iN/   [ĩ:N]   'committee member"

In these forms, the lexically prohibited long vowel [i:] is derived, and any phonological alternation that blocks its realization, such as consonant insertion, is not operated. These facts suggest that the lexical prohibition on long vowels, if any, is not much influential at the surface level. In other words, the long vowel restriction can block denasalization in some SJ words because it is not obligatory but an optional phonological alternation, which is not essential in SJ morphophonology.

3.3 Morphological Boundary

Another possible factor that obstructs denasalization is the clarification of the morphological boundary in an SJ word. In some CVN.VN words in which the two vowels are identical, denasalization is blocked to clarify the

---

[3]This restriction also blocks denasalization in a CaN.iN word because /a:/ is also impossible in the SJ lexicon. However, /maN-iN/ can be optionally pronounced as [mã:ĩN], in which the moraic nasal loses its consonantal place, as shown in the Appendix below. I believe this case is exceptional because, besides the two moraic nasals, the onset of the first syllable is also a nasal, and the whole word is always nasalized. In other words, the nasality in the first morpheme is guaranteed by the onset nasal. Under such a phonologically specific context, the consonantal place of the moraic nasal is much easier to lose than in other cases.

morphological boundary. If denasalization occurs in a word with such a CV structure, the morphological boundary becomes obscure; therefore, phonological alternation is not preferred to avoid such a situation.

This view can explain the statistical difference between CeN.iN words, in which denasalization often takes place, and words with CeN.eN or CiN.iN structure, in which the phonological alternation is relatively suppressed, as shown in Table 2. In other words, the moraic nasal serves to mark the morphological boundary. In a word with CeN.iN structure, the morphological boundary is not obscure even in its denasalized form because the two morphemes have different vowels from each other. Therefore, denasalization is not obstructed. If this view is accurate, the internal morphological information of SJ words, most of which are highly lexicalized, is psychologically real and still active for phonological grammar.

Similar to the argument in the previous section, this blocking factor is only active in denasalization and cannot exclude the nonpreferred structure from the surface level. Consider the following examples:

(7) a. /tee-eN/   [te:.ẽN] 'garden'
    b. /tʃi-iki/   [tʃi:.ki] 'area'

In these words, the vowel in the first morpheme and that in the second morpheme are identical, and the morphological boundary is obscure in the surface forms. However, no phonological alternation happens to cancel this situation. Again, these facts suggest that the requirement of clear morphological boundary, if any, is not much influential at the surface level. It emerges only in the case of the optional alternation in SJ phonology.

4   Summary

In this article, I examined denasalization of moraic nasals in SJ bimorphemic words, a phenomenon that has been overlooked in previous studies of Japanese phonology. The statistical survey of the speech corpus showed that denasalization often takes place in words with CeN.iN structure but not in others. As shown in Section 3, the analysis of this morphophonological alternation revealed important evidence to understand SJ phonology and morphology and their interface, which are sometimes covered in more dominant alternations.

References

Ito, J. and A. Mester. 1995a. The Core-Periphery Structure of the Lexicon and Constraints on Reranking. *Papers in Optimality Theory*, ed. J. Beckman, L. Walsh, and S. Urbanczyk, 181-210. Amherst: University of Massachusetts, GLSA.

Ito, J. and A. Mester. 1995b. Japanese Phonology. *The Handbook of Phonological Theory*, ed. J. Goldsmith, 817-838. Oxford: Blackwell.

Ito, J. and A. Mester. 1996. Stem and Word in Sino-Japanese. *Phonological Structure and Language Processing: Cross-Linguistic Studies*, ed. T. Otake and A. Cutler, 13-44. Berlin: Mouton de Gruyter.

National Institute for Japanese Linguistics and Language. 2008. *The Corpus of Spontaneous Japanese*, Ver. 2. Database.

Nishimura, K. 2018. Phonological Optionality in Japanese Loanwords. *IELS* 35· *Papers from the 35ᵗʰ Conference of English Linguistic Society of Japan*.

Selkirk, E. 1982. *The Syntax of Words*. Cambridge, MA: MIT Press.

Tateishi, K. 1990. Phonology of Sino-Japanese Morphemes. *General Linguistics*, ed. G. Lamontagne and A. Taub, 209-235. University of Massachusetts Occasional Papers in Linguistics, 13. Amherst: University of Massachusetts, GLSA.

Vance, T. J. 1987. *An Introduction to Japanese Phonology*. New York: SUNY Press.

Vance, T. J. 2008. *The Sounds of Japanese*. Cambridge: Cambridge University Press.

Appendix

The following table shows the full research results of denasalization in SJ bimorphemic words with CVN.VN structure found in CSJ, classified by the vowel combination. "TOTAL," "DNED," and "%" indicate the number of tokens, including any variant forms, the number of tokens that show denasalization, and the frequency of denasalization, respectively.

STRUCTURE	EXAMPLE	TOTAL	DNED	%
CeN-iN	geN-iN 'cause'	1028	637	62.0%
CiN-iN	dʒiN-iN 'workforce'	19	5	26.3%
CaN-iN	maN-iN 'full crowded'	47	9	19.1%
CaN-eN	kaN-eN 'hepatitis'	32	2	6.3%
CeN-eN	deN-eN 'rural area'	326	20	6.1%
CuN-oN	dʒuN-oN 'pure tone'	122	2	1.6%
CoN-iN	oN-iN 'phoneme'	475	7	1.5%
CaN-oN	kaN-oN 'hearing'	79	1	1.3%
CiN-eN	kiN-eN 'nonsmoking'	66	0	0.0%
CeN-oN	geN-oN 'original sound'	37	0	0.0%
CiN-aN	ʃiN-aN 'new plan'	8	0	0.0%
CeN-aN	geN-aN 'original plan'	7	0	0.0%
CuN-eN	buN-eN 'separation of smoking areas'	6	0	0.0%
CiN-uN	kiN-uN 'luck with money'	3	0	0.0%
CuN-iN	buN-iN 'branch hospital'	3	0	0.0%
CaN-aN	kaN-aN 'consideration'	2	0	0.0%
CuN-aN	buN-aN 'draft'	2	0	0.0%
CiN-oN	ʃiN-oN 'warble tone'	1	0	0.0%
CeN-uN	seN-uN 'war cloud'	1	0	0.0%
CaN-uN	-	0	0	-
CoN-eN	-	0	0	-
CoN-aN	-	0	0	-
CoN-oN	-	0	0	-
CoN-uN	-	0	0	-
CuN-uN	-	0	0	-

APPENDIX The full results of SJ denasalization in CVN.VN words in CSJ

Identity Avoidance Effects on *Rendaku* in the Process of Producing Japanese Noun Compounds: Evidence from Three Oral Production Experiments

MASAKI SONE AND YUKI HIROSE
The University of Tokyo

1 Introduction

1.1 *Rendaku* (Sequential Voicing)

Rendaku is a morphophonological process where the initial voiceless obstruent of the second constituent in a compound becomes voiced (Vance 1987; Ito and Mester 2003; Kubozono 1995). For example, in (1), when the two words *umi* ('sea') and *kame* ('turtle') form a compound, the initial consonant of the second constituent /k/ in *kame* becomes voiced to /g/.

(1) *umi* + *kame* > *umi-game*
    sea   turtle >   sea turtle

Japanese/Korean Linguistics 25.
Edited by Shin Fukuda, Mary Shin Kim, and Mee-Jeong Park.

However, there are many cases in which *rendaku* does not occur. Numerous studies have investigated what factors affect the occurrence of *rendaku*, some taking experimental approaches (Vance 1979; Ihara and Murata 2006; Tamaoka and Ikeda 2010; Ihara et al. 2011; Kawahara and Sano 2013, 2014). Experimental studies allow researchers to control target variables without relying on existing lexical items by flexibly manipulating phonological conditions of both the input and the potential output. This makes it possible to test whether the factors that are claimed to affect *rendaku* in the lexicon based on observations of naturally occurring examples are psychologically real, or grammaticalized, in native speakers' minds (Kawahara and Sano 2013). Such experimental approaches are useful for avoiding frequency issues related to how often *rendaku* is applied to the target words and the degree to which compounds in tasks are lexicalized.

1.2 The Obligatory Contour Principle (OCP)

The Obligatory Contour Principle (OCP) was first put forward as a morpheme-structure constraint that prohibits two consecutive high tones or two consecutive low tones in a morpheme's lexical entry (Leben 1973). Extending this constraint, McCarthy (1986) proposed that the OCP can block applications of phonological rules in various languages. Yip (1988) also demonstrated that the OCP could trigger some phonological processes.

Sasaki (2011) reported that, in the Hokkaido dialect of Japanese, syllable deletion applies to [sa] in a [sasa] sequence that results from the suffixation of a morpheme marking a 'spontaneous' meaning to some verb roots (e.g., /hagemas-rasar-ru/ 'encourage' + spontaneous marker + present tense marker > *hagemasaru*, instead of **hagemasasaru*). Sasaki explained this deletion as the effect of a "mora-sized OCP," which prohibits the moraic sequence within the same segmental content. On the other hand, Kawahara and Sano (2016) reported that the OCP plays a role not only at the moraic level but also at the consonantal level in Japanese. Thus, the scope of the OCP in Japanese is still a controversial matter.

1.3 Background of the Current Study

1.3.1 Identity Avoidance and *Rendaku* Application (Exp. 1 and 2)

Sato (1989) argued that *rendaku* does not occur in the second constituent of a compound of two adjacent voiceless fricative–initial syllables (e.g., *haha* 'mother,' *susu* 'soot'). However, Sato's proposal was not confirmed by statistical evidence from a database analysis by Irwin (2014).

Kawahara and Sano (2014) found that *rendaku* could be both triggered and blocked to avoid adjacent identical moras across a morpheme boundary. They first demonstrated that compounds containing two identical CV moras (where C is a voiceless obstruent) with a morpheme boundary between the first constituent and second constituent as in (2a) are more likely to undergo *rendaku* compared with compounds that do not have adjacent identical moras as in (2b). They also examined cases in which Identity Avoidance would inhibit the application of *rendaku*. For example, two adjacent identical CV moras across a morpheme boundary would result from the application of *rendaku* in (2c), *iga-ganiro*, but not in (2d), *kuda-ganiro*. The results showed that the condition in (2c) was less likely to undergo *rendaku* than the condition in (2d). This is accounted for as avoidance of adjacent identical CV moras (i.e., **ga-ga**). Kawahara and Sano (2016) further demonstrated that, in adjacent moras across a morpheme boundary, a sequence with identical mora-initial consonants (e.g., *iga+geniro*) is more likely to trigger *rendaku* than a sequence with nonidentical consonants (e.g., *iga+zeniro*).

(2) Kawahara and Sano (2014)

a. *ika*   +   *kaniro*   > *ika-kaniro* or *ika-ganiro*
   squid   nonce word

b. *kusa*   +   *kaniro*   > *kusa-kaniro* or *kusa-ganiro*
   grass   nonce word

c. *iga*   +   *kaniro*   > *iga-kaniro* or *iga-ganiro*
   spiky   nonce word

d. *kuda*   +   *kaniro*   > *kuda-kaniro* or *kuda-ganiro*
   pipe   nonce word

While Kawahara and Sano (2014, 2016) examined the proactive effects of sequences of identical moras or identical mora-initial consonants across morpheme boundaries, we investigated the effects of such sequences within morphemes in the two experiments reported in section 2. Employing CVCVCV-structured nonce words, and looking at their first and second moras, we focused on the remedial effects of Identity Avoidance on a sequence of identical moras (e.g., **kakara**; Experiment 1) or identical mora-initial consonants (e.g., **kakura**; Experiment 2).

1.3.2   Inhibiting Effects of the OCP-Labial and OCP-Voiced (Sonorant) on *Rendaku* Application (Experiment 3)

This section focuses on cases when Identity Avoidance (i.e., OCP) inhibits *rendaku* application. When, as in (3a), the second constituent already contains a voiced obstruent, *rendaku* application is blocked (i.e., "Lyman's Law"; Lyman 1894).

Lyman's Law is often seen as an effect of the OCP on a sequence of voiced obstruents within the second constituent of compounds (i.e., OCP-voiced (obstruent)). In contrast, in morphemes containing a sequence of a nasal and an approximant, *rendaku* application is not blocked, as (3b) shows (Ito and Mester 1986; Kubozono 1999). This suggests that the OCP-voiced (sonorant) in Japanese is not accounted for by Lyman's Law.

(3)
a. *aki*   + *kaze*   >   *aki-kaze* (*aki-gaze)
   autumn   wind   autumn wind

b. *umi*   + *kame*   >   *umi-game*
   sea   turtle   sea turtle

Based on dictionary data, Kawahara et al. (2006) examined the effects on *rendaku* application of initial consonants with the same place of articulation in two adjacent moras. They reported that stems with [h] in the first mora and [m] in the second mora did not usually undergo *rendaku*, as in (4a). On the other hand, stems with [h] in the first and [n] in the second mora did tend to undergo *rendaku*, as in (4b). Note that *ha* becomes *ba* by *rendaku*; it acquires [+bilabial] in addition to [+voice].

(4)
a. combination of [b…m] blocked:
   suna   + *hama* >   *suna-hama* *suna-bama
   sand   shore

b. combination of [b…n] not blocked:
   ai   + *hana* >   *ai-bana* *ai-hana
   purple   flower

Kawahara et al. (2006) explained the inhibition of *rendaku* as in (4a) in terms of a co-occurrence restriction on two consecutive bilabial features on the first and second consonants in the stem. The stem in (4a) has the /h…m…/ sequence; the place of articulation of [h] and [m] are different. However, changing [h] into [b] by *rendaku* would result in two sequential labials within the same stem, which is to be avoided. Kawahara et al. suggested a possibility that the OCP (i.e., Identity Avoidance) could restrict a sequence of two similar phonological features (i.e., labial features in this case) in the process of *rendaku* application. Kumagai (2017) also explored cases in which OCP-labial effects on the second constituent of a compound inhibit *rendaku*, and demonstrated that the applicability of /h/ to /b/ *rendaku* differed by the degree of similarity among the labial consonants in the subsequent moras in the input. In other words, the consonants create a cline of *rendaku* probability: /Φ/ > /w/ > /m/. For example, the probability of *rendaku* would decrease with second constituents as follows: *hV*hara > *hV*Φ*ura* > *hV*w*ara* > *hV*m*ara* (V = /a/, /i/, or /u/).

Based on Kumagai's (2017) results, we hypothesize that *rendaku* would be motivated by eliminating a sequence of not only the labial feature but also other overlapping features in adjacent moras within the input. In experiment 3, we focus on a sequence of [+voiced] features, testing the effects of [+voiced] in sonorants. Whether sonorant voicing plays a role in Japanese is a controversial issue repeatedly discussed in theoretical literature. Most studies (e.g., Ito and Mester 1986; Mester and Ito 1989) propose that sonorants do not have [+voiced] features influencing phonological processes in Japanese because, as shown (4a-b), voicing on sonorants is ignored in the process of the application of Lyman's Law. But Rice (1993) proposed that Japanese sonorants have an underlying [+voiced] feature that yields voicing in following segments (i.e., voicing on sonorants is active to some extent). Rice's proposal was based on the observation that nasals induce postnasal voicing in the past tense formation in Japanese (e.g., /kam + ta/ → [kan-*da*] 'chewed').

If Japanese speakers tend to avoid a sequence of [+voiced] features and if [+voiced] features in sonorants affect the phonological process in Japanese, words such as *hanara* (whose *rendaku* form is *banara*) would be less likely to undergo *rendaku* than words that do not contain a voiceless consonant in the second mora such as *hasara* (whose *rendaku* form is *basara*).

Furthermore, the control conditions in Kumagai's (2017) study included words containing two adjacent identical moras such as **hahara**. Because we suspect this could potentially influence the results if Identity Avoidance is at work at the moraic level, Experiment 3 (section 3) investigates the effects of the OCP-labial and the OCP-voiced by eliminating such mora sequences in our experimental conditions.

2 Experiments 1 and 2

Experiments 1 and 2 investigate cases in which the OCP is predicted to facilitate *rendaku* application.

2.1 Experiment 1

Experiment 1 examines cases in which a sequence of two identical moras within an input word could be avoided by *rendaku* application.

2.1.1 Participants, Design, and Prediction

Experiment 1 recruited eighteen adult speakers of Tokyo Japanese, who took part in the experiment in exchange for a small remuneration.

Experiment 1 utilized five existing words for the first constituent: *sato* 'countryside', *mori* 'forests', *yama* 'mountain', *oo* 'big', and *ko* 'small'. Forty-eight nonce words were created for the second constituent. As illustrated in (5), half of the forty-eight nonce words included two identical adjacent CV moras (Identical) as in (5a). In contrast, the other half of the nonce words had all different CV moras (Nonidentical) as in (5b). Of the targets, twenty-four were unaccented and twenty-four had initial accents. As the present research focuses on the effect of a sequence of identical moras, we report the effects of the accent type of the nonce words elsewhere (Sone and Hirose, under review).

The prediction is that if OCP applies to two successive moras in the second constituent, the second constituents that include two adjacent identical moras (i.e., Identical) as in (5a) should undergo *rendaku* application more often than the second constituents that consist of all different moras (i.e., Nonidentical) as in (5b).

(5)

a. *mori* + *kakara* (Identical) > *mori-kakara* or *mori-gakara*
   forest   nonce word

b. *mori* + *kasara* (Nonidentical) > *mori-kasara* or *mori-gasara*
   forest   nonce word

2.1.2 Procedure

In a practice session, the participants were first familiarized with the concept of possible phonological change in compound formation (i.e., that pronunciation can sometimes change when compounds are created). The goal was to ensure the participants felt free to make changes to the phonological form of the presented items so as to sound the most natural. In each trial, they saw a simple picture (e.g., 6a) and heard an audio file of a nonce word describing the item in the picture, such as *kasara* 'flower's name'. They were asked to repeat the nonce word, and the experimenter checked that they repeated it correctly in isolation. Then the participants were presented a second picture, depicting the item in a context, and prompted to create an original compound to describe the picture (e.g., in the case of (6b), the participants were asked, "How would you call a *kasara* which blooms in the forest?"). Their utterances were recorded, and each form they produced was later coded as to whether it showed *rendaku* or not (e.g., *mori-kasara* or *mori-gasara*).

(6)   a   b

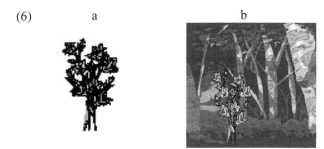

2.1.3 Analysis

The data were analyzed with logistic linear mixed effects models using the R statistical program's lme4 package (Jaeger 2008). The participants' application/nonapplication of *rendaku* was treated as a binominal dependent variable, and the presence/absence of adjacent identical moras was entered as a fixed effect. Participants and items were entered as random effects. The best-fit model was selected using a backward selection approach.

2.1.4 Results

The vertical bars in Figure 1 represent the percentages of *rendaku* application in the two conditions: with and without a sequence of identical moras in the second constituent. The analysis shows that words containing two adjacent identical moras underwent *rendaku* more often than words composed of all different moras ($\beta = -1.650$, $z = -1.998$, $p = 0.045$). The average percentages of *rendaku* application in the Identical condition and Nonidentical condition are 28.7% and 18.5%, respectively.

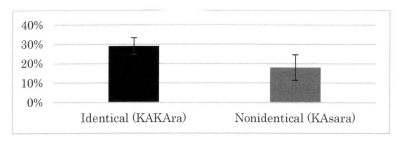

FIGURE 1 Percentage of *rendaku* application by mora identity in the second constituent. The error bars represent the standard error based on subject means in each condition.

2.2   Experiment 2

Experiment 2 focused on the degree of feature overlap between consonants in adjacent moras in C**V**CVCV-structured nonce words (e.g.,
kakura vs. *kasura*).

2.2.1   Participants, Design, and Prediction

Experiment 2 recruited twenty-three native speakers of Tokyo dialect who
participated in exchange for a small remuneration.

Experiment 2 employed two real words for the first constituent (*umi*
'sea' and *mori* 'forest'), and forty-eight nonce words for the second constituent. Half of the forty-eight nonce words included two consecutive consonants (Identical condition) as in (7a). In contrast, the other half of the nonce
words had all different consonants (Nonidentical condition) as in (7b).
Twenty-four targets were unaccented and twenty-four were initial-accented.
We discuss the possible effects of accent type elsewhere (Sone and Hirose,
under review).

If the OCP plays a role in a sequence of mora-initial consonants in adjacent moras such as *kakara*, the Identical condition as in (7a) would be
more likely to trigger *rendaku* than the Nonidentical condition as in (7b).

(7)
a. *mori*   + **ka**ku**ra** (Identical)   > *mori-**ka**ku**ra** or *mori-**ga**ku**ra**
   forest   nonce word

b. *mori*   + **ka**su**ra** (Non-identical) > *mori-**ka**su**ra** or *mori-**ga**su**ra**
   forest   nonce word

2.2.2   Procedure and Analysis

The procedure of Experiment 2 was the same as that of Experiment 1. The
data analysis procedure was also the same, except that the fixed effect was
the presence/absence of identical consonants in adjacent moras.

2.2.3   Results

The vertical bars in Figure 2 represent the percentages of *rendaku* application in the two conditions: with and without a sequence of identical mora-
initial consonants in the second constituent. No reliable effect of identical
consonants was observed ($\beta = -0.025$, $z = -0.084$, $p = 0.932$).

The percentage of *rendaku* application in the Identical condition and
the Nonidentical condition amounted to 27% and 28%, respectively.

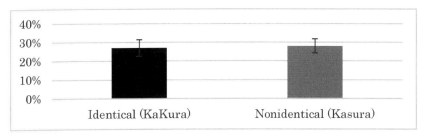

FIGURE 2 Percentage of *rendaku* application by consonant identity in the second constituent. The error bars represent the standard error based on subject means in each condition.

2.3   Discussion (Experiments 1 and 2)

The results of Experiments 1 and 2 show that second constituents with two adjacent identical CV moras, but not second constituents in which only the initial consonants of the adjacent moras were identical, underwent *rendaku* application more often than second constituents that consisted of all different CV moras.

These results suggest that *rendaku* can affect a phonological sequence that already exists in the input, indicating that identity avoidance is at work in this process.

3   Identity Avoidance in Conflict: Within and across Morpheme Boundaries (Exp. 3)

Experiment 3 simulated a tug-of-war situation between the triggering effect of *rendaku* across morpheme boundaries and the inhibiting effect of *rendaku* within a single morpheme in the compounding input. The goal of this experiment was to see how the two factors would affect each other.

3.1   Participants, Design, and Prediction

The stimuli in Experiment 3 again used nonce words. The stimuli were structured to cross two factors. One was mora-level identity (Identical vs. Nonidentical) across the morpheme boundary (*nara#ha...* vs. *naha#ha...*). The other was degree of feature overlap between the consonants in the second constituent, as shown in (8); the consonant was [h] in the first mora, and the second mora's consonant overlapped with [h] to varying degrees: [m] [+bilabial, +voiced], [n/r] [-bilabial, +voiced], or [s/t/k] [-bilabial, -voiced].

(8)

a. *nara* + *hamara* [+bilab, +voi]/*hanara* [-bilab, +voi]/*hasura* [-bilab, -voi]
   Nara (name of a city)

b. *naha* + *hamara* [+bilab, +voi]/*hanara* [-bilab, +voi]/*hasura* [-bilab, -voi]
   Naha (name of a city)

When the first constituent is *naha* as in (8b), the resulting compound would have two identical CV moras between the first constituent and second constituent, as in *naha-hamara*. On the other hand, when the first constituent is *nara*, as in (8a), the resulting compound would not have an identical CV mora sequence. Based on previous findings (Kawahara & Sano 2014), we predicted that the two identical CV moras (*naha-hamara*) would facilitate *rendaku* more often than two nonidentical CV moras (*nara-hanara*).

We also predicted a gradient effect countering *rendaku* application, based on the degree of similarity in both voicing and bilabial features between the first two moras in the second constituent (e.g., *hamara* < *hanara* < *hasara* (%*Rendaku*)). This prediction was based on the expectation that the *rendaku* forms selected would avoid violating the OCP-bilabial (e.g., blocking *hamara* to ***bamara***) and the OCP-voiced (e.g., blocking *hanara* to ***banara***).

3.2 Procedure and Analysis

Experiment 3 utilized forty-eight nonce words for the second constituent. Twenty-four nonce words included two potential adjacent bilabial features if the compounds were to undergo *rendaku* (e.g., *hamara*). The other twenty-four nonce words were divided into two types. The Voiced Consonants condition had fourteen items with a sonorant consonant such as a nasal (e.g., *hanara*) or an approximant (e.g., *harura*) in the second mora. The Voiceless Consonants condition had ten nonce words with voiceless consonants (e.g., *hasara*) in the second mora. In addition, Experiment 3 used ten real words as filler items: eight that would undergo *rendaku* (e.g., *kaeru* 'flog') and two that would not (e.g., *hituzi* 'sheep').

The procedure in Experiment 3 was the same as that in Experiment 1. The process of analysis was the same as well, except that the fixed effects were mora-identity (e.g., *naha-hamara* vs. *nara+hamara*) and consonant features in the second mora of the second constituent (e.g., *hamara* [+bilabial, +voiced], *hanara* [-bilabial, +voiced], *hasara* [-bilabial, -voiced]).

3.3   Results

The analysis of the effects of identicality found, as expected, a significant main effect (Identical [*naha*] > Nonidentical [*nara*]; β = 0.556, z = 2.476, p = 0.013). The average *rendaku* response ratios in the Identical condition and Nonidentical condition were 17% (*naha-hamara*) and 12% (*nara-hamana*), respectively.

The analysis of the consonant features found a significant effect in the predicted order: *hamara* [+bilabial, +voiced] < *hanara* [-bilabial, +voiced] < *hasara* [-bilabial, -voiced]. Each comparison showed a significant difference (β = 0.949, z = 3.279, p = 0.001 and β = -1.243, z = -4.116, p < 0.001). The average *rendaku* response ratios in the bilabial, voiced, and voiceless conditions were 8% (*hamara*), 15% (*hanara*), and 30% (*hasara*), respectively. No reliable interaction between the effects of identicality across morpheme boundaries and the effects of consonant features was observed.

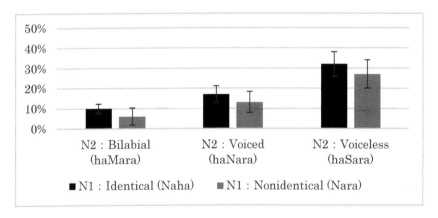

FIGURE 3 Percentage of *rendaku* application by consonant identity across morpheme boundaries and by consonant features (bilabial, voiced, and voiceless) in the second constituent. The error bars represent the standard error based on subject means in each condition.

4   Discussion

This study has looked at various aspects of cases in which the OCP might trigger or inhibit *rendaku* within or across morpheme boundaries in the production of compounds. The results of Experiments 1 and 2 provide evidence that the OCP has a facilitation effect in the application of *rendaku* as a means of improving the sound sequence existing in the input (at the cost of altering the original form of the input) when the second constituent includes identical adjacent moras (e.g., *kakara*) but not when only the moras' initial consonants are identical (e.g., *kakura*). This finding is consistent with Sasaki's (2011) argument for "mora-sized OCP." Our results also demonstrated that the mora-sized OCP can have a stronger effect than the OCP applying to identical consonants intervened by a vowel.

Next, the results of Experiment 3 show that two adjacent identical CV moras across a morpheme boundary (e.g., *naha-hamara*) facilitate *rendaku*, replicating Kawahara and Sano's (2014) results. Moreover, we concurrently showed the effects of both the OCP-bilabial (*hamara* → *bamara*) and the OCP-voiced (*hanara* → *banara*) within the second constituent, the former being more salient than the latter. While the OCP-bilabial effect of *rendaku* is a replication of Kumagai (2017), our results further demonstrated that a sonorant can actually inhibit the process of *rendaku* application. This provides an experimental support for Rice's (1993) argument that Japanese sonorants have a [+voiced] feature that influences Japanese phonological processes. It should be noted that the Identity Avoidance effect triggering *rendaku* across a morpheme boundary and the Identity Avoidance effect inhibiting *rendaku* within a single morpheme in the input did not interact with each other. We therefore conclude that these are independent effects.

References

Ihara, M. and Murata, T. 2006. Nihongo no *rendaku* ni kansuru ikutsu-ka no jikken. On'in Kenkyū 9:17–24.

Ihara, M., Tamaoka, K. and Lim, H. 2011. *Rendaku* and markedness: Phonetic and phonological effects. Paper presented at the July meeting of the Tokyo Circle of Phonologists, Tokyo.

Irwin, M. 2014. *Rendaku* across duplicate moras. *NINJAL Research Papers* 7:93–109.

Ito, J. and Mester, A. 1986. The phonology of voicing in Japanese: Theoretical consequences for morphological accessibility. *Linguistic Inquiry* 17: 49–73.

Ito, J. and Mester, A. 1988. Markedness and word structure: OCP effects in Japanese. Ms., UC Santa Cruz.

Ito, J. and Mester, A. 2003. Japanese morphophonemics: Markedness and word structure. Cambridge, MA: MIT Press.

Jaeger, T. F. 2008. Categorical Data Analysis: Away from ANOVAs (transformation or not) and towards Logit Mixed Models. Journal of Memory and Language 59(4): 434–446.

Kawahara, S. and Sano, S. 2013. Testing Rosen's Rule and Strong Lyman's Law. Ms., Keio University and Okayama Prefectural University.

Kawahara, S. and Sano, S. 2014. Identity Avoidance and *rendaku*. Proceedings of Phonology 2013. (Online publication)

Kawahara, S. and Sano, S. 2016. *Rendaku* and identity avoidance: Consonantal identity and moraic identity. In T. Vance and M. Irwin (eds.), Sequential voicing in Japanese compounds: Papers from the NINJAL *Rendaku* Project. Amsterdam: John Benjamins. pp. 47–55.

Kawahara, S. Ono, H. & Sudo, K. 2006. Consonant co-occurrence restrictions in

Yamato Japanese. *Japanese/Korean Linguistics* 14, 27–38. Stanford: CSLI Publications.

Kubozono, H. 1995. Gokeisei to on'in kōzō [Word formation and phonological structure]. Tokyo: Kurosio.

Kubozono, H. 1999. Nihongo no Onsei [The sound system of Japanese]. Tokyo: Iwanami.

Kumagai, Gakuji (2017) Testing OCP-labial effect on Japanese *rendaku*. Ms. Revsion submitted.Downloadable at http://ling.auf.net/lingbuzz/003290

Leben, W. 1973. Suprasegmental Phonology. Doctoral dissertation, MIT.

Lyman, B. 1894. Change from surd to sonant in Japanese compounds. Oriental Club of Philadelphia, 1–17.

McCarthy, J. J. 1986. OCP effects: Gemination and antigemination. Linguistic Inquiry 17:207–263.

Mester, Armin, and Junko Ito. 1989. Feature predictability and underspecification: Palatal prosody in Japanese mimetics. *Language* 65: 258–93.

Rice, K. 1993. A reexamination of the feature [sonorant]: The status of sonorant obstruents. *Language* 69:308–344.

Sasaki, K. 2011. Syllable deletion as a prosodically conditioned derived environment effect. In: W. McClure and M. den Dikken (eds.), Japanese/Korean Linguistics Vol. 18, 214–225. Stanford: CSLI.

Sato, H. 1989. Fukugōgo ni okeru akusento kisoku to *rendaku* kisoku. [The accent rule and the *rendaku* rule in compounds]. In: M. Sugito (ed.), Kooza nihongo to nihongo kyooiku [Lectures on Japanese and Japanese education], vol. 2, 233–265. Tokyo: Meiji Shoin.

Tamaoka, K. and Ikeda, F. 2010. Whiskey or bhiskey? Influence of first element and dialect region on sequential voicing of shoochuu. Gengo Kenkyu 137:65–79.

Vance, T. J. 1979. Nonsense word experiments in phonology and their application to *rendaku* in Japanese. Doctoral dissertation, University of Chicago.

Vance, T. J. 1987. An introduction to Japanese phonology. New York: SUNY Press.

Yip, M. 1988. The Obligatory Contour Principle and phonological rules: A loss of identity. Linguistic Inquiry 19: 65–100.

Part IV

Psycholinguistics

Effects of Grammatical Variations on Predictive Processing

NAYOUNG KWON
Konkuk University

1 Introduction

Prediction is one of the most fundamental principles of human cognition. It operates in various cognitive domains including theory of mind, visual processing, and motor control (Friston & Stephan 2007; Frith & Frith 2006; Mehta & Schaal 2002; Wolpert & Flanagan 2001) as well as language (DeLong, Urbach, & Kutas 2005; Federmeier 2007; Pickering & Garrod 2007; Van Berkum, Brown, Zwitserlood, Kooijman, & Hagoort 2005). However, while there has been ample evidence that language processing is predictive, it is not clear whether predictiive processing always takes place whenever relevant information is available. Here, I discuss studies suggesting the limits of predictive processing, focusing on the formation of various types of long-distance dependencies, and contrasting their processing profiles to those involved in preactivation of semantic features.

Language processing has been argued to be highly incremental and predictive. That is, langue users immediately process and interpret incoming words despite rampant ambiguity in human language. This

Japanese/Korean Linguistics 25.
Edited by Shin Fukuda, Mary Shin Kim, and Mee-Jeong Park.

sometimes results in processing difficulty at the point of structural disambiguation when the intially built structure turns out to be incorrect. This phenomenon was dubbed the garden path effect and has been taken as evidence that structural processing is incremental and predictive (Rayner & Frazier 1987; Frazier & Rayner 1982).

The predictive nature of language processing has also been examined in the context of semantic processing. For example, Federmeier and Kutas (1999) examined brain responses to semantic category violation using ERPs. In the study, they presented a lead in sentence (e.g., *They wanted to make the hotel look more like a tropical resort*) followed by a target sentence (e.g., *So along the driveway, they planted rows of …*), which ended either with the predicted lexical item (e.g., *palms*), a within-category violation (e.g., *pines*; an unexpected lexical item that belongs to the same taxonomic category with the expected item), or a between-category violation (e.g., *tulips;* a likewise unexpected item from a different taxonomic category). The results showed that while both violation conditions elicited larger N400s than the expected condition at the critical position, even larger N400s were elicited in response to the between-category violation condition than to the within-category violation condition. This was so even when their cloze probabilities were equally low. These results have been taken to suggest that some semantic features of a predicted word are preactivated ahead of time, facilitating the processing of unexpected words which overlap in semantic features with the predicted word (see also DeLong et al. 2005; Federmeier, McLennan, De Ochoa, & Kutas 2002; Kutas 1993; Kutas & Hillyard 1984; Lau, Stroud, Plesch, & Phillips 2006; Thornhill & Van Petten 2012; Wicha, Moreno, & Kutas 2003; Wicha, Bates, Moreno, & Kutas 2003; Van Petten & Luka 2012; Van Berkum et al. 2005).

However, while these results are compelling, they are also compatible with the integration hypothesis such that lexical items are easier to integrate with the previous context when they share a larger number of semantic features with an expected word. In addition, it is also not clear whether preactivation of semantic features is limited to salient semantic features such as categorical information (Federmeier and Kutas 1999) or grammaticalized features such as gender (Spanish: Wicha et al. 2003; Dutch: Van Berkum et al. 2005) or animacy (Polish: Szewczyk & Schriefers 2013). I address this issue in Section 2 based on an ERP study using the classifier system in Chinese. By examining effects at a sentential position before a predicted word, I show that fine-grained semantic features of a predicted word can be pre-activated before bottom-up input. In Section 3, turning to structural prediction, I discuss the processing of long-distance dependency formation. I first compare the processing of relative clauses in English with that in Korean, showing that cognitive mechanisms underlying the processing of anaphora and cataphora are similar. Nonetheless, however, based on eye-tracking studies of dependency formation, I argue that predictive processing is more limited in cataphora than in anaphora. Section 4 concludes.

2   Pre-activation of Semantic Features

Chinese, Korean and Japanese are classifier languages. Thus, for example in Chinese, a noun must be preceded by a *classifier* when it is accompanied by a numeral, a demonstrative or a quantifier (Li & Thompson 1989). This is illustrated in (1), where the classifier 张 is used for 纸 'paper', signalling perceived characteristics of 纸 'paper' as a flat object. This suggests that the classifier system is a way of representating noun classification in Chinese.

(1)   三   张   纸
      three   classifier   paper
      'three sheets of paper'

However, the semantic classification of a given classifier is not always associated with a homogeneous group in Chinese. For example, the classifier 部 is used with 'novels', 'movies', 'telephones' and 'cars', and thus may represent at least two semantic classifications, with 'literature' and 'movies' forming one semantic category and 'cars' and 'telephones' the other. However, it is not easy to define these classifications in a way that they can be exclusively distinguished from other similar concepts such as 'train' or 'performance', both of which require a different classifier. This suggests that the semantic content of classifiers is often quite abstract. Furthermore, when not used as classifiers, these characters can have different meanings. For example, the classifier 部 means 'department' when used as a noun. Thus, given that the agreement between a classifier and its associated noun is rather specifically defined, if prediction of a noun affects the processing of its preceding classifier, this could be taken as evidence for predictive processing. This is the research question that Kwon, Sturt, & Liu (2017) investigated in their ERP study.

Kwon et al. (2017) designed their study similar to Federmeier and Kutas (1999) but, crucially, examined ERP effects at a classifier position before a predicted noun. The results were compatible with those reported in Federmeier and Kutas (1999); in a highly constrained context as in (2) (e.g., ~ *that Zhang Yimou directed*; mean cloze probabilty for predicted classifiers and nouns: .68 and .85 respectively), classifiers that mismatched a predicted noun (e.g., *movie*) elicited an N400 effect compared to a matching classifier. Furthermore, the N400 effect was graded such that it was bigger for classifiers that were semantically unrelated to the predicted word (e.g., 座, a classifier for *building*) than for classifiers that were related (e.g., 场, a classifier for *performance*). This was so even when the cloze probabilities of these mismatching classifiers (and their following nouns) were all zero.

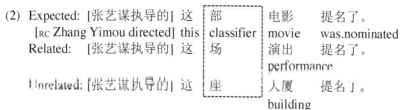

(2) Expected: [张艺谋执导的] 这 部 电影 提名了。
    [rc Zhang Yimou directed] this classifier movie was.nominated
    Related: [张艺谋执导的] 这 场 演出 提名了。
    performance
    Unrelated: [张艺谋执导的] 这 座 大厦 提名了。
    building
'This movie/performance/building that Zhang Yimou directed was nominated.'

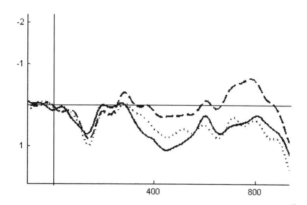

FIGURE 1 Grand average ERP waveforms time-locked to the classifier position at a right posterior region (E38; EGI EEG system, 64-channel HydroCel Geodesic Sensor Nets) for expected (solid line), unrelated (dashed line) and related conditions (dotted line) with the 300 ms pre-classifier baseline (figure reconstructed from Kwon et al. 2017)

These results suggest that at least with highly constraining contextual information, language processing is predictive. Furthermore, the graded N400 effects at the classifier position before the predicted noun suggest that the predictions are fine-grained enough to include information about the wide range of semantic classifications that the classifier system in Chinese represents (see Szewczyk & Schriefers 2013 for similar results based on animacy in Polish).

In the next section, I turn my attention to structural prediction, focusing on active dependency formation.

3   Predictive Dependency Formation

Predictive dependency formation has been frequently discussed in the context of the Active filler strategy (Frazier & Clifton 1989; Boland, Tanenhaus, Garnsey, & Carlson 1995; Garnsey, Tanenhaus, & Chapman 1989; Pickering & Traxler 2003; Traxler & Pickering 1996), which argues that once a displaced element (filler henceforth; *who* in (3)) is detected, the parser immediately postulates its gap position without waiting for further information. Thus, when there is an overt pronoun (*us*) in the predicted gap position (i.e., object of the embedded verb, *bring*), processing difficulty results, as can be shown by slower reading times at *us* in (3a) than in (3b) (Filled-gap effects: Crain & Fodor 1985; Stowe 1986).

(3) Filled-gap experiment sentences (Stowe 1986)
a. My brother wanted to know who Ruth will bring us home to __ at Christmas.
b. My brother wanted to know if Ruth will bring us home to Mom at Christmas.

However, while there are various types of dep anaphoric dependency endencies, most of the studies to date have focused on a syntactic anaphoric dependency, where a linguistic element is displaced as a result of syntactic movement and precedes its gap position as in relative clause or wh-question sentences in English. Accordingly, it is not clear whether predictive dependency formation is a general parsing heuristic or is limited to this specific type of dependency. To address this question, based on ERP studies of a syntactic anaphoric dependency (English), a syntactic cataphoric dependency (Korean) and a referential cataphoric dependency (Korean), I first show that neuro/cognitive mechanisms underlying the processing of these different types of dependencies are similar. Then I discuss predictive processing in a cataphoric dependency, comparing its processing profiles to those of an anaphoric dependency.

3.1   Previous ERP Studies of Anaphoric vs. Cataphoric Dependencies

One of the most studied constructions in the field of psycholinguistics is the relative clause construction, especially in the context of the processing of subject and object relative clauses. This has been an important topic for psycholinguistics, as it provides a good testing ground for various processing accounts and/or theories (see Kwon, Gordon, Lee, Kluender, & Polinsky 2010 for relevant discussion). Importantly to the goal of the current paper, studies have shown that object relative clauses elicit a LAN effect (left anterior negativity; Kluender & Kutas 1993) compared to subject relative clauses at the point that a dependency is completed (relevant sentential position in a box in (4) and (5)). This has been attested in relative clauses in English with an anaphoric dependency ((4); King & Kutas 1995; also see Weckerly & Kutas 1999; Müller, King & Kutas 1997; Münte, Schwirtz, Wieringa, Matzke & Johannes 1997; Vos, Gunter, Kolk & Mulder 2001), as well as in relative clauses in Korean ((5); Kwon, Kluender, Kutas, & Polinsky 2013) and Japanese (Ueno & Garnsey 2008) with a cataphoric dependency, despite potentially different processing procedures that could have been necessitated by different surface orders of these two types of dependencies.

(4) Relative clauses in English (King & Just 1991; King & Kutas 1995)
a. SR: The reporter*i* who __*i* harshly attacked the senator[____]the error.
b. OR: The reporter*i* who the senator harshly attacked __[____]the error.

(5) Relative clauses in Korean

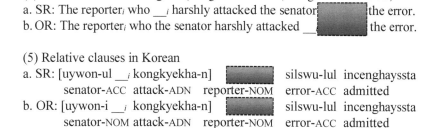

a. SR: [uywon-ul __*i* kongkyekha-n]   silswu-lul incenghayssta
        senator-ACC attack-ADN reporter-NOM error-ACC admitted
b. OR: [uywon-i __*i* kongkyekha-n]   silswu-lul incenghayssta
        senator-NOM attack-ADN reporter-NOM error-ACC admitted

Previous studies have suggested that left anterior negativity (LAN) is related to working memory among others, such that a bigger LAN effect is elicited in response to sentences taxing working memory compared to control sentences (cf. King & Kutas 1995; Fiebach, Schlesewsky & Friederici 2002; Vos, Gunter, Kolk, & Mulder 2001). Likewise, the LAN effect elicited to object relative clauses when compared to subject relative clauses has also been interpreted as indexing higher working memory costs in the processing of object relative clauses, either because of multiple processes taking place about the same time (King & Kutas 1995) or processing difficulty that arises from language-universal parsing heuristics (see Kwon et al. 2010 for relevant discussion). In addition, it was found that a referential dependency involving *pro* as in (6) similarly elicits a LAN at the point when *pro* is associated with its antecedent (relevant sentential position in a box), compared to control sentences without such dependency (Kwon 2008).

(6) An adjunct clause with *pro* in Korean
[hwalang-uy taypyo-ka ___*i*   kwukceycek censihoy-eyse   nophi
gallery-GEN representative-NOM international exhibition-at   highly

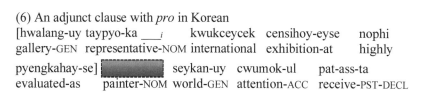

pyengkahay-se]   seykan-uy cwumok-ul   pat-ass-ta
evaluated-as   painter-NOM world-GEN attention-ACC receive-PST-DECL

'Because the representative of the gallery highly evaluated (him$_i$) at the international exhibition, the painter$_i$ gained the attention of the world.'

For the goal of our current paper, these remarkably similar brain responses to syntactic anaphoric (e.g., relative clauses in English) and cataphoric (e.g., relative clauses in Korean and Japanese) dependencies on the one hand and to syntactic and referential cataphoric dependencies (e.g., relative and adjunct clauses in Korean) on the other suggest that despite different surface and/or grammatical features, similar cognitive mechanisms underlie the processing of these dependencies. However, in the next section I discuss experimental findings suggesting that these depedencies differ in the strength of predictive dependency formation.

3.2 Predictive Dependency Formation in Anaphoric vs. Cataphoric Dependencies

Dependency formation has been shown to be active in various linguistic contexts. As already discussed, in sentences with syntactic dependencies a displaced filler activates a search for its gap position (Active filler strategy; Frazier & Clifton 1989). Likewise, in sentences with a referential dependency, an anaphorical expression without an antecedent triggers an active search of its antecedent, leading to processing difficulty when features of the anaphoric expression are not compatible with those of the first available antecedent. For example, Kreiner, Sturt, & Garrod (2008) found a gender mismatch cost at *the king* after a gender mismatching reflexive, *herself.* Similarly, van Gompel and Liversedge (2003) found processing difficulty at *the girl* after a masculine pronoun *he,* even though pronouns are relatively free in their domain of interpretation such that *he* docs not necessarily require an intra-sentential antecedent.

(7) Kreiner et al. (2008), Experiment 2
After reminding himself/herself about the letter, the king immediately went to the meeting at the office.

(8) van Gompel and Liversedge (2003), Experiment 1
When he was fed up, the boy/girl visited the girl very often.

In addition, active dependency formation interacts with structural ambiguity such that it can override an otherwise strong structural preference. For example, according to Late closure, a parsing principle that is assumed to guide structural parsing in the Garden path theory (Frazier 1987), a structurally ambiguous NP following a verb is likely to be parsed as the direct object of the verb (e.g., Because Ralph [vp threaten [np the neighbour]]...). Thus, when the NP turns out to be a main clause subject instead (e.g., Because Ralph [vp threaten] [s [np the neighbour recorded...]), processing difficulty results (e.g., Pickering, Traxler and Crocker 2000). However, using the object cleft construction Cai, Sturt, & Pickering (2013) showed that this garden path effect can be removed when the structurally ambiguous NP is preceded by a displaced filler. This is because the object position of the verb is the first available gap position for the clefted object (*John* in (9)) and is thus immediately parsed as such according to the Active filler strategy, which requires the ambiguous NP (*the neighbour* in (9)) to be parsed as the main clause subject. This suggests that strongly predictive dependency formation based on Active filler strategy may override Late closure in the processing of a syntactic anaphoric dependency.

(9) Experimental sentences in Cai et al. (2013)
Because it was John that Ralph threatened(,) the neighbour recorded their conversation.

Given this, an important question is whether strongly predictive dependency formation can also be found in a cataphoric dependency. Kwon & Sturt (2014) examined the processing of the nominal control construction (10) and the adjunct control construction (11) to address this question. These constructions are ideal test cases to examine the generality of predictive dependency formation, as dependency formation between sentential elements is semantically (or syntactically) motivated (for relevant theoretical discussion, please see Culicover & Jackendoff 2001, 2006; cf. Hornstein 1999), and, based on immediate use of control information during the early processing stage (Kwon & Sturt 2016), an obligatory (Kwon & Sturt 2014; norming study) cataphoric dependency can be formed.

(10) Kwon & Sturt (2014), Experiment 1 sample stimuli
a. Giver control
Before Andrew$_i$'s refusal PRO$_{i/*k}$ to wash(,) the kids$_k$ came over to the house.
b. Recipient control
Before Andrew$_i$'s order PRO$_{*i/k}$ to wash(,) the kids$_k$ came over to the house.

(11) Kwon & Sturt (2014), Experiment 2 sample stimuli
a. Giver control
Before Andrew's failure to wash(,) the kids came over to the house.
b. Adjunct control
Before PRO$_i$ failing to wash(,) the kids$_i$ came over to the house.

The experimental sentences in Kwon & Sturt (2014) were thus created such that while a controller (e.g., *Andrew*) is already available at the point of processing PRO in the giver control sentences (10a & 11a), no controller is available for PRO in the recipient control (10b) and the adjunct control (11b) sentences PRO is processed. Eye-tracking experiments were conducted to when investigate whether active search of PRO's controller will be launched in the recipient and adjunct control constructions, and if so, whether the search will override Late closure, as in the cleft construction. If dependency formation takes priority over Late closure, then a structurally ambiguous NP (e.g., *the kids*) will be parsed as the main clause subject, not as the direct object of the embedded verb. This is because if the NP is parsed as the object, it cannot be assigned to PRO as its controller due to the Princicple C violation (i.e., [PRO$_i$ to wash the kids$_i$]. On the other hand, if parsed as the main clause subject, *the kids* can be assigned to PRO as its controller (i.e., [PRO$_i$ to wash] [the kids$_i$...). If so, then the recipient control and the adjunct control condition sentences should not elicit a garden path effect at the disambiguating position (e.g., *came over*) when the NP is confirmed to be the main clause subject. In contrast, processing difficulty is predicted in the corresponding subject control sentences. However, the results (Figure 2) showed that while active search for a controller launched in the recipient and adjunct control constructions, a garden path effect was observed in all the ambiguous sentences regardless of control type. The effect of experimental manipulation was found only during the recovery processes from the intial misanalysis, which were easier in the recipient and adjunct control sentences, where PRO-controller dependency formation facilitated the structural reanalysis compared to giver control sentences.

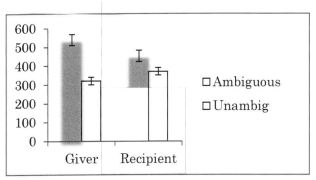

FIGURE 2 Go-past reading times at the disambiguating verb position in Exp 1 (reconstructed from Kwon & Sturt, 2014)

Combined with previous studies, these results suggest that although control information can be used immediately, predictive dependency formation is not as strong in cataphora as in anaphora, and may not override Late closure.

4 Discussion and Conclusions

Prediction is a mental process that generates information about future states based on available knowledge or information. In this paper, I discuss how prediction shapes on line sentence processing by discussing previous studies of preactivation of semantic features and structural prediction.

Previous evidence for semantic prediction has been mainly conducted in Indo-European languages based on unilateral and highly grammaticalized semantic features such as animacy or gender (Szewczyk & Schriefers 2013; Van Berkum et al. 2005; Wicha et al. 2003) or based on straightforward taxonomic relations (Federmeier and Kutas 1999). On the other hand, Chinese classifiers represent a broad spectrum of noun classifications including (but not limited to) animacy, shape, size, and function (Allan 1977; Tai 1994). Accordingly, the gradient semantic prediction effects in Kwon et al. (2017) confirm the generality of semantic predictions across languages; at least with highly constraining contextual information, semantic features from a wide spectrum of semantic relations can be predicted even when they do not correlate with overt morpho-syntactic markers.

On the other hand, studies of structural predictions suggest that structural predictions can be more constrained by surface or gramamtical characteristics. That is, in contrast to highly predictive dependency formation in a syntactic anaphoric dependency (as in the object cleft construction examined by Cai et al. 2013), the influence of predictive dependency formation is more limited in a cataphoric dependency (as in the control construction examined by Kwon et al. 2014). It is possible that this is because control information is a rather weaker cue for dependency formation. While control information is immediately used to form a long-distance dependency during the on-line sentence processing (Kwon & Sturt 2016), the interpretation of the control construction may be more sensitive to semantic or pragmatic relations between sentential elements, posing a relatively weaker grammatical requirement on dependency formation.

Another possibility is that cataphoric dependency is not a preferred type of dependency in general. In fact, previous studies have shown that, in general, cataphoric dependency is more limited in distribution than anaphoric dependency within a language. For example, sentence (12b) illustrates a violation of Principle C and thus is considered to be unaccetable. On the other hand, sentence (12d) sounds less natural and less favored when compared to sentence (12c), even when it does not violate any grammatical constraint.

(12) Sentences from Kuno (1972)
a. anaphoric: Mark$_i$ said he$_i$ won the prize.
b. cataphoric: * He$_i$ said Mark$_i$ won the prize.
c. anaphoric: Before I scolded Harry$_i$, I calmed him$_i$.
d. cataphoric: ??Before I scolded him$_i$, I calmed Harry$_i$.

Likewise, cataphora seem more limited in their distribution across-languages as well. In the context of relative clauses for example, 98% of head-initial languages (60 of 61 examined in Dryer 1992) and 59% of head-final languages (26 of 63 examined in Dryer 1992) have relative clauses with an anaphoric dependency (i.e., post-nominal relative clauses). This means that there are many more relative clauses with an anaphoric dependency than those with a cataphoric dependency cross-linguistically. If we adopt a proposal by Hawkins (2004) on the close relation between processing efficiency and structural complexity, this could suggest that cataphora is less efficient to process than anaphora, and thus is more limited in general. Alternatively, it is possible that cataphoric dependency is more limited in distribution, and thus it is harder to predict a cataphoric dependency than an anaphoric dependency. Thus, ambiguous stuctures are less likely to be predicted to be   instances of a cataphoric dependency despite grammatical cues available.

To conclude, prediction operates in language processing as well as in other cognitive domains. Highly constraining contextual information may lead to preactivation of fine-grained semantic features in advance of bottom-up input even in a language without overt morpho-syntactic markers that correlate with these semantic features. On the other hand, structural predictions can be limited depending on the nature of a stucture. Cataphoric dependencies, for example, are less strongly predicted than anaphoric dependencies, at least when the dependency is motivated by control information. We need further studies, however, to confirm the generality of this observation using various structures with a cataphoric dependency.

References

Allan, K. 1977. Classifiers. *Language*, 285-311.

Boland, J. E., Tanenhaus, M. K., Garnsey, S. M., & Carlson, G. N. 1995. Verb argument structure in parsing and interpretation: Evidence from wh-questions. *Journal of Memory and Language* 34: 774-806.

Cai, Z., Sturt, P., & Pickering, M. 2013. The effect of non-adopted analyses on sentence processing. *Language and Cognitive Processes* 27: 1286-1311.

Crain, S., & Fodor, J. D. 1985. How can grammars help parsers. In D. Dowty, D. Kartunnen, & A. M. Zwicky Eds., *Natural language parsing: Psycholinguistic, computational, and theoretical perspectives* pp. 94–128. Cambridge, UK: Cambridge University Press.

Culicover, P. W. & Jackendoff, R. 2001. Control is not movement. *Linguistic Inquiry* 32: 493-512.

Culicover, P. W. & Jackendoff, R. 2006 Turn over control to the semantics. *Syntax* 9: 131-152.

DeLong, K. A., Urbach, T. P., & Kutas, M. 2005. Probabilistic word pre-activation during language comprehension inferred from electrical brain activity. *Nature neuroscience* 8: 1117-1121.

Dryer, Matthew S. 1992. The Greenbergian word order correlations. *Language* 68: 81-138.

Federmeier, K. D., & Kutas, M. 1999. A rose by any other name: Long-term memory structure and sentence processing. *Journal of memory and Language* 41: 469-495.

Federmeier, K. D., McLennan, D. B., De Ochoa, E., & Kutas, M. 2002. The impact of semantic memory organization and sentence context information on spoken language processing by younger and older adults: An ERP study. *Psychophysiology* 39: 133-146.

Federmeier, K. D. 2007. Thinking ahead: The role and roots of prediction in language comprehension. *Psychophysiology* 44: 491-505.

Fiebach, C., J., Schlesewsky, M., & Friederici, A. D. 2002. Separating syntactic memory costs and syntactic integration costs during parsing: The processing of German *wh*-questions. *Journal of Memory and Language* 47: 250-272.

Vos, S. H., Gunter, T. C., Kolk, H. H. J., & Mulder, G. 2001. Working memory constraints on syntactic processing: An electrophysiological investigation. *Psychophysiology* 38: 41-63.

Frazier, L. & Rayner, K. 1982. Making and correcting errors during sentence comprehension: Eye movements in the analysis of structurally ambiguous sentences. *Cognitive Psychology* 14: 178-210.

Frazier, L. 1987. Sentence processing: A tutorial review. In M. Coltheart Ed., *Attention and performance XII: The psychology of reading*. Hillsdale, NJ: Erlbaum

Frazier, L., & Clifton, C. 1989. Successive cyclicity in the grammar and parser. *Language and Cognitive Processes* 4: 93–126.

Friston, K. & Stephan, K. 2007. Free energy and the brain. *Synthese* 159: 417–458.

Frith, C. D., & Frith, U. 2006. How we predict what other people are going to do. *Brain Research* 1079: 36-46.

Garnsey, S. M., Tanenhaus, M. K., & Chapman, R. M. 1989. Evoked potentials and the study of sentence comprehension. *Journal of Psycholinguistic Research* 18: 51-60.

Hawkins, John A. 2004. *Efficiency and complexity in grammars* Oxford University Press.

Hornstein, N. 1999. Movement and Control. *Linguistic Inquiry* 30: 69-96.

King, J., & Just, M. A., 1991. Individual differences in syntactic processing: The role of working memory. *Journal of Memory and Language* 30: 580-602.

King, J., & Kutas, M. 1995. Who did what and when? Using word- and clause-level ERPs to monitor working memory usage in reading. *Journal of Cognitive Neuroscience* 7: 376-395.

Kluender, R., & Kutas, M. 1993. Bridging the gap: Evidence from ERPs on the processing of unbound dependencies. *Journal of Cognitive Neuroscience* 52: 196-214.

Kreiner, H., Sturt, P., & Garrod, S. 2008. Processing definitional and stereotypical gender in reference resolution: Evidence from eye-movements. *Journal of Memory and Language* 58: 239-261.

Kuno, S. 1972. Functional Sentence Perspective: A Case Study from Japanese and English. *Linguistic Inquiry* 3: 269-320.

Kutas, M., & Hillyard, S. A. 1984. Brain potentials during reading reflect word expectancy and semantic association. *Nature* 307: 161 – 163

Kutas, M. 1993. In the company of other words: Electrophysiological evidence for single-word and sentence context effects. *Language and cognitive processes* 8: 533-572.

Kwon, N. 2008. Processing of syntactic and anaphoric gap-filler dependencies in Korean: Evidence from self-paced reading time, ERP and eye-tracking experiments. Doctoral dissertation, University of California, San Diego

Kwon, N., Lee, Y., Gordon, P. C., Kluender, R., & Polinsky, M. 2010. Cognitive and linguistic factors affecting subject/object asymmetry: An eye-tracking study of pre-nominal relative clauses in Korean. *Language* 86: 546-582.

Kwon, N., Kluender, R., Kutas, M., & Polinsky, M. 2013. Subject/Object processing asymmetries in Korean relative clauses: Evidence from ERP data. *Language* 89: 537-585.

Kwon, N., & Sturt, P. 2014. The use of control information in dependency formation: An eye-tracking study. *Journal of Memory and Language* 73: 59-80.

Kwon, N., & Sturt, P. 2016. Processing control information in a nominal control construction: An eye-tracking study. *Journal of Psycholinguistic Research* 45: 779-793.

Kwon, N., Sturt, P, & Liu, P. 2017. Predicting semantic features in Chinese: evidence from ERPs. *Cognition* 166: *433-446.*

Lau, E., Stroud, C., Plesch, S. & Phillips, C. 2006. The role of structural prediction in rapid syntactic analysis, *Brain and Language* 98: 74-88.

Li, C. N., & Thompson, S. A. 1989. *Mandarin Chinese: A functional reference grammar.* University of California Press.

Mehta, B. & Schaal, S. 2002. Forward models in visuo-motor control. *Journal of Neurophysiology* 88: 942–953.

Müller, H. M., King, J. W., & Kutas, M. 1997. Event-related potentials elicited by spoken relative clauses. *Cognitive Brain Research* 5: 193-203.

Münte, T. F., Schwirtz, O., Wieringa, B. M., Matzke, M., & Johannes, S. 1997. Elektrophysiologie komplexer Sätze: Ereigniskorrelierte Potentiale auf der Wort- und Satz-Ebene. *Zeitschrift für Elektroenzephalographie, Elektromyographie und verwandte Gebiete* 28: 11-7.

Pickering, M. J., Traxler, M. J. & Crocker, M. W. 2000. Ambiguity resolution in sentence processing: Evidence against frequency-based accounts. *Journal of Memory and Language* 43: 447-475

Pickering, M. J., & Traxler, M. J. 2003. Evidence against the use of subcategorisation information in the processing of unbounded dependencies. *Language and Cognitive Processes* 18: 469-503.

Pickering, M. J., & Garrod, S. 2007. Do people use language production to make predictions during comprehension? *Trends in Cognitive Sciences* 11: 105-110.

Rayner, K., & Frazier, L. 1987. Parsing temporarily ambiguous complements. *Quarterly Journal of Experimental Psychology* 39: 657-673.

Stowe, L. A. 1986. Parsing wh-constructions: Evidence for on-line gap location. *Language and Cognitive Processes* 1: 227-245.

Szewczyk J., Schriefers H. 2013. Prediction in language comprehension beyond specific words: An ERP study on sentence comprehension in Polish. *Journal of Memory and Language* 68: 297-314.

Tai, J. H. 1994. Chinese classifier systems and human categorization. *In honor of William S.-Y. Wang: Interdisciplinary studies on language and language change*, 479-494.

Thornhill, D. E., & Van Petten, C. 2012. Lexical versus conceptual anticipation during sentence processing: frontal positivity and N400 ERP components. *International Journal of Psychophysiology* 83: 382-392.

Traxler, M. J., & Pickering, M. J. 1996. Plausibility and the processing of unbounded dependencies: An eye-tracking study. *Journal of Memory and Language* 35: 454-475.

Ueno, M., & Garnsey, S. M. 2008. An ERP study of the processing of subject and object relative clauses in Japanese. *Language and Cognitive Processes* 23: 646-688.

van Berkum, J. J., Brown, C. M., Zwitserlood, P., Kooijman, V., & Hagoort, P. 2005. Anticipating upcoming words in discourse: evidence from ERPs and reading times. *Journal of Experimental Psychology: Learning, Memory, and Cognition* 31: 443-467.

van Gompel, R.P.G., & Liversedge, S.P. 2003. The influence of morphological information on cataphoric pronoun assignment. *Journal of Experimental Psychology: Learning, Memory, and Cognition* 29: 128-139.

van Petten, C., & Luka, B. J. 2012. Prediction during language comprehension: Benefits, costs, and ERP components. *International Journal of Psychophysiology* 83: 176-190.

Vos, S. H., Gunter, T. C., Kolk, H. H. J., & Mulder, G. 2001. Working memory constraints on syntactic processing: An electrophysiological investigation. *Psychophysiology* 38: 41-63.

Weckerly, J., & Kutas, M. 1999. An electrophysiological analysis of animacy effects in the processing of object relative sentences. *Psychophysiology* 36: 559-570.

Wicha, N. Y., Bates, E. A., Moreno, E. M., & Kutas, M. 2003. Potato not Pope: human brain potentials to gender expectation and agreement in Spanish spoken sentences. *Neuroscience Letters* 346: 165-168.

Wicha, N. Y., Moreno, E. M., & Kutas, M. 2003. Expecting gender: An event related brain potential study on the role of grammatical gender in comprehending a line drawing within a written sentence in Spanish. *Cortex* 39: 483-508.

Wolpert D.M., & Flanagan J.R. 2001. Motor prediction. *Current Biology* 11: R729–732.

Processing is not Facilitated by Exposure to Violations of Burzio's Generalization

JUNNA YOSHIDA

University of Tsukuba

EDSON T. MIYAMOTO
Future University Hakodate

1   Introduction

Recent work has provided exquisitely-detailed understanding of the role of frequency in language acquisition (Santolin & Saffran 2018 for a summary and inter-species comparison) and language comprehension (Levy 2008; *inter alia*). Here we suggest that much like in learning in non-human animals (Garcia & Koelling 1966), frequency of exposure is important in human language comprehension, but it is unlikely to override learners' internal constraints, such as those related to putatively-universal grammatical biases.

Previous experimental work in sentence comprehension suggests that readers habituate and get faster as the experiment proceeds. Moreover, the speedup is larger for constructions that are rare in everyday language because

Japanese/Korean Linguistics 25.
Edited by Shin Fukuda, Mary Shin Kim, and Mee-Jeong Park.
Copyright © 2018, CSLI Publications

their relative frequency is much higher during experiments (Fine et al. 2013). Participants seem to be able to rapidly finetune their expectations so that sentences that were hard to understand at the beginning of the experimental session, become increasingly easy and, in some cases, easier than baseline sentences. In other words, learning takes place along the experimental session as exposure is immediately incorporated into readers' experience, and expectations are modified accordingly. This jibes well with models of comprehension where difficulty in comprehension is in large part explained by expectation generated from exposure (Levy 2008), and grammatical constraints are irrelevant (Sasaki & McWhinney 2006, and references therein, for discussion for Japanese).

The work by Fine and colleagues is methodologically interesting for its use of statistical analyses to investigate how readers' behavior changes along the experiment. But it is also theoretically important for making explicit predictions about the behavioral changes that should occur if exposure is responsible for the reading time differences observed in experiments. We build on their work by using ungrammatical sentences to test their predictions. Crucially, their predictions should extend to ungrammatical sentences, as long as the constructions used are relatively rare.

The grammatical constraint adopted here is *Burzio's generalization*, according to which only verbs that can assign an external theta role can assign accusative case (Burzio 1986). This constraint has been implicated in the distribution of the accusative marker *o* with verbal nouns in Japanese (Miyagawa 1989; *inter alia*). Verbal nouns (see (2ab)) are often followed by the light verb *suru* "do" and the accusative marker *o* can intervene as in (2c).

(2) a. Verbal noun
    ryoko
    travel
    'travel'

   b. Verbal noun + light verb
    ryoko suru
    travel do
    'to travel'

   c. Verbal noun + *o* + light verb
    ryoko o   suru
    travel acc do
    'to travel'

Some types of intransitive verbal nouns as in (3a) cannot be followed by the accusative marker as shown in (3b) (Miyagawa 1989; Tsujimura 1990; Kageyama 1993; Kobayashi 2004; but see Grimshaw and Mester 1988).

(3) a.

Ya	ga	mato	ni	meityuu		-sita.
arrow	nom	target	dat	strike		do-past

b. *

Ya	ga	mato	ni	meityuu	o	sita.
arrow	nom	target	dat	strike	acc	do-past

(Miyagawa 1989: 659)

'The arrow struck the target.'

The accusative marker is unacceptable in (3b) because the verbal noun *meityu* is unaccusative, therefore it does not have an external theta role and, according to Burzio's generalization, the verbal noun plus *suru* complex cannot assign the accusative marker (Miyagawa 1989; but see Uchida & Nakayama 1993, for an alternative account; also the general discussion).

2 Experiment

We conducted a reading-time experiment to confirm that unaccusative constructions such as (3b) are unacceptable, and therefore slow to process. Moreover, we conducted analyses to test the claim that such a slowdown decreases with exposure to the construction (Fine et al. 2013).

2.1 Method

2.1.1 Participants

Forty native speakers of Japanese were paid to participate in the experiment.

2.1.2 Materials

A two by two design was adopted to investigate the effect of the accusative marker (with or without) depending on the type of predicate (unaccusatives or unergatives; see (4) for example sentences).

The first factor was *marker* so that within each pair of sentences, one version had the accusative marker *o*, and the other version omitted it. The second factor varied *predicate type* between items so that half of the items used unaccusative predicates, and the other half used unergative predicates.

To avoid possible ambiguities in the type of predicate, the subject (region R4) of the unaccusative items was inanimate, whereas the subject of the unergative items was animate (common Japanese surnames).

R5 is the crucial region where the verbal noun was presented with or without the accusative marker *o*. If unaccusative predicates are strange with the accusative marker *o* (Unaccusative/With condition, for short), they should be read more slowly compared to the Unaccusative/Without condition. Unergative verbal nouns should be perceived as natural regardless of the presence of the accusative marker *o*; therefore, reading times to the Unergative/With and the Unergative/Without conditions should not differ.

(4) a. Unaccusative item

	R1			R2			
Kimura-san	ni	yoruto,	/ asa	10 ji		goro	/
Kimura	to	according	morning	10 o'clock		around	

	R3		R4		R5		R6
nyuin-tyu	no	/ Matumoto-san	ga	/ sanpo	(-o)	sita /	youda.
hospitalized	gen	Matumoto	nom	walk	(acc)	did	aux-v

'According to Mr. Kimura, Mr. Matsumoto who is in the hospital took a walk around ten o'clock in the morning.'

b. Unergative item

	R1			R2	
Intânetto	ni	yoruto,	/ 80 nen-dai	ni /	
Internet	to	according	1980s	in	

	R3		R4		R5		R6
nihon	-sya	no	/ yusyutu	ga	/ zouka	(-o)	sita /	youda.
Japanese car		gen	export	nom	increase	(acc)	did	aux-v

'According to the Internet, Japanese car exports increased in the 1980s.'

Apart from the two factors above (marker and predicate type), a third factor was included so that each sentence had a code-switched version where the Japanese predicate was replaced with an equivalent English word.

Ten unaccusative verbal nouns and Ten unergative verbal nouns were used twice each to create forty sets of items. The forty sets were distributed into four lists according to a Latin Square design, so that each list contained the same number of items of each type and no more than one version from each set. The code-switching conditions are not of interest here, and are not reported. Therefore, in the analyses reported, each participant saw twenty test items in the crucial two by two design (marker versus predicate type).

Each participant saw one list interspersed with ninety-two filler sentences and presented pseudo-randomly so that test items did not follow consecutively. Thirty fillers were monolingual Japanese sentences, and the remaining sixty-two were Japanese sentences with one or two words in English.

2.1.3 Procedure

Before the experiment, participants were told that they were about to read sentences uttered by bilingual speakers who mix English and Japanese. Japanese characters were used to present Japanese words; the code-switched English words were presented using the Latin alphabet. Participants read individual sentences in a non-cumulative self-paced moving window fashion presented with Doug Rohde's Linger program, then rated acceptability on a 6-point scale (1 = "very strange"; 6 = "very natural"), and answered a yes/no comprehension question with feedback.

2.1.4 Analyses

R was used to analyze the data (version 3.3.0; R Core Team 2016). Comprehension question accuracy was analyzed using mixed logit models, and reading times were analyzed with linear mixed-effect models (lme4 package, version 1.1-12; Bates et al. 2015). Analyses of acceptability ratings were conducted using random-effects ordered logit models (ordinal package, version 2015.6-28; Christensen 2015). Main effects were calculated with the Anova function (car package, version 2.1-3; Fox & Weisberg 2011) and Satterthwaite approximations were used to compute the degrees of freedoms. Post hoc pairwise comparisons were conducted with the lsmeans function (lsmeans package, version 2.23-5; Lenth 2016).

The interaction between predicate type (unergative vs. unaccusative) and marker (with/without the accusative marker *o*) was the crucial effect of interest. However, participants tend to speed up along the experimental session, therefore scaled log-transformed number of trials which included the number of test and filler items seen (*trial number*, for short) was also included (analyses without this variable yielded similar trends). All factors were centered to decrease collinearity. Random effects included subject- and item-specific intercepts to each analysis. The best model for each analysis was selected using backward selection.

Analyses for acceptability ratings and reading times only included trials for which the comprehension question was answered correctly. Reading times were trimmed (points below 100 ms and above 3000 ms were discarded, affecting less than 1.15% of the data) and log-transformed to decrease skewness (raw RT analyses revealed similar trends). Reading times were model-trimmed and refitted (Baayen 2008) resulting in an additional loss of 1.34% data.

2.2 Results

Comprehension accuracy was lower in the With *o* conditions (β = -.95, z = -2.26, p = .024; see Table 1).

In the acceptability ratings, there was an interaction between predicate and marker ($\beta = -1.03$, $z = -2.88$, $p = .004$; see the last column of Table 1). Post hoc analyses revealed higher ratings in the Unaccusative/Without condition than in the Unaccusative/With condition ($\beta = .14$, $z = 2.24$, $p = .025$), but no difference in the Unergative conditions ($\beta = -.10$, $z = -1.24$, $p = .215$).

Predicate	Marker	Accuracy (%)	Acceptability
Unaccusative	With o	93.00	5.42
	Without o	97.50	5.62
Unergative	With o	96.00	5.38
	Without o	98.00	5.18

TABLE 1 Mean Comprehension Question Accuracy and Acceptability per Condition.

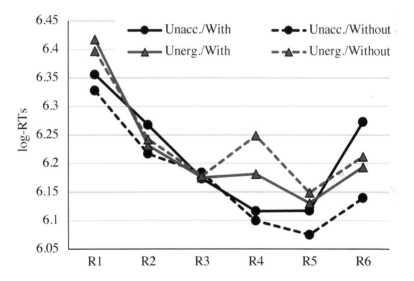

FIGURE 1 Region-by-Region Mean Log-Transformed Reading Times.

Results for the reading times were as follows (see Figure 1 for the region-by-region mean log-transformed reading times). Across all regions, there was a main effect of trial number as reading times got faster as the experiment progressed ($ps < .001$). Moreover, there was a main effect of predicate type in R1 ($\beta = -.08$, $t = -2.67$, $p = .011$) and in R4 ($\beta = -.09$, $t = -2.82$, $p = .008$), such that the Unaccusative conditions were read faster than the Unergative conditions. This main effect was likely due to the type of words used across conditions, as surnames were used for the Unergative conditions, whereas common nouns were used for the Unaccusative conditions.

R5 is the crucial region where the verbal noun was presented. The predicted interaction between predicate type and accusative marker was observed (β = .03, t = 2.02, p = .043). However, post hoc analyses revealed no difference between the Unaccusative conditions (β = -.03, t = -1.38, p = .168), or between the Unergative conditions (β = .03, t = 1.48, p = .139).

In R6 (the auxiliary verb), the interaction from the previous region persisted (β = .05, t = 2.90, p = .004). The Unergative conditions did not differ (β = -.002, t = -.06, p = .950), while for Unaccusatives, With o was slower than Without o (β = -.14, t = -4.14, p < .001).

The results are compatible with the observation that unaccusative verbal nouns are less natural with the accusative marker o (Miyagawa 1989; Tsujimura 1990; Kageyama 1993; Kobayashi 2004). However, rather than ungrammaticality per se, the results may be related to the low frequency of this construction. Participants slow down, not because a grammatical constraint was violated, but because they are not used to seeing such construction. A corpus-frequency count was conducted to test this possibility.

Corpus frequency

A corpus count was conducted on the Balanced Corpus of Contemporary Written Japanese (BCCWJ: National Institute for Japanese Language and Linguistics 2017). The occurrence of the verbal nouns used in the reading-time experiment revealed that the Unaccusative/With condition is relatively infrequent ($\chi 2(1)$=448.76, p<.000; see Table 2).

Predicate	Marker	
	With o	Without o
Unaccusative	4 (0.13%)	3076 (99.87%)
Unergative	248 (14.38%)	1477 (85.62%)

TABLE 2 Occurrence of Verbal Nouns Used in the Experiment

Therefore, there are two different ways of accounting for the reading-time data reported. One possibility is that grammatical violations affect comprehension directly, causing slow reading times. Alternatively, grammatical violations only affect production by decreasing frequency of use (as attested by the corpus count). This infrequent use in turn decreases exposure, therefore readers slow down because they are not used to seeing this construction. It is often difficult to tease apart these two possibilities. But, analyses proposed by Fine et al. (2013) allow us to test the two types of explanations. In the following, we report analyses to investigate how reading times and acceptability ratings changed along the reading-time experiment.

Analyses investigating the changes along the experimental session

Apart from the factors used in the first set of analyses (predicate type, accusative marker, and trial number), a new variable, *test trials*, was included to investigate changes along the experimental session. Test trials is the number of Unaccusative/With sentences a participant saw at each point along the experiment (from 0 to 3; similar trends were observed when the total number of test trials was used). All factors were centered to decrease collinearity, and numerical factors were also scaled.

Recall that trial number includes test trials and filler trials to account for overall speedups that occur along the experiment as participants get used to the experimental procedure. In contrast, test trials measures how speedup varied between conditions along the experiment. The Unaccusative/With condition is relatively infrequent (in the corpus count it is less than 1.5% of the Unaccusative/Without condition, but during the experiment the two conditions are presented with equal frequency). Therefore, exposure to this construction should be particularly effective and its speedup should be steeper than in the Unaccusative/Without condition. A similar improvement may be observed in the acceptability ratings.

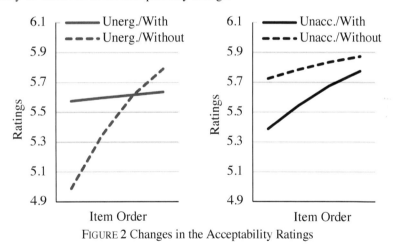

FIGURE 2 Changes in the Acceptability Ratings

Results were as follows (see Figure 2). There was a trend in all four conditions for acceptability to increase with test trials ($p = .077$). The pace of improvement did not differ between the Unergative/Without and the Unergative/With conditions ($\beta = -.27, z = -1.44, p = .150$). However, the pace of improvement for the Unaccusative/With condition was greater than in the

Unaccusative/Without condition ($\beta = 0.84$, $z = 2.22$, $p = .026$), as predicted by experience-based models (see Snyder, 2000 for related results). Recall that the acceptability ratings were collected after each sentence was read, but adaptation should be observed earlier, when the crucial word was read. Therefore, we report relevant reading-time analyses next.

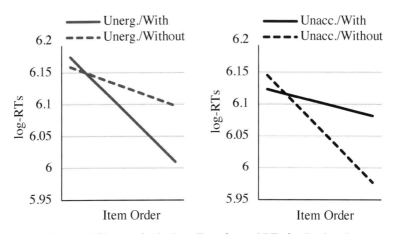

FIGURE 3 Changes in the Log-Transformed RTs for Region 5

In R5, the crucial region with the verbal noun, there were speedups in all conditions. There was no difference between the unergative conditions ($\beta = .004$, $t = .23$, $p = .819$). In contrast, the speedup in the Unaccusative/With condition was smaller compared to the Unaccusative/Without condition ($\beta = .08$, $t = 2.25$, $p = .025$), even though the Unaccusative/With condition is less frequent (see the corpus results). This is the opposite of what previous exposure models predict (Fine et al. 2013), suggesting that exposure to the ungrammatical construction is unlikely to explain the results reported.

In R6, speedups between the unaccusative conditions ($\beta = -.004$, $t = -.08$, $p = .934$), and between the unergative conditions did not differ ($\beta = -.02$, $t = -1.02$, $p = .310$).

2.3 Discussion

Overall, the ungrammatical Unaccusative/With condition was rated lower and read more slowly than the Unaccusative/Without condition. There were no comparable differences between the Unergative conditions. These results are compatible with claims that unaccusative verbal nouns are less natural when followed by the accusative marker o (Miyagawa 1989; Tsujimura 1990; Kageyama 1993; Kobayashi 2004).

Further analyses revealed that the reading-time result is unlikely to be related to the low frequency of the Unaccusative/With condition, as the speedup in this condition was smaller than in the Unaccusative/Without condition. This is the opposite of what experience-based models would predict (Fine et al. 2013).

Results in the acceptability ratings were in line with these models' predictions as the rise in the Unaccusative/With condition was larger than in the Unaccusative/Without condition, with no comparable difference between the Unergative conditions. However, these results are much too late to be related to expectation processes since they occurred long after the words where the crucial predictions were made. One possible explanation is that caser-marker omission is often associated with informal speech, therefore inclusion of the accusative marker could make the sentences sound more prescriptively correct. The insertion of the marker with unaccusative predicates in particular may lend them a stilted style (somewhat akin to saying "waste did an increase" instead of saying "waste increased") and it may explain why it is favored by politicians as in (5).

(5) Syouhikatudou ga   zouka   itasimasu   to
    consumption   nom   increase do-polite   if
    seikatuhaikibutu mo zouka   wo   suru to iu   koto
    waste   also increase acc   do   that mean which
    de   gozaimasu.
    cop   polite
    'It is the case if consumption increases, waste also increases.'
    (Transcripts of the Diet (Japanese Parliament) Sessions, 1978 in BCCWJ)

One concern in the results presented is the effect that the code-switched conditions may have had on the other sentences in the experiment. It is possible that they would make participants more likely to expect unusual sentences; therefore, it should be easier for participants to accept ungrammaticalities and consequently easier for reading times to reveal adaptations similar to those reported for grammatical sentences (as in Fine et al. 2013). Another possibility is that participants were willing to ascribe idiosyncrasies in the sentences to peculiarities of the bilinguals' style, and associate it with some politicians' overcorrected style. Whatever the case, trends in an ongoing experiment tend to replicate the results reported in this paper suggesting that the overall conclusions are likely to hold even when all sentences in the experiment are in Japanese.

3   General Discussion

Experimental work in the 1950s indicated that frequency of exposure, although important, was not sufficient to explain learning as it could not override learners' internal constraints (see Garcia & Koelling 1966, and references therein, on constraints in rats' acquired food avoidance). Recent work on language acquisition and processing has concentrated on frequency, but once again ignoring learner's internal biases. This paper is part of an ongoing project trying to at least partly correct this oversight by examining the interplay between frequency and grammatical constraints.

It is not our goal to deny the importance of frequency. Our results indicate an overall adaptation as readers get faster as they see more sentences (the effect of the variable *trial number*). But there is also a more specific adaptation as participants get faster as they see similar constructions (verbal nouns followed by a light verb, with or without the accusative marker). Therefore, it is undeniable that frequency of exposure is having an effect on behavior. Our interest, however, was in the claim that the pace of change (i.e., the rate of reading-time acceleration), differs between conditions, and that it is steeper for infrequent conditions because of their relatively high incidence during experiments (Fine et al. 2013). However, the differences we observed were in the opposite direction of what Fine and colleagues predicted. Namely, acceleration in the infrequent Unaccusative/With condition was less steep than in its Unaccusative/Without counterpart, suggesting that seeing an ungrammatical condition repeatedly induces limited facilitation.

We have emphasized the ungrammatical nature of the sentences we used. However, there is another aspect that differs in our sentences. In Fine and colleagues' experiment, the infrequent construction was probably salient and there may have been some premedidation from the part of the participants in expecting an ambiguous form (e.g. *the witness examined...*) to be used in its less preferred form (as a participial as in *the witness examined by the lawyer*) rather than in its more common form (as a simple past). In our items in contrast, the ungrammatical Unaccusative/With sentences are not very salient. Their surface form is identical to that of the grammatical Unergative/With. In fact, even linguists with extensive training have failed to notice the ungrammaticality (see the judgments in Grimshaw & Mester 1988). But the kinds of processes advocated by experience-based models do not require events to be salient in order for expectation to be adjusted. Nevertheless, this is clearly an area that is worth exploring in the future.

An area where we are conducting further studies is related to the exact nature of the ungrammaticality itself. In this paper, we couched the discussion in terms of Burzio's generalization (following Miyagawa 1989). However, the phenomenon may be more general, and Burzio's generalization may be a special case of the way the accusative marker is constrained by the subject's ability to have control over the event (Kageyama 1993; Uchida & Nakayama 1993). This is often illustrated with transitive verbal nouns' internal argument, which can be marked with the accusative marker *o* as in (6a), or the genetive marker *no* as in (6b).

(6) a. NP *o* construction

Gakusei ga   kyoositu   wo   soozi-sita,
student   nom   classroom acc   clean-do past
'The student cleaned the classroom.'

   b. NP *no* construction

Gakusei ga   kyoositu   no   soozi o   sita.
student   nom   classroom gen   clean acc   do-past
(lit.) 'The student did the cleaning of the classroom.'

(Miyamoto & Kishimoto 2016: 440)

Some transitive verbal nouns are unacceptable in the genitive construction as in (7b) (Tanomura 1988; Kageyama 1993; Uchida & Nakayama 1993).

(7) a. NP o construction

Keikan   ga   suri   o   taiho-sita.
policeman nom   pickpocket acc   catch-do-past
'The policeman caught the pickpocket.'

   b. NP no construction

*Keikan   ga   suri   no   taiho o   -sita.
policeman nom   pickpocket gen   catch acc   do-past
(lit.) 'The policeman did a catch of the pickpocket.'

(Uchida & Nakayama 1993: 440)

The subjects in both (6) and (7) have external theta roles, therefore Burzio's generalization cannot differentiate between (6b) and (7b). A new study is under preparation to investigate this type of construction. But for the purposes of this paper, it suffices that the accusative marker cannot appear in certain environments (perhaps due to Burzio's generalization, or perhaps because it requires an event that is under the control of the subject). Our point then is that violations of such a constraint are not easily overridden by exposure.

References

Baayen R. H. 2008. *Analysing Linguistic Data*. New York: Cambridge University Press.

Bates, D., Maechler, M., Bolker, B., & Walker, S. 2015. Fitting Linear Mixed-Effects Models Using lme4. *Journal of Statistical Software* 67(1): 1-48. doi:10.18637/jss.v067.i01.

Balanced Corpus of Contemporary Written Japanese (BCCWJ). 2017. Tokyo: National Institute for Japanese Language and Linguistics. Data version 1.1., accessed on February 27th 2017. https://chunagon.ninjal.ac.jp/

Burzio, L. 1986. *Italian Syntax*. Dordrecht: Reidel.

Christensen, R. H. B. 2015. Ordinal - Regression Models for Ordinal Data. R package version 2015.6-28. http://www.cran.r-project.org/package=ordinal/.

Fine, A. B., Jaeger, T. F., Farmer, T. A., & Qian, T. 2013. Rapid Expectation Adaptation during Syntactic Comprehension. *PLoS ONE*, 8, e77661.

Fox, J. & Weisberg, S. 2011. *An {R} Companion to Applied Regression, Second Edition*. Thousand Oaks CA: Sage. http://socserv.socsci.mcmaster.ca/jfox/Books/Companion

Garcia, J. & Koelling, R. 1966. Relation of Cue to Consequence in Avoidance Learning. *Psychonomic Science* 4: 123-124.

Grimshaw, J., & Mester, A. 1988. Light Verbs and θ-Marking. *Linguistic Inquiry* 19: 205-232.

Kageyama, T. 1993. *Bunpo to gokeisei [Grammar and Word Formation]*. Tokyo: Hituzi Syobo.

Kobayashi, H. 2004. *Gendainihongo no kangodoumeisi no kenkyu [Research on Sino-Japanese verbal nouns in contemporary Japanese]*. Tokyo: Hituzi Syobo.

Lenth, R. V. 2016. Least-Squares Means: The R Package lsmeans. *Journal of Statistical Software* 69(1): 1-33. doi:10.18637/jss.v069.i01

Levy, R. 2008. Expectation-Based Syntactic Comprehension. *Cognition* 106:1126–1177.

Miyagawa, S. 1989. Light Verbs and the Ergative Hypothesis. *Linguistic Inquiry* 20: 659-668.

R Core Team. 2016. R: A language and environment for statistical computing. R Foundation for Statistical Computing, Vienna, Austria. https://www.R-project.org/.

Santolin, C. & Saffran J. R. 2018. Constraints on Statistical Learning across Species. *Trends in Cognitive Sciences* 22: 52-63. doi: 10.1016/j.tics.2017.10.003.

Sasaki, Y. & McWhinney, B. 2006. The Competition Model. *The Handbook of East Asian Psycholinguistics*, eds. M. Nakayama, R. Mazuka, Y. Shirai, & P. Li, 307-314. Cambridge, UK: Cambridge University Press

Snyder, W. 2000. An Experimental Investigation of Syntactic Satiation Effects. *Linguistic Inquiry* 31: 575–582.

Tanomura, T. 1988. Heya o soji suru to heya no soji o suru [Heya o soji suru and heya no soji o suru]. *Nihongogaku* 7(11): 70-80.

Tsujimura, N. 1990. Ergativity of Nouns and Case Assignment. *Linguistic inquiry* 21: 277-287.

Uchida, Y. & Nakayama, M. 1993. Japanese Verbal Noun Constructions. *Linguistics* 31: 623-666.

Part V

Sociolinguistics and Discourse Analysis

From False Promises, Fake Quotations, and Feigned Questions into Grammar: Grammaticalization of Manipulative Discourse Strategies

SEONGHA RHEE
Hankuk University of Foreign Studies

1 Introduction[*]

There is a general agreement among grammaticalizationists that discourse is where grammaticalization is triggered, or that discourse and grammar are in mutual feeding relationship in their formation (Givón 1979; Lichtenberk 1991; Heine et al. 1991, inter alia). Discourse is the locus of active meaning negotiation filled with various kinds of rhetorical and discourse strategies to fulfill intended persuasion. A large body of grammaticalization studies in Korean presents many instances in which rhetorical and discursive strategies

[*] I am thankful for the comments made by the JK 25 audience. Also thanks go to Shaun Manning for kindly reading an earlier version of the paper. This research was supported by the Hankuk University of Foreign Studies research fund.

Japanese/Korean Linguistics 25.
Edited by Shin Fukuda, Mary Shin Kim, and Mee-Jeong Park.

played crucial roles. This paper presents some linguistic 'bad guys' that may be labeled as false promises, fake quotations, and feigned questions.

2   A Note on Basic Concepts

Before we discuss the grammaticalization of manipulative discourse strategies in earnest, a brief mention on a few related concepts is in order. First of all, the notion of grammaticalization has been defined in a number of ways, notably by Kurylowicz (1975[1965]: 52), as change of a morpheme advancing from lexical to grammatical, or from less grammatical to more grammatical status, and by Hopper and Traugott (2003: xv), as the change whereby lexical terms and constructions in certain linguistic contexts to serve grammatical functions, and, once grammaticalized, continue to develop new grammatical functions.

Discourse markers (DMs) have been a subject of controversy with respect to their status, i.e., as to whether they are 'grammatical' forms or not. Their status determines whether their development can be viewed as an instance of grammaticalization or not (see Waltereit 2006 vs. Diewald 2006, 2011). Following Diewald (2006, 2011), Wischer (2000), Traugott (1995), Rhee (2014), and many others, this paper takes the position that DMs are indeed grammatical forms and thus their development is rightfully considered as an instance of grammaticalization.

Another notion that bears relevance to the present paper is rhetoric. Keith and Lundberg (2008: 4) define rhetoric as the study of producing discourses and interpreting how, when, and why discourses are persuasive. From this perspective, rhetoric is concerned with language for persuasion (see also Leech 1983; Leith and Myerson 1989; Wales 2001: 344-346). Since all, or nearly all, instances of language use concern successful conveyance of the speaker's intention, rhetorical strategies are expected to surface among the most researched subjects of grammaticalization. Indeed certain grammatical markers have been analyzed as having discourse-pragmatic origins, e.g. Givón (1979), Herring (1991) for clause subordinators, Hopper (1982) and Herring (1988) for perfective aspect markers. Discussing the role of rhetoric in grammaticalization, Rhee (2008b) argues that the motivation for adopting rhetorical strategies is to increase illocutionary force of the statement by making it more dramatic and vivid.

3   Case studies

3.1   False Promises: Disguised Imperative

The speech act of command is impositive and thus often avoidable across languages (Narrog 2010). The Korean language, which shows fastidious concern in marking interpersonal relationship, presents itself as one of the languages that avoid to an extreme level the impositive speech act, i.e. imperative (Koo 2004a,b). Thus, alternative speech acts are well developed, e.g. using hortative 'let's' marked with honorification, using pseudo-monologue questions marked with politeness thus signaling its non-monologic intention, using future-marked declaratives, etc. Korean seems to have continually developed alternative strategies throughout history, and these idiosyncrasies in Korean seem to be responsible for the development of an imperative in the disguise of a promissive in Present-Day Korean (PDK), which will be presented momentarily.

In PDK there are multiple sentence-final particles (SFPs) for imperatives and for promissives. These multiple forms signal different levels of formality, honorification, and politeness toward the addressee. One form specializing in the promissive speech act is -*lkey*, used at the intimate level, which has a polite-level variant -*lkeyyo*. The polite promissive -*lkeyyo* is being innovated as polite imperative, despite frequent criticism by prescriptivists. As a promissive marker -*lkey* is not compatible with subject honorification since the actor of the promise is the speaker and as a general rule a speaker cannot honorify himself or herself. When the form was innovated as a polite imperative marker, however, it can be, and is often, modulated with honorification, i.e., -*lkeyyo* [-HON] and -*silkeyyo* [+HON] for request and command. [1]

(1) a. Promissive -*lkey*
    nay-ka   tow-acwu-lkey
    I-NOM   help-BEN-PROM
    'I will help you.'

---

[1] The following abbreviations are used in glossing: ACC: accusative; ADN: adnominal; ANT: anterior; BEN: benefactive; CAUS: causal; COMP: complementizer; CT: concessive topic; DEC: declarative; DGR: degree-marker; DM: discourse marker; END: sentence-ender; FUT: future; GEN: genitive; HON: honorific; IMP: imperative; INST: instrumental; INT: interrogative (=Q); INTEN: intentional; INTJ: interjective; MN: measure noun; NOM: nominative; NOMZ: nominalizer; PASS: passive; POL: polite; PRES: present; PROH: prohibitive; PROM: promissive; PST: past; PT: pejorative topic; PURP: purposive; Q: question (=INT); QUOT: quotative; REAS: reason; REPT: reportative; RETRO: retrospective; SFPD: sentence-final particle of discontent; SIM: simultaneous; SM: stance-marker; TOP: topic; TRL: trial.

b. Imperative (Polite Request) (a dentist to a young patient)
ca   ip   com   khukey   pelli-lkey-yo
now mouth a.little widely   open-IMP-POL
'Now, please open your mouth wide.'

c. Imperative (Polite Request) (a nurse to an adult patient)
yeki chimtay-ey nwuw-si-lkey-yo
here bed-at   lie.down-HON-IMP-POL
'Please lie on the bed over here.'

d. Imperative (a head-beautician to her assistant)
3-pen   sonnim mence tow-atuli-lkey-yo
3-number client first   help-BEN-IMP-POL
'Help the Number 3 client first.'

In appearance (1b) and (1d) are ambiguous between promissive and imperative. The addressee infers the intended imperative meaning only from the context. In terms of discursive strategy, the speaker is talking about opening the mouth and attending to a client as if she would do so, but addressee reads the speaker's mind and acts accordingly, thus building solidarity between interlocutors. This development involves diverse discursive and rhetorical strategies (see section 4 for more discussion).

3.2 Fake Quotations

3.2.1 Borrowed Mouth

Korean complementizers (COMPs) incorporate the markers of the embedded clause type markers, e.g., *-tako* and *-lako* for declarative (DEC), *-nyako* for interrogative (INT), *-lako* for imperative (IMP) and *-cako* for hortative (HORT). However, these COMPs have undergone functional extension from embedding quoted or reported speech to diverse functions, as shown in part below:

(2) a. DEC-COMP *-tako* > Reason marker (REAS)
ku-nun pappu-tako   setwulu-n-ta
he-TOP be.busy-REAS hurry-PRES-DEC
'He hurries because he is busy.'
(< lit. He, saying, "(I) am busy," hurries.)

b. DEC-COMP -*lako* > Concessive Topic marker (CT)
uysa-lako   pyeng-ul   ta   kochi-nun ke-y   ani-ta
doctor-CT illness-ACC all cure-ADN NOMZ-NOM be.not-DEC
'Even doctors cannot cure all illnesses.'
(< lit. Saying, "(she) is a doctor," (she) cannot cure all illnesses.)

c. INT-COMP -*nyako* > Pejorative Topic marker (PT)
thomatho-nyako toykey   cak-ney
tomato-PT   very   be.small-INTJ
'What a small tomato!'
(< lit. Saying, "({Is it, Are you}) a tomato?", ({it's, you're} very small.)

d. IMP-COMP -*lako* > Purposive marker (PURP)
somwun-na-lako   way   kul-ay?
rumor-exit-PURP   why   do.so-END
'Are you trying to stir up a rumor?'
(< lit. Why are you doing so, saying, "Let there be a rumor!"?)

e. HORT-COMP -*cako* > Intentional/Purposive marker (INTEN)
na ne sonhay-ip-hi-cako   ile-nun   ke-ø   ani-ya
I you loss-suffer-CAUS-INTEN do.this-ADN NOMZ-NOM be.not-END
'I'm not doing this in order to make you suffer loss.'
(< lit. I'm not doing this, saying, "Let's make you suffer loss!")

The extended functions of the COMP-based markers given above and many others all show subjectification in that the speaker is attributing an imaginary utterance to the sentential subject as if he or she is saying so, thus a phenomenon labeled as 'through a borrowed mouth' in Rhee (2009). The 'borrowed mouth' phenomenon with complementizers is not only frequent in grammaticalization but also in lexicalization, as in *cwukelako* 'desperately' (< 'saying, "Die!"'), *cwukkeysstako* 'desperately' (< 'saying, "I will die."'), *payccaylako* 'non-committedly' (< 'saying, "Cut open my belly!"'), etc.

3.2.2 Pseudo-Quotative/Reportative for Stance Marking

Among the quotative/reportative (QUOT/REPT) forms is -*tanta* which originated from a construction with the COMP -*tako*. Incidentally, the SFP -*tay* carries a similar function as -*tanta* (cf. Sohn & Park 2003), and it has been observed that reported thoughts often carry evaluation/assessment-marking function (Kim 2014). The development of QUOT/REPT -*tanta* can be schematically presented as below:

(3) *-tako   ha-n-ta   >> -tanta*
    COMP   say-PRES-DEC   QUOT/REPT
                                          '(x) says that ⋯'
                                          '(x) says that⋯/ it is said that⋯'

The QUOT *-tanta* becomes the REPT *-tanta*, without involving formal change (cf. Japanese QUOT/REPT *-to/tte*, Oshima & Sano 2012) as in (4). The major change in this is that the author of the reported speech is now no longer identifiable, as shown in (5).

(4) QUOT/REPT sentence-ender *-tanta*
ku-ka   kot   o-keyss-tanta
he-NOM   soon   come-FUT-QUOT/REPT
QUOT: 'He says that he will come soon.'
REPT: 'They say that he will come soon.'

(5) REPT sentence-ender *-tanta*
twi-s-cip   kim-tolyeng-i   cyuk-ess-tanta
back-GEN-house   [name]-bachelor-NOM   die-PST-REPT
'They say that the young bachelor Mr. Kim the neighbor in the back died.'
(Late 19th c., *Akpwu* 1)

Originally a QUOT/REPT marker, *-tanta* further develops into a stance marker (SM), again without formal change, as it becomes recruited for rhetorical effects, such as friendliness, emphasis, feigned mirativity, among others.

(6) Attitudinal stance of friendliness [A child and his mother on a weekend]
Child: [How come Daddy is not playing with me today, Mom?]
Mother: *appa-nun ton   pe(l)-si-nula   pappu-si-tanta*
            dad-TOP   money earn-HON-because   very be.busy-HON-SM
            '(Son,) Daddy is very busy making money (for us) these days.'

For the friendliness signaled by *-tanta*, it is commonly used in child-directed language (cf. Son 1998; Kim 2000), and thus children's books or even impromptu stories use this SFP frequently, a phenomenon also found in other languages including Quechua (Aikhenvald 2004).

(7) *swuph-sok-maul-ey   kkoymanh-ko   yengliha-n*
    forest-inside-village-at be.cunning-and be.clever-ADN
    yewu-ka   sal-ass-tanta
    fox-NOM   live-PST-SM

'(Once upon a time,) there lived a cunning and clever fox in a village deep in a forest.' (PDK, Narrated fairy-tale, *Yewuwa twulwumi*)

The SM *-tanta* is a marker of friendliness and in examples like (7) above, it invites the addressee (the child) into the vivid story-line. It engages the addressee in the joint construction of a representation (cf. 'negotiation of common ground' Jucker and Smith 1998: 172). Aikhenvald (2004: 137, 313) argues that reported evidential is used as 'a stylistic token of folk tales and narratives' in Kham, Quechua, Baniwa, Achagua, Piapoco, among others. Similarly, Goddard (1983) notes that the reported evidential is often used for children's 'pretend' games.

In addition to the stance of friendliness toward the addressee, the SM *-tanta* is also used for marking other interactional stances such as emphasis, feigned mirativity, news-breaking, boastful talks, and even pejoration, as exemplified in part below:

(8) a. Emphasis
etise kamhi ··· ne-kathun ke-n nwun-ey an cha-ø.
where daringly··· you-like thing-TOP eye-at not fill-END
na-n kkwum-i khu-tanta
I-TOP dream-NOM be.big-SM
'How dare you (ask me out)! I have no eyes for someone/something like you. I do have a great dream (yes, I sure do!).' (2005, Drama *Pimil namnye* Episode #1)

b. News-breaking
(Context: The speaker is breaking news to his children that their mother is pregnant.)
kuliko cohun sosik-i hana te iss-tanta.
and good news-NOM one more exist-SM
ni-tul tongsayng sayngki-lkey-a
you-PL baby.sibling be.born-FUT-END
'(Guess what?) There is one more piece of good news. You guys will have a baby brother/sister.' (2008, Drama, *Wekhingmam* Episode #14)

c. Pejoration
(A woman to her daughter with regard to her long-waited-for would-be son-in-law who, to her great dismay, returned with an appearance of a wretched beggar)
ney syepang ni-tolyeng-i ne-lAl po-la o-ass-tanta
your boyfriend [name]-Mr.-NOM you-ACC see-PURP come-PST-SM

'Your boyfriend Mr. Ni (who has become a beggar) has impudence to come to see you.' (19th c., *Namwenkosa* 212)

The development of *-tanta* into a marker of a speaker's stance is largely based on its former REPT function. That is, the speaker's stance is necessarily subjective whereas reported speech is non-subjective because its authorship is speaker-external. Thus, by marking a statement with REPT, the speaker is objectifying the proposition being presented. The speaker is saying in effect, "This is not my personal opinion but someone else's. The SM sometimes signals discontent along with emphasis as in (8a), and further the speaker's pejorative attitude as in (8c), in which the speaker displays her pejorative attitude toward the man or toward the proposition that he has presumptuously come to see her daughter. By using the REPT *-tanta*, i.e., by adopting someone else's voice, the speaker is distancing herself from the state-of-affairs as if she were only an observer of the scene. This disconnection capitalizes inherent 'otherness' (Bakhtin 1981: 339) in reported speech.

3.3 Feigned Questions

3.3.1 Approximative Derivational Morphemes

Korean has a number of interesting derivational morphemes involving question forms (Rhee 2008a). They defy any neat and tidy formal treatment, and thus have been avoided or neglected in linguistic analyses, or they are treated as idiosyncratic, idiomatic expressions (cf. Lee & Lee 2010). They are approximative adjectivers and adverbializers, such as V-*lkkamalkkaha(nu)n* ('that says, "Shall (I) V or not?"'), N-*manhalkkaha(nu)n* ('that says, "Shall (I) be the size of N?"'), MN-*toylkkamalkkaha(nu)n* ('that says "Shall (I) become MN or not?"; MN: measure noun), V-*lkkamalkka* ('Shall (I) V or not?'), etc. Some of them are analytically exemplified below:

(9) a. V-*lkkamalkkaha-* 'with a quality bordering on V-ing'
po-i-l-kka-ma-l-kka-ha-nun   *sem*
see-PASS-FUT-Q-not.do-FUT-Q-say-SIM.ADN island
'a barely visible island' (lit. 'an island that says, "Shall I be seen or not?"')

b. N-*manhalkkaha-* 'with a quality bordering on being N'
oleynci-man-ha-l-kka-ha-n   *wupak*
orange-DGR-do-FUT-Q-say-ANT.ADN   hail
'hail about the size of an orange' (lit. 'hail that said, "Shall I be the size of an orange?"')

c. MN-*toylkkamalkkaha-* 'with a degree close to MN'
30 acre-toy-l-kka-ma-l-kka-ha-nun   *swuph*
30 acre-become-FUT-Q-not.do-FUT-Q-say-ADN forest
'a forest of about 30 acres' (lit. 'a forest that says, "Shall I become 30 acres or not?"')

d. V-*lkkamalkka* 'hesitating about V-ing'
kunye-nun kyelhon-ul   ha-l-kka-mal-kka komin   cwung-i-ta
she-TOP   marriage-ACC do-FUT-Q-not.do-Q worry middle-be-DEC
'She is wondering if she should marry.' (lit. 'As for her, "Shall (I) marry or not marry?," (she) is wondering.')

The development of these derivational morphemes from question forms in the above, though complex in appearance, may be analyzed as involving many conceptual manipulations, including personification, perspective shift, etc. But the most fundamental aspect of it is that the notion of 'indeterminacy' inherent in question forms is recruited to signal inconclusiveness or approximation in word derivation. For instance, in (9a) by attributing "Shall I be seen or not?" to an island as if it were saying the monologual question, the language user innovates a grammatical marker that describes the state of affairs of an island with approximation or inconclusiveness, i.e., the island is barely visible.

3.3.2   Indefinite Pronouns & Indefinite Adverbs

Another class of forms developed from feigned questions is that of indefinite pronouns and indefinite adverbs. These forms involve interrogative pronouns and many of them are full-fledged question sentences in appearance. For instance, personal interrogative pronoun *nwukwu* 'who' functions as an indefinite pronoun 'someone', but the interrogative constructions involving it also function as pronoun with the meaning 'someone', as below:

(10) Indefinite pronouns derived from *nwukwu* 'who'
a. *nwukwu* 'someone' < *nwukwu* 'who'
b. *nwuka* 'someone' < *nwukwu-ka* [who-NOM] 'who is?'
c. *nwukw(i)unka* 'someone' < *nwukwu-(i)-nka* [who-be-Q] 'who is it?'
d. *nwukwu(i)nci* 'someone' < *nwukwu-(i)-nci* [who-be-Q] 'who is it?'

The general patterns of using an interrogative pronoun/adverb as an indefinite pronoun/adverb and of using such interrogative forms in question constructions are productive lexicalization and grammaticalization patterns, e.g. with *nwukwu* 'who' (as shown above), *mwe* 'what', *mwues* 'what', *encey* 'when', *eti* 'where', *ettehkey* 'how', and *way* 'why'. This pattern of rhetorically recruited pseudo-questions is exemplified in the following examples in which such indefinite pro-forms are morphologically broken down with separate glosses:

(11) a. *nwukwunka* 'someone'
wuli cwung-ey nwukwu-ø-nka   *paysin-ul*   *ha-yss-ta*
we   middle-at   who-be-Q(=someone)   betrayal-ACC   do-PST-DEC
'Someone among us betrayed us.'
(lit.: <u>Who-is-it</u> among us betrayed us.)

b. *mwenka* 'something'
ku-nun ecey   *kakey-eyse mwe-ø-nka-lul*   *sa-ss-ta*
he-TOP   yesterday store-at   what-be-Q(=something)-ACC buy-PST-DEC
'He bought something at the store.'
(lit.: He bought <u>what-is-it</u> at a store.)

c. *waynka* 'for some reason'
ku salam way-ø-nka mam-ey an tul-e
that person why-be-Q   mind-at not enter-END
'I don't like the person for some reason.'
(lit. He does'nt <u>why-is-it</u> enter into (my) heart.)

The development of interrogative pronouns into indefinite pronouns is an instance of conversion and reification also attested in Classical Greek (*tís* 'who?' and *tis* 'someone', *poû* 'where?' and *pou* 'somewhere'), Chinese (*shéi* 'who?' 'someone', *shénme* 'what?' 'something'), Hopi (*hak* 'who?' 'someone'), Dyirbal (*wanya* 'who?' 'someone' and *minya* 'what?' 'something'), etc. (Haspelmath 1997: 170). Full-fledged interrogative constructions developing into fully lexicalized indefinite pro-forms are also attested in English, e.g. *what-d'you-call-it* (Enfield 2003), *whatchamacallit* (< *what you may call it*), *dontcherknow* (< don't you know), etc.

3.3.3 Discourse Markers

Korean has many DMs that originated from question constructions. DMs in this category are so numerous and their functions are so diverse across various domains, e.g. pause-filling, mitigation, attention attraction, affirmation, negation, etc., that discussing them in detail is beyond the scope of this paper. Thus exemplification of a few instances may suffice the purpose.

Korean interrogative pronouns, which often can stand alone as full-fledged questions, are often used as DMs, as illustrated by *way* 'why' and *eti* 'where' in (12).

(12) a. Attention-attractor *way* 'why'
ke   way   kimpaksa   mal-i-ya
that why (=DM) Dr.Kim   talk-be-END
'Look, (I am going to talk about) Dr. Kim.'
(lit.: That, why, the talk is about Dr. Kim.)

b. Emphatic negator *eti* 'where'
A: [Isn't he really smart?]
B: *eti!   cenhye an ttokttokha-y*
    where (=DM) at.all not be.smart-END
    'Absolutely not. He's not smart at all.'
    (lit.: Where! He's not smart at all.)

In a more complex fashion, certain constructions involving interrogative forms develop into DMs. In this case, the constructions comprise a structural template along with a slot, thus resembling 'formal idioms' in construction grammar (Fillmore et al. 1988). This is exemplified below:

(13) a. Pause-filler *ku x-nya* 'x is it?' (*x*= what, who…)
ku salam-un   ku hoysa-uy ku mwe-nya   isa-la-te-la
that person-TOP the firm-GEN that what-Q (=DM) executive-COMP-RETRO-DEC
'They say he is … an executive of the firm.'
(lit. He is the firm's what-is-it executive, I recall.)

b. Mitigator *x-(i)lalkka* 'shall (I) say x?' (x=NP)
ku salam-un   kiin-i-la-l-kka   *com   isangha-n*
that person-TOP eccentric-be-COMP-FUT-Q(=DM) a.little be.strange-ANT.ADN
tey-ka   iss-e
place-NOM exist-END
'The person is strange in some respects, sort of an eccentric, maybe.'
(lit. The person is, *shall-I-say*-an-eccentric, (he) has some places that look strange.)

The DM *ku mwenya* 'what is it?' illustrated in (13a) is an instance of the *ku x-nya* DMs which can accommodate an interrogative pronoun in the *x*-slot. This DM is usually recruited to fill in the speech gap. Similarly, the expression *kiinilalkka* 'shall I say (he is) an eccentric?' in (13b) is an instance of *x-ilalkka*, the *x*-slot of which is filled in with a NP. The speaker usually employs this DM to signal his or her reluctance to use a particular expression, thus mitigating the assertion. This type of discourse strategy is widely manifested across languages with the forms labeled as "parentheticals" (Dehé & Kavalova 2007), "comment clauses" (Brinton 2008), and "theticals" (Heine 2013; Kaltenböck et al. 2011; Heine et al. 2017), among others.

3.3.4 Sentence-Final Particles of Discontent

Still another category of feigned questions that triggered grammaticalization is that of sentence-final particles of discontent (SFPDs) (Koo & Rhee 2013; Rhee & Koo 2017). These SFPDs were developed from feigned monologual questions adjoined to the end of a sentence. For instance, SFPDs -*nam* and -*kam* developed from [SFP -*na* + *mwe* 'what?'] and [SFP -*ka* + *mwe* 'what?'], in each of which the question *mwe* 'what?' is fused with the preceding SFPs through erosion. Some of such uses are exemplified in (14).

(14) a. SFPD -*kam*
(One who was not aware of the passing of time utters in surprise.)
sikan-i   way ilehkey ppalli ka-nun-kam
time-NOM why like.this fast   go-PRES-SFPD
'How fast time is passing?! [Oh, no! It's getting late!]'

b. SFPD -*nam*
(A parent grumbles noticing that her child is not serious about studying.)
paywu-ese nam-ø   cwu-nam
learn-and others-ACC give-SFPD
'(Do you think) studying will benefit others?! [No! It will benefit YOU!]'

As indicated earlier, -*kam* and -*nam* originated from the [SFP+what?] complex. The challenging or discontent meaning in the SFPDs was inherited from the question 'what?' in the source structure. The source constructions are monologual questions, as evidenced by the use of the so-called 'audience-blind' enders, e.g., -*ka* and -*na* (Rhee & Koo 2017), but these monologues are 'feigned' monologues as they are spoken with the intention of being heard and thus with sufficient audibility.

(15)a. -*na mwe* > -*nam*
na-n caconsim-to   eps-na   mwe? (> -*nam*)
I-TOP self-esteem-also not.exist-SFP what (> -SFPD)
'(Do you think) I don't even have a sense of self-esteem?'
(Lit. Do I not even have self-esteem, what?)

b. *-ka mwe > -kam*
nay-ka   kulehkey   hankaha-n-<u>ka   mwe</u> (> *-kam*)
I-NOM   like.that   be.leisurely-CR-<u>SFP   what</u> (> -SFPD)
'(Do you think) I am so leisurely?'
(Lit. Am I that leisurely, what?)

Similar states of affairs are attested across languages (Mesthrie 1982; Smith 1985; Beeching 2002; Kuteva et al. 2018). In a number of languages, a short, yet complete, question 'What?' attached to the end of a sentence signals speaker's emotion and attitude (Kuteva et al. 2018). This is in line with the observation that sentence-final positions are often favored by stance particles in Korean (cf. Sohn 1994; Sohn 1995, 2015; Sohn & Park 2002; Kim & Sohn 2015; Ahn 2016).

4   Issues for Discussion

The development of diverse grammatical markers described above reveals diverse discourse and rhetorical strategies. We will briefly look at some of the prominent cases from these strategic points of view.

4.1   Discourse Strategies

One of the most notable aspects of the grammaticalization instances is the development of attitudinal stance markers. For instance, the development of the imperative from the promissive shows that the speaker seeks to build solidarity with the addressee, by strategically saying something as if he or she intended to do it himself or herself. The same development also exhibits the politeness strategy. When the command takes the form of a promise, the face-threatening becomes mitigated because the utterance *prima facie* is not addressed to the discourse partner.

Similarly, in the case of the development of QUOT/REPT, the speaker's diverse stances came to be signaled by it, such as pejorative attitude (attitudinal stance), or friendliness (emotional stance), distancing attitude (epistemic stance), among others. Similar states of affairs involving evidentials developing into epistemic markers have been reported in Quechua and Bulgarian (Floyd 1999: 72). The notion of 'otherness' (Bakhtin 1981: 339) inherent in reported speech and the non-committal function of reported speech (Gvozdanović 1996: 63 as cited in Aikhenvald 2004: 138) are closely related to the stance function

It is also evident that the development of the SFPDs marking the speaker's discontent is an instance of grammaticalization of the stance. The speaker's display of affect plays a crucial role in coconstruction of attitudinal common ground among interlocutors.

4.2   Interactivity Modulation

Another aspect manifest in the development of the diverse markers described above is the strategic manipulation of interactivity. For instance, the functional extension of QUOT/REPT into stance marking brought forth such interactive stance functions as signaling emphasis, mirativity, news-breaking, and boastful talk. The same development also led to the emergence of the function of marking the speaker's intention to negotiate or seek common ground. In addition the SM -*tantu* also functions as a mirative, which creates a strong engaging effect on the part of the addressee. It signals the speaker's desire to 'share' the information as well as the feeling it arouses, an excellent instance of 'intersubjectification' (Traugott 2003).

In the case of the development of indefinite pronouns and adverbs as well as the DMs from question forms, strategic manipulation of interactivity is prominent. The use of question forms, though not directed, creates an engaging effect on the addressee and enhances interactivity among interlocutors. The inherent nature of engagement in question forms explains in part why question words are susceptible to grammaticalization of interactivity markers (for discussion in Korean, see Kim 2002; Lee 1999; Koo 1999, 2000; Rhee 2008; Kim 2010, among others).

Similarly, the functional extension of COMPs and the lexicalization of adverbs from COMPs also show the strategic interactivity modulation. The use of feigned other-originated utterances enhances interactivity. The speaker expresses the desire for the addressee's active engagement by saying something 'through a borrowed mouth' (Rhee, 2009).

In the case of SFPDs, it has been pointed out that they are built on non-interactional SFPs, i.e., audience-blind forms, and non-interactional utterance types ('feigned monologues'). SFPDs feign audience-blindness and monologuality, thus strategically lowering the visibility of the audience. When SFPDs are employed, the speaker intends to have his or her utterance heard by the discourse participant. They also serve as a strategic loophole to avoid blame, if confronted. Thus, SFPDs are excellent examples of strategic interactivity modulation in grammaticalization of discourse functions.

4.3   Dramatizing Presentation

The development of the forms described above also exhibits rhetorical strategies operating in grammaticalization, most notably, dramatizing presentation. For instance, in the case of approximatives, indefinite pronouns and adverbs, innovative COMP functions, COMP-based adverbs, and interrogative-based DMs all seem to have been motivated by the speaker's desire to use dramatic or graphic means in order to be creative in language use (cf. 'creativity'; Heine et al. 1991; Heine & Stolz 2008).

Similarly, the development of stance marking functions from QUOT/REPT also suggests the recruitment of rhetorical strategies. The use of quotations for validity borrowing, feigned mirativity to dramatize the information, and rejection of accommodation of the on-going situation, i.e., distancing, all share the common characteristics of employing rhetorical strategies. When the speaker reports something of his or her authorship by using the QUOT/REPT marker -tanta, the speaker is feigning the authorship as if the information is from a third party. Thus, the self-reporting may create connotation of mirativity (cf. Aikhenvald 2004: 185, 195-215).

4.4 Perspective Management

The last noteworthy rhetorical strategy in the development of the grammatical forms elaborated above is perspective management. It is evident that the speaker's and the addressee's perspectives are manipulated, i.e., shifted or mixed, in the development of the 'borrowed mouth' COMPs, COMP-based adverbs, approximatives, promissives, and stance markers.

Since reported speech involves multiple authors, QUOT/REPT inherently represents 'multiple perspectives' (Evans 2006; cf. 'speech within speech and speech about speech', Vološinov 1930: 115; 'multivoicedness' or 'polyphony of voices', Bakhtin 1986; for similar observations, see Buchstaller 2014). The SM -tanta developed from QUOT/REPT inherits such multiple perspectives from the latter. The voices of the two speakers may completely concur or differ. A peculiarity with the SM -tanta is that the original speaker may not exist at all, and thus it is a kind of 'hypothetical discourse' (Golato 2012), i.e., the two tiers of voices consist of the voice of a hypothetical speaker and that of the current speaker. Thus, it is possible for -tanta to function as a signal of refusal of 'accommodative process' (cf. Giles et al. 1991). This is in line with Goffman's (1986[1974]: 512) observation that reported speech carries reduced personal responsibility, as "[h]e [the speaker] splits himself off from the content of the words by expressing that their speaker is not he himself or not he himself in a serious way."

It is also noteworthy that the development of the innovative imperative goes beyond the speaker-addressee intersubjectification, i.e., it was strongly motivated by the consideration of the people present in the scene. Its use is often observed among service providers especially in businesses catering to high-class clientele. The use of the promissive-turned imperative is a service-providers' in-group discourse strategy employed while clients are present in the scene within the earshot. The rationale behind this is that employers or high-ranking employees issuing a command to their low-ranking employees in the presence of their clients may negatively affect the atmospheres of classy and posh businesses patronized by high-profile clients. The desire to avoid issuing commands in the presence of clients seems to have strongly motivated this grammatical change in which a mild form of speech act, i.e. promissive has been co-opted to encode a more potentially face-threatening speech act, i.e. imperative.

5   Summary & Conclusion

Grammaticalization of certain grammatical markers involves discursive and rhetorical strategies. Speakers use available linguistic forms often manipulating them discursively or rhetorically in order to solve communicative problems. By doing so they try to be attentive to the addressee or even to the people who are present in the discourse scene. Thus grammaticalization is indeed a multi-faceted process influenced by many ambient linguistic and extra-linguistic, situational factors that are present in individual instances of language use. Language speakers use available language materials to fulfill immediate discursive needs, and thus, Rhee and Koo (2014: 334) assert that "Speakers of a language are not mere consumers of linguistic forms but are active manipulators of the existing forms, and thus creators and innovators of language." Involvement of diverse aspects in grammaticalization calls for the necessity of analyzing language use and grammatical change from multiple perspectives.

References

Ahn, Mikyung. 2016. Surprise in discourse: The mirative meanings of *ta(ha)*-derived sentence final particles in Korean. *Language and Linguistics* 71: 95-114.

Aikhenvald, Alexandra. 2004. *Evidentiality*. Oxford: Oxford University Press.

Bakhtin, Mikhail M. 1981. *The Dialogic Imagination: Four Essays*. (Ed. by Michael Holquist, trans. by Caryl Emerson and Michael Holquist). Austin: University of Texas Press.

Bakhtin, Mikhail M. 1986. *Speech Genres and Other Late Essays*. (Ed. by Caryl Emerson and Michael Holquist, trans. by Vern W. McGee. Austin: University of Texas Press.

Beeching, Kate. 2002. *Gender, Politeness and Pragmatic Particles in French*. Amsterdam: Benjamins.

Brinton, Laurel J. 2008. *The Comment Clause in English: Syntactic Origins and Pragmatic Development*. Cambridge: Cambridge University Press.

Buchstaller, Isabelle. 2014. *Quotatives: New Trends and Sociolinguistic Implications*. Oxford: Wiley Blackwell.

Dehé, Nicole, and Yordanka Kavalova, 2007. Parentheticals: an introduction. In: Nicole Dehé & Yordanka Kavalova (Eds.), *Parentheticals*, 1-22. Amsterdam: Benjamins.

Diewald, Gabriel. 2006. Discourse particles and modal particles as grammatical elements. In: Kestin Fischer (Ed.), *Approaches to Discourse Particles,* 403-425. Amsterdam: Elsevier.

Diewald, Gabriel. 2011. Pragmaticalization (defined) as grammaticalization of discourse functions. *Linguistics* 49.2: 365-390.

Enfield, Nicholas. 2003. The definition of *what-d'you-call-it*: Semantics and pragmatics of recognitional deixis. *Journal of Pragmatics* 35: 101-117.

Evans, Nicholas. 2006. A view with a view: Towards a typology of multiple perspective constructions. *Berkeley Linguistics Society* 31: 93−120.

Fillmore, Charles J., Paul Kay, and Mary Kay O'Connor. 1988. Regularity and idiomaticity in grammatical constructions: The case of *let alone*. *Language* 64: 501-538.

Floyd, Rick. 1999. *The Structure of Evidential Categories in Wanka Quechua*. Dallas: SIL and the University of Texas at Arlington Press.

Giles, Howard, Nicholas Coupland, and Justine Coupland. 1991. Accommodation theory: Communication, context, and consequence. In: Howard Giles, Nicholas Coupland, & Justine Coupland (Eds.), *Contexts of Accommodation: Developments in Applied Sociolinguistics,* 1-68. Cambridge: Cambridge University Press.

Givón, Talmy. 1979. From discourse to syntax: Grammar as a processing strategy. In: Talmy Givón (Ed.), *Discourse and Syntax,* 81-112. New York: Academic Press

Goddard, Cliff. 1983. A Semantically-Oriented Grammar of the Yankunytjatjara Dialect of the Western Desert Language. Ph.D. dissertation. Australian National University, Canberra.

Goffman, Erving. 1986[1974]. *Frame Analysis: An Essay on the Organization of Experience*. York, PA: Northeastern University Press.

Golato, Andrea. 2012. Impersonal quotation and hypothetical discourse. In: Isabelle Buchstaller, & Ingrid Van Alphen (Eds.*), Quotatives: Cross-linguistic and Cross-disciplinary Perspectives*, 3-36: Amsterdam: Benjamins.

Gvozdanović, Jadranka. 1996. Reported speech in South Slavic. In: Theo A. Janssen, & Wim van der Wurff (Eds.). *Reported Speech: Forms and Functions of the Verb,* 57-71. Amsterdam: Benjamins.

Haspelmath, Martin. 1997. *Indefinite Pronouns*. Oxford: Clarendon Press.

Heine, Bernd. 2013. On discourse markers: Grammaticalization, pragmaticalization, or something else? *Linguistics* 51.6: 1205-1247.

Heine, Bernd, Ulrike Claudi, and Friederike Hünnemeyer. 1991. *Grammaticalization: A Conceptual Framework*. Chicago: The University of Chicago Press.

Heine, Bernd, Gunther Kaltenböck, Tania Kuteva, and Haiping Long. 2017. Cooptation as a discourse strategy. *Journal of Linguistics* 55.4: 813-856.

Heine, Bernd, & Thomas Stolz. 2008. Grammaticalization as a creative process. *STUF* 61.4: 326-357.

Herring, Susan C. 1988. Aspect as a discourse strategy in Tamil. *Berkely Linguistic Society* 14: 280-292.

Herring, Susan C. 1991. The grammaticalization of rhetorical questions in Tamil. In: Elizabeth C. Traugott, & Bernd Heine (Eds.) *Approaches to Grammaticalization,* 2 vols., Vol. 1: 253-284, Amsterdam; Benjamins.

Hopper, Paul J. 1982. Aspect between discourse and grammar. In: Paul J. Hopper (Ed.), *Tense Aspect: Between Semantics and Pragmatics,* 3-18. Amsterdam: Benjamins.

Hopper, Paul J., and Elizabeth C. Traugott. 2003. *Grammaticalization.* Cambridge: Cambridge University Press.

Jucker, Andreas H., and Sara W. Smith. 1998. And people just you know like 'wow': Discourse markers as negotiating strategies. In: Andreas H. Jucker, & Yael Ziv (Eds.), *Discourse Markers: Descriptions and Theory,* 171-201. Amsterdam: Benjamins.

Kaltenböck, Gunther, Bernd Heine, and Tania Kuteva. 2011. On thetical grammar. *Studies in Language* 35.4: 848-893.

Keith, William M., and Christian O. Lundberg. 2008. *The Essential Guide to Rhetoric.* Boston: Bedford/St. Martins.

Kim, Alan Hyun-Oak. 2010. Rhetorical questions as catalyst in grammaticalization: Deriving Korean discourse marker ketun from conditional connective. *Journal of Pragmatics* 43: 1023-1041.

Kim, Jong-Hyun. 2000. The attitudinal force of quasi-quotation sentences in Korean. *Eneohag: Journal of the Linguistic Society of Korea* 26: 75-104.

Kim, Mary Shin. 2014. Reported thought as a stance-taking device in Korean conversation. *Discourse Processes* 51.3: 230-263.

Kim, Stephanie Hyeri, and Sung-Ock S. Sohn. 2015. Grammar as an emergent response to interactional needs: A study of final *kuntey* 'but' in Korean conversation. *Journal of Pragmatics* 83: 73-90.

Kim, Tae-Yeop. 2002. A study on the grammaticalization of discourse marker. *The Korean Language and Literature* 26: 61-80.

Koo, Jong-Nam. 1999. On the discourse 'eodi'. *Linguistics* 7.3: 217-234.

Koo, Jong-Nam. 2000. Tamhwaphyoci *mwe*-uy mwunpephwawa tamhwa kinung [On grammaticalization of the discourse marker *mwe* and its discourse functions]. *Kwukemwunhak* 35: 5-32.

Koo, Hyun Jung, and Seongha Rhee. 2013. On an emerging paradigm of sentence-final particles of discontent: A grammaticalization perspective. *Language Sciences* 37: 70−89.

Kuryłowicz, Jerzy. 1975[1965]. The evolution of grammatical categories. Reprinted in J. Kuryłowicz, *Esquisses linguistiques,* vol. 2, 38-54. Munich: Fink.

Kuteva, Tania, Seongha Rhee, Debra Ziegeler, and Jessica Sabban. 2018. On sentence-final "what" in Singlish: Are you the queen of England, or what? *Journal of Language Contact* 11: 32-70.

Lee, Heeja, and Jong-Hee Lee. 2010. *Emi Cosa Sacen* [The dictionary of particles]. Seoul: Hankook Publisher.

Lee, Han-gyu. 1999. The pragmatics of the discourse particle *mwe* in Korean. *Discourse and Cognition* 6.1: 137-157.

Leech, Geoffrey N. 1983. *Principles of Pragmatics*. New York: Longman.

Leith, Dick, and George Myerson. 1989. *The Power of Address: Explorations in Rhetoric*. London: Routledge.

Lichtenberk, Frantisek. 1991. On the gradualness of grammaticalization. In: Elizabeth Closs Traugott, & Bernd Heine (Eds.), *Approaches to Grammaticalization*, 2 vols., Vol. I, 37-80. Amsterdam: Benjamins.

Mesthrie, Rajend. 1982. *English in Language Shift: The History, Structure, and Sociolinguistics of South African Indian English*. Cambridge: Cambridge University Press.

Narrog, Heiko. 2010. (Inter)subjectification in the domain of modality and mood-- Concepts and cross-linguistic realities. In: Kristin Davidse, Lieven Vandelanotte, & Hubert Cuyckens (Eds.), *Subjectification, Intersubjectification and Grammaticalization*, 385-429. Berlin: Mouton.

Oshima, David Y., and Shin-ichiro Sano. 2012. On the characteristics of Japanese reported discourse: A study with special reference to elliptic quotation. In: Isabelle Buchstaller, & Ingrid Van Alphen (Eds.), *Quotatives: Cross-linguistic and Cross-disciplinary Perspectives*, 145-171. Amsterdam: Benjamins.

Rhee, Seongha. 2008a. Subjectification of reported speech in grammaticalization and lexicalization. *Harvard Studies in Korean Linguistics* 12: 590−603.

Rhee, Seongha. 2008b. From rhetoric to grammar: Grammaticalization of rhetorical strategies in Korean. *Japanese/Korean Linguistics* 13: 359−370.

Rhee, Seongha. 2009. Through a borrowed mouth: Reported speech and subjectification in Korean. *The LACUS Forum* 34: 201−210.

Rhee, Seongha. 2014. "I know you are not, but if you were asking me": On emergence of discourse markers of topic presentation from hypothetical questions. *Journal of Pragmatics* 60: 1-16.

Rhee, Seongha, & Hyun Jung Koo. 2014. Grammaticalization of causatives and passives and their recent development into stance markers in Korean. *Poznań Studies in Contemporary Linguistics* 50.3: 309-337.

Rhee, Seongha, & Hyun Jung Koo. 2017. Audience-blind sentence-enders in Korean: A discourse-pragmatic perspective. *Journal of Pragmatics* 120C: 101-121.

Smith, Ian. 1985. Multilingualism and diffusion: A case study from Singapore English. *Indian Journal of Applied Linguistics* 11.2: 105-128.

Sohn, Ho-Min. 1994. *Korean*. London: Routledge.

Sohn, Sung-Ock S. 1995. On the development of sentence-final particles in Korean. *Japanese/Korean Linguistics* 5: 219-234.

Sohn, Sung-Ock S. 2015. The emergence of utterance-final particles in Korean. In: Sylvie Hancil, Alexander Haselow, & Margje Post (Eds.), *Sentence-Final Particles*, 181-195. Berlin: de Gruyter.

Sohn, Sung-Ock S., and Mee-Jeong Park. 2002. Discourse, grammaticalization, and intonation: The analysis of *-ketun* in Korean. *Japanese/Korean Linguistics* 10: 306-319.

Sohn, Sung-Ock S., and Mee-Jeong Park. 2003. Indirect quotations in Korean conversation. *Japanese/Korean Linguistics* 11: 105-118.

Son, Se-mo-dol. 1998. {-(nun/n)tanta}uy emihwa [Development of *-(nun/n)tanta* into an ending]. *Hankwuk Enemwunhwa: Journal of the Society of Korean Language and Culture* (Hanyang University) 16, 105−130.

Traugott, Elizabeth Closs. 1995. The role of the development of discourse markers in a theory of grammaticalization. Paper presented at the 12th International Conference on Historical Linguistics. Manchester, UK.

Traugott, Elizabeth Closs. 2003. From subjectification to intersubjectification. In: Raymond Hickey (Ed.), *Motives for Language Change*, 124-139. Cambridge: Cambridge University Press.

Vološinov, Valentin N. 1930. *Marxism and the Philosophy of Language* (Trans. by L. Matejka, I. R. Titunik from Russian Marksizm i filosofija jazyka, in 1973). Cambridge: Harvard University Press.

Wales, Katie. 2001. *A Dictionary of Stylistics*. New York: Longman.

Waltereit, Richard. 2006. The rise of discourse markers in Italian: a specific type of language change. In: Kerstin Fischer (Ed.), *Approaches to Discourse Particles*, 61-76. Amsterdam: Elsevier.

Wischer, Ilse. 2000. Grammaticalization versus lexicalization. 'Methinks' there is some confusion. In: Olga Fischer, Anette Rosenbach, & Dieter Stein (Eds.), *Pathways of Change: Grammaticalization in English,* 355-370. Amsterdam: Benjamins.

From Tasty Adjective to Succulent Metaphor: What the Language of Food Reveals

Natsuko Tsujimura
Indiana University

1 Introduction

Food and food preparation form an essential part of our daily life. Some people eat to live, while many of us are fortunate enough to enjoy living to eat. Naturally, food and food preparation are strongly culture-bound. Although their nature is subject to change especially in the modern world's globalizing and glocalizing climate, conscious or subconscious adherence to an individual's culinary tradition, in many ways, reflects our identity, as is well said by the cliché "We are what we eat."

Food and language are both something we often take for granted, but when put together, they could become a powerful force in diverse and surprising ways. Research in multi- and inter-disciplinary areas related to food studies has produced a number of intriguing results to date. To report just one, Wansink et al. (2005) presented one group of cafeteria patrons

Japanese/Korean Linguistics 25.
Edited by Shin Fukuda, Mary Shin Kim, and Mee-Jeong Park.

(Group A) with detailed descriptions like "Traditional Cajun Red Beans and Rice", "Succulent Italian Seafood Filet", and "Tender Grilled Chicken"; and another group (Group B) with minimal descriptions such as "Red Beans and Rice", "Seafood Filet", and "Grilled Chicken". The food items under the two names in each pair were identical. After eating meals, the patrons were asked to rate the taste of what they ate and to comment on their eating experiences. Group A rated the taste of the food significantly higher than Group B; and Group A reported their experiences of the dishes more favorably than Group B. This experiment shows that descriptive words and phrases in food names can influence our sensory evaluation. Thus, the language we communicate with can be a powerful means not only to inform us but to manipulate our thoughts and judgments, whether positively or negatively.

It is not difficult to find how our linguistic knowledge can inform us about everyday situations involving food. Such knowledge ranges, for example, from word formation, loanwords, sound symbolism, and lexicalization, to metaphor. I give one illustration of a beverage advertisement that effectively uses the structure of language to promote a product. On a bottled iced-coffee appears what seems to be the name of the product, *otoko-no koohii* [man-Gen coffee] 'coffee for men', suggesting that it targets male consumers. In smaller letters, the caption in (1)—all in the hiragana syllabary—is added to the product name.

(1) にがみば・しった [nigamiba・shitta]

The combined captuion, *nigamibashitta otoko-no koohee*, displays multi-layered interpretations that are of linguistic significance. First, *nigamibashitta* (苦み走った)is a descriptor for a good looking, manly man, but *nigami* literally means "bitterness". At least for marketing purposes, the bitter taste is well associated with masculinity as opposed to the connection between the sweet taste and females. Bottles of sake shown in the background on the photo seems to have a staging effect for the masculinity advanced by this ad. Second, of more interest from a morphosyntactic perspective, the caption にがみば・しった [nigamiba・shitta] on the label is intentionally written in hiragana, and with the dot marker for a pause between the two parts. Other information on the label indicates that this coffee product is made available in the local market of Kumamoto prefecture in Kyushu. Interestingly, *ba* in *nigamiba* indicates the object marker in this dialect instead of more standard accusative marker -*o*, and with the morpheme break given in (1), the phrase means "know bitterness." That is, one interpretation of the caption in the local dialect is "coffee for men who know the bitterness," where bitterness is the essence of coffee. Together, this coffee product is meant for ruggedly handsome men who are coffee connoisseurs, precisely achieving the commercial goal to capture male consumers' attention especially in the local context. It is intriguing to see advertisers make remarkably creative use of a wide range of linguistic knowledge to communicate with a target audience.

Academic research on the language of food, on the relation between language and food, or on food as a specific subject embedded in discourse and sociolinguistic investigations, is by no means new. For example, Adrienne Lehrer's book *Wine and Conversation* (1983, 2009) and her articles investigating culinary terms demonstrate the systematic architecture of the lexicon by showing that cooking terms and wine vocabulary can be coherently analyzed based on conceptual and methodological tools like semantic fields and componential analysis. Jurafsky (2014) informs us that history, cognitive science, and sociolinguistics all contribute to our understanding of how the language of food affects and reflects the way we think. The volumes compiled by Seto (2003, 2005) take an extensive look at the richness of the taste vocabulary and expressions in Japanese from a semantic perspective. With a narrower focus, Culy (1996) diachronically investigates the distribution of null objects in English recipes as a genre of writing. Similarly, Strauss (2005) makes sociocultural and sociolinguistic comparisons of American, Japanese, and Korean food commercials, particularly focusing on taste terms used in those corpora (commercials). As attested by yet other work, food seems to be dealt with more indirectly. For instance, many of the chapters contained in Hosking et al. (2010), Gerhand et al. (2013), and Szatrowski (2014) present spoken discourse in which food is a topic of conversation that undergoes analysis. Importantly, regardless of the type of approach one takes to language and food or to the language of food, foundational concepts and methodological and analytical tools in linguistics as a discipline serve—and have served—as a lynchpin to our explorations.

Language plays an important role in food descriptions and more broadly, in food-related matters, as the existing literature and ongoing research have amply shown; but it is not my intention to advocate or speak of what might be labeled as "culinary linguistics". On the one hand, sub-fields of applied linguistics such as computational linguistics, anthropological linguistics, and forensic linguistics have each developed their own unique ways of applying linguistic concepts and methodology that are specific to and cater toward these narrowly-defined areas. For instance, forensic linguistics applies linguistics to the context of the law and the judicial system and procedures. On the other hand, linguistic investigations of food-related matters do not seem to aim at capturing systematic patterning or reaching generalizations that pertain to the language of food. Instead, researchers have used the language of food as a data source, just as they could examine the language used in sports or fashion for analysis. For the same reason that we do not have sub-areas like "sports linguistics" or "fashion linguistics", I do not subscribe to a view that "culinary linguistics" establishes a disciplinary home for research on the language of food. I will be more concerned with questions like, why we can describe food taste with language so richly, even though we have so few words that directly describe those basic food tastes, or how the language of food affects and mirrors the way we think. These are indeed the questions that the existing literature has looked at, and constitute a line of research that a number of linguists and cognitive scientists are engaged in. Understanding the language of food from a linguistic perspective by using linguistic terms, concepts, and analytical tools is beneficial to answering these and related questions.

While there are various linguistic phenomena—including word formation patterns, loanwords, and sound symbolism—that reflect such a premise and are worthy of investigations, for the remainder of this article, I would like to have a closer examination of two topics, lexicalization and metaphor.

2   Lexicalization

Semantic issues of lexicalization have been explored from various perspectives, but one of the most rigorously explored is probably motion events. With Leonard Talmy and Dan Slobin as leaders, this line of research is concerned with which meaning components are internally specified as part of the lexical property and which semantic elements are expressed externally to the lexical item. (See McCawley 1968; Slobin 1996, 2006; Talmy 1985, 2000) (cf. Jackendof 1990; Pustejovsky 1995) In analyzing motion verbs, for instance, meaning components that constitute a motion event include motion, figure, path, ground, manner, and cause. The ways in which these components are incorporated in a verb's meaning are different depending on the language, and they have been typologized into a few patterns.

Just as motion verbs are structured and their systematic patterning is subject to linguistic analysis, so too are cooking terms, as illustrated in Adrienne Lehrer's important work on cooking verbs (Lehrer 1969, 1972), the wine vocabulary (Lehrer 1983, 2009), and general taste terms (Lehrer 1975). In particular, Lehrer's examinations of cooking terms in various languages have shown useful applications of semantic fields and componential analysis. Briefly put, the idea of semantic fields—originated from Lyons (1963, 1968) and is summarized in Lehrer (1972)—is such that "the vocabulary of a language is organized into a number of conceptual or semantic fields", (Lehrer 1972: 155) and that each field is structured in terms of semantic relations including hyponymy, synonymy, antonymy, and incompatibility, among others. Lehrer (1972) analyzed cooking terms in nine different languages: English, French, German, Chinese, Japanese, Jacaltec, Yoruba, Navajo, and Amharic. According to her investigation, there are at least thirty-five cooking verbs in English, and she organized some of them in Figure 1. This taxonomical structure is supposed to reflect particularly the hyponymy and synonymy relations among them. For example, *boil₁, fry, broil*, and *bake* are types of cooking; *poach* and *stew* are types of simmering; and so on.

cook								
boil₁			fry			broil	bake	
simmer		full boil₂		sauté	French fry deep fry	grill	barbe-cue, char-coal	roast
poach	stew	par-boil	stew-ing					
	braise							

FIGURE 1 Cooking verbs in English (Lehrer 1972: 157)

However, the organization would look vastly different depending on the language. For example, Lehrer's analysis of Japanese cooking verbs in Figure 2 gives quite a different outlook from its English counterpart in Figure 1. I will come back to this figure later for elaboration.

niru 'boil'	musu 'steam'	yaku 'bake, roast, grill, pan-fry'	ageru 'deep fry'
yuderu 'hard-boil eggs'	taku 'boil followed by steam'	itameru 'stir-fry'	

FIGURE 2 Cooking verbs in Japanese (Lehrer 1972: 163)

Different lexical structures of cooking terms in Lehrer's sample languages have been organized by way of componential analysis. Meanings of the cooking words are dissected, and semantic components are recognized that are relevant to capturing similar and different meaning characteristics among each other. For instance, use of water-based liquids (e.g. stock, wine, milk) is a semantic feature—indicated by [+water]—that is lexicalized in the meanings of *boil, simmer*, and *niru* 'boil,' whereas lack of it—indicated by [-water]—characterizes the specific cooking processes of *broil* and *bake*. Similarly, use of fat ([+/-fat]), vigorous vs. gentle cooking action ([+/-Vigorous]), and long vs. short cooking time ([+/-long time]) partake in the criteria for

componential analysis. And, combinations of these components lead to semantic relations like hyponymy, synonymy, and incompatibility. This may
be likened to distinctive features in phonology, which have been helpful to
identify natural class in sound inventories. (2) presents Lehrer's (1969) componential analysis, corresponding to Figure 1 (English) above.

(2)

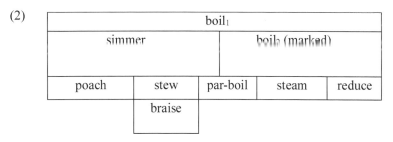

```
simmer:  [+water] [-vigorous action] [+liquids] [+solids]
boil₂:   [+water] [+vigorous action] [+liquids] [+solids]
poach:   [+water] [-vigorous action][+preserve shape] [+solids]
stew:    [+water] [-vigorous action] [+long cooking time]
         [+solids]
parboil: [+water] [-long cooking time] [+solids]
steam:   [+water] [+vigorous action] [+rack, sieve] [+solids]
reduce:  [+water] [+vigorous action] [+reduce bulk] [+liquids]
braise:  [+water] [-vigorous action] [+lid] [+solids]
```
                                                    (Lehrer 1969)

Shared features, opposite features, special features, and their combinations
result in a structural organization of one aspect of cooking terms. In (2), the
last features [+liquids] [+solids] refer to relevant parameters that specify collocation. For example, the presence of the collocational feature [+solids] but
not the [+liquids] feature for *poach* is reflected by the contrast between *poach
the fish* and **poach the broth*. Similarly, *reduce the sauce* is reasonable while
**reduce the fish* is anomalous. This difference is attributed to the colloca-
tional feature of [+liquids] and the absence of [+solids] associated with the
verb *reduce*.

   (3) demonstrates a componential analysis of Japanese cooking verbs, corresponding to Figure 2. Once again, shared features, opposite features, special features, and their combinations make it possible to catalog these Japanese cooking verbs into a coherent lexical organization.

(3)

niru 'boil'	musu 'steam'
yuderu 'hard-boil eggs'	taku 'boil followed by steam'

niru 'boil':   [+water] [+submerged]
musu 'steam': [+water] [-submerged]
yuderu 'hard-boil (eggs)': [+water] [+submerged] [+long cooking
                       time] [+special food (eggs)]
taku: <niru followed by musu>

(Lehrer 1972)

For the Japanese verbs in (3), I have extracted only the organization of cooking terms in Figure 2 that share the [+water] feature. Lehrer uses slightly different sets of features in Lehrer (1969) and Lehrer (1972), but they are essentially the same in the basic tenet of the analysis. She consulted a Japanese speaker who informed her that *yuderu* is specific to boiling eggs, contrary to a more general use of the verb.

In (4) I have reworked Lehrer's original analysis, especially by modifying *yuderu* and including two additional verbs, *wakasu* and *yugaku*.

(4)

wakasu 'boil water'	yuderu 'boil'		musu 'steam'
	yugaku 'parboil'	niru 'boil in a special broth'	taku 'boil+steam (rice)'

wakasu: [+water]
yuderu: [+water] [+submerged] [+solids]
musu: [+water] [-submerged] [+solids]
yugaku: [+water] [+submerged] [-long time] [+solids]
niru: [+water] [+submerged] [+special cooking liquid]
        [+solids]
taku: YUDERU followed by MUSU [+special food (rice)]

The verb *wakasu*, not in Lehrer's original analysis, is generally used for boiling water. The verb takes (o)*yu* 'hot water' but not *mizu* '(cold) water' as its object. It suggests that the object refers to a final "product" resulting from the cooking process that the verb denotes. This is reminiscent of the English verb *bake* in the creation sense as in *bake a cake* (as opposed to the change-of-state sense in *bake a potato*). *Wakasu* has quite narrowly defined semantic characteristics with their syntactic consequence of restricting its choice of direct object to (o)*yu*. Since there is no other cooking process that further elaborates on or overlaps with the basic water boiling denoted by *wakasu*, the verb does not seem to have hyponyms.

It is worth noting that although not common, *gyuunyuu* 'milk' may be found as the object of *wakasu* besides *(o)yu* 'hot water', especially in social media. In *gyuunyuu-o wakasu* [milk-Acc (water-)boil], the verb means heating or boiling milk, but unlike *(o)yu-o wakasu*, the object, *gyuunyuu*, is not understood to refer to what is created as a result of the boiling process. Instead, the verb has a more general sense of changing the state of the liquid from cold to reasonably hot. Additionally, I have found a phrase, *misoshiru o wakasu* [miso.soup-Acc (water-)boil] in the novel *Kiriha-e* (2010), written by the 2008 Naoki Prize winner Arano Inoue. As is the case with *gyuunyuu-o wakasu*, the combination of *wakasu* and miso soup strikes me as almost anomalous because *wakasu* is virtually reserved for boiling plain water. *Wakasu* in the presence of miso soup as its object does not have the creation sense, but in this case, too, the verb bears a more general meaning of bringing liquids to a reasonably hot temperature. If the range of collocation is widening beyond hot water to include other liquids to be heated, it may suggest that the componential analysis of *wakasu* calls for a further (collocational) feature specification of [+liquids].

In (4), also added to Lehrer's original list is *yugaku*, which can be characterized by a similar set of semantic components that we see with the English verb *parboil*. The term describes quick cooking in boiling water. In (4) *yuderu* in the first row and *niru* in the second have been reversed from Lehrer's analysis, changing the hyponymy relation between the two verbs: *yuderu* refers to a more general cooking process with water than just boiling eggs, while *niru* requires boiling in a broth that is not simply water. For instance, such broth may consist of water or dashi, soy sauce, sugar, and mirin. Finally, following Lehrer's analysis, *taku* has been dissected into the combination of *yuderu* 'boil' and *musu* 'steam'. The dialectal variation associated with this verb is noteworthy. In the western region of Japan, *taku* can be used as an alternative to *niru*, especially for slow-cooking, while in the eastern part of Japan in general, the term is almost exclusively used for cooking rice. For speakers in the eastern region, then, *gohan* '(cooked) rice' is virtually the unique direct object of the verb *taku*.

Although the way individual vocabulary items are grouped into semantic fields may not be identical across languages, the set of components (semantic features)—such as presence of liquid, presence of fat, direct heat—provide basic tools to capture the systematic patterning of cooking terms in a coherent semantic field. This further indicates that word meanings are not random, and that words can achieve a highly structured organization based on their meaning components.

Let us go back to the contrast between English and Japanese in (2) and (4) again. The Japanese cooking tradition is world renowned—enough to have garnered the recognition of the UNESCO Intangible Cultural Heritage—whereas its English counterpart is perhaps more modestly perceived. In that light it feels as if there should be more variety of verbs or expressions in Japanese that refer to the cooking process. While the exact number of cooking verbs in Japanese may not be overwhelmingly large, there are in fact other ways we can describe cooking preparation quite richly. As is well known, Japanese mimetics form a word class with an extensive membership, and they play an important role in elaborating the cooking processes. So, the general cooking verb *niru* can be further detailed by a wide array of mimetics, as expressions in (5) illustrate. Furthermore, compounding widely participates in word formation in Japanese, and makes a crucial contribution to detailing the cooking process as well. The list in (6) shows various V-V compounds where the first member is consistently the root of the general cooking verb *niru*.

(5) gutsugutsu 'boiling, bubbling'
    kotokoto 'simmering'
    satto   'quickly'   niru 'cook'
    gotogoto 'boiling, bubbling'
    guragura 'boiling rigorously'

(6) ni-komu   'boil well, stew'
    ni-tateru 'boil up'
    ni-tsumeru 'boil down'
    ni-kaesu   'reboil'
    ni-kobosu 'boil and then throw away the liquid   (usually followed by another around of boiling)'
    ni-shimeru 'boil x hard (down)'
    ni-dasu   'extract the essence by boiling'
    ni-tsukeru 'boil x hard with soy (and sugar)'

The use of mimetics and compounding in cooking expressions is not arbitrary or accidental. Motions verbs in (7-8) illustrate patterns that are very similar to those of cooking terms in (5-6).

(7) Mimetics with motion verbs
    dosadosa   'with a loud noise'
    daradara   'slowly without enthusiasm'
    zorozoro   'in great number'   aruku 'walk'
    dokadoka   'noisily and violently'
    sassato   'speedily'   (Hamano 1998: 2)

(8) Compounding with motion verbs
  a. kake-agaru   'run up'
      hai-agaru   'crawl up'
      hane-agaru   'jump up'
      tobi-agaru   'fly up'
  b. kake-mawaru   'run around'
      aruki-mawaru   'walk around'
      hashiri-mawaru   'run around'
      kogi-mawaru   'paddle around'
      koroge-mawaru   'roll around'
      tobi-mawaru   'fly around'
      haizuri-mawaru   'crawl around'
      hane-mawaru   'jump around'
  c. tobi-aruku   'run about'
      hai-aruku   'crawl about'
      ukare-aruku   'wander about'
      hottsuki-aruku   'wander about'

In (7) manner of motion is expressed by different mimetic words appearing together with a general verb of manner of walking, *aruku* 'walk'. Compounding in (8) provides a way in which motion verbs like *agaru* 'go up', *mawaru* 'go around', and *aruku* 'walk' receive finer-grained descriptions complementing the basic meaning of these motion events. (Kageyama 1993, Matsumoto 1996) In order to elaborate on detailed circumstances, we make good use of linguistic mechanisms that are available for manner expressions across semantic fields.

In this section, we have discussed lexicalization as it pertains to cooking terms. It is demonstrated that semantic fields and componential analysis provide conceptual bases and analytical tools helpful to examine cooking verbs in Japanese. By componentially dissecting the vocabulary internally to the cooking field and by comparing lexicalization patterns across semantic fields, we are reminded that the lexicon is uniformly organized in terms of a set of concepts and components that form them.

3 Metaphor

Metaphors are enormously prevalent in our daily communication (Lakoff and Johnson 1980), and their broad application cannot be overlooked in considering various ways in which language and food interact. Our tastes are limited to five—sweet, sour, salty, bitter, and umami—and these five words are far from sufficient to describe our intricate food experiences. Metaphors are very efficient and effective to that end, as is extensively catalogued in Seto (2003, 2005).

The intimate connection between food and our life beyond eating is also manifested by metaphors that express or describe non-food experiences by referring to food items. Extreme examples are attested by sexist remarks using food items and food-related expressions. For instance, Japanese references to women who are older than twenty-five as *kurisumasu-keeki* (クリスマスケーキ) "Christmas cake" and those over thirty-one as *toshikoshi-soba* (年越し蕎麦) "soba noodles eaten on the new year's eve" suggest that women who have passed the ideal age of twenty-five or thirty-one for marriage are unable to fit the social mold and thus have little value, just as Christmas cake after December 25th and end-of-year soba noodles after December 31st find little or no use. These expressions are typical testaments that show how aspects of our language can mirror the ideologies of the society and its people.

Our discussion of semantic fields in Section 2 has an important implication to metaphors. Metaphorical extension is widely discussed in various linguistic contexts, but of more direct relevance to our current discussion is the observation that the members of the same semantic field and semantic relations among them are metaphorically extended to another semantic field (Lehrer 1978; also see Rappaport Hovab and Levin 1998). For example, members of the field of cooking in English, such as *boil, burn*, and *simmer*, are together metaphorically extended to the field of emotional states. This allows the verbs to be used to describe emotions like anger and rage, as in *His comments made me boil* or in the newspaper headline *Emotions simmer after bad loss to the Jets*. Likewise in Japanese, the cooking terms discussed in Section 2 can be metaphorically extended to describe emotions and mental states. In (9) *waku* 'boil (water)' is used to depict the audience's excitement; and in (10), expressions with compounds formed around the intransitive counterpart of *niru* 'boil (in a special broth)'—*nieru*—all refer to angry states of humans.

(9) Subarashii engi-ga   kanshuu-o   <u>wak</u>-ase-ta.
     wonderful performance-NOM audience-ACC boil-CAUS-PAST
     'The wonderful performance excited the audience.'

(10) a. <u>nie</u>-kaeru omoi
         boil   feeling
         'blood-boiling rage'
      b. ikari-ga   <u>nie</u>-tagiru
         anger-NOM   boil
         'The rage stews in the body.'
      c. harawata-ga   <u>nie</u>-kurikaeru
         intestines-NOM boil
         'boiling rage inside'

Since these cooking words are all extended to describe emotional states, instead of analyzing each instance of a metaphor individually, we can try to collectively capture a conceptual thread that allows for the meaning extension. The conceptual metaphor (Johnson and Lakoff 1980) offers an analytical tool for such an approach. Using the concept and terminology of the conceptual metaphor framework, the metaphor examples in English and Japanese illustrated above are all captured by the conceptual metaphor, EMOTION IS COOKING, where emotion is the target and cooking is the source.

In a similar vein, Tsujimoto (2003, 2005) give detailed analyses of metaphors where the vocabulary of non-food fields are used to portray attributes and tastes of food. The two seemingly unrelated fields are analogized in terms of conceptual metaphors. Some of her examples are shown in (11-14) where relevant conceptual metaphors are indicated by the headings in capital letters. All the examples are taken from Tsujimoto (2003). The underlined expressions belong to non-food fields but are metaphorized to describe food items and tastes. In my English translations, I tried to preserve their literal meanings (i.e. the meanings in the source domain) so that the metaphorical relations are clearly detected.

(11) FOOD/TASTE IS HUMAN
    a.   <u>shitsukoi</u> aji
           persistent taste
           'persistent taste'
    b.   <u>jikoshuchoo-no</u>   tsuyoi yasai
           self.assertion-GEN strong vegetable
           'vegetable with strong self-assertion'
    c.   <u>sunaona</u>   wain
           gentle/obedient wine
           'gentle/obedient wine'

(12) FOOD/TASTE IS LIVING BEING
    a.   sozai-no   mochiaji-o   <u>ikasu/korosu</u>
           ingredients-GEN natural.flavor-ACC revive/kill
           'revive/kill the best of the ingredient's natural flavor'
    b.   biihushichuu-yori tsukeawase-ga <u>katsu</u>
           beef.stew-than   sides-NOM   win
           'the sides defeat the beef stew'

(13) INGREDIENT IS CONTAINER
    a.   umami-o   tojikomeyoo-to-suru ryoori
          flavor-ACC lock.in-try   cuisine
          'a cuisine that tries to lock in the flavor'
    b.   shizen-no   umami-ga hisondeirunda
          nature-GEN flavor-NOM hiding
          'the natural flavor is hiding'
    c.   kusami-o   nuite-oku
          smell-ACC remove
          'remove the smell'

(14) TASTE IS A MOVING OBJECT
    a.   aji-ga   nigeru
          flavor-NOM escape
          'the flavor escapes'
    b.   amami-ga   dete-kuru
          sweetness-NOM come.out
          'sweetness comes out'
    c.   niku-no   naka-made aji-ga   hairu
          meat-GEN inside-to flavor-NOM enter
          'the flavor goes into the meat'

In these metaphors, analogy between food and non-food is made through the conceptual metaphors as guiding principles. So, food and tastes are viewed to have personalities and behave like humans (11), to have a life with the ability to live, fight, and survive (12), and to have physical dimensions for static presence and dynamic movement (13-14). Thus, a variety of descriptions of food and tastes in (11-14) are able to maintain coherence and cohesion by virtue of conceptual metaphors.

The target-source relation between food and non-food, as is demonstrated in (11-14), can be reversed. That is, we can use food vocabulary to describe non-food items. Below, examples are drawn from fashion advice in a commercial magazine that targets women in their fifties as its readership. Copious instantiations of food and cooking vocabulary metaphorically illuminating a wide array of aspects in fashion coalesce into the conceptual metaphor of FASHION IS COOKING. Based on professional advice by a fashion specialist, the following captions appear along with colorful photos for visual supplements.

(15) a. kakushi-aji-o   oshiete-moraimasu
         hidden-taste-ACC   have.her.teach
         '(we will) have her teach us hidden/secret tastes'

    b. konsaba-huku-koso   shehu-shidai
         conservative-outfit-EMPH.   chef-up.to
         'conservative outfits are up to the chef'

    c. koko-ga   supaisu
         here-NOM spice
         '(you need to use) spice here'

(16) shinpuru-wanpi-mo reshipi-shidaide hiru-mo yoru-mo
      simple-dress-also   recipe-depend day-also evening-also
      gochisoo-ni
      feast-into
      'a simple dress can be turned into a feast depending on a recipe'

(17) jaketto-ni   ajitsuke
      jacket-onto season
      'season (=add flavor/taste) a jacket'

The three inviting lines in (15) appear on the first page of this fashion segment, where Ms. Takahashi is introduced as the fashion advisor. Details in
smaller prints that accompany the photos fill the rest of the page, further sup-
plementing the phrases in (15). In (15a) *kakushiaji* 'hidden/secret taste' an-
ticipates to-be-disclosed fashion tips that Ms. Takahashi is going to reveal to
the reader. (15b) encourages the reader to serve as a "chef" who is in charge
of coordinating the outfit from head to toe. There are three occurrences of the
phrase in (15c), each pointing to a coat jacket, a necklace, and a belt. These
three "spices" are important items to be added to a conservative-looking base
outfit, so that the entire fashion appearance will be enhanced. Secondary
items like accessories are viewed as one of the *kakushiaji* 'hidden/secret taste'
of fashion that the reader learns from Ms. Takahashi. The caption in (16) uses
two cooking-related word, *reshipi* 'recipe' and *gochisoo* 'feast'. Recipes have
ingredients and instructions. The fashion tip is concerned with how to make
a simple dress versatile according to day-time and evening activities. So, a
simple dress is a main ingedient, and the reader is instructed to add to it an
extra shirt for a workplace during the day, or accessories and shoes that could
be more ostentatious for evening activities. Results of the "recipe" are stylish
appearances that are gorgerous and "feast"-like, while at the same time, fitting to the time (day vs. evening) and purpose (work vs. pleasure). Similarly,
(17) advises the reader that a simple-looking jacket can be "seasoned" by
coordinating it with a tie, a belt, and fashionable pants. The jacket is a primary
ingredient, and the reader is suggested to enhance it with additional accessary

items, just as extra seasoning would improve on the taste of the food. The result is a transformation of something that is unassuming to a little more eye-catching outfit that is likened to rich flavors in food.

The examples in (15-17) are representative of specific ways in which the conceptual metaphor FASHION IS COOKING is instantiated. Added to this collection are the vocabulary and expressions of food and cooking such as *ryoori-suru* 'to cook', *ryoori-hoo* 'cooking method', *kakushiaji-o kikaseru* 'bring out hidden/secret flavor', *manisshu-na ajitsuke* 'mannish seasoning', and *shun-no huumi-o kuwaeru* 'add a seasonal flavor'. These are all embedded in fashion advice as part of concrete suggestions to improve on fashion coordination. Throughout the series of fashion tips, the coordination of stylish and trendy outfits is conceptually analogized to the cooking process, and the food vocabulary is accordingly used to refer to each step of the process. Thus, the conceptual metaphor FASHION IS COOKING provides a broad thread to unite these individual expressions into a coherent idea, lending credence to a regularity in our analogical process at the conceptual level.

4 Conclusion

Language is powerful in the food and cooking field, and our linguistic research has much to contribute to understanding how closely language and food interact and influence each other. The language of food contains resources rich with potential for linguistic analysis; and reciprocally, linguistic knowledge helps us dissect many a ways in which we think and express in words. We communicate through food, and the language we speak serves as a flavorful ingredient and often as a succulent hidden spice in our communication.

References

Culy, C. 1996. Null Objects in English Recipes. *Language Variation and Change* 8: 91–124.

Gerhard, X. M. Frobenius, and S. Ley. (Eds.) 2014. *Culinary Linguistics: The Chef's Special*. Amsterdam: John Benjamins.

Hamano, S. 1998. *The Sound-Symbolic System of Japanese*. Stanford: CSLI.

Hosking, R. (Ed.) 2010. *Food and Language*. London: Prospect Books.

Inoue, A. 2010. *Kiriha-e*. Tokyo: Shincho Bunko.

Jackendoff, R. 1990. *Semantic Structure*. Cambridge, MA: The MIT Press.

Jurafsky, D. 2014. *The Language of Food*. New York: W.W. Norton & Company.

Kageyama, T. 1993 *Bunpoo to Goikeisei* [Grammar and Word Formation]. Tokyo: Hitsuzi Shobo.

Lakoff, G. and M. Johnson. 1980. *Metaphors we Live By*. Chicago: The University of Chicago Press.

Lehrer, A. 1969. Semantic Cuisine. *Journal of Linguistics* 5: 39–56.

Lehrer, A. 1972. Cooking Vocabularies and the Culinary Triangle of Lévi-Strauss. *Antropological Linguistics*. 155–71.

Lehrer, A. 1975. Talking about Wine. *Language* 51.4: 901–23.

Lehrer, A. 1978. Structures of the Lexicon and Tansfer of Meaning. *Lingua* 45: 95–123.

Lehrer, A. 1983. *Wine and Conversation*. Bloomington: Indiana University Press.

Lehrer, A. 2009. *Wine & Conversation*. 2nd ed. Oxford: Oxford University Press.

Lyons, J. 1963. *Structural Semantics*. Oxford: Blackwell.

Lyons, J. 1968. *Introduction to Theoretical Linguistics*. Cambridge, UK. Cambridge University Press.

McCawley, J. 1968. *The Phonological Component of a Grammar of Japanese*. The Hague: Mouton.

Matsumoto, Y. 1996. *Complex Predicates in Japanese: A Syntactic and Semantic Study of the Notion 'Word'*. Stanford: CSLI.

Pustejovsky, J. 1995. *The Generative Lexicon*. Cambridge, MA: The MIT Press.

Rappaport Hovav, M. and B. Levin. 1998.Building Verb Meaning. *The Projection of Arguments*, eds. M. Butt and W. Geuder, 97–134. Stanford: CSLI.

Seto, K. (Ed.) 2003. *Kotoba-wa Aji-o Koeru* [Words Exceed Taste]. Tokyo: Kaimeisha.

Seto, K. (Ed.) 2005. *Ajikotoba-no Sekai* [The World of Taste Vocabulary]. Tokyo: Kaimeisha.

Slobin, D. 1996. From "Thought and Language" to "Thinking for Speaking". *Rethinking Linguistic Relativity*, eds. J.J. Gumperz and S.C. Levinson, 70-96. Cambridge: Cambridge University Press.

Slobin, D. 2006. What Makes Manner of Motion Salient? Explorations in Linguistic Typology, Discourse, and Cognition. *Space in Languages: Linguistic Systems and Cognitive Categories*, eds. M. Hickmann and S. Robert, 59-81. Amsterdam: John Benjamins.

Strauss, S. 2005. The Lingistic Aestheticization of Food: A Cross-Cultural Look at Food Commercials in Japan, Korea, and the United States. *Journal of Pragmatics* 37: 1427–55.

Szatrowski, P. (Ed.) 2014. *Language and Food: Verbal and Nonverbal Experiences*. Amsterdam: John Benjamins.

Talmy, L. 1985. Lexicalization Patters: Semantic Structure in Lexical Forms. *Language Typology and Syntactic Description*, vol. 3, ed. T. Shopen, 57–149. Cambridge: Cambridge University Press.

Talmy, L. 2000. *Toward a Cognitive Semantics*, Vol. II. Cambridge, MA: MIT Press.

Tsujimoto, 2003. Aji-kotoba-no Kakushi-aji [Secret Taste of Taste Vocabulary]. *Kotoba-wa Aji-o Koeru* [Words Exceed Taste], ed. K. Seto, 156–183. Tokyo: Kaimeisha.

Tsujimoto, 2005. Hiyu-de Ajiwau [Taste Through Metaphors]. *Ajikotoba-no Sekai* [The World of Taste Vocabulary], ed. K. Seto, 137–161. Tokyo: Kaimeisha.

Wansink, B., K. van Ittersum, and J.E. Painter. 2005. How Descriptive Food Names Bias Sensory Perceptions in Restaurants. *Food Quality and Preference* 16: 393–400.

Interactional Functions of Verbalizing Trouble: Self-addressed Questions in Japanese Conversation

TOMOKO ENDO
Seikei University

DAISUKE YOKOMORI
Kyushu University

1 Introduction

In the spoken mode of language use, speakers are not always fully prepared for what to say next and occasionally encounter trouble producing their utterances. Conversational behaviors occurring during such speech production trouble, which have been collectively called "self-repair" (Schegloff et al. 1977; Schegloff 2013), vary from less language-specific options such as silence, word cut-off, sound prolongation (Den 2009), and false-starts to more language-specific ones such as fillers (e.g., *uun, aaa, eeto, anoo*, etc. in Japanese) and what Tian et al. (2017) call "self-addressed questions" (henceforth SAQs)—questions explicitly addressing a speech

Japanese/Korean Linguistics 25.
Edited by Shin Fukuda, Mary Shin Kim, and Mee-Jeong Park.
Copyright © 2018, CSLI Publications

production problem.[1] Examples of English SAQs cited in previous Conversation Analytic studies of self-repair are as follows.

(1) "B't, a-another one that wentuh school with me wa:s a girl na:med uh, (0.7) °**W't th'hell wz er name.**° Karen." (Schegloff et al. 1977: 363)
(2) "He ha:d u:m (1.0) **Whuh wuz iht.** (0.3) Oh. He had some paint: (.) da:mage. on is car." (Lerner 2013: 99)

Although these parts (What the hell was her name, What was it) have the form of questions, the speaker is not really asking the recipient to provide information.

Among various methods to deal with speech production trouble, Both fillers and SAQs use specific linguistic forms to deal with speech production troubles; therefore,, analyzing them will greatly contribute to our understanding of each language. However, while fillers have been a popular topic in the literature (Clark & Fox-Tree 2002; Sadanobu & Takubo 1995; Watanabe 2009), SAQs did not receive much attention until Tian et al. (2017) conducted a cross-linguistic study of SAQs in English, Mandarin, and Japanese.

For Japanese SAQs, Tian et al. (2017) examined three recurrent formats, *nanteyuuno* 'what do you call it,' *nandaroo* 'what would it be,' and *nandakke* 'what was it (again),' and compared them in terms of whether the SAQ is anticipating a noun phrase (NP) or a clause. As a result of a corpus survey, they found that *nanteyuuno* tends to be used when a speaker is anticipating a clause and, on the other hand, *nandakke* tends to be used when a speaker is anticipating an NP, while *nandaroo* is used in both contexts (see Table 1).

	Total	Anticipating	
		Noun phrase	Clause
nanteyuuno 'what do you call it'	52	7 (13.5%)	45 (86.5%)
nandaroo 'what would it be'	33	12 (36.4%)	21 (63.6%)
nandakke 'what was it'	14	12 (85.7%)	2 (14.3%)
Total	99	31 (31.3%)	68 (68.7)

TABLE 1 Results from Tian et al. (2017) (modified from Table 9 in Tian et al. (2017: 915))

---

[1] We do not intend the term "question" here to refer to a kind of social action (e.g., requesting information or requesting confirmation); rather, we use it to refer to it as a category of grammatical formats which have features of interrogative morphsyntax (e.g., question words like *nan(i)* 'what').

Furthermore, under an assumption that the use of an NP-anticipating SAQ indicates a speaker's problem with remembering while a clause-anticipating SAQ indicates a speaker's problem with finding an appropriate formulation, Tian et al. suggest that it is a characteristic of SAQ use in Japanese, which sharply contrasts with SAQ use in English and Mandarin, that SAQs are more likely to be used when speakers have trouble finding appropriate phrasings than when speakers have trouble remembering particular items.[2]

Although Tian et al. (2017) first shed light on the systematicity of the usage of SAQs, their findings do not fully account for why and when speakers use each format of SAQs (e.g., *nanteyuuno, nandaroo, nandakke*). In fact, having trouble is one thing and verbalizing the trouble is another. That is, while a speaker may have trouble finding the right words or remembering them, she or he does not necessarily have to verbalize the trouble. Conversely, even if a speaker has no cognitive obstacles in producing an utterance, she or he can pretend to have trouble by using an SAQ or another kind of trouble verbalization. People do not verbalize speech production trouble only because they are actually having such trouble in their minds. Making speech production trouble public by uttering an SAQ can be used as a resource for an action in the ongoing interaction, since the trouble is heard by the recipient once it is verbalized. The present paper investigates what outcomes such explicit verbalizations of speech production trouble (i.e., SAQs) have in the ongoing interaction. We address this issue by analyzing the sequential environments of SAQs and the social actions that speakers can achieve by using them.

2 Data and Methodology

The data used for this study are recordings of everyday conversation among friends, family members/relatives, or acquaintances, which amount to approximately twenty-five hours in total. They are taken from the *CallHome* and *CallFriend* corpora (MacWhinney 2007) as well as our own video-recordings of face-to-face interactions.

From our data set, we assembled collections of three formats of Japanese SAQs and their variants: *nanteyuuno* 'What do you call it,' *nandakke* 'What was it (again),' and *nandaroo* 'What would it be'—the same three variants as Tian et al. (2017). The composition of each of these formats is as follows: *Nanteyuuno* is composed of *nan(i)* 'what,' *te* (Quotation marker), *yuu* 'say,' and *no* (Final Particle); *Nandakke* is

---

[2] Examples of the English SAQs that Tian et al. (2017) examined include *how shall I say it, what's the word I want, what is it, what's his name*, and *when was it*; while the Mandarin SAQs consisted of *shenme* 'what,' *shei* 'who,' *zenme jiang* 'how to say it,' and *na* 'where.'

composed of *nan(i)* 'what,' *da* (Copula), and *kke* (Past);[3] and *Nandaroo* is a combination of *nan(i)* 'what' and *daroo* (Copula with a modal element). In our collection, variations of these forms are included. For example, a sentence-final particle *kana* can be added after *nanteyuuno*, forming *nanteyuuno kana* 'what do you call it, I wonder'. Sometimes *teyuu* (Quotation particle *te* + verb *yuu* 'to say') is truncated as *tyuu*, as in *nantyuuno* 'what do you call it.' Table 2 shows the distribution of SAQs and linguistic units produced after them.[4,5] In this study, we focus on SAQs after which a clause was produced.

	Total	Anticipating		
		Noun phrase	Clause	Others
nanteyuuno 'what do you call it'	35	8 (22.9%)	22 (62.9%)	5 (14.3%)
nandaroo 'what would it be'	41	10 (24.4%)	17 (41.5%)	14 (34.2%)
nandakke 'what was it'	49	32 (65.3%)	14 (28.6%)	3 (6.1%)
Total	125	50	58	17

TABLE 2 Distribution of three SAQ formats in our data

We examined the examples using the methodology of Interactional Linguistics (Couper-Kuhlen & Selting 2017; Thompson et al. 2015). Excerpts are transcribed in accordance with the standard transcription conventions in Conversation Analysis (Jefferson 2004).[6]

3 *Nanteyuuno* 'What Do You Call It' in Tellings of Delicate Issues

Nanteyuuno 'what do you call it' expresses trouble in phrasing, or formulation in CA's term. The speaker is trying to find an appropriate expression for what she or he has in mind. When we look at the

---

[3] See Hayashi (2012) for the epistemic stance indexed by *kke* and its interactional consequences.

[4] Following Tian et al. (2017), we use the term 'anticipating' to refer to the item produced after an SAQ, but this does not mean that we assume the speaker always has the item in mind when she or he produces an SAQ.

[5] The differing results in the frequency of SAQs from Tian et al. (2017) (see Table 1) might be due to the differences in the activities with which participants are engaged and in the relations between participants. The Japanese data used in Tian et al. (2017) come from the conversational sub-corpus in the *Corpus of Spontaneous Japanese*, which is a collection of mock interviews and task-oriented dialogues, with partipants who did not know each other before the interviews. In contrast, as the particpants in our data are friends, family members, or relatives, they have many memories and pieces of knowledge in common.

[6] Word-by-word glosses are given only for the utterances featuring SAQs.

conversational environment, we find that *nanteyuuno* is often used when the speaker is producing a telling about a delicate issue. The example below is a case in point. In (3), Fumi, who has been living in the US for many years, is talking with her niece, Ruka, who has just gotten admitted to the English literature department at a university in Japan. Ruka had sent a letter in English to Fumi before the call, and prior to the excerpt, Fumi has started correcting grammatical mistakes in the letter.

(3) [English letter] CH2074_4:50
01 Fumi: *"for"::: (.) ano "entrance examination of university" tte kaite aru kedo,*
            '"for", well, you wrote "entrance examination of university",'
02 Ruka: *un.*
            'yeah'
03 Fumi: *kooiu baai wa "to go university" tte iu no. Amerika de wa ne.*
            'In this case, we say "to go university". In America."
04 Ruka: *(.) aa:::[:::*
            'Oh::::'
05 Fumi: *[sore ka "for university" tte iu no ne.*
                 'Or we say "for university".
06 Ruka: *(.) aa sonna fuu ni icchau no?*
            'Oh (you) say it in that way?'
07 Fumi: *un sonna fuu ni icchau no.*
            'Yeah (we) say it in that way.'
08 Ruka: *hu:::[::n.*
            'Oh:::'
09 Fumi: *[toka ne, iroiro ano >**nanteyuno** kana.< machigae de wa nai*
                 like FP various FL   what.do.you.call.it FP mistake COP TOP NEG
10   *nda keredomo:::,*
                 SE but
                 'Like that, there are various, **what do you call it**, not wrong but,'
11 Ruka: *u[n. motto-]*
            'Yes. more-'
12 Fumi: *[motto ko]u iu hoo ga ii tte iu no to:, (.)*
             'there are better ways to say those things.'
13   *.hh [sore]kara ano nandakke? ano::: machigae no to ne. aru kara sa.*
             'And well, what was it? Well, there are mistakes (in your writing).'
14 Ruka: *[n-]*
15 Fumi: *.hh [ano] shikkari (.) obenkyoo <chinatai>ne. e[he he huh huh huh]*
            'Well, study hard.'
16 Ruka: *[un.]*   *[aa:: soo desu ne::.]*
                 'Yes'   'Oh, that's right.'
17   *chotto saikin daraketeta n de:=*

'I've been lazy these days, so,'
18 Fumi: =u::n.
'Yeah'
19 Ruka: a ganbara nakya dame ya ha ha
'Oh I need to work hard. (laughter)'

One possible reason for Fumi's use of *nanteyuuno* 'what do you call it' might be merely the lack of a one-word description: as what Ruka had written is not totally wrong, it is not technically a *machigae* 'mistake,' which makes it hard for Fumi to refer to the issue in a straightforward way. It should also be noted, however, that Fumi is engaging in a socially difficult task. Advice-giving is highly delicate and face-threatening, even though Fumi has been living in the US for a long time and is thus entitled to correct Ruka's mistakes or unnatural English phrases. This delicate nature of the ongoing activity can also be seen in line 15, where Fumi uses a baby-talk register when she says *obenkyoo chinatai ne* '(You) study.'[7] This baby-talk register makes her utterance sound like a joke, and Fumi's laughter right after saying it also indicates the laughable-ness of this utterance. In this way, *nanteyuuno* 'what do you call it' in this example is working as a mitigation of the face-threatening act of advice-giving.

Another type of tellings of delicate issues occurs with negative assessments, as shown in the next example. The example is taken from a conversation between two female speakers, Setsu and Yuka. Yuka has recently moved from Colorado to Wyoming.

(4)[Wyoming] CFjapn 1605_1:00   (Prior to the excerpt, Sestu talked about a music event she had attended.)
01 Yuka: nanka urayamashii desu soo yuu koo, isogashii:: (.) naka ni:,
'Well I envy you for being in such a busy ,'
02 Setsu: un un [hhh   ]
'Yeah.'
03 Yuka: [ano, irutte] iu no ga.
'situation.'
04 Setsu: dooshite::.
'Why?'
05 Yuka: ya atashi:, wa[ioming ni, kite]::, =
'I, after coming to Wyoming,'
06 Sestu: [u::n.   ]
'Yeah.'

---

[7] The form *shinasai* is the unmarked imperative form of *suru* 'do'. With the alternation of *shi* to *chi* and *sa* to *ta*, *chinatai* sounds like child-directed speech.

07   =*un un.*
         'Yeah.'

08   *h*[*hhhh*   ]

09 Yuka: [*tottemo koko*] *inaka nandesu yone?* =
              'This place is a very rural area, you know?'

10 Setsu: =*soo datte nee.* [*un un hh*   ]
              'I heard so. yeah.'

11 Yuka: [*moo:, <u>hon%to</u> hidoi ndesu*]*yo. .h*=
                    'It's really terrible.'

12 Setsu: =*u::*[*n.*   ]
              'Yeah.'

((12 lines omitted. Yuka explains that her life had a harmony when she was in Colorado, but the harmony was lost after she moved to Wyoming.))

25   [*(de)* (.) *kazoku dake desho*]*o.* [*.hh*]
         'And I only have my family'

26 Setsu: [*un un. hh*   ] [*un*] *un* [*un.*]

27 Yuka: [*tomo*]*dachimo, inaishi:,*=
                        'I have no friends,'

28 Setsu: =*mada tomodachi dekinai?*
              'You haven't made friends yet?'

29 Yuka: *tte iu ka:, .hh* [*ano:,*]
              'Or (to put it more precisely,) well,'

30 Setsu: [*un.*] *h un.* [*hhh*]
              'Yeah.   Yeah.'

31 Yuka: [*zenzen*] *koo:,* >**nanteyuuno** *kana.*<=
              at.all this.way How.to.say.it FP
              'Totally, well, **what do you call it,**'

32 Yuka: =*chi*[*gau*]*n desu yo ano, (0.2) kyoo*[*tsuu no*] *ten ga nai ndesu zenzen.*
         different SE COP FP well common GEN aspect NOM not.exist SE at.all
         '(they are) different, well, (we) have nothing in common.'

33 Setsu: [*un.*]   [*un.*   ]
            'Yeah.'   'Yeah.'

34   *u:n, u*[*n,*   *u*]*n.* [*hhh*   ]
         'Yeah. Yeah.'

35 Yuka: [*dakara,*] [*.h yappari ano:*]*, muzukashii. .hh*=
         'So,'   'after all, well, it's difficult.'

36 Setsu: =*a so::o hh*
         'Oh is it so.'

In this example, the speaker is talking about a complicated situation which could not be summed up by a one-word description. Yuka is making negative evaluations about her neighbors and trying to find a better way of phrasing them. We should note, however, that the difficulty in phrasing is also due to the delicateness of the issue being discussed. As Du Bois (2007) has argued, a speaker positions herself or himself by making an evaluation about a topic. Making a negative assessment about others is a risky action as the speaker might sound too self-confident or judgemental. Note that her phrasing is extremely straightforward when she characterizes Wyoming, a place where she lives: she says *tottemo koko inaka nandesu yone?* 'This place is very rural, okay?' (line 09). By contrast, Yuka produces *nanteyuuno* 'what do you call it' when she is talking about her neighbors, positioning herself as not certain about the appropriateness of the phrasing of the negative evaluations she is going to make.

Also note that the tokens of *nanteyuuno* are articulated at a faster tempo than their surrounding words. While *nanteyuuno* can be used for buying time (cf. Iwasaki 2009), the use of this SAQ in this example might be better described as Yuka taking a stance of distancing herself from the formulation of her turn. That is, by saying *nanteyuuno*, the speaker warns the recipient that the phrasing may not be the best and that the speaker is not fully committed to all of the implications that the phrasing might invoke.

In this section, we analyzed the uses of *nanteyuuno* and argued that the speaker is employing it to verbalize trouble in phrasing when she is doing a telling that requires a delicate formulation, such as advice-giving or a negative assessment. By verbalizing this trouble with formulation, the speaker can project the delicate nature of the talk, warn the recipient that what is going to be said right after *nanteyuuno* may not be the best formulation, and thus distance herself from the formulation. In this way, *nanteyuuno* is used as a resource for stance-taking.

4   *Nandakke* 'What Was It' and *Nandaro* 'What Would It Be'

The sequential environments for *nandakke* 'what was it' and *nandaroo* 'what would it be' are different from that of *nanteyuuno*. Some tokens of *nandakke* and *nandaroo* are found in the environments of topic-shift and list-making. *Nandaroo* is also found when a speaker is answering a question or elaborating an answer.

Nandakke 'what was it (again),' which is said to express trouble with memory-retrieval (Tian et al. 2017), often occurs when a speaker is shifting topics or making a list. Due to space limitations, we will only focus on the cases involving topic-shifts in this paper. In the following example, a couple is talking on the phone.

(5) [Kid's crying] CH1012_04:25
01 Waka: [*tokorode-*
        'By the way,'
02 Hiro: [( ) *zuibun naiteru na.*
        '(He's) crying a lot.'
03 Waka: *un?*
        'Huh?'
04 Hiro: *zuibun naiteru na.*
        '(He's) crying a lot.'
05 Waka: (0.8) *un.* (0.2) *ima chotto ochita kana.* (.) [*isu kara.*
        'Yeah'   'I guess (he) just fell. (.) From the chair.'
06 Hiro: [*un.*
                                            'Yeah.'
07 Waka: (1.0) *un.* (0.5) *.h* [*h*]
        'Yeah.'
08 Hiro: [*toko*]*rode nani*
                        '(By) "by the way", what (were you going to say)?'
09 Waka: (0.7) *u::::nto.* (.) **nandakke** (0.5)
        INJ   what.was.it
        'Um, what was it.'
10   *a soo da socchi kara sa tegami daseba ikura gurai kakan no?*
        'Oh yeah, how much does it cost to send a letter from there (the U.S.)?'

When Waka, the wife, produces a topic-shift marker, *tokorode* 'by the way,' Hiro, the husband, notices that their baby is crying in the background on Waka's side. After Waka explains what has just happened, in line 08 Hiro asks what she was going to say after *tokorode* 'by the way.'

Although it is Waka who was launching a new topic with *tokorode* in line 01, she was distracted by Hiro's question and seems to have trouble in remembering what she was going to talk about. After producing an interjection *unto* 'well' and *nandakke*, she asks a question, which starts a completely new topic.

Nandaroo 'what would it be' is found in a similar environment. In the next example, a mother (Mom) and her son (Son) are talking. After Mom finishes giving a suggestion to Son regarding a phone call he should make, Son says that he understands. Here they reach the end of a topic, as is indicated by *sonnna kanji kana* 'I guess that's it' and *ne. un soo ne* 'Yeah, Right.' When Mom moves on to the next topic, she says *nandaroo* 'what would it be' in line 06.

(6) [Grandma] CH1290_08:20

01 Mom: *ano:: aisatsu suru yooni tte iwaremashita kara tte kakete gorannasai?*

    'Well, call (them) saying that (you) were told to say hi (to them).'

02 Son: *hai (.) wakarimashita.*

    'Yes. I understand.'

03   (0.5)

04 Son: *sonnna kanji [kana.*

    'I guess that's it '

05 Mom: [*ne. un soo ne.*

        'Yeah. Right.'

06   *sorede:: ato wa:: <**nandaroo** na>.=*

    CONJ remaining TOP what.would.it.be FP

    'And, the remaining (topic) is, **what would it be.**'

07   *=obaachama, oge- ogenki?*

    'Grandma, is- is she fine?'

08 Son: *un. genki da yo. [kinoo wa:: obachan no*

    'Yeah, she's fine. Yesterday, auntie's'

09 Mom: [*kokontoko-*

    'These days-'

10 Son: *(sankei) no happyookai ga ate, [sore:: mi ni itte*

    '(sankei) concert, she went to see it'

In line 06, Mom first produces a conjunction, *sorede* 'and,' and *ato wa* 'the remaining (topic) is,' which strongly projects a shift of topic. Then she says *nandaroo na* 'what would it be' in a slow tempo, expressing that she is trying to come up with what she wanted to talk about next. Right after *nandaroo na*, she rushes to ask about the grandmother, and Son starts talking about how the grandmother is doing.

What is common between *nandakke* and *nandaroo* in these two examples is that the participants have arrived at a boundary of talk. In this kind of environment, both participants are aware that the prior topic is already over and that they have to move on to another topic or end the call.[8] By using *nandaroo* or *nandakke* in such a position, the speaker indicates that she or he is going to start a new topic, thereby preparing the recipient for the unfolding new phase of the ongoing conversation.

---

[8] For common features at the end of a topic, see Hayashi and Yoon (2009).

One sequential environment observed only with *nandaroo* 'what would it be' is when the speaker is answering a question or elaborating an answer. In this environment, *nandaroo* indicates a state of thinking-in-progress. That is, the speaker is trying to come up with an answer or an explanation, thus the trouble the speaker is dealing with is related to neither memory-retrieval nor phrasing. In the example below, a researcher, Asami, is interviewing Banta about how his stance on child-raising has changed after the Great East Japan Earthquake of 2011.[9] After Banta explains his thoughts, Asami turns to Banta's wife Chika for her thoughts. Since Asami and Chika are close friends, they speak in a casual style.

(7)[face of "ittekimasu"]
01 Asami: *Chii chan wa,* (0.3) *doo omou?*
        'What do you think, Chii chan (= Chika's nickname)?'
02   (0.2)
03 Chika: *atashi wa,* (.) <u>*kanarazu*</u> *ittekimasu no* <u>*kao*</u> *o miru.*
        'I, take a look at (my kid's) face of "Ittekimasu (I'm leaving)".'
04   (0.2)
05 Asami: *aa::, soo*[*nanda.*]
        'Oh, is it so.'
06 Chika: [*moo na*]*n*[*ka,*
                 'Well,'
07 Asami: [*.h un.*
                    'Yeah'
08 Chika: **nandaroo.** (0.3) *yappari nakunatta hito mo ippai iru* <u>*kara:,*</u>
        What.would.it.be after.all die.PST person too many exist so
        'What would it be. (0.3) Because lots of people died (in the earthquake),'
11 Asami: *un un.*
        'Yeah, yeah.'
12   (0.7)
13 Chika: *i*[*tsu-   soo,   i*]*tsu,*
        'anytime- right, anytime,'
14 Asami: [<u>*hanaretete* ↑*ne*</u>]
        'While (they are) away (from their family), right?'
15 Chika: [*itsu   so*]*oyuufuuni,* (.) *nattemo okashikunai jookyoo da*<u>*kara:,*</u>
        'Because in the present situation, such things can happen anytime,'
16 Asami: [<u>*soo da yone*</u>_]
        'Right.'

---

[9] This example is from a face-to-face conversation, while other examples are all from telephone conversations. Whether the function of indicating thinking-in-progress is more common in face-to-face conversations needs further examination using quantitative analysis.

Chika's answer in line 03 'I take a look at my kid's face when he says he's leaving' is somewhat abstract and it is not clear what she means by this answer. The 0.2-second gap in line 04 and Asami's response *aa soo nanda* 'Oh is it so' in line 05 seem to be reacting to this unclearness in Chika's answer, since *aa soo nanda* 'Oh is it so' only receipts the previous turn as new information and does not show an affiliative stance (cf. Endo 2017). Starting in line 06 Chika elaborates her answer, and she says *nandaroo* before providing a substantial elaboration.

Here, Chika is indicating that she is in the process of thinking. As explained above, she has already given her answer to the question, but the answer only explains what she does (i.e., to take a look at her son when he leaves home), while the reason behind her behavior is yet to be explained. By saying *nandaroo* 'what would it be,' Chika indicates that she is going to produce further explanation, which keeps Asami in the recipient's position, as shown by her response tokens in line 11.

5 Summary and Conclusion

In this paper, we have shown that SAQs, or verbalizations of speech trouble, are interactionally motivated. Our finding is that different SAQs inhabit different sequential environments. *Nanteyuuno* 'what do you call it,' which expresses that the speaker is having trouble in formulation (phrasing), is often used when the speaker is dealing with delicate issues. In contrast, *nandakke* 'what was it' and *nandaroo* 'what would it be' are found in the environments of topic-shifts or list-making. *Nandaroo* is also found when the speaker is answering a question or elaborating an answer, and is used to show that the speaker is in a state of 'thinking-in-progress.'

In spontaneous speech, speakers face several tasks: thinking about what to say, finding the right expression, making sure what is going to be said does not cause any big problems in the ongoing interaction, etc. While having trouble in speech production might be a speaker-internal problem, verbalizing trouble makes the trouble public, which inevitably has interactional outcomes. In analyzing linguistic items in actual interaction, we have to consider what those items enable the participants to do in the ongoing interaction.

References

Clark, H. & Fox-Tree, J. 2002. Using *Uh* and *Um* in Spontaneous Speaking, *Cognition* 84: 73-111.

Couper-Kuhlen, E. & Selting, M. 2017. *Interactional Linguistics: An Introduction to Language in Social Interaction.* Cambridge: Cambridge University Press.

Den, Y. 2009. Prolongation of Clause-initial Mono-word Phrases in Japanese. *Linguistic Patterns in Spontaneous Speech*, ed. S-C Tseng, 167–92, Taipei: Institute of Linguistics, Academia Sinica.

Du Bois, J. 2007. Stance Triangle. *Stancetaking in Discourse,* ed. R. Englebretson, 139-82. Amsterdam/Philadelphia: John Benjamins.

Endo, T. 2017. The Japanese Change-of-State Tokens *A* and *Aa* in Responsive Units. *Journal of Pragmatic*s 123: 151-66.

Hayashi, M. 2012. Claiming Uncertainty in Recollection: A Study of *Kke*-Marked Utterances in Japanese Conversation. *Discourse Processes* 49: 391-425.

Hayashi, M. & Yoon, K. 2009. Negotiating Boundaries in Talk. *Conversation Analysis: Comparative Perspectives*, ed. J. Sidnell, 248-76. Cambridge: Cambridge University Press.

Iwasaki, S. 2009. Time Management Formulaic Expressions in English and Thai. *Formulaic Language,* eds. R. Corrigan, E. A. Moravcsik, H. Ouali, and K. M. Wheatley, 589-614. Amsterdam/Philadelphia: John Benjamins.

Jefferson, G. 2004. Glossary of Transcript Symbols with an Introduction. *Conversation Analysis: Studies from the First Generation*, ed. G. H. Lerner, 13-31. Amsterdam/Philadelphia: John Benjamins.

Lerner, G. H. 2013. On the Place of Hesitating in Delicate Formulations: a Turn-Constructional Infrastructure for Collaborative Indiscretion. *Conversational Repair and Human Understanding*, eds. M. Hayashi, G. Raymond & J. Sidnell, 95-134. Cambridge: Cambridge University Press.

MacWhinney, B. 2007. The TalkBank Project. *Creating and Digitizing Language Corpora: Synchronic Databases, Vol.1.* eds. J. C. Beal, K. P. Corrigan & H. L. Moisl, 163-80. Houndmills: Palgrave-Macmillan.

Sadanobu, T. & Takubo, Y. 1995. Danwa niokeru Shinteki Soosa Monitaa Kikoo: Shinteki Soosa Hyooshiki *Eeto* to *Ano(o)* [The Monitoring Devices of Mental Operations in Discourse: a Case of "eeto" and "anoo"]. *Gengo Kenkyu* 108: 74-93.

Schegloff, E. 2013. Ten Operations in Self-Initiated, Same-Turn Repair. *Conversational Repair and Human Understanding*, eds. M. Hayashi, G. Raymond & J. Sidnell, 95-134. Cambridge: Cambridge University Press.

Schegloff, E. A., G. Jefferson, & H. Sacks. 1977. The Preference for Self-Correction in the Organization of Repair in Conversation. *Language* 53(2): 361-82.

Thompson, S. A., B. Fox & E. Couper-Kuhlen. 2015. *Grammar in Everyday Talk: Building Responsive Actions.* Cambridge: Cambridge University Press.

Tian, Y., T. Maruyama & J. Ginzburg. 2017. Self Addressed Questions and Filled Pauses: A Cross-linguistic Investigation. *Journal of Psycholinguistic Research,* 46(4): 905-22.

Watanabe, M, 2009. *Features and Roles of Filled Pauses in Speech Communication: A Corpus-based Study of Spontaneous Speech*, Tokyo: Hitsuji Shobo.

The Korean Vocative Interjection *Ya*: Functions Beyond Summoning Actions

MARY SHIN KIM
University of Hawai'i at Mānoa

1 Introduction

Drawing on the framework and methodology of conversation analysis, this study examines the unexplored functions of the Korean vocative interjection *ya* 'hey' for a variety of actions beyond summoning. As a vocative interjection, *ya* is used for calling or summoning a fairly closely related addressee of the same age or younger as the speaker (Chang 1996), as seen in excerpt 1.[1] This segment comes from a telephone conversation between two friends who are recording their telephone call for a corpus project.

[1] The exclamatory interjection *ya* 'wow', which serves to display the speaker's affective stance, such as surprise or pleasure (see example below), is not discussed here.

ya: kyengchi   cengmal   coh-ta.
wow   view   really   good-DC
'Wow, the view is really nice!'

Japanese/Korean Linguistics 25.
Edited by Shin Fukuda, Mary Shin Kim, and Mee-Jeong Park.
Copyright © 2018, CSLI Publications

341

Excerpt 1 [KO_6694]

1 B: hhh [hh hh

2→A: [ya ya >ya ya ya<
         'Hey, hey, hey, hey, hey'

3→B: e.
         'Yeah'

4 A: ilum-un   tay-ci   mal-ca.
       name-TOP state-NML do.not-PRP
       'Let's not state our names.'

5 B: e.
       'Yeah.'

6 A: Okay.

Lines 2–3 show a generic summon-answer sequence. Speaker A summons speaker B, who is engaged in a different activity (laughing), before she proceeds with her main action in line 4, which is requesting they not reveal their names during the recording. Here, *ya* stands by itself and functions as a pseudo-address term, which can be roughly translated as 'hey' in English.

However, an investigation of naturally occurring interactions shows that this account is incomplete. *Ya* appears when there is no need for calling or summoning an addressee. For instance, *ya* occurs in dyadic telephone conversations where there is no ambiguity in understanding whom the speaker is addressing and when the addressee is already engaged in the ongoing interaction, as seen in excerpt 2.

Excerpt 2 [KO_4296]

1 A: Columbia   mwul   coh-a?
       Columbia   water   good-IE
       'Does the water feel good at Columbia (University)?'

2→B: **ya** mwul-i concayha-ci   anh-nun-ta-nikka   ne-n--
       ya water-NOM exist-NML   not-PRS-DC-said.so you-TOP
       'YA water does not exist (here), I told you.'

Here, speaker A asks a question and speaker B starts her response with *ya*, although she already has speaker A's attention. *Ya* even appears in the middle of a speaker's turn, as seen in excerpt 3, line 4.

Excerpt 3 [KO_6725]

```
1   B:    kulehci.   han tal-ey       phalsip pwul.
          right      one month-per    eighty  dollar
          'Right. It's eighty dollars a month.'

2   A:    ssa-ci-to             anh-ko.
          cheap-NML-either      not-and

3         pissa-ci-to           anh-ko      kuleh-kwuna
          expensive-NML-either  not-and     be.SO-UNASSIM
          'It's neither cheap nor expensive.'

4→B:     pissa-ci      ya    hankwuk-ey pihaysen     pissa-ci:.
          expensive-COMM ya   Korean-compared.to  expensive-COMM
          'It's expensive YA compared to Korea, it's expensive:.'
```

Despite the high frequency of *ya* in unexpected occurrences in interaction, there does not appear to be any empirical research focusing on the diverse uses of *ya*.[2] This paper aims to investigate what functions and actions *ya* performs beyond the act of summoning in interaction.

2   Data and Methodology

The analysis is based on 375 instances of *ya* found in 32 different telephone calls (960 minutes) from the Linguistic Data Consortium Korean Corpus of Telephone Speech and 31 instances of *ya* found in a personal data collection of two videotaped multi-party interactions among speakers of Korean (120 minutes). The paper examines representative cases from the collection. The study deploys a conversation analytic approach that focuses on examining how participants in interaction compose and position turns at talk so as to realize one another's actions (Schegloff 2007). This framework is essential for examining when and how speakers deploy *ya* at various interactional moments.

---

[2] Vocative *ya* appears in 77 out of 100 telephone calls in the Linguistic Data Consortium Korean Corpus, which demonstrates its high frequency in interactions across different age groups and genders.

3   Disjunctive Topic Shift

The analysis first shows that *ya* systematically occurs in turn-initial position or at the beginning of a turn constructional unit and serves important functions in the organization of turns and turn-taking. *Ya* frequently occurs in first position when a speaker is initiating a new action sequence. In this position, *ya* functions to mark disjunctive topic shift, as seen below. The following exchange comes from a telephone conversation between two friends. Just prior to this segment, A was telling B about her acquaintance's sudden death due to an unexpected accident.

Excerpt 4-1   [KO_4296]

1   A: khayp   pwulssangha-ci¿
             real   pitiful-COMM
             'It's a real pity (she died), isn't it?'

2   B: khayp-i-ta.
             real-be-DC
             'It's a real (pity).'

3   A: ung.
             'Yeah.'

4→   <**ya** itongwu   nemwu   chakha-ci anh-ni?
             ya NAME   so   nice-NML not-Q
             'YA isn't Yi Dong Woo so nice?'

5   B: ung.
             'Yes.'

6   A: >maynnal cenhwaha-y.<
             everyday call-IE
             'He calls me everyday.'

7   B: cincca   chakha-ta.
             really   nice-DC
             'He's really nice.'

In lines 1–2, the story reaches its closure as A and B assess the event as very unfortunate. In line 3, A brings her turn to a point of possible completion using a sequence-closing *ung* 'yeah', but then, in line 4, she abruptly picks up the turn again with *ya* (the angle bracket < in front of *ya* marks an abrupt utterance) and shifts to a different topic, her boyfriend, who she has talked about earlier in their telephone call. Because the recipient is already engaged in the talk, this *ya* does not function to summon, but rather serves to alert the recipient of, and prompt her to shift her attention to, the new disjunctive topic sequence the speaker is about to launch. The conversation continues in excerpt 4-2.

Excerpt 4-2   [KO_4296]

8   A: khayp-i-ci¿
           excellence-be-COMM
           'He is great, isn't he?'

9   B: e. .h weyniliya.
           yes   wow
           'Yes. .h Wow'.

10→   .hh   **ya**   ne   nacwungey   manyakey cengmallo
                  ya   you   later   if   really

11   New York-ulo   ol   ke-mye:n
            New York-to   will.come-if
            'YA if you're really going to come to New York later,'

12 A: ung.
           'Uh huh.'

13 B: ney   kes-kkaci hayse   Phantom   opera   kathi
           your   thing-including   Phantom   opera   together

14   yeyyakhay noh-umyen   coh-keyss-ta:.
            have.it.reserved-if   good-DCT:RE-DC
            'it would be a good idea to reserve your ticket as well for the Phantom of the Opera.'

The practice of deploying *ya* for topic transition is not limited to a single speaker. This time, as A's talk about her boyfriend reaches its closure in lines 8–9 with their assessment that the boyfriend is a great guy, it is B who shifts the topic. In line 9, B brings her turn to a point of possible completion, but then in line 10 rushes straight into an in-breath (.hh) and an emphatic *ya* (underline marks higher pitch or loudness) and shifts to a different topic, from A's boyfriend to A's upcoming visit to New York where B lives. As shown here, speakers regularly preface a disjunctive topic shift with *ya*.

4 Abrupt Activity Shift

Ya not only marks abrupt transition at the topic level (what speakers are talking about), but also at the action and activity level (what speakers are doing). And *ya* is not limited to turn-initial position, but also occurs in turns-in-progress. The following segment from another telephone conversation between two friends shows such an example. Here, speaker A begins to deliver self-flattering news about getting admitted to Ewha Woman's University. As B displays that she is aware of the news (line 2), A begins to provide an additional piece of news that B may not know (line 3). Note how A then momentarily departs from this main activity in progress.

Excerpt 5 [KO_4478]

```
1  A:   ah   na   itay ka-ss-e. = itay       ka-n [ke  al-a?
        oh   I    Ewha go-PST-IE Ewha        go-RL fact know-IE
        'Oh, I got into Ewha. Do you know I got into Ewha?'

2  B:                                    [e:  al-e kulay:.
                                         yes know-IE yeah
                                         'Ye:s, I know, yeah.'

3  A:   ung      itay       mwullihak-kwa    ka-ss-kwu:
        yeah     Ewha       physics-dept.    go-PST-and
        'Yeah, I got into the Ewha Physics Department, and'

4→      <ya sengmi--  sengmi-nka?
        ya  NAME      NAME-Q
        'YA Seongmi- is it Seongmi?'

5  B:   ung
        'Yes.'

6  A:   kyay-nu:n ceki itay pwule   kyoyuk-i-nka   ka-ss-te-la.
        she-TOP   DM   Ewha French  education-be-Q go-PST-RT-DC
        'she got into Ewha's French Department.'
```

In line 4, A departs from her unfolding talk and engages in a side activity, eliciting B's help in remembering their mutual friend's name, Seongmi. Here, A explicitly marks this abrupt departure with *ya* to redirect the recipient's attention to this side activity. Identifying the person properly is important as the recipient needs to recognize the person the speaker is just about to mention. With B's confirmation of the friend's name in line 5, A returns to the halted main activity, reporting another piece of news, that their mutual friend got admitted to the same university, in line 6.

As illustrated above, speakers regularly use *ya* when departing from one topic to another or from one activity to another in a disjunctive manner. *Ya* is used in turns that are not cohesive with prior talk in terms of either the topic or the activity.

5   Disalignment and Disaffiliation

This section examines cases where *ya* is deployed in turns that are not only disaligned with the activity in progress, but disaffiliated with the stance of others. This function of *ya* is observed when *ya* appears in second position in response to a sequence-initiating turn, as shown in excerpt 6 (which includes excerpt 2).

Excerpt 6   [KO_4296]

1→A: Columbia   mwul   coh-a?
       Columbia   water   good-IE
       'Does the water feel good at Columbia (University)?'

2→B: **ya** mwul-i   concayha-ci   anh-nun-ta-nikka   ne-n--
       ya water-NOM exist-NML   not-PRS-DC-said.so   you-TOP
       'YA water does not exist (here), I told you.'

3   A: yeca   mwul-un?
         woman   water-TOP
         '(Then) what about women?'

Speaker A's question to speaker B in line 1 uses an idiom to ask whether the people at B's university are attractive. The question requires a yes or no response. The recipient, B, prefaces her response with *ya*, signaling that B is not going to abide by the terms of the question. Instead, she challenges the question itself by disputing its presupposition: the water does not exist, so asking whether it is good or not is irrelevant. B also claims that she has already given A this information ('I told you.'). As seen here, the *ya*-prefaced response displays disalignment and disaffiliation, thus problematizing both the act of asking the question and the question itself. In response, A amends her question (line 3). Such uses of *ya* can also be observed in various other interactional contexts beyond question and response sequences.

Excerpt 7 comes from a face-to-face conversation among three friends in which one of them, Y, reports a piece of news: The new Pope can speak ten different languages (lines 1–2). The two other participants, B and W, show different responses to this news.

Excerpt 7 The New Pope

1→Y: ipen-ey   saylo   ppophin   kyohwang-i
       this.time-at new   elected   Pope-NOM

2 →   sip kay kwuke   ha-n-tay
       ten CL   language do PRS HEARSAY
       'I heard the new Pope can speak ten languages.'

3 B: HA:: cincca-yo¿= ((Speaks with excitement))
       wow really-POL
       'WO:W, really?'

4→W: =**ya** kuke-nun--   cepen-ey--   ta   ha-canh-a.=
       ya   that-TOP   last.time-at everyone do-you.know-IE
       'YA that's- everyone can, you know.'

5   =sip kay kwuke-ka   nungthongha-ta-nun ke-ya?
       ten CL language-NOM   fluent-DC-RL   thing-be:IE
       'You mean, he is fluent in ten languages?'

6 B: anim hi cengto ha-n-ta-nun   ke-yey-yo?
       or   hi about   do-PRS-DC-RL   thing-be-POL
       'or you mean, he can say simple greetings like "hi"?'

7 W: kulay   kukey   kwungkumhay.
       right   that:NOM be.curious-IE
       'Right, that's what I would like to know.'

8 Y: hi   cengto ha-myen na-to   ilcwuil-man
       hi   about   do-if   I-too   one.week-only

9   kongpwuha-myen   na-to   sip kay kwuke   ha-n-ta.
       study-then   I-too   ten CL language do-PRS-DC
       '(It would not have been in the news report) if it is only to say "hi",
       which (even) I could speak ten languages after studying for a
       week.'

In line 3, B responds to the news as noteworthy by expressing excitement and surprise. However, in line 4, the other participant, W, begins his response with *ya*, signaling that he will take a different stance. In fact, he challenges the noteworthiness of the report by claiming that it is something everyone can do. Furthermore, in line 5, W asks for clarification on the extent to which the Pope can speak ten different languages, casting doubt on the way in which Y treats the report as noteworthy. Interestingly, as W challenges Y, B starts to align with W and co-constructs W's question challenging Y in lines 5–6. Facing these challenges from the other participants, Y disputes their questions in lines 8–9. As such, the *ya*-prefaced response disrupts the progressivity of the talk and undermines the action and stance of the prior speaker.

As Schegloff (1996) noted, early turn beginnings are regularly occupied by resources that mark the relationship between the current turn-in-progress and that which precedes it. They also project the ensuing turn and action. As we have seen, *ya* regularly occurs turn-initially or at the beginning of a turn constructional unit, and in this position, *ya* indexes disjunctive transitions or departures from the prior turn or talk, or the trajectory of the interaction.

6   A Turn-Constructional Pivot

Ya is also regularly observed in turn-final position or at the end of a turn-constructional unit, as shown in excerpt 8, line 2. Its position demonstrates that, here, *ya* is not functioning to summon an addressee, which would not be necessary at the end of a speaker's turn. Similar to excerpts 6 and 7, *ya* in excerpt 8 occurs when the speaker takes a disaffiliative stance. Here, B disapproves of A's extravagant behavior. Speaker B's disaffiliative stance in line 2 is demonstrated by A's response in line 3, where A begins to defend her lavish behavior.

Excerpt 8 [KO_6744]

1	A:	ttokkathun	kakey-eyse	sey kay-lul	sa-ss-ketung?
		same	store-at	three CL-ACC	buy-PST-CORREL

'(I) bought three (pairs of pants) at the same store.'

2→	B:	hh	manhi	sa-ss-ta	**ya**. hh
			many	buy-PST-DC	**YA**

'Hh (You) bought many YA. hh'

3	A:	ani	paci-ka	nemwu	ttak	pwuthe-se
		well	pants-NOM	too	exactly	stick-because

'Well, my pants were too tight, so.'

Ya sometimes appears in turn-medial position, where it operates as a *turn-constructional pivot*, which is a resource for extending a turn at talk (Schegloff 1979; Walker 2007; Clayman 2012). In other words, because *ya* can occur in both turn-initial and turn-final positions, it can belong to the talk before and/or after it, serving as pivot between them. Recent studies by Clayman (2012) and Clayman and Raymond (2015) show how address terms often serve as modular pivots in English. Excerpt 9 shows a similar example in Korean. In this telephone conversation, A and B, mothers of preschoolers, are talking about the monthly cost of preschool, B states the cost (line 1), and A assesses it as neither inexpensive nor expensive in lines 2–3.

Excerpt 9 [KO_6725]

```
1  B:   kulehci.   han tal-ey       phalsip pwul.
        right      one month-per   eighty dollar
        'Right. It's eighty dollars a month.'

2→A:   ssa-ci-to            anh-ko    .
        cheap-NML-either     not-and

3→      pissa-ci-to             anh-ko      kuleh-kwuna.
        expensive-NML-either    not-and     be.SO-UNASSIM
        'It's neither cheap nor expensive.'

4→B:    pissa-ci      ya    hankwuk-ey pihaysen      pissa-ci:.
        expensive-COMM ya   Korean-compared.to  expensive-COMM
        'It's expensive YA compared to Korea, it's expensive:.'

5  A:   hankwuk-ey pihaysen      pissa-ntey:,
        Korea-compared.to        expensive-but
        'Compared to Korea, it's expensive, but'
```

Note how B responds to A's assessment. In line 4, B first disagrees, but then quickly elaborates on her prior talk with no gap. Here, *ya* pivots between "It's expensive." and "Compared to Korea, it's expensive." *Ya* can syntactically and prosodically belong to both the preceding and the subsequent units of talk. The pitch track of this utterance (Figure 1) clearly shows the continuous intonational trajectory across both junctures.[3]

---

[3] Studies by Walker (2007, 2010) and Clayman (2012) show that the intonation pattern of a pivot differs from that of a "rush through." Although both compress the transition place and extend the turn, in the case of a pivot, the prior and subsequent talk maintain a seamless pitch trajectory across both junctures, as shown in Figures 1 and 2. In the case of a rush through, the prior talk shows the terminal pitch contour characteristic of a turn-constructional unit completion.

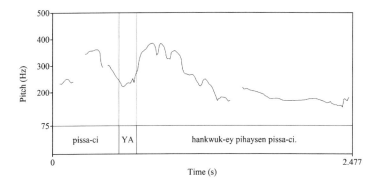

FIGURE 1 Pitch track for Excerpt 9

Ya thus serves to extend a turn beyond a projected or incipient point of possible completion, enabling the speaker to secure a longer turn and further elaborate her prior unit of talk. Similar to Clayman's (2012) findings regarding the use of English address terms, here we observe a speaker using *ya* immediately after making a claim that is at odds with a recipient's claim or stance, and is therefore vulnerable to the recipient's challenge; apparently to forestall any such challenge, the speaker leaves no gap, instead quickly providing elaboration on her own prior talk.[4] In response, in line 5, the recipient changes her stance and displays at least partial agreement to the speaker's claim.

Excerpt 10 from a telephone conversation shows another example of *ya* serving as a turn-constructional pivot. Prior to this segment, speaker A has been complaining about her recent hardships. The segment begins with another complaint by A (line 1).

Excerpt 10 [KO_4296]

```
1  A:   kuleko    na    khayp    nulk-ess-e.
        and       I     really   age-PST-IE
        'And, I have aged so much.'

2       nemwu    soksanghan    il--     soksanghan    il-i
        so       upsetting     matter   upsetting    matter-NOM
```

---

[4] Questions remain regarding whether full address terms and pseudo-address terms such as the interjection *ya* show subtle differences in their usages and functions.

3   manhi   sayngki-nikka nulk-te-la: salam-i::.
           much   occur-because age-RT-DC   person-NOM
           'Because I had so many upsetting incidents-
           so many upsetting incidents, I noticed myself aging so much.'

4 B: <u>cin [cca</u>?
          'Really?'

5 A: [kewul   po-ko   na   khayp   nolla-ss-ta-nikka.
           mirror   look-and I   really   shock-PST-DC-said.so
           'I was shocked when I looked at myself in the mirror.' .

6→   wancen   <u>halmeni</u> tway-ss-e   **ya**   ne-- ne-twu
           totally   grandma become-PST-IE ya   you you-also

7→   na po-myen nollalkel⌐
           I   see-if   will.be.shocked
           'I totally became a <u>grandma</u> YA if you- you see me
           you will be shocked, too!'

When speaker A describes how she has aged (lines 1–3), which can be considered a self-deprecatory comment, B displays disbelief by asking for confirmation ('Really?'). The environment is similar to that in excerpt 9, in that the speaker's claim is vulnerable to the recipient's disbelief or challenge. As soon as A and B's overlapping talk ends, in line 6, A further upgrades the severity of her complaint, from simply 'aged' to 'became a grandma'.[5] Further, without pausing, she uses *ya* and then continues her turn with an utterance that strengthens her claim by stating that the recipient would agree if she could see for herself (lines 6–7). *Ya* is prosodically continuous with the adjacent talk and serves to simultaneously complete the prior unit and launch the next with no gap between them, as shown in the pitch track in Figure 2.

---

[5] The preferred response to self-deprecation is disagreement, which denies the deprecated attributes of the deprecator (Pomerantz 1984). In excerpt 10, line 4, B displays disbelief of A's self-deprecatory assessment. However, as noted by Kim (2015), there are many cases in which the deprecator disagrees with the recipient and continues to deprecate herself, as seen here in lines 6–7.

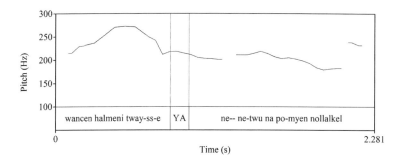

FIGURE 2 Pitch track for Excerpt 10

Excerpts 9 and 10 both show examples of how *ya* is used as a pivot when implementing assessments different from those of the recipients. The speakers continue their talk past a point of possible syntactic and pragmatic completion to preempt further disagreements or challenges from the recipients. As this section demonstrates, in turn-medial position, *ya* continues to play an important role in the organization of turns and turn-taking.

7   Discussion and Conclusion

This examination of the vocative interjection *ya* in naturally occurring conversational data has uncovered diverse functions beyond its summoning action. As a pseudo-address term, *ya* appears in various turn positions (initial, medial, and final) and sequential positions (first and second) and serves to initiate or extend turns at talk in situations where the speaker may be at odds or in competition with other speakers in terms of topic, activity, action, or stance.

The multifaceted functions of the vocative interjection *ya* can be explained by its original summoning property. The summoning function of *ya* serves to alert the recipient that the speaker is about to make some kind of departure from the prior turn and talk. Speakers make such disjunctive moves because they have imminent tasks or actions to which they need to orient. In excerpt 5, in the midst of the speaker's turn, the speaker quickly confirms the name of a third party with the help of the recipient, before moving on to talk about that person. In excerpts 9 and 10, the speakers quickly elaborate on their claim with no gap because their talk is vulnerable to a recipient's challenge. In excerpt 4, both speakers abruptly shift the topic of the talk according to their action agenda. In excerpts 6 and 7, speakers treat the prior talk and stance as inadequate and disrupt the progressivity of the talk before it develops further. Whether *ya* occurs in turn-initial, turn-medial, or turn-final position, it serves essential functions in the organization of turns and turn-taking.

This study expands our understanding of the usages and roles of interjections in interaction. Many other interjections remain to be examined for their uses in a range of interactional contexts.

References

Chang, S. J. 1996. *Korean.* Amsterdam: John Benjamins.

Clayman, S. 2012. Address Terms in the Organization of Turns at Talk: The Case of Pivotal Turn Extensions. *Journal of Pragmatics* 44: 1853–1867.

Clayman, S. and Raymond, C. 2015. Modular Pivots: A Resource for Extending Turns at Talk. *Research on Language and Social Interaction* 48: 388–405.

Kim, M. S. 2015. The Complexity and Variability of Self-Deprecation in Korean Conversation. *Pragmatics and Society* 6(3): 398–420.

Pomerantz, A. 1984. Agreeing and Disagreeing with Assessments: Some Features of Preferred/Dispreferred Turn Shapes. *Structures of Social Action*, ed. M. Atkinson and J. Heritage, 57–101. Cambridge: Cambridge University Press.

Schegloff, E. A. 1979. Identification and Recognition in Telephone Conversation Openings. *Everyday Language: Studies in Ethnomethodology*, ed. G. Psathas, 23–78. New York: Irvington.

Schegloff, E. A. 1996. Turn Organization: One Intersection of Grammar and Interaction. *Interaction and Grammar*, eds. E. Ochs, E. A. Schegloff, and S. A. Thompson, 52–133. Cambridge: Cambridge University Press.

Schegloff, E. A. 2007. *Sequence Organization in Interaction.* Cambridge: Cambridge University Press.

Walker, G. 2007. On the Design and Use of Pivots in Everyday English Conversation. *Journal of Pragmatics* 39: 2217–2243.

Walker, G. 2010. The Phonetic Constitution of a Turn-Holding Practice: Rush-Throughs in English Talk-in-Interaction. *Prosody in Interaction*, eds. D. Barth-Weingarten, E. Reber, and M. Selting, 51–72. Amsterdam: John Benjamins.

Abbreviations

ACC	Accusative	CL	Numeral classifier
COMM	Committal	CORREL	Correlative
DC	Declarative suffix	DCT:RE	Deductive reasoning
DM	Discourse marker	HEARSAY	Hearsay marker
IE	Informal ending	NOM	Nominative
NML	Nominalizer	POL	Polite speech level
PRP	Propositive suffix	PRS	Present
PST	Past suffix	Q	Question marker
QT	Quotative construction	RL	Relativizer suffix
RT	Retrospective	TOP	Topic marker
UNASSIM	Unassimilated		

The Role of Intonation in Discourse: The Analysis of *Ani* in Korean

MEE-JEONG PARK
University of Hawaii at Manoa

1 Introduction

The purpose of this study is to investigate the role of intonation in discourse by examining the Korean expression *ani* 'no', the two main functions of which can be determined by the type of intonation it is used with. In Korean, *ani* 'no' can have two main functions: (1) that of negative (NEG) answer to a prior utterance, most commonly used as an answer to polar questions, or (2) that of discourse marker (DM) as in the following examples:

(1) NEG *ani*   A: swukcey hay-ss-e?
                     Did you do your HW?
                 B: **ani**. an hay-ss-e.
                     No, I didn't (do it).

(2) DM *ani*   A: ikes com pwa-pwa
                     Take a look at this.

Japanese/Korean Linguistics 25.
Edited by Shin Fukuda, Mary Shin Kim, and Mee-Jeong Park.
Copyright © 2018, CSLI Publications

> B: **ani** ikey mwe-ya?
> *What! What is this?*

Naver.com Korean-English dictionary also defines *ani* as (a) an adverbial 'no, nope, nay'; or (b) an interjection 'what!, Good heavens!' *Ani* is often used with the polite style suffix *-yo*, as in *aniyo* used as a declarative sentence as in the context of (1). Even in the context of (2), *ani* may be used with the polite *-yo* although it is not very common. Another related form of *ani* is *anita* 'to be not', which can be conjugated with many different suffixes, either in non-polite or polite forms (e.g., *ani-ya*, *ani-eyyo*, *ani-pnita* 'It's not').

According to Koo (2008), the use of *ani* was found in 15-18th century texts as negation marker. After this period, *ani* was replaced by the shorter form *an* during late 19th century (Lee 2008), and around that time, it obtained its discourse functions, which can be summarized in the following (M. Kim 1997; Koo 2008):

(i) a way of expressing unacceptable/negative attitude,
(ii) to call one's attention to a change in topic, and
(iii) as a repair maker for an error

Yang (2002) provides further details on the functions of DM *ani* as politeness, marking uncertainty, sarcasm, commitment avoidance, correction, topic shift, monitoring prior talk, and initiating turns. In addition, it is claimed that *ani*-prefaced responses to questions are used to resist responding to a challenge (H. Kim 2011) as well as the question's expectation (S. Kim 2015).

The purpose of this study is to investigate the role of intonation, Korean prosodic boundary tones (BT) in particular, in marking different functions of Korean *ani* in terms of (i) what types of BTs they are being used, and (ii) how these BTs demarcate the two different functions of *ani,* that of negation and discourse marker.

2   Data and Method

This study includes a total of 148 instances of *ani*[1] taken from twenty 60-minute episodes of Korean TV dramas aired within the past 3 years: *sangsokjatul* 'The heirs' and *pyeleyse on kutay* 'My love from stars'. From the 148 instances of *ani*, 33 were used as NEG response to a prior utterance and 115 as DM. All instances were analyzed using Pitch Works speech analysis software to determine the exact type of BT for each occurrence of *ani* in these 20 hours of scripted speech.

---

[1] *Ani* with the polite suffix *-yo* was not included in this study as majority of DM *ani* appear without *-yo*. Therefore, this study will compare NGE and DM *ani* without the polite *-yo* to avoid any possible influence it might place on the use of *ani*.

3   Korean Intonation Model

According to Jun's model of Korean intonation (1998, 2000)[2], an Accentual Phrase (AP) contains one or more words, and an Intonation Phrase (IP) can have one or more APs and is marked by a phrasal tone known as boundary tone (BT) such as H%, L%, HL%, LHL% etc.

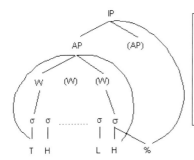

Intonational Structure of Seoul Korean
IP: Intonation Phrase,
AP: Accentual Phrase
w: phonological word,
s: syllable   T= H, when the syllable initial segment is aspirated/tense, otherwise,
T=L%: Intonation phrase boundary tone

FIGURE 1 K-ToBI (Korean Tones and Break Indices) [Reprint from Jun (2000)]

Although Jun includes up to nine types of BTs in her model, Park (2003, 2012) classifies them mainly in two groups based on their final tone type: Low-final (L%, HL%, LHL, HLHL%, LHLHL%) and High-final (H%, LH%, HLH%, LHLH%), as the L-final BTs do not show similar compatibility as is the case of the final-H BTs.

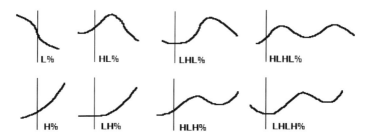

FIGURE 2 Korean Prosodic Boundary tones [Reprint from Jun (2000)]

4   Data Analysis

Based on the analysis of types of BT for all occurrences of *ani*, there are frequently used tone types associated with the two functions of *ani*, NEG

---

[2] The newly added Intermediate Phrase (ip) will not be included in this study as the new version of K-ToBI is not yet officially available and is not relevant to this study.

and DM respectively. Below is the summary of frequency on the occurrence of the two functions of *ani* and the number of words in each IP (Intonation Phrase) that includes the two types of *ani*.

	NEG *ani*	DM *ani*
Sole IP	33	27
Non-sole IP	-	88
Total	**33**	**115**

TABLE 1 Number NEG *ani* and DM *ani* occurring as sole vs. non-sole IPs

The analysis reveals that 88 out of 115 DM *ani* are part of an IP with two or more words as in example (3), where *ani kuntey* 'well but' form one IP with a single BT LHL%. On the other hand, 27 out of 115 DM *ani* are used as a sole IP, that is, *ani* forming one sole IP as in example (4), which also gets LHL%. It is noteworthy that all cases of DM *ani* carry a L-final BTs (i.e., L%, HL%, LHL%, HLHL%).

(3)   **ani** kuntey[LHL%] way nay-ka ha-yya toy-nuntey.
        well but   why I-NM   do -must-CIRCUM
        Well, why do I have to do it.

(4)   **ani**[LHL%] nay-ka mwe-l   calmoshay-ss-nya-kwu~
        well   I-NM   what-ACC do wrong-PST-Q-QT
        Well, what did I do wrong.

As for NEG *ani*, in contrast, all 33 occurrences of *ani* form a sole IP. Of these 33 IPs, 25 of them carry a H-final BT (e.g., H%, LH%, HLH%) and 8 a L-final BT (e.g., HL%, LHL%, HLHL%), as summarized in Table 2 below.

BT Types	NEG *ani*	DM *ani*
H%	23	-
LH%	1	-
HLH%	1	-
L%	-	8
HL%	6	1
LHL%	1	13
HLHL%	1	5

TABLE 2 Types of BTs occurring with NEG *ani* and DM *ani*

All 25 cases of IP with H-final BTs were all responses to clear cases of polar questions. On the other hand, out of the 8 occurrences of NEG *ani* forming sole IPs with L-final BTs, 6 of them were not direct answers to polar questions, but instead, negative comments to the prior utterance as in example (5), where a male speaker M suggests a female speaker W to give her a ride. Then, W declines the offer using NEG *ani* with a L-final BT HL%.

(5) M: nay-ka teyly-eta cwu-lkey.
I-NM   escort-give-PRP
I'll give you ride.

W: **ani**[HL%] pesu tha-ko ka-nun key phyenhay.
ani   bus ride-and go-REL   comfortable
No, I'm more comfortable riding a bus.

Now, going back to the numbers in Table 2 above, it is very important to note that the majority of occurrences of NEG *ani* takes H-final BTs (25 out of 33), whereas DM *ani* does not take any H-final BTs. In other words, H-final BTs are only associated with NEG *ani*, whereas L-final BTs are mainly associated with DM *ani* and some NEG *ani* which are not direct responses to polar questions. Below are examples of NEG *ani* with a H-final BT (6) and DM *ani* with a L-final BT (7).

(6) NEG *ani*: Excerpt from *My Love from the Star* [Ep.10]

1	W	ne hoksi kang-taephyo yenlak wa-ss-ti?
		you by chance Kang-CEO contact come-PST-RT
		Did you get a call from Mr. Kang by chance?

2	Songi	**ani**[H%] a response to a
		No. Yes-no question

3	W	kulen michin casik..
		like that crazy bastard
4		ku inkan-hanthey yenlak o-myen patci ma. al-ass-e?
		that human-to contact come-if get-do not know-PST-Q
		That crazy bastard.
		If he calls you, don't answer him, alright?

5	Songi	al-ass-e.
		Know-PST-DC
		Okay.

In this excerpt, Songi responds to her mother's question with *ani* 'no' in line 2. This is a clear case of *ani* being used as one of the two options 'yes' or 'no' to a polar question of whether or not Mr. Kang has contacted her. Between the two options, Songi uses *ani* 'no' with H%. H-final BT used in a non-interrogative expression NEG *ani* serves to set forth a basis for further elaboration in responding to a polar question. By using the NEG *ani* with H-final BT, the speaker conveys that his/her own response to a polar question is added to the speaker and hearer's 'mutual belief' (Hirschberg & Ward 1995), and in cognition whether the hearer can relate the content of the just released response to his/her own propositional content (Park & Sohn 2001).

In this way, H-final NEG *ani* enhances the interactional aspect of this topic initiated by a polar question by projecting the speaker's attempt to elicit the hearer's involvement into further development of discourse.

The L-final DM *ani*, on the other hand, mainly serves to organize the flow and structure of discourse without such a strong elicitation of the hearer's involvement. In the following excerpt, W1 is being contentious to W2, who works for W1 as a housemaid. W1 is suspicious about W2 who could have possibly been eavesdropping on W1. When W2 denies that she has intentionally eavesdropped on her but it just happened, W1 responds with *ani* to express her negative attitude toward W2's response. In this case, *ani* 'well' is used with a L-final BT as in line 4.

(7) DM *ani*: Excerpt from *The heirs* [Ep.3]

1	W1	encey-pwuthe keki iss-ess-eyo?
		When-since there be-PST-POL
2		ta yestul-ess-eyo?
		all eavesdrop-PST-POL
		How long were you there?
		Were you eavesdropping?

3	W2	yestulun key ani-la kunyang tul-ly-ess-eyo.
		eavesdrop-RL not-but just hear-PAS-PST-POL
		I wasn't eavesdropping but I could just hear you.

4	W1	**ani**[HLHL%] nay-ka thonghwa-lul
		ani I-NM phone call-ACC
5		hako iss-ess-umyen inkichek-ul nay-ya-ci.
		do be-PST-if indication of presence-ACC make-must-COMM
		Well, if I was on the phone, then you
		should've made yourself known!

a way of expressing a negative attitude

Figure 3 below shows the pitch tracks of the two types of *ani*, NEG with H-final BT and DM with L-final BT, respectively.

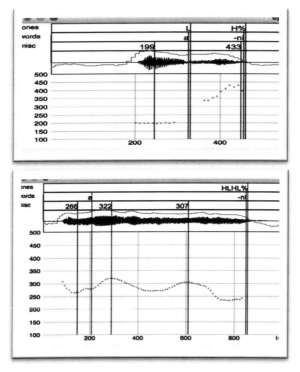

FIGURE 3 Pitch tracks of (a) NEG *ani* with H% and (b) DM *ani* with HLHL%

5   H% in Non-interrogative Utterances

There are two streams of studies that dealt with the occurrence of H% with non-interrogative sentences: (a) interactional and (b) epistemic.

(a) Interactional functions: McLemore's (1991) is one of the first studies on rising intonation using naturally occurring conversation data within a socially constructed contextualization. She examined the way members of a sorority use rising intonation to convey different ranges of social functions beyond uncertainty, such as sign of solidarity. Britain (1992) claims that high rising BT (high rising terminal contour, HRTs in his term) in declarative sentences in New Zealand English is used as a positive politeness marker. Moreover, the Korean sentence ending suffix -*ketun* 'you see, that fact is..' is very frequently used with H% to signal 'other-directed' utterances which elicit a response or reaction from the hearer (Park & Sohn 2001; Park 2003, 2012).

(b) Epistemic functions: Speakers of English use falling tone in declarative sentences to mark speakers' commitment toward the propositional content, whereas rising tone to signal lack of commitment (Gunlogson 2002). According to Park (2003, 2012), Korean speaker (Sp) and hearer's (Hr) epistemic status is conveyed within the combination of sentence ending suffixes and H-final or L-final BTs. When Hr's awareness of information conveyed within the utterance about to be made is low, Korean sentence ending suffixes such as -ketun 'you see, the fact is…' is used with H% very frequently. On the other hand, when Hr's awareness of information conveyed within the utterance is high, suffixes such as -canha 'you know' is used with L% most frequently. Furthermore, when Sp's awareness of information conveyed within the utterance is low, some yes-no question suffixes (e.g., -na/nka?) are used with H%, but L% is used with some yes-no question suffixes (e.g., -ci?) when Sp's awareness of information conveyed within the utterance is high. The summary of this finding is summarized in Figure 4.

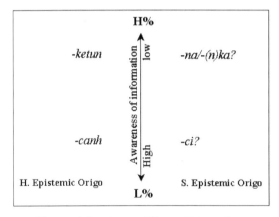

FIGURE 4 Speaker and Hearer Epistemic
Status [reprint from Park (2012)]

Typologically, there are three different answering systems for polar interrogatives: (i) yes/no systems, (ii) agree/disagree systems, and (iii) echo systems (Sadock & Zwicky 1985; Konig & Siemund 2007: 320). In languages like English and German, for instance, asnwers to both positive and negative polar questions are simply type-confirming responses (Raymond 2003) as in (8). In languages like Korean and Japanese, for instance, asnwers to negative polar questions are either acceptance/approval or denials /disapproval of the content of the question as in (9).

(8) English: yes/no system

    (a) A: Did he bring a present?
        B: Yes. (confirmation)
        A: Did he bring a present?
        B: No. (non-confirmation)

    (b) A: Did he not bring a present?
        B: Yes, he did (non-confirmation)
        A: Did he not bring a present?
        B: No. (confirmation)   (Konig & Siemund 2007: 321)

(9) Korean: agree/disagree system

    (a) A: pap meke?
            Are you eating?
        B: ung
            Yes. (You're right. I'm eating).
        A: pap meke?
            Are you eating?
        B: ani
            No. (You're wrong. I'm not eating).

    (b) A: pap an meke?
            Aren't you eating?
        B: ung
            Yes. (You're right. I'm not eating).
        A: pap an meke?
            Aren't you eating?
        B: ani
            No. (You're wrong. I'm eating).

When answering a negative polar question in Korean, 'yes' means the respondent agrees with the content of the negative question; on the other hand, when answering with *ani* 'no' it means the respondent disagrees with the content of the negative question. Therefore, *ani* can be used to negate the truth-conditional meaning of the prior utterance.

In the following excerpt, speaker M is the older brother of Tan, who is the boyfriend of the speaker W. W runs into M in a party and wonders if

Tan came with him. With the expectation that Tan would also be there, W asks M a yes-no question in line 1.

(10) Excerpt from *The Heirs* [Ep.3]

1   W   hoksi   thani-to   kathi   wa-ssess-eyo,   yeki?
             Maybe Tan-too together come-PST-POL here
             Did Tan come here with you too?

2   M   ani[H%]

challenging the assumption made by the Q

Sp's lack of commitment to *ani*; eliciting Hr's reaction and/or continued participation, which can weaken the challenge made by *ani*

3   ecceta poni ni-ka   cheum-ita.   Way?
             By chance you-NM first-be-DEC why
             No. You are the first one. Why?

4   W   thani-ka   cilthwuha-keyss-ta.
             Tan-NM   envy-MD-DEC
             Tan would be jealous.

Although the utterance in line 1 is a question, the way the question is designed (polar question) shows that W is inclined to believe Tan would be there too. When M asnwers the question with *ani* 'no' in line 2, he is challenging the assumption made by W in her polar question. As mentioned earlier, the use of *ani* to answer a polar question, the respondent disagrees with the assumption, and therefore, providing a dispreferred answer creating a challenge to the speaker (Yoon 2010; Heritage & Raymond 2012). Therefore, H% is used with *ani* to signal the speaker's lack of commitment toward the proposition expressed in *ani*. Furthermore, the use of H% weakens the challenge imposed by *ani* by eliciting continued participation from the questioner speaker. Since the respondent is not in agreement with the speaker, is willing to continue this discussion until this dispreferred situation is resolved. Therefore, M not only denies the question but provides additional information clarifying that she is the first visitor since Tan is not there. M also asks her why she is asking about Tan and he is willing to continue the conversation about the topic with W.

6   Production Test

So far, it was confirmed how DM *ani* never occurred with H-final BTs, whereas NEG *ani* most frequently occurred with H-final BTs but L-final BTs were also used case by case. A mini production test was conducted to confirm whether the occurrences of L-final BTs with NEG *ani* are stylistic or not by asking six native speakers of Korean to do a dubbing to the short excerpt taken from the commercial movie *Notting Hill* (1999).

In this excerpt, William offers different types of drinks and food to Anna who is about to leave. They had an akward encounter and were not feeling comfortable about each other. Anna declines every single offer but William keeps asking. Each of the six participants watched the excerpt with the audio off during the first round, and during the second round, they were asked to dub Anna's answers 'no' in Korean using *ani-yo*, the polite form to make sure all participants use the same form with the same attitude (i.e., politeness) and number of syllables. The movie excerpt is provided below.

(11) Excerpt from *Notting Hill*

William	Uh, would you like a cup of tea before you go?
Anna	**No.**
William	Coffee?
Anna	**No.**
William	Orange juice… probably not.
	Something else cold… coke, water?
	Some disgusting sugary drink pretending to have something to do with fruits of the forest?
Anna	**No.**
William	Would you like something to nibble… apricots soaked in honey.. yours if you want them.
Anna	**No.**
William	Do you always say 'no' to everything?
Anna	**No.**
	I better be going. Thanks for your… help.
William	You're welcome.

Based on each of the six participant's dubbing exercise, everyone used H% with all five instances of *ani* 'no' except for the following three: third 'no' from the second participant, fourth 'no' from the fourth participant, and the last 'no' from the fifth participant. Although this is a small sample, it is very clear that the choice of non H% for NEG *ani* is a stylistically driven variation.

7 Conclusion

H-final NEG *ani* enhances the interactional aspect of the topic initiated by a polar question by projecting the speaker's attempt to elicit the hearer's involvement into further development of discourse. At the same time, however, the challenge conveyed within *ani* 'no' can be taken as challenging, and therefore, impolite. By using a H-final BT, the speaker alleviates his/her commitment toward the disapproval/disagreement made by NEG *ani*. The L-final DM *ani*, on the other hand, mainly serves to organize the flow and structure of discourse without such a strong elicitation of the hearer's involvement.

8 Future Studies

This is a preliminary study and does not include naturally occurring conversation data. In future studies, natural speech data will be included to see more variation in terms of context and situations where *ani* occurs with H%, such as the use of the polite ending suffix *-yo* as well as turn structure. In addition, further functions of L-final BTs associated with the DM *ani* will also be included in these studies.

References

Britain, D. 1992. Linguistic change in intonation: The use of high rising terminals in New Zealand English. *Language Variation and Change, 4*(1): 77-104.

Gunlogson, C. 2002. Declarative questions. In *Proceedings of Semantics and Linguistic Theory 12*, B. Jackson (ed.). Ithaca, NY: CLC Publications.

Heritage, J. & Raymond, G. 2012. Navigating epistemic landscapes: Acquiescence, agency and resistance in responses to polar questions. In J. P. de Ruiter (Ed.), *Questions: Formal, functional and interactional perspectives*. pp. 179–192. University Press.

Hirschberg, J. & Ward. G. 1995. The Interpretation of the High-Rise Question Contour in English. *Journal of Pragmatics*, 24, 4: 407-412.

Jun, S.-A. 2000. K-ToBI (Korean ToBI) Labelling Conventions. http://www.linguistics.ucla.edu/people/jun/ktobi/k-tobi.html

Jun, S.-A. 1998. The Accentual Phrase in the Korean prosodic hierarchy. *Phonology*, 15.2: 189-226.

Kim, H.R.S. 2011. Ani 'No'-prefaced responses to Wh-questions as challenges in Korean conversation. *Japanese/Korean Linguistics 20* [Edited by B. Frellesvig and P. Sells]. CSLI Publications.

Kim, S.H. 2015. Resisting the Terms of Polar Questions Through Ani ('No')-Prefacing in Korean Conversation. *Discourse Processes*, 52: 311-334.

Kim, M.S. 1997. Some Functions of ani in a Conversational Structure of Korean. *Discourse and Cognition*. 4.2: 77-101.

Lee, J-Y. 2008. Hankwuke Yongenpwucengmwunuy Yeksacek Pyenhwa [Diachronic Changes of Korean Predicate Negation]. Seoul: Thayhaksa.

Koo, H. J. 2008. Grammaticalization of Negation Markers in Korean. *Discourse and Cognition*, 15.3: 1-27.

McLemore, Cynthia 1991. *The pragmatic interpretation of English intonation: Sorority speech*. Unpublished doctoral dissertation, University of Texas at Austin.

My Love from the Star. 2013. A Korean TV drama aired by SBS.

Notting Hill. 1999. British romantic comedy film by Universal Pictures.

Park, M.-J. 2003. *The Meaning of Korean Prosodic Boundary Tones*. Unpublished Dissertation, UCLA.

Park, M.-J. 2012. *The Meaning of Korean Prosodic Boundary Tones*. Brill.

Park, M.-J. & Sohn, S.O. 2001. Discourse, Intonation, and Grammaticalization: An analysis of the Korean sentence ender -*ketun*. *Japanese/Korean Linguistics*, 10: 307-320.

Raymond, G. 2003. Grammar and social organization: Yes/no interrogatives and the structure of responding. *American Sociological Review*, 68: 939–967.

Konig, E., & Siemund, P. 2007. Speech act distinctions in grammar. In T. Shopen (Ed.), *Language typology and syntactic description, vol. 1. Clause structure* (pp. 276–324). Cambridge, UK: Cambridge University Press.

Sadock, J. & Zwicky, A. 1985. Speech act distinctions in syntax. In T. Shopen (Ed.), *Language typology and syntactic description*, vol.1, clause structure, pp. 155–196. Cambridge University Press.

The Heirs. 2013. Korean TV drama aired by SBS.

Yoon, K.E. 2010. Questions and responses in Korean Conversation. *Journal of Pragmatics*, 42: 2782–2798.

Appendix: Abbreviations

ACC	Accusative case
COMM	Committal
DC	Declarative suffix
DM	Discourse marker
NEG	Negative adverbial
NM	Nominative case
NML	Nominalizer
PAS	Passive suffix
POL	Polite speech level suffix
PRP	Prospective suffix
PST	Past suffix
Q	Question suffix
RL	Relativizer
RT	Retrospective
TOP	Topic marker

Productive Use of Indexicalized Variable in Social Interaction: The Case of *Ranuki* in Japanese

SHIN-ICHIRO SANO
Keio University

1   Introduction

Recent sociolinguistic studies have offered a multi-dimensional perspective of style, characterized by the display of identities in interaction or indexicality, where social meanings of linguistic forms are defined by interactional moves through which speakers take stances, create alignments, and construct personas (e.g., Eckert 1989 et seq.), beyond the earlier uni-dimensional model based on direct mapping between the standard /vernacular dichotomy and social categories (e.g., Labov 1966 et seq.).

This paper presents a case study of style/index focusing on the morphophonological variation in verbal inflection called *ranuki* (*ra*-Deletion) in spoken Japanese (e.g., Ito and Mester 2004). In particular, this study demonstrates (i) novel stylistic aspects of *ranuki* and its functions, and (ii) the process by which speakers develop such functions by utilizing the variable tied to existing norms for their own interactional purposes. This

Japanese/Korean Linguistics 25.
Edited by Shin Fukuda, Mary Shin Kim, and Mee-Jeong Park.

study confirms that the productive use of *ranuki* indexically signals fine-grained stylistic information.

2 Background

2.1 The Variable *Ranuki*

Ranuki (also known as *ra*-Deletion) is a morphophonological variation in potential forms. It is an ongoing change observed since the 1920s (Kindaichi et al. 1995) as part of the global change in potential forms in Japanese over the past 100 years (e.g., Sano 2015).

Potential forms in Japanese comprise a verb stem and a potential suffix. The verb stems are classified into two types according to their ending, being either vowel-final (e.g., *mi-* 'see', *tabe-* 'eat') or consonant-final (e.g., *ik-* 'go', *nom-* 'drink'). The potential forms show morphophonological alternations according to stem type, as vowel-final stem verbs take the potential suffix *-rare*, while consonant-final stem verbs take *-e*. *Ranuki* affects only verbs with vowel-final stems, where it variably deletes the syllable *ra* from the potential suffix *-rare*, resulting in the reduced form *-re*. This produces the morphophonological variation in potential forms with vowel-final stems comprising *-rare* (full form) and *-re* (reduced form) (Ito and Mester 2004). As exemplified in Table 1, the potential forms of vowel-final stems such as *mi-* and *tabe-* are traditionally full forms, such as *mi-rare* and *tabe-rare*; if these forms undergo *ranuki*, novel reduced forms such as *mi-re* and *tabe-re* are produced.

stem (vowel-final)	full form	*ranuki* (reduced) form
mi- 'see'	mi-rare 'can see'	mi-re 'can see'
tabe- 'eat'	tabe-rare 'can eat'	tabe-re 'can eat'

Table 1. Examples of full and reduced potential forms of vowel-final stem verbs

Although *ranuki* is still diffusing, there is an established attitude towards it, as (i) it has been more than 100 years since its appearance, and *ranuki* is now widely used, and (ii) *ranuki* has been covered in the media and in education by highlighting the non-standard status of the reduced form, so the distinction between the full form (standard) and the reduced form (non-standard) is recognized even by non-experts.

2.2 History of Research on Style

Next, I will briefly sketch the history of research on style, which can be linked to the development of sociolinguistics (see Eckert 2012, 2016). The earlier dominant model can be characterized as "macro-scale" and "uni-dimensional." In this model, primary focus is placed on the link between linguistic forms, namely the standard/vernacular dichotomy, and pre-determined socio-demographic categories, such as age, gender, class, and ethnicity, with social meaning based on prestige vs. stigma. Here, style is interpreted in a formality continuum, as attention paid to speech. Furthermore, style is closely connected to class stratification (Labov 1966, 1972; Wolfram 1969; Trudgill 1974, among others, cf. Labov 1963).

On the other hand, the recent model is characterized as "micro-scale" and "multi-dimensional" (Eckert 2000 et seq.; Eckert and Rickford 2001; Mendoza-Denton 2002; Shilling-Estes 2004; Coupland 2007). Apart from pre-determined categories, this model assumes that, through their use of variation, speakers create personal and social styles. In other words, through interactional moves or social practice, speakers intentionally create new categories and social meanings, such as identity and persona, based on the community's ideology, with sound symbolism and iconization playing an important role (Eckert 2000; Podesva 2004; Zhang 2005, 2008; Campbell-Kibler 2007, among others).

Among the concepts introduced in recent research on style, especially relevant to this study is indirect indexicality (Silverstein 1976), which states that non-referential meaning is constructed or conventionalized by social practices based on a particular cultural ideology and context (as opposed to an "index" or denotation). In other words, the association between a linguistic form and a category or label produces an ideological meaning. In Table 2, I exemplify indirect indexicality by showing the referential and non-referential meanings of some Japanese sentence-final particles (Ochs 1990, see Kataoka 2002).

	referential (direct)	non-referential (indirect)
zo, ze	forcefulness	masculinity
wa	softness, hesitancy	femininity

Table 2. Referential and non-referential meanings of Japanese sentence-final particles

As illustrated in Table 2, as *zo* and *ze* are preferentially used by male speakers to directly encode forcefulness (referential), they can also indirectly encode masculinity (non-referential). Similarly, as *wa* is preferentially used by female speakers to directly encode softness and hesitancy (referential), it can also indirectly encode femininity (non-referential). The following two questions then arise: 1) What is the non-referential meaning produced by the association between full form (standard) vs. reduced form (vernacular) and social categories?; 2) How is this association interpreted?

2.3   Issues to Be Addressed

Thus far, *ranuki* has been studied in the variationist paradigm, with the focus placed on the link between the dichotomy of full (standard) vs. reduced (vernacular) forms and pre-determined categories. The characteristics of *ranuki* that this prior work revealed mainly concerned linguistic or internal factors (Matsuda 1993; Sano 2011). However, recent usage-based studies have shed light on previously unnoticed extra-linguistic aspects of *ranuki*, such as the fact that the reduced form is more compatible with younger speakers, informal style, female speakers, and a lower level of education (Sano 2011). Furthermore, beyond this category-based approach, the recent multi-dimensional approach has demonstrated that the use of *ranuki* patterned by formality reflects gender and workplace stereotypes in Japan (Sherwood 2014, 2016).

Additionally, sociolinguistic surveys in Japanese have observed the recent trend of speakers, especially in younger generations, productively using non-standard forms to design their interpersonal relationships and the interactional atmosphere, as observed in cellphone and email communication (Tanaka 2001), as well as accesorizing their dialects (Tanaka 2001; Kobayashi 2004), with their vernacular playing the role of a stylistic variant rather than a stigmatized or local variant. Moreover, the role of the vernacular is defined with respect to the standard variety. With this background, the goal of this study was to demonstrate that speakers create novel communicative functions of *ranuki* based on the standard/non-standard dichotomy linked to the existing norm, especially focusing on indirect indexicality.

3   Method

3.1   Corpus

The corpus employed in this study was the *Meidai Conversation Corpus* (data version 2016.12, henceforth MC corpus), a collection of 120 conversation samples amounting to around 100 hours of speech. All participants were native speakers of Japanese. The corpus provides the information in the following format. Transcription follows the Japanese orthography consisting of Chinese characters and the kana syllabary. The annotated morphological information was analyzed using the parser *MeCab* (ver. 0.98) and the dictionary *UniDic*. Meta-linguistic information includes speaker attributes (e.g., age, gender, birthplace), relationship between speakers, and setting; this study considered only the relationship between speakers and the setting. All annotated information is accessible via the *Chuunagon* online search engine (ver. 2.2.2.2).

3.2 Procedure

This study examined every sample in the corpus, particularly targeting utterances involving the full form (*rare*) or the reduced form (*re*). The data were collected using *Chuunagon* by selecting from the items listed in the pull-down menu and specifying the targeted letters in the required fields. To search for the full form, the lexeme was specified as られる (*rareru*); to search for the reduced form, the type of inflection was specified as 下一段-ラ行 (*ra*-line lower unigrade).

From the retrieved data, I filtered out certain irrelevant information. The full form られる covers four meanings: potential, passive, honorific, and spontaneous; thus, I excluded tokens with meanings other than potential. Likewise, the reduced form 下一段-ラ行 can false-hit other verbal categories (e.g., *re*-final stem verbs, potential forms of consonant-final stem verbs); thus, I excluded categories other than the reduced form.

3.3 Quantitative Analysis

An exhaustive search for data in the MC *Corpus* and the aforementioned filtering resulted in the dataset presented in Table 3.

	frequency	ratio
full form	387	0.59
reduced form	269	0.41

Table 3. Distribution of full and reduced forms in the MC *Corpus*[1]

The variable consists of the full form and the reduced form. The primary measure in the quantitative analysis is the ratio of the reduced form among all potential forms, based on token frequency count. The ratio is calculated for each context and compared according to the relationship between speakers and the setting. Based on the annotation provided by the corpus, the factors and levels were arranged as in Table 4.

This study employed a quantitative method as an objective way to analyze indexicality. The distributional skews were tested with the logistic regression analysis using the glm function in R (R Development Core Team 1993-2018), and with Fisher's exact test for a certain distribution. Post-hoc tests (multiple comparisons) were conducted using the Steel-Dwass method. The dependent variable was the choice of full/reduced form. The predictors were the relationship between speakers and the setting.

---

[1] The collected tokens were produced by 153 speakers with the following characteristics: gender: male (21), female (130); age: 10s (12), 20s (68), 30s (24), 40s (19), 50s (15), 60s (10), 70s (2), 90s (1).

relationship between speakers
1. lovers, parents-children, friends
2. peers, seniors-juniors
3. neighbors, acquaintances, strangers

setting
1. while traveling, at home, in a public place, and in the workplace
2. in shops: *-ya* (e.g., *izaka<u>ya</u>* 'pub'), *-ten* (e.g., *kissa<u>ten</u>* 'café')
3. at restaurants: family restaurant, Italian restaurant, restaurant (general), restaurant (hotel)

Table 4. The factors and levels considered in the analysis

4 Results

4.1 Relationship between Speakers

4.1.1 Lovers, Parents-Children, Friends

The first category of the relationship between speakers comprises conversations between lovers, between parents and their children, and between friends.[2] Here I assume that the non-referential meaning of *ranuki*, if any, should manifest in a distributional gap in the use of the full vs. the reduced form in social interaction. The distributional gap was examined by comparing the ratio of reduced form use in each context, as shown in the following figure.[3]

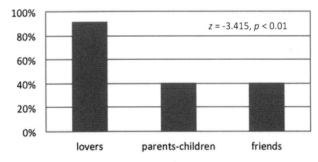

Figure 1. The distribution of *ranuki*: lovers, parents-children, friends

Figure 1 shows that the ratio of the reduced form is significantly higher in "lovers" than in "parents-children" or "friends." Assuming that the lovers

---

[2]Note that the "parents-children" relationship does not involve small children, but rather adults or adolescents.

[3]In the following text, generalizations are made based on the results of the post-hoc tests, although their details are left out due to space limitations.

relationship involves more affection or intimacy than parents-children or friends, we can argue that the distribution of the reduced form corresponds with the level of affection or intimacy in the relationship. The generalization drawn from this pattern is that the higher the level of affection/intimacy in the relationship, the more speakers use the reduced form. Together with the prior finding that the reduced form is more compatible with an informal and relaxed context (Sano 2011), this suggests that the association between full or reduced form and formality can indirectly encode affection or intimacy as a non-referential meaning.

4.1.2   Peers, Seniors-Juniors

The next category of the relationship between speakers comprises conversations between peers, and between seniors and juniors. The seniors and juniors here represent a relative status based on age (school year) differences.

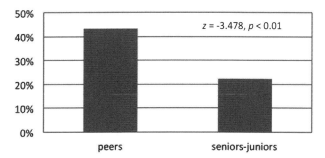

Figure 2. The distribution of *ranuki*: peers, seniors-juniors

As illustrated in Figure 2, the ratio of the reduced form is significantly higher in "peers" than in "seniors-juniors." In terms of seniority hierarchy, peers are considered to be equal, while seniors are superior to juniors; this dynamic also involves levels of power. Based on the data, we can argue that the distribution of the reduced form corresponds with the seniority hierarchy: the smaller the seniority gap between the speakers, the more they use the reduced form. In connection with the prior finding that the reduced form is more compatible with an informal and relaxed context, this suggests that the association between full or reduced form and formality can also indirectly encode seniority or power as a non-referential meaning.

4.1.3   Neighbors, Acquaintances, Strangers

For the last category of the relationship between speakers, let us consider conversations between neighbors, acquaintances, and strangers. Figure 3 shows that no reduced form was observed in "neighbors" and "acquaintances," while the ratio of the reduced form in "strangers" was close to 40 percent. Assuming that the neighbors relationship is more intimate than acquaintances, which in turn is more intimate than strangers, we can argue that the distribution of the reduced form follows the reverse order of the level of intimacy. The generalization drawn from this pattern is that the lower the level of intimacy, the more speakers use the reduced form.

Figure 3. The distribution of *ranuki*: neighbors, acquaintances, strangers

This may seem somewhat counterintuitive because speakers tend to use a formal speaking style in less intimate interactions, such as with strangers. However, consider that neighbors cannot misbehave, because they know one another well, while strangers do not necessarily have to be as careful about their language use. This has some parallels with internet communication, where participants tend to be faceless and thus more lax in their language use. Coupled with the prior finding that the reduced form is more compatible with an informal and relaxed context, this suggests that the association between full or reduced form and formality (in particular, prestige vs. stigma) can indirectly encode appearance or decency as a non-referential meaning.

4.2   Setting

4.2.1   While Traveling, at Home, in a Public Place, in the Workplace

Next, we turn our attention to the setting in which the conversation takes place. The first category comprises interactions while traveling, at home, in a public place, and in the workplace. As Figure 4 shows, the ratio of reduced form use decreases in the following order: "while traveling," "home," "public place," and finally "workplace." In terms of atmosphere, relaxedness/nervousness, face, or role, these settings are ordered on a scale from while traveling, to home, to public place, to workplace. From this, we can argue that reduced form use is compatible with a better atmosphere and being more relaxed; the less speakers have to care about their face or role, the more they use the reduced form. As speakers are careful about their language use in the workplace because it relates to their face or role, the ratio of reduced forms in such a setting is lowest. In connection with the prior finding that the reduced form is more compatible with an informal and relaxed context, this suggests that the association between full or reduced form and formality can indirectly encode atmosphere, relaxedness/ nervousness, face, or role as a non-referential meaning.

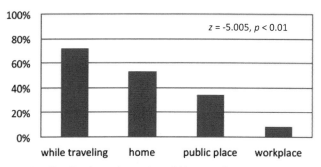

Figure 4. The distribution of *ranuki*: while traveling, at home, in a public place, in the workplace

4.2.2   In Shops

The next category comprises conversations at two kinds of shops, *-ya* (e.g., *izakaya* 'pub') and *-ten* (e.g., *kissaten* 'café'). In terms of the class or rank of shops, *-ten* is higher than *-ya*. Specifically, *-ya* provides a more casual setting, while *-ten* provides a more refined setting.

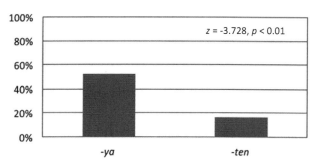

Figure 5. The distribution of *ranuki* at two kinds of shops

Figure 5 shows that the ratio of the reduced form is significantly higher in "*-ya*" than in "*-ten*." This suggests that the distribution of the reduced form follows the reverse order of class or rank of shops. The generalization drawn from this pattern is that the lower the class or rank of the shop, the more speakers use the reduced form. Coupled with the prior finding that the reduced form is more compatible with an informal and relaxed context, this suggests that the association between full or reduced form and formality can indirectly encode harmony or consistency with the space as a non-referential meaning.

4.2.3 At Restaurants

A similar pattern is observed in conversations at restaurants, with the final category comprising family restaurants, Italian restaurants, general restaurants, and hotel restaurants. In descending order of class or rank of restaurant, it goes: hotel restaurant, general restaurant, Italian restaurant, and finally family restaurant. This ranking partly reflects the fact that there are many chains of casual Italian restaurants nowadays, even though they have traditionally had an image of luxury or high class.

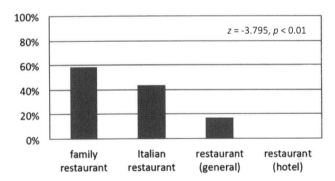

Figure 6. The distribution of *ranuki* at four kinds of restaurants

As Figure 6 illustrates, the ratio of reduced form use decreases in the order of "family," "Italian," "general," and "hotel." This suggests that the distribution of the reduced form follows the reverse order of the class or rank of restaurants. That is, the lower the class or rank of the restaurant, the more speakers use the reduced form. Given that the reduced form is more compatible with an informal and relaxed context, this result suggests that the association between full or reduced form and formality can indirectly encode harmony or consistency with the space as a non-referential meaning.

5 Discussion

The results of the examination suggest that the manner in which speakers deploy *ranuki* indexically encodes fine-grained stylistic information, namely, non-referential meaning regarding interpersonal relationships, such as seniority-based hierarchy and intimacy/solidarity, and settings associated with the purpose of interaction and the class/rank of the space.

In considering the functions of *ranuki*, ideology plays an important role. The ideology in the current context involves the stereotypical images of, for example, the gentle boyfriend, the trusty neighbor, the skilled business person, or the high-quality restaurant. The question to be addressed is how these images can be indexed/perceived in linguistic practice. A community's ideology is created by the media and the linguistic norm, as in the case of considering the full *-rare* form to be correct and the reduced *-re* form incorrect. In terms of the association between *ranuki* and social categories, the full form is closely connected with formal, educated, and traditional aspects, while the reduced form is closely connected with informal, uneducated, and innovative aspects. When it comes to ideological perceptions of interpersonal relationships or settings, use of the full form can index decent, educated, respectful, and noble images, as observed in conversations between neighbors and between seniors-juniors, in workplaces, and at hotel restaurants. In contrast, use of the reduced form can index affectionate, happy, and approachable images, as observed in conversations between lovers and between peers, while traveling, and at family restaurants. By making use of these resources, speakers create an atmosphere or construct a persona that conforms to the context.

Finally, let us consider *ranuki* in connection with the accesorization of dialects (Kobayashi 2004, Tanaka 2011). Originally, the function of local dialects was as a means of communication for certain communities within the standard/local dialect dichotomy, with the latter being stigmatized. As the standard became more common, the function of local dialects changed to a stylistic choice, whereby a local dialect can be used to index solidarity, create an atmosphere, and for fun. Nevertheless, this function is still built upon the standard/local dialect dichotomy. In the case of *ranuki*, the non-referential meaning of the reduced form is built upon the dichotomy between the full form and the reduced form; in order to perform their stylistic functions, both the full and the reduced form need to survive and co-exist, even though *ranuki* is an ongoing change in which the reduced form is replacing the full form.

6 Summary

This corpus-based quantitative study demonstrated novel stylistic aspects of *ranuki*, its communicative functions, and how such functions are developed by utilizing the variable tied to existing norms for interactional purposes, such as interpersonal relationships, and the interactional atmosphere associated with indirect indexicality. In performing social actions based on the community's ideology, speakers derive *ranuki*'s new indexicalized functions (non-referential meanings) for their interactional purposes, in addition to the status imposed on the form by linguistic norms/prescriptive grammar, which is difficult to explain using the uni-dimensional model. Future work should include a qualitative analysis and a time-sensitive analysis of any changes or developments in the use of *ranuki* in interaction.

References

Campbell-Kibler, K. 2007. Accent, (ING) and the Social Logic of Listener Perceptions. *American Speech* 82: 32-64.

Coupland, N. 2007. *Style: Language Variation and Identity*. Cambridge: Cambridge University Press.

Eckert, P. 1989. *Jocks and Burnouts: Social Identity in the High School*. New York: Teachers College Press.

Eckert, P. 2000. *Language Variation as Social Practice*. Oxford: Blackwell.

Eckert, P. 2008. Variation and the Indexical Field. *Journal of Sociolinguistics* 12(4): 453-476.

Eckert, P. 2012. Three Waves of Variation Study: The Emergence of Meaning in the Study of Sociolinguistic Variation. *Annual Review of Anthropology* 41: 87-100.

Eckert, P. 2016. *Third Wave Variationism*. Oxford Handbooks Online, DOI: 10.1093/oxfordhb/9780199935345.013.27

Eckert, P. and J. R. Rickford, eds. 2001. *Style and Sociolinguistic Variation*. Cambridge: Cambridge University Press.

Ito, J. and A. Mester. 2004. Morphological Contrast and Merger: Ranuki in Japanese. *Journal of Japanese Linguistics* 20: 1-18.

Kataoka, K. 2002. Shijiteki, Hishijitekiimi-to Bunkatekijissen: Gengo Shiyooniokeru 'Shihyosei'-nitsuite [Referential/Non-referential Meaning and Cultural Significance: 'Indexicality' in Language Use]. *Syakaigengo Kagaku* [The Japanese Journal of Language in Society] 4(2): 21-41.

Kindaichi, H., T. Shibata and O. Hayashi, eds. 1995. *Nihongo Hyakka Daijiten* [Encyclopedia of the Japanese Language]. Tokyo: Taishukan Syoten.

Kobayashi, T. 2004. Akusesarii-toshiteno Gendaihoogen [Contemporary Dialect: Accessories of the Language]. *Shakaigengo Kagaku* [The Japanese Journal of Language in Society] 7(1): 105-107.

Labov, W. 1963. The Social Motivation of a Sound Change. *Word* 18: 1-42.

Labov, W. 1966. *The Social Stratification of English in New York City*. Washington, DC: Center for Applied Linguistics.

Labov, W. 1972. *Sociolinguistic Patterns*. Philadelphia: University of Pennsylvania Press.

Matsuda, K. 1993. Dissecting Analogical Leveling Quantitatively: The Case of the Innovative Potential Suffix in Tokyo Japanese. *Language Variation and Change* 5(1): 1-34.

Mendoza-Denton, N. 2002. Language and Identity. *The Handbook of Language Variation and Change*, eds. J. K. Chambers, P. Trudgill and N. Schilling-Estes, 475-499. Oxford: Blackwell.

Ochs, E. 1990. Indexicality and Socialization. *Cultural Psychology: Essays on Comparative Human Development*, eds. J. W. Stigler, R. A. Shweder and G. Herdt, 287-308. Cambridge: Cambridge University Press.

Podesva R. 2004. *On Constructing Social Meaning with Stop Release Bursts*. Paper presented at Sociolinguistics Symposium 15, Newcastle upon Tyne.

R Development Core Team. 1993-2018. *R: A Language and Environment for Statistical Computing*. R Foundation for Statistical Computing, Vienna, Austria.

Sano, S. 2011. Real-time Demonstration of the Interaction among Internal and External Factors in Language Change: A Corpus Study. *Gengo Kenkyuu* [The Journal of the Linguistic Society of Japan] 139:1-27.

Sano, S. 2015. Optimization of the Verbal Inflectional Paradigm by the Cyclic Application of Morphophonological Processes: Evidence from Potential Forms in Japanese. *Open Linguistics* 1(1): 580-595.

Sherwood, S. 2014. *Social Pressures Condition Ranuki in the Potential Form of Japanese Verbs*. Talk presented at NWAV-AP3 at Victoria University of Wellington.

Sherwood, S. 2016. *Indicating and Perceiving Social Hierarchy through Language Variation: The Case of Ranuki in Japanese*. BA thesis, Western Sydney University.

Silverstein, M. 1976. Shifters, Linguistic Categories, and Cultural Description. *Meaning in Anthropology*, eds. K. H. Basso and H. A. Selby, 11-55. Albuquerque: University of New Mexico Press.

Schilling-Estes, N. 2004. Constructing Ethnicity in Interaction. *Journal of Sociolinguistics* 8(2): 163-195.

Tanaka, Y. 2001. Kectaidenwa-to Denshimeiru-no Hyoogen [Expressions in Cellphone and Email Communication]. *Gendai Nihongo Kooza*, vol. 2, eds. Y Hida and T. Sato, 98-127. Tokyo: Meiji Syoin.

Tanaka, Y. 2011. *'Hoogenkosupure'-no Jidai: Nise-kansaiben-kara Ryoomago-made* [Generation of 'Dialect Cosplay': From Psuedo Kansai Dialect to Ryooma-Language]. Tokyo: Iwanami Syoten.

Trudgill, P. 1974. *The Social Differentiation of English in Norwich*. Cambridge: Cambridge University Press.

Wolfram, W. 1969. Linguistic Correlates of Social Differences in the Negro Community. *Georgetown Monograph Series on Languages and Linguistics* 22, ed. J. Alatis, 249-257. Washington, DC: Georgetown University Press.

Zhang, Q. 2005. A Chinese Yuppie in Beijing: Phonological Variation and the Construction of a New Professional Identity. *Language in Society* 34(3): 431-466.

Zhang, Q. 2008. Rhotacization and the 'Beijing Smooth Operator': The Social Meaning of a Linguistic Variable. *Journal of Sociolinguistics* 12(2): 201-222.

On the Rise of *Douride* 'no wonder' as a Projector and the Reformulation of Discourse Sequential Relations in Japanese*

REIJIROU SHIBASAKI
Meiji University

1 Introduction

Regardless of which of the possible argument structure types in Japanese is examined, verbal or adjectival predicates tend to be placed in either sentence- or clause-final position (Iwasaki 2002: 83-84) apart from in the case of some particular emotive constructions (Ono 2006). Verbal or adjectival predicates can be realized in a variety of forms, often with

* I am grateful to Sung-Ock Sohn, Tomohide Kinuhata, Hiroaki Tanaka, Naoki Otani, Hiro Yuki Nisisawa, Ryoko Suzuki, and Heather Oumounabidji for their helpful comments in preparation for the current paper. Any remaining faults are my own. Note that this study is part of Grant-in-Aid for Scientific Research (B) project (PI: Ryoko Suzuki, No. 17KT0061) by the Japan Society for the Promotion of Science.

Japanese/Korean Linguistics 25.
Edited by Shin Fukuda, Mary Shin Kim, and Mee-Jeong Park.

various types of tense-aspect-mood morphemes or particles. Nominalization patterns in Japanese have been studied synchronically, diachronically or typologically (Shibatani 2017). On the other hand, the fact that nominal predicates occurring with with some particular lexical nouns have changed into adverbial connectors seems to have hitherto gone unnoticed. It is true that Shinya (2014) addresses the usage of nominal predicates in contemporary Japanese and that Narumi (2015) investigates the change from nouns to adverbial phrases in the history of Japanese; however, the versatility of nouns as shown in (1) and (2) has not come under close scrutiny especially from diachronic and theoretical perspectives. Elements in point are underlined from here on.[1]

(1) Nominal predicate use: *douri ga nai*

Konna	*mutsukasii*	*hon*	*ga*	*kodomo*	*ni*	*yomeru*
such	difficult	book	NOM	child	DAT	read.can

douri	*ga*	*nai*
reason	NOM	be.not

"It's absurd to think that a child should be able to read such a difficult book." (Group Jammassy 2015: 338)

(2) Adverbial use: *douride*

A:
Kanojo	*no*	*ryooshin*	*wa*	*gakusha*	*da*	*yo*
she	GEN	parents	TOP	scholars	COP	FP

"Both of her parents are scholars."

B:
Douride	*kanojo*	*mo*	*atamagaii*	*hazu-da*
no.wonder	she	too	be.smart	must-COP

"So that explains why she's so smart too!" (ibid.)

Group Jammassy (2015: 338) describes the nominal-predicate use *douri ga nai* as an expression that means "no matter how one thinks about something, there is no reason or basis to accept it as correct" (ibid.). However, they make no mention of the corresponding affirmative use, e.g. *douri ga aru* ('reason' + NOM + 'exist') or *douri dearu* ('reason' + COP), which means to 'be reasonable, be in the right, accord with reason.' The adverbial use of *douride* is described as being used "when someone learns the most reasonable explanation for a state of affairs and accepts it, with the sense of "of course, that makes sense/that must be why"" according to Group Jammassy (ibid.). The adverbial *douride* serves to make either addressees or

---

[1] The glossing conventions are follows: ACC=accusative; AUX=auxiliary; COP=copula; DAT=dative; DEM=demonstrative; FP=final particle; GEN=genitive; N=noun; NML=nominalizer; NOM=nominative; PREF=prefix; PT=particle; S=sentence; SUF=suffix; TOP=topic.

readers anticipate upcoming discourse, which Hopper and Thompson (2008: 105) call *projector* (see Shibasaki 2018 for further discussion). Note that *douride* can also be used to make an appropriate response, i.e. *aizuchi* in Japanese, while the interlocuter is speaking. However, because of limitations of space, I will leave this use aside from this current study.

So which of the two expressions appeared earlier in the history of Japanese and which derived from the other? According to Kitahara (2006), i.e. the unabridged dictionary of the Japanese language, the earliest example of *douri* 'reason, truth' as a noun is recorded in the eighth century. Later in the eleventh century, a nominal predicate use of *douri* can be witnessed as in (3), while several forms of adverbial connectors such as *douride* ('reason' + PT [< adnominal form of COP]), *dourika* ('reason' + PT), *dourikoso* ('reason' + emphatic PT), etc. began life around the middle of the eighteenth century as in (4). Nouns as well as verbs are known to have the potential to become used as other grammatical categories such as adverbs and conjunctions across languages (Heine and Kuteva 2007: 111); *douri* can thus be considered to have followed this direction of change.

(3) Nominal predicate use: *douri nari*
    Toodaiji   *go-shoryoo*   *shokoku*   *sanjo,*
    temple.name PREF-possession everywhere   no.authority
    shooen   *shukoo*   *kouhai*   <u>*douri-nari*</u>
    private.estate   deprivation   wasteland   reason-COP
    "(Since) estates in the property of Todai Temple have no authority all over the place, (it) is no wonder (that such) private properties (are) terminated." (1053 *Toodaijimonjo*; Kitahara 2006)
(4) Adverbial use: *douride*
    <u>*Douride*</u>   *mago*   *ga*   *me-ni-kakari...*
    no.wonder   grandchild   NOM   eye-in-hang
    "No wonder, (one) caught sight of (his/her) grandchild and..."
    (1749 *Yorokobigarasu*; Kitahara 2006)

The functional derivation of adverbial forms from their nominal forms is not restricted to the case of *douride*. Table 1 provides us with the emergence of adverbial forms from similar nominal expressions in the history of Japanese. It is interesting that, while the years in which each noun or nominal predicate appears for the first time differ greatly, the years in which its adverbial expression appears for the first time begin from the middle of the eighteenth century onward, as shown in the table. Although both *kihon* 'basic, basis' and *gensoku* 'principle' are labeled only as nouns in Kitahara (2006), a corpus search of their adverbial expressions, albeit not comprehensively, results in the following consequences: *kihon-teki-ni* ('basis'-SUF-PT) 'basically' (1947) > *kihon* 'basically' (2002) and *gensoku-teki-ni ieba* ('principle'-SUF-PT + 'saying') 'generally speaking' (1925) > *gensoku* 'in principle, as a rule' (2001); the corpora used for this study are introduced in Section 2. In a nutshell, these changes seem to be paradigmatic in creating newer adverbial expressions from quite a few erstwhile nominal predicates, beginning from the middle of the eighteenth century or mostly emerging around the turn of the twentieth century.

Example	The earliest nominal use	The earliest nominal predicate use	The earliest adveribal use
douri 'truth, reason	718	1053	1749
jijitsu 'fact, in fact'	1017	1017	1914[2]
shoujiki 'truth, frankly'	1060	1060	1838
mochiron 'sure thing'	1275	1275	1795
touzen 'a matter of course, no surprise'	Late 14C	Late 14C	1923-27
kihon 'basic, basically'	1709	1709	NA
muron 'taken for granted, sure thing'	1771	?1771	1868-72
gensoku 'principle, in principle'	1885-86	1885-86	NA

TABLE 1 The Earliest Examples of Nominal and Adverbial Uses of Nouns (based on Kitahara 2006 with the author's comments added)

Such a direction of change in grammatical category is not always granted unqualified approval. Noguchi (2016: 62-64), who is a kind of prescriptivist, shows wariness of the use of adverbial expressions of *kihon* and *gensoku* especially in written language. Iima (2017: 74-76), as a compiler of Japanese dictionaries, contemplates these on-going changes with equanimity. That said, these noun-based adverbial expressions can be witnessed frequently in informal texts such as blogs (but not so frequently in conversation) according to several corpus-based surveys shown in Section 3. This genre-specific distributional pattern might be a reflection of *uchi kotoba* in daily lives, i.e. dictions, phrases, or texts when one types expressions using computers or smartphones, namely, another type of linguistic expression in contrast to or in the midst of written and spoken language (Agency for Cultural Affairs 2018).

This article is structured as follows. Section 2 introduces the corpora and coding properties used for this study; Section 3 shows the results of the

---

[2] Shibasaki (2018) found one older example of the adverbial use of *jijitsu* in a text published in 1901.

corpus-based surveys. Section 4 examines and discusses the distributional patterns from syntactic and pragmatic perspectives, accompanied by brief concluding remarks and future issues.

2   Corpora and Coding Properties

Table 2 summarizes the set of corpora mainly used for the study. Since one type of adverbial expression is found in the middle of the eighteenth century as shown in (4), I referred to the following two historical corpora of particular genres, i.e. *Sharebon* (gay-quarter novelettes) and *Ninjoobon* (love stories) in the eighteenth and nineteenth centuries (Ichimura 2015 and Fujimoto and Takada 2015), respectively. However, any earlier example of adverbial use could not be attested. Therefore, I will focus on the development of the adverbial *douride* from the Meiji period (c.1868-1912) onwards, based on the examples from the corpora in Table 2.

Corpus (period)		Number of words
Modern Japanese Corpora	*Meirokuzasshi* (1874-1875)	approx. 180,000 words
	Kokuminnotomo (1887-1888)	approx. 1 mil. words
	Kindai Josee Zasshi (1894-1895, 1909, 1925)	approx. 2 mil. words.
	Taiyo Corpus (1895, 1901, 1909, 1917, 1925)	approx. 5.34 mil words[3]
Contemporary Japanese Corpora	*Balanced Corpus of Contemporary Written Japanese* (=BCCWJ) (1971-2005, varying according to genre)	approx. 150 mil. words
	Nagoya University Conversation Corpus (=*Meidai Corpus*) (2001-2003)[4]	approx. 1.4 mil. words

TABLE 2 The Japanese Corpora Used for This Study

The coding properties for nominal predicates and adverbial expressions are illustrated in (5) and (6), respectively. As for *douride*, some relevant forms are examined for comparison.

(5) Nominal predicate use:
   douri 'reason' + *-nari/dearu/da/desu/*etc. (various types of copulas)[5]

---

[3] Tanaka (2012) approximates the number of words for each period of *Taiyo Corpus*: 1.3 mil. words for 1885; 1.2 mil. words for 1901; 1.0 mil. words for 1909; 0.97 mil. words for 1917; 0.87 mil. words for 1925.

[4] See Fujimura et al. (2012) for a fuller description of the corpus.

(6) Adverbial use:
    douri-de ('reason'-adnominal form of copula)

3   Survey Results

3.1   Results from Modern Japanese Corpora

The following are the survey results based on Modern Japanese Corpora (Mod-J Corpora). Around the turn of the twentieth century, the form *douri* was nominal predicate (or nominal itself) oriented, while adverbial use was in a germinal stage. '± others' means the presence or the absence of other elements.

	douri + COP ± others (nominal predicate)	*douride* (adverbial)	Total
douri	92.5% (148 tokens)	7.5% (12 tokens)	100% (N=160)

TABLE 3 The Frequency of Adverbial and Nominal Predicate Uses of *Douri* in Mod-J Corpora

The distributional pattern of the nominal predicate use of *douri* in Mod-J Corpora is summarized in Table 4; the numbers are the raw frequencies of each expression.

douri + COP (nominal pred.)	1874-75	1888-89	1894-95	1901	1909	1917	1925	Total
-*nari*	...	8	22	6	7	10	...	53
-*aru*	2	7	16	6	5	2	2	40
-*dearu* ±	...	...	1	4	12	7	9	33
-*da* ±	...	...	4	1	5	1	3	14
-*desu*	...	...	...	1	2	...	1	4
-*dearimasu*	...	...	...	...	1	...	...	1
-*degoza(r)imasu*	...	...	3	...	...	...	...	3
Total	2	15	46	18	32	20	15	148

TABLE 4 The Distributional Pattern of the Nominal-Predicate Use of *Douri* in Mod-J Corpora

What we can learn from this survey result is that the nominal *douri* can be attached to a variety of copulas. Furthermore, the oldest form of copula, i.e.

---

[5] Fukushima (2014: 371) states that the word formation 'noun (especially words of Chinese origin) + copula' is characteristic of Modern Japanese (c. 1868-1926) based on Abe (2009). In other words, the derivation of adverbial forms from this period-specific formation, i.e. N+COP, is worth an in-depth examination.

-*nari*, as shown in (3), is found to have been used for a prolonged period of time and to be frequently observed up until 1917. Presumably, the other variant forms such as *douri-da*, *douri-dearu*, or *douri-desu*, were created over time by analogy with the frequently used constructional schema, i.e. *douri* + -*nari*, as seen in Table 4. The other expressions listed in Table 1 also seem to have affected one another, gradually giving rise to the abstract schema, i.e. N + COP. The whole historical pathway of this construction thus serves as a good case that can be accounted for in the framework of usage-based appoarches to grammar (e.g. Bybee 2006).

Table 5 lists the breakdown of the adverbial expressions of *douri* in Mod-J Corpora. Notice that the three different but relevant expressions are included in the table for comparison. In contrast to the flourishing of the nominal predicate use of *douri*, the adverbial use of *douri* was in germ in terms of frequency.

douri (adverbial)	1874-75	1888-89	1894-95	1901	1909	1917	1925	Total
douri-de 'no wonder, indeed'	...	...	4	1	3	...	4	12
mottomona douri-de 'for a good reason'	...	...	...	...	...	...	1	1
douri-jou-yori-shite 'in all reason'	4	...	...	...	...	...	...	4
douri-jou 'in all reason'	...	...	1	1	6	...	1	9
Total	4	0	5	2	9	0	6	26

TABLE 5 The Distributional Pattern of the Adverbial Use of *Douri* in Mod-J Corpora

3.2   Results from BCCWJ

The survey results based on BCCWJ are summarized in Table 6. It is obvious that *douri* 'truth, reason' has been mostly adverbialized (i.e. 84.7 %) as *douride* or *dooride*, while its nominal predicate use has been in a sharp decline (15.3%). In what follows, I will briefly explain the points in the survey results based on Tables 7 and 8.

	douri + COP ± others (nominal predicate)	*douride* (adverbial)	Total
douri	15.3% (28 tokens)	84.7% (155 tokens)	100% (N=160)

TABLE 6 The Frequency of Adverbial and Nominal Predicate Uses of *Douri* in BCCWJ (All Genres)

Firstly, regardless of the usage types, *douri* turns out to be highly skewed towards particular genres, especially Book (65.2%, 101 out of 155 tokens) and *Yahoo!* Blogs and its online question-and-answer services (28.4%, 44 out of 155 tokens).

Genre	-da±	-dearu±	-desu	-nari	-dearimasu	Total
Book	4	10	8	2	...	24
Yahoo!Blogs	1	...				1
Magazine	...	1	...	...	...	1
Newspapers	...	1	...	...	...	1
Diet Minute	...	...	1	...	...	1
White Book	...	...	...	...	...	0
Textbook	...	...	...	...	...	0
Public Rel. Mag.	...	...	...	...	...	0
Verse	...	...	...	...	...	0
Law	...	...	...	...	...	0
Total	5	12	9	2	0	28

TABLE 7 The Distributional Pattern of the Nominal-Predicate Use of *Douri* in BCCWJ

Genre (literation)	*douride* (道理で)	*douride* (どうりで)	*dooride* (どおりで)	Total
Book	57 (56.4%)	41 (40.6%)	3(3.0%)	101
Yahoo!Blogs	8 (18.2%)	27 (61.4%)	9(20.4%)	44
Magazine	3	4	1	8
Newspapers	1	...	...	1
Diet Minute	1	...	...	1
White Book	...	...	...	0
Textbook	...	...	...	0
Public Rel. Mag.	...	...	...	0
Verse	...	...	...	0
Law	...	...	...	0
Total	70 (45.2%)	72 (46.4%)	13 (8.4%)	155

TABLE 8 The Distributional Pattern of the Adverbial Use of *Douri* in BCCWJ

Secondly, the relation between character literation and language function is worthy of remark: when *douride* is written in *hiragana*, it always serves as an adverb (see *projector* in Section 1), not as a nominal predicate. On the other hand, when *douride* is written in *kanji* (Chinese characters) accompanied by the *hiragana* form of the adnominal inflection of COP, i.e.

道理で, some functional variations can be confirmed: adverb (66.3%), nominal predicate (31.4%), and some indeterminate phrasal expressions (2.3%, e.g. *douri-de-motte* 'reasonably').

According to Iwasaki (2002: 11), Japanese has a general rule "that content words are written in *kanji*, function words in *hiragana*, and Western loans and sound-symbolic words such as onomatopoeia in *katanaka*." In other words, *douri* is located still on the midway of the content-function word continuum, which suggests that even the adverbialized *douride* cannot be strongly preferred in conversational discourse. In fact, only two examples of *hiragana*-written adverbial *douride* can be found in the *Meidai Corpus*.

Thirdly, one variant phonetic pattern *dooride* instead of *douride* is produced, albeit in small numbers, presumably due to a type of progressive assimilation through repeated use (15.3%, 13 of 85 *hiragana* examples).

4   Discussion and Concluding Remarks

In this section, I will probe deeper into the historical pathway of the functional expansion of *douri* and briefly account for how it changes in certain discourse-syntactic contexts, based on the following representative examples at each historical stage.

(7) Stage 1: [clause$_{NML}$ + *wa*$_{TOP}$ + *douri*-COP] SENTENCE 1
 Kyonen   no   koto   o   omoidashi-te   kanashiku
 last.year   GEN   thing   ACC   remember-and   sadly
 omou   no   wa   douri-da
 think   NML   TOP   no.wonder-COP
 "(It) is no wonder that (we) feel sad when (we) remember what (happened) last year." (1895 *Azumanishikie*; *Taiyo*)

(8) Stage 2: [clause 1$_{(NML)}$ (+ *wa*$_{TOP}$) + *douri*-COP, clause 2] SENTENCE 1
 ...Yoron   no   nozomi   o   ou   hito   ga
  public.opinion GEN   hope   ACC   have.a.duty person NOM
 daijin   to-naru   (Ø)   (Ø)   douri-dearu-ga...
 minister   PT-become   (NML)   (TOP)   no.wonder-COP-but
 "(It's) no wonder (that) those who can be supported by ordinary people become a minister, but..."
 (1901 *Shakainohuhaikyuujiiken*: *Taiyo*)

(9) Stage 3 [...] SENTENCE 1 [DEM + *douri*-COP, ...] SENTENCE 2
 Soko ga   sunawati   kyoosoo-ni-naru   no   dearu.
 that   NOM in.other.words competition-PT-become   NML   COP

 Sayoona-douri-dearu-kara   miginogotoki
 such/left-reason-COP-because   following/right

genshiseibutsu	*ni*	*atte*	*mo*	(...)	*hitsuzen-no-koto*
protobiont	PT	meet	PT		dead.cert-GEN-NML

dearu	*to*	*shinzuru*
COP	COMP	believe

"Namely, this turns out to be a competition. For this reason, (I) believe that it is inevitable even when (one) comes across the following primeval forms of life."

(1919 *Shizen no Majari to Shinka Tairan*)

(10) Stage 4: [...] SENTENCE 1 [*douride*, ...] SENTENCE 2

Douride	*eigo*	*ga*	*tassha-na*	*hazu.da*
no.wonder	English	NOM	good-be	AUX.COP

"No wonder, (he) speaks English fluently."

(1990 *Tagen'uchu*; BCCWJ)

At Stage 1, the embedded clause is nominalized by *no* and topicalized by *wa*, and immediately followed by the nominal predicate *douri-da* as in (7). Structurally, the *douri*-predicate is inside the bi-clausal sentence, while pragmatically, the thematic clause is accompanied by the rhematic *douri*-predicate. Namely, the theme-rheme relation is realized in one sentence.

At Stage 2, one can witness the *douri*-predicate with the subordinate conjunction *ga* 'but' as in (8), which serves a clause-chaining function. This particular example includes neither the nominalizer *no* nor the topic marker *wa* unlike (7), simply because they are grammatically omissible around this stage. What is important in this example is the inflectional form of the verb in the preceding clause, i.e. *naru* 'become': this form can be interpreted either as the adnominal form or as the sentence-end form of the verb. If one regards this discourse-syntactic sequence as a case of adnominal form, the interpretation of the example is just like the English translation in (8). On the other hand, another language user might have read or heard this example as a case of sentence-end form; the source of this example is a type of written opinion, which is considered to have been a colloquial form of those days. If some language users of those days preferred the second interpretation, the example can be translated: "those who can be supported by ordinary people become a minister. (It's) no wonder, but..." Such a grammatical ambiguity would have facilitated the stand-alone adverbial use of *douri* as is more clearly illustrated in the next example (9).

At Stage 3, *douri* is used as part of the independent adverbial phrase *sayoona-douri-dearu-kara* 'for this reason' as in (9). Interestingly, the modifier *sayoona*, which literally means 'as in the left' (左様な), makes anaphoric reference to the preceding discourse, while the next expression *miginogotoki*, which literally means 'as in the right' (右の如き), makes cataphoric reference to the following discourse. In other words, the *douri*-

adverbial expression as a *projector* occupies the intermediate position between preceding and following sentences/clauses, serving to lubricate the flow of information: the theme-rheme relation is expanded from a biclausal construction to a sequenced-sentence construction. At Stage 6, the form of the adverbial use is mostly fossilized as *douride* and serves as a *projector* between sentences or clauses.

Figure 1 is a schematic representation of the above-mentioned change in discourse-syntactic structure. At Stage 2, the form of the nominal predicate is specified as *douri*-COP (LK=linking form of the verb). SYN=syntax; PRAG=pragmatics.

Stage 1: S-final nominal predicate (S-end form) = (7)
     [clause$_{NML}$ + *wa*$_{TOP}$ + *douri*-COP   ] SENTENCE 1
SYN: clausal subject   predicate
PRAG: theme   rheme

Stage 2: S-medial nominal predicate (linking form)=(8)
     [clause 1$_{(NML)}$ + (*wa*$_{TOP}$) + *douri*-COP (LK),   clause 2] SENTENCE 1
SYN: clausal subject   predicate/projecting
PRAG: theme (effect)   rheme (cause/reason)

Stage 3: S-initial adverbial phrase (projector) = (9)
     [...   ...] SENTENCE 1   DEM + *douri*-COP, [......] SENTENCE 2
SYN: preceeding S   projecting   following S
PRAG: theme (effect)   rheme (cause/reason)

Stage 4: S-initial adverb(projector) = (10)
     [...   ...] SENTENCE 1   *douride*,   [......] SENTENCE 2
SYN: preceeding S   projecting   following S
PRAG: theme (effect)   rheme (cause/reason)

Figure 1: The Discourse-Syntactic Reformulation of the *Douri*-Construction

What Figure 1 tells us about this structural change is as follows. Syntactically, *douri* undergoes the change from the inside of the sentence as a nominal predicate to the outside of the sentence as a *projector*; pragmatically, the theme-rheme relation realized in one sentence becomes reformulated over history, connecting preceding (thematic) and following (rhematic) information, forming a larger discourse unit. In a nutshell, the syntactic change of *douri* involves an increase in structural scope, i.e. from a bi-clausal sentence to a sequenced-sentence construction, in a very similar way to that suggested in Traugott and Dasher (2002: 152-189).

Some researchers, especially those who address language change within the purview of sentence grammar, might receive the impression that the change from the sentence-final predicate to the sentence-initial *projector* is a radical change in syntax. However, if we widen our horizons to reconsider how to combine sentences in a stretch of discourse, such a radical structural change would not be unusual (see Onodera 2004 for relevant phenomena).

Radical changes in the syntax of *douri* cannot fully be explained in the framework of traditional approaches including grammaticalization. Conversely, constructionalization (Traugott and Trousdale 2014) may give a better account of this phenomenon, as shown in the analysis of another change, i.e. *jijitsu* from the inside to the outside of the sentence (Shibasaki 2018). I will leave this issue for my future study due to space limitation.

References

Abe, S. 2009. Imi kara Mita Goishi (A Semantic View of Lexical History). *Goishi* (Lexical History), eds. S. Abe, M. Saito, A. Okajima, K. Hanichi, M. Ito, and T. Maeda, 73–104. Tokyo: Iwanami.

Agency for Cultural Affairs, Government of Japan. 2018. Wakariau tameno Gengo Komyunikeeshon (Houkoku) ni tsuite ('On the Report: Language Communication for Mutual Understanding), 2 March 2018.

(www.bunka.go.jp/koho_hodo_oshirase/hodohappyo/1401904.html)

Bybee, J. 2006. From Usage to Grammar: The Mind's Response to Repetition. *Language* 82 (4): 711–733.

Fujimura, I., S. Chiba, and M. Ohso, 2012, Lexical and Grammatical Features of Spoken and Written Japanese in Contrast: Exploring a Lexical Profiling Approach to Comparing Spoken and Written Corpora. *Proceedings of the VIIth GSCP International Conference. Speech and Corpora*, 393–398.

Fukushima, T. 2014. Juuzokusetsu ni oite Ishi/Suiryoo ga Genshooshita no wa Naze ka (Why Volition/Inference Decline in Subordinate Clauses). *Form and Meaning in Japanese Complex Sentence Constructions(written in Japanese)*, eds. T. Masuoka, M. Oshima, O Hashimoto, K. Horie, N. Maeda, and T. Maruyama, 347–382. Tokyo: Hituzi Syobo Publishing.

Group Jammassy (Supervising editors: Yuriko Sunakawa and Priscilla Ishida). 2015. *A Handbook of Japanese Grammar Patterns for Teachers and Learners.* Tokyo: Kurosio Publishers.

Heine, B. and T. Kuteva. 2007. *The Genesis of Grammar: A Reconstruction.* Oxford: Oxford University Press.

Hopper, P. J. and S. A. Thompson. 2008. Projectability and Clause Combining in Interaction. *Cross-Linguistic Studies of Clause Combining*, ed. Ritva Laury, 99–123. Amsterdam: John Benjamins.

Iima, H. 2017. *Shoosetsu no Kotobajiri o Toraetemita* (Trapping Someone in the Wording of His/Her Novel). Tokyo: Kobunsha.

Iwasaki, . 2002. *Japanese*, 1st ed. Amsterdam: John Benjamins.

Narumi, S. 2015. *Studies in the Japanization of Chinese Loanwords: Focusing on Adverbialization (written in Japanese)*. Tokyo: Hituzi Syobo Publishing.

Noguchi, K. 2016. *"Hobo-hobo" "Ima-ima"?!: Kuizu Okashina Nihongo* ("Approximate-approximate" "Now-now"?!: Funny Japanese Quizzes). Tokyo: Kobunsha.

Ono, T. 2006. An Emotively Motivated Post-Predicate Constituent Order in a 'Strict Predicate Final' Language. *Emotive Communication in Japanese*, ed. S. Suzuki, 139–153. Amsterdam: John Benjamins.

Onodera, N. O. 2004. *Japanese Discourse Markers*. Amsterdam: John Benjamins.

Shibatani, M. 2017. Nominalization. *Handbook of Japanese Syntax*, eds. M. Shibatani and S. Miyagawa, 271–331. New York: De Gruyter Mouton.

Shibasaki, R. 2018. From the Inside to the Outside of the Sentence: Forming a Larger Discourse Unit with *Jijitsu* 'fact' in Japanese. *New Trends on Grammaticalization and Language Change*, eds. S. Hancil, T. Breban, and J. V. Lozano, 333–360. Amsterdam: John Benjamins.

Shinya, T. 2014. *Studies on Noun Orientation of Japanese Language (written in Japanese)*. Tokyo: Hituzi Syobo Publishing.

Tanaka, M. 2012. Meijikooki kara Taishooki no Goi no Reberu to Goshu (Levels and Types of Words from Late Meiji to Taisho Eras). Tokyo: National Institute for Japanese Language and Linguistics.

(http://pj.ninjal.ac.jp/corpus_center/cmj/doc/09Tanaka.pdf)

Traugott, E. C.and R. B. Dasher. 2002. *Regularity in Semantic Change*. Cambridge: Cambridge University Press.

Traugott, E. C. and G. Trousdale. 2014. *Constructionalization and Constructional Change*. Oxford: Oxford University Press.

Corpora and Dictionary

Balanced Corpus of Contemporary Written Japanese (BCCWJ).
(http://www.kotonoha.gr.jp/shonagon/)

Kindai Josee ZasshiCorpus, eds. A. Kondo, Y. Mabuchi and N. Hattori, 2012. Tokyo: National Institute for Japanese Language and Linguistics (NINJAL).

Kokuminnotomo Corpus, ed. A. Kondo, 2014. Tokyo: NINJAL.

Meirokuzasshi Corpus, ed. A. Kondo, Y. Mabuchi and N. Hattori, 2012. Tokyo: NINJAL.

Nihon Kokugo Daijiten (The Dictionary of the Japanese Language), ed. Y. Kitahara, 2006. Tokyo: Shogakkan.

Ninjoobon, eds. A. Fujimoto and T. Takada, 2015. Tokyo: NINJAL.

Sharebon, ed. T. Ichimura, 2015. Tokyo: NINJAL.

Taiyo Corpus (CD-ROM), 2005. Tokyo. Hakubunkan Shinsha.

Reporting Past Experience with the Immediate Perception Marker -ney in Korean Conversation

HYE YOUNG SMITH
University of Hawai'i at Mānoa

1   Introduction

In Korean, sentence enders are productively used to express the speaker's epistemic stance (Heritage 2012) by revealing how information was acquired, when information is incorporated into the speaker's knowledge system, and how strong the speaker's belief in her knowledge is. One of the Korean sentence enders that can express all these aspects of one's knowledge is *-ney*, which has been identified as an epistemic modal suffix (Chang 1985, 1995; Lee 1991; Park 1999; Kwon 2013, 2015), an evidential marker (Choi 1995; Strauss 2005; Song 2007, 2014, 2015), and a mirative marker (Strauss 2005; Chung 2012; Cho 2016).

Chang (1985, 1995) labeled *-ney* as an epistemic modal suffix that signals the speaker's perception of information through sensory observations. More comprehensive accounts for properties of *-ney* were

Japanese/Korean Linguistics 25.
Edited by Shin Fukuda, Mary Shin Kim, and Mee-Jeong Park.
Copyright © 2018, CSLI Publications

provided by Lee (1991[1], 1993), who defined -*ney* as a "factual realization marker" conveying "newly perceived information" that is considered factual and definitve by the speaker (Lee 1991, P. 381). In (1), for example, the utterance by a doctor indicates that the doctor has examined the patient and recognized a problem with the patient's liver. Kwon (2013) also stated that -*ney* is an epistemic modal suffix that expresses the speaker's strong conviction and assertion.

(1) *kan-i   nappu-si-**ney**-yo.*
     liver-NOM   bad-HON-***ney***-DEF
     [It turns out that] you have a problem with your liver.

(Lee 1991: 403)

On the other hand, some researchers focused on the source of information conveyed with -*ney*: as an evidential marker, it reveals that the speaker has acquired the information from firsthand experience or observation. Song (2007, 2014) asserted that -*ney*, as a direct evidential marker, signals the speaker's present sensory observation, as in (2a), and mental realization, as in (2b), both of which are triggered by firsthand experience. Strauss (2005), highlighting the distinction between evidentiality and epistemic modality, manifested how -*ney* expresses the speaker's "knowledge state" rather than "belief state," while signaling "consciousness shift" within the speaker as a result of inductive reasoning (p. 437). Strauss regarded -*ney* as an evidential marker, but more specifically, as a mirative marker.[2]

(2) a. *yepcip-un   nemwu   sikkulep-**ney***
        next:door-TOP   too:much   noisy-***ney***
        The house next door is too noisy.   (Song 2014: 822)

    b. *kapcaki   ku   cangmyen-i sayngkakna-**ney***
       suddenly   that scene-NOM come:to:mind-***ney***
       Suddenly that scene comes to mind.   (Song 2014: 822)

Mirativity, defined by DeLancey (2001) as "linguistic marking of an utterance as conveying information which is new or unexpected to the speaker (pp. 369–370)," is another label that has been given to -*ney* by recent studies (Park 2011; Chung 2012; Cho 2016). It is believed that -*ney*

---

[1] Lee (1991) labeled -*ney* as an immediate evidential, but in his analysis, evidentiality was regarded as a subcategory of epistemic modality.

[2] In Strauss (2005), mirativity was discussed within the system of evidentiality.

fits into this category well because there is a general consensus among researchers that signaling new information and counterexpectation (Sohn 1999) or surprise are the main features of -*ney*.

The grammatical category of -*ney* still remains controversial, although a large number of previous studies have contributed to clarifying it. As DeLancey (2001) noted, however, epistemic modality, evidentiality and mirativity are conceptually related, and it is not surprising that "forms from one kind of system develop functions of another, as when evidential senses developed into fundamentally mirative constructions (p. 380)." Thus, this paper takes an agnostic stance in that illustrating the functional uses of -*ney* is more important than defining its grammatical category.

The semantic and pragmatic profiles of -*ney* have been established by many previous studies. In addition to its aforementioned fundamental functions as an epistemic modal, direct evidential, and mirative marker, -*ney* is also used to express deferred realization, reinterpretation, and recollection (Park 2011; Moon 2014), as exemplified in (3). Moreover, Chung (2012) pointed out that the speaker can play the role of a perceiver, an objective observer or a messenger of the given event or information when using a -*ney* utterance. Thus, by using -*ney*, the speaker can distance herself as a third person from her own experience and provide a more objective description of the event (Park 2011).

(3) a. *chelswu-ka   pemin-i-ess-**ney**!*
    Cheolsu-NOM culprit-be-PST-**ney**
    (Now I realize) Cheolsu was the culprit!   (Park 2011: 13)

    b. *kulekoponikka cemsim-ul an-mek-ess-**ney**-yo.*
    By:the:way   lunch-ACC not-eat-PST-**ney**-DEF
    By the way, (we) didn't have lunch.   (Moon 2014: 93)

However, the functional and interactional aspects of -*ney* have been still underexplored in the previous research. Strauss (2005) noted that it is common for a -*ney* utterance to occur in the second pair part of an adjacency pair (Sacks et al. 1974) in activities such as assessment, compliment, or showing empathy. In a study that analyzed natually occuring talks between a child and a caregiver, Kim and Suh (2004) analyzed the caregiver's uses of -*ney* that brought the child's attention to the current event and performed various actions such as rebuking, complimenting and teasing.

This study aims to explore the pragmatic expansion of the Korean sentence ender -*ney* in reporting the speaker's past experience. In the following sections, I will illustrate how utterances ending with -*ney* reenact the speaker's past perception or observation in reporting or narrative telling. Additionally, I will discuss the pragmatic effects achieved by the use of -*ney*, such as (a) adding immediacy to the event and inviting the participant to co-assess the new information; (b) highlighting noteworthiness of the event while providing a post-event summary; (c) describing the reported event as uncontrollable and claiming a reduced accountability for the consequences.

2 Data and Methodology

In order to investigate the pragmatic contexts where -*ney* can be deployed, approximately 600 minutes of Korean telephone conversations from Linguistic Data Consortium (LDC) corpus were analyzed using conversation analytic (CA) methods. The participants in the conversations are international students, temporary residents, or immigrants living in the United States or in Canada. Most conversations took place between close friends or family members, and the participants were aware that they were being recorded.

Among 191 occurrences of -*ney* as a sentence ender, 35 tokens were used in reporting or recounting a narrative, which is an atypical use of -*ney*, considering its fundamental feature as an immediate perception marker signaling direct evidence. There has been only few studies on -*ney* that anlyzed naturally occurring conversation data, therefore, the CA framework will provide a new perspective to the analysis and development of the functional profiles of -*ney*.

3 -*ney* in Reporting Past Perception

This section illustrates the use of -*ney* in the present moment of utterance to report one's past sensory perception or past observation.

Excerpt (4) is a conversation between two female friends who are both international students studying in the US. The excerpt begins with Sun's story preface (Sacks et al. 1974) in lines 1-3 that projects a forthcoming narrative about her typical day.

(4) 12 O'clock
01 Sun: °*ya*°= *Na*:: *cincca* hhh
       hey   I   really hhh
02   *y(h)a- na- nauy onul halwu-nun mwe-*
       hey   I   my   today day-NOM what
03   *mwen-ci   a-nya¿*
       what-DISJ know-INTERR

Hey, really, do you know what my day was like today?

04 *(0.2)*

05→Sun: *ca-ko ilena-ss-teni*::   *yeltwu-si-**ney**¿ hh*
     sleep-and wake:up-PST-RETRO twelve-o'clock-***ney*** hh
     I woke up, and it is 12 o'clock-***ney***!

06 Mee: *hh*

07 Sun: *hh a*: *yeltwu-si-kwuna*::   *hhh sin:nakey mek-ko*: *hh*
    hh ah twelve-o'clock-UNASSIM hhh intensely eat-and hh
    (I thought) Oh, it's 12 o'clock! I pigged out, and

08    $*mek-ul-key ttelecy-ess-ta*¿$
    things:to:eat run:out-PST-DECL
    I ran out of food,

In this excerpt, Sun is reporting her lazy day to her friend by reenacting her past sensory experience. After calling Mee's attention to the background of the story (*cako ilenassteni* 'I woke up, and'), Sun reenacts her immediate response to the new information she has perceived (*yeltwusiney*¿ 'it is 12 o'clock!') as if she has just waken up now (line 5). By verbally demonstrating her past reaction with a moderately rising tone (¿), Sun displays her surprise at the unexpected information and invites Mee to attend to the ridiculousness of the perceived event. In lines 5-6, Sun's utterance with *-ney* is immediately followed by the laughter of both participants (which implies that the information is somewhat noteworthy and/or laughable). In line 7, there is another reenactment of Sun's reaction to her perceptional experience, this time in a more internalized way with the use of *-kwuna*, which has been distinguished from *-ney* in many aspects, one of which is being more speaker-centered than *-ney* (Strauss 2005). What is notable here is that Sun's present utterance with *-ney* is not a response to the immediately preceding experience. Rather, it is a reenactment of her past sensory experience.

4 *-ney* in Post-Event Report

In this section, *-ney* used in reporting the summary of a past event will be discussed.

  Excerpt (5) exhibits Jun's short narrative on his get-together with friends. The story is initiated by telling the consequence of the event: he is hungover from drinking too much yesterday (lines 1-2). Jun's report summary of his drinking party (lines 6-7) is conveyed with the sentence ender *-ney*, adopting a distanced and self-observing stance, implying that overdrinking was beyond his control. I suggest that a semantic feature of *-ney*, i.e., signaling 'surprise', provides a background here for the upcoming information: the astonishing amount of vodka he drank with his friends. Moreover, the noteworthiness and ridiculousness of the story is also portrayed in the expression *kkutcangul nayssta* "completely drained" (line 10). In this excerpt, *-ney* is used to provide a summary of a past event in the sense that the speaker is now looking back to what has caused his current condition, i.e., hangover.

(5) A gallon of vodka

01 Jun: *na-nun ecey   ↑swul-ul   >nemwu manhi masy-ekacko<*
     I-TOP yesterday alcohol-ACC too   much to:drink-so

02 *onul opaitu   hay-ss-ta.*
     today throw:up to:do-PST-DECL
     I drank too much yesterday, so I threw up today.

03 Pyo: *mwe ha-n↑tako¿*
     what to:do-because
     What for?

04 Jun: *ecey   ku- mweya San Francisco-eyse wass-canha::*
     yesterday that- DM   San Francisco-from came-you:know
     Yesterday, (my friends) came from SF, you know.

05 Pyo: *ung:*
     Yeah.

06 Jun: *>kulaykaciko< ku- >ku-ma-tul-hako   tto<*
     so   that that.dude-PL-with DM

07→ *swul han can-ul   hay-ss-**ney**:*
     drink one shot-ACC to:do-PST-**ney**
     So I had a drink with them-**ney**.

08 Pyo: *ung.*
     Yeah.

09 Jun: *ku potukha il gallon-ul   sey myeng-ise*
     DM vodka one gallon-ACC three people-as

10 *kkutcang-ul   nay-ss-ta   ecey.*
     completion-ACC to:make-PST-DECL yesterday
     The three of us completely drained a gallon of vodka yesterday.

5   Pragmatic Expansion of *-ney* and the Effects

As illustrated in the previous two excerpts, the immediate perception marker *-ney* can be used in reporting a past perception, experience, observation, or event. However, there has been no previous research that has recognized or investigated this special use of the sentence ender *-ney*.

This paper not only illustrates this phenomenon but also attemps to answer the question: what does this pragmatic expansion tell us? From an agnostic stance, the phenomenon is described in terms of the three effects that result from expanding the pragmatic boundary of -*ney*.

5.1 Immediacy

One of the effects of using -*ney* in reporting or telling narrative is adding immediacy to the reported past experience. Immediacy, according to Lee (1993), is a discourse-pragmatic factor of -*ney* in that perception of the information is limited to the present moment. By deploying -*ney*, Sun in Excerpt (4), made her retrieved past perceptual memory immediately available to the other participant. Similarly, the following conversation between the same participants from Excerpt (4), exhibits how -*ney* adds immediacy and vividness to the report of the speaker's accumulated past observations.

(6) Shopping
```
01 Sun:   na-nun (.) yo-   yeki on   ay-tul-i    ta  ka-pon
          I-TOP      this- here came kid-PL-NOM all have:been:to
02        ku khun paykhwacem      Macy's lanun tey-to
          that big  department:store Macy's called place-even
03        hanpen-to   mos    ka pwass-e =(   ).
          once-even   cannot have:been-IE
          I haven't even been to that big department store, Macy's
          that everyone (international students) here has been to.
04 Mee:   ne kongpu-man ha-nun-kwuna¿
          you study-only  to:do-ATTR(RL)-UNASSIM
          (I guess) all you do is study?
05 Sun:   a:ni¿ (0.4) hh na-lang  chinhan
          no          hh me-with close
06        ku  Brazil enni  iss-canh[a::
          that Brazil sister exist-you:know
          No. You know my friend from Brazil?
07 Mee:                     [e::]
                            Yeah.
08 Sun:   ku enni-ka    shopping-ul    keuy   an-ha-ney¿
          that sister-NOM shopping-ACC  almost not-to:do-ney
          (I found that) She rarely goes shopping-ney.
09 Mee:   e:: neney  ↑maynnal kati       tanye?
          oh you:guys everyday together hang:out
          Oh, you guys hang out together everyday?
```

In this excerpt, Sun complains about her monotonous lifestyle by highlighting her lack of shopping experience in New York, with an extreme case formulation (Pomerantz 1986) (*aytuli ta ka pon* 'everyone has been to', *hanpento mos* 'not even once'). Mee, in response, proffers a candidate understanding of untold reason for not going shopping (line 4), by using -*kwuna*, a sentence ender frequently used to seek confirmation of inference (Lee 1991; Park 1999) or formulating what might have been alluded to (Schegloff 1996), in a moderately rising tone. Disconfirming Mee's inference in lines 5-6, Sun solicits a recognition of a person at the beginning of her short narrative. Then, Sun reports her past observations, which has led her to the conclusion that her roommate rarely goes shopping (line 8). It is notable that, although her utterance is not directly triggered by immediate perception, Sun uses -*ney* as if she has just recognized the fact. By recounting her past perception, Sun invites Mee to participate in completing her story by inferring the reason Sun does not go shopping, hence achieving intersubjectivity.

5.2 Noteworthiness

Surprise, as one of the emotional stances which -*ney* expresses, is triggered by new information that is unexpected or even contrary to the speaker's existing knowledge or belief (Lee 1993). In storytelling, the climax or punchline of the story is often marked with reported speech or reported thought (Holt 1996; Kim 2014). I argue that the speaker's epistemic and/or emotional stance toward a past event - and more precisely, their assessment of the noteworthiness, unusualness, or ridiculousness of the event - can be expressed with -*ney* as a result of pragmatic expansion. For example, Sun in Excerpt (4) and (6) expressed her surprise at her past perceptual event (i.e., finding out she woke up at noon, figuring out her roommate's disinterest in shopping), both in a moderately rising intonation. According to Park (2003), when produced with -*ney*, a high boundary tone (H%) and a rising boundary tone (LH%) express the speaker's surprise and newness, respectively. Likewise, in excerpt (5), the story summary (*ku-ma-tul-hako tto swul han can-ul hay-ss-ney*: 'So I had a drink with them.') is provided with the use of -*ney*, followed by an exaggerative expression (*kkutcang-ul nay-ss-ta ecey* 'completely drained') to support the event's ridiculousness and noteworthiness.

5.3 Reduced Accountability

Another effect from using the immediate perception marker -*ney* for reporting a past perception is that the speaker can claim reduced accountability for the event. I argue that objectification or distancing, the discourse-pragmatic feature of -*ney* (Park 2011; Chung 2012; Kwon 2013), takes effect when the speaker uses -*ney* to describe his/her own past experience. It indicates that the distancing effect of -*ney* as a direct evidential has developed to imply reduced accountability when applied in a particular context (i.e., reporting or narrative). Excerpt (7) illustrates the interactional function of -*ney* when a participant distances himself from the trouble he is accused of having caused.

(7) Busan

01 Hun: *way yenlak an hay-ss-e::* [*ccacung na-key.*
         why contact not to:do-PST-IE annoyance get-RESUL
         Why didn't you call me? It pissed me off.

02 Soo: [*ung? ung?*]
                                        huh? huh?

((Lines omitted))

14 Soo: *nay-ka ku mwe calendar wi-eyta ku-ke-l*
         I-NOM that DM calendar on-LOC that-thing-ACC

15   *cenhwapenho-lul   ttak   cek-e   noh-ko*
         phone:number-ACC right   write-CONN put-and

16   *emma-hantey con:na honna-ko.*
         mom-from   a:lot   get:scolded-and
         I wrote the phone number right on the- the calendar and
         got scolded by my mom, and...

17 Hun: *mwe?*
         What?

18 Soo: *ney cenhwapenho-lul,*
         your phone:number-ACC
         Your phone number.

19 Hun: *e*
         mmhm.

20 Soo: *cip-ey   ku   congi- congi-ka   eps-ese*
         home-at that paper paper-NOM not:exist-because
         Because there wasn't paper at home,

21   *calendar wi-eyta cek-ess-ta,*
         calendar on-LOC   write:down-PST-DECL
         I wrote it on the calendar.

22 Hun: *ung*
         Yeah.

23 Soo: *malu-ey   iss-nuntey,*
         living:room-LOC exist-CIRCUM
         It was in the living room.

24 Hun: *ung*

Yeah.

25 Soo: *i:ke-y   mwe-nyako mak* (.) *co:nna honna-n   taumey*
       this-NOM what-QT DM   a:lot get:scolded after

26   *a: olmky-e   cek-nuntako thak   nwatwu-ko icey*
       ah move-CONN write-COMP right leave-and DM
       After my mom scolded me like "What the heck is this,"
       I left it right there to copy it, and

27 Hun: *ung*
        Yeah.

28 Soo: *pusan-ul   ka-ss-**ney**¿*
        Pusan-ACC go-PST-***ney***
        I went to Busan-***ney***.

29   (0.4)

30 Hun: *um a tto namca-ka pingkyey-lul tay-myen an toy-ci:*
        um ah DM man-NOM excuse-ACC tell-if   not okay-COMM
        Um, ah well, it's not cool when a man makes an excuse.

Beginning with Hun's accusation of Soo not calling him, immediately followed by a strong expression of his emotional state (*ccacungnakey* 'It pissed me off'), this excerpt shows Soo's storytelling in the context of giving an excuse. After a short repair sequence in the omitted lines, Soo begins telling his story in an attempt to defend his integrity against Hun's accusation. Notably, Hun produces response tokens such as "mmhm" and "yeah" that allow Soo to continue his storytelling (Gardner 2002; Young & Lee 2004). From line 14, Soo puts his mom onto the stage to dilute his involvement in the incident, especially by repeatedly highlighting the fact that he was very harshly scolded by his mom for writing Hun's number on the calendar in the living room. In line 28, the story comes to a climax when Soo nonchalantly says that he left to go to Busan, using the immediate perception marker *-ney*. By giving an account of a past event as if he has just perceived the fact, Soo can avoid blame for neglecting the situation (not having contacted Hun) and for not explaining the situation to Hun in the meantime before Hun makes the complaint. Hun also understands Soo's action as making an excuse, and in response, he teasingly criticizes him for it (*namcaka pingkyeylul taymyen an toyci* 'It's not cool when a man makes an excuse') (line 30).

6   Conclusion

In this paper, Korean speakers' use of the immediate perception marker *-ney* in naturally occurring conversation was examined. In addition to the semantic and pragmatic features that have been previously revealed, this study attempted to illustrate how -*ney* is used in reporting or recounting a narrative. The interactional effects that arise from these deviant cases are as follows: First, using -*ney* in a narrative has a general effect of adding immediacy and vividness to the story. I contend that this effect stems from the basic semantic feature of -*ney* that denotes the speaker's direct or firsthand experience. Second, -*ney* utterances used in a post-event report objectifies the speaker's personal experience, and at times, allows speakers to avoid responsibility for an undesirable situation. I believe that this effect is derived from the meaning of -*ney* as 'differred realization.' By picturing a past event as one that has been just realized, the speaker exempts herself from having to disclose her emotional stance toward the described event. Finally, the use of -*ney* in a narrative emphasizes surprising and noteworthy characteristics of the story itself. In this case, the speaker's surprise does not necessarily arise from an immediate perceptual event. Rather, the speaker adopts the mirative sense inherent in -*ney* to underscore the noteworthiness of the story.

The uses of -*ney* in reporting perception exemplified in this paper differ from the general profile of -*ney* (used in signalling immediate, present perception), in that it is used strategically to report a past event and the speaker's cognitive/emotional stance in a present voice, as if the speaker is still in the effect of the past perception. Therefore, I propose that the pragmatic context expansion which caused atypical uses of -*ney* needs more attention in future research.

References

Chang, K. H. 1985. *Hyentay Kwukeuy Yangsang Pemcwu Yenkwu* [A Study of Modality Categories in Modern Korean]. Seoul: Tower.

Chang, K. H. 1995. Categorical independence and subcategories of Korean modality. *Korean Journal of Linguistics* 20(3): 191-205.

Cho, Y. J. 2016. *Hankwukeuy Uyoyseng Pemcwuuy Silhyenkwa Ku Yangsang* [Mirativity in Korean: Its Design and Realizations]. *Korean Language Research* 40: 251-278.

Choi, S. J. 1995. The Development of Epistemic Sentence-ending Modal Forms and Functions in Korean Children. *Modality in Grammar in Discourse*, ed. J. L. Bybee & S. Fleischman, 165-204. Amsterdam: John Benjamins.

Chung, K. S. 2012. The Semantics of the Korean Sentence-final Suffix -*ney*: In Relation to Evidentiality and Mirativity. *Korean Journal of Linguistics* 37(4): 995-1016.

DeLancey, S. 2001. The Mirative and Evidentiality. *Journal of Pragmatics* 33(3): 369-382.

Gardner, R. 2002. *When Listeners Talk: Response Tokens and Listener Stance.* Amsterdam: John Benjamins.

Heritage, J. 2012. Epistemics in Action: Action Formation and Territories of Knowledge. *Research on Language & Social Interaction* 45(1):30-52.

Holt, E. 1996. Reporting on Talk: The Use of Direct Reported Speech in Conversation. *Research on Language and Social Interaction* 29(3): 219-245.

Kim, K. H. & Suh, K. H, 2004. An Analysis of Korean Sentence-ending Suffixes in Caregiver-Child Interaction. *Language Research* 40(1): 923-950.

Kim, M. S. 2014. Reported Thought as a Stance-Taking Device in Korean Conversation. *Discourse Processes* 51(3): 230-263.

Kwon, I. S. 2013. The Semantics of the Korean Sentence-final Suffix *-ney* Revisited: Response to Chung (2012). *Korean Journal of Linguistics* 38(1): 53-66.

Kwon, I. S. 2015. Revisiting the Korean Sentence-final Suffix *-ney* Once More: Response to Chung (2014). *Korean Journal of Linguistics* 40(3): 287-305.

Lee, H. S. 1991. Tense, Aspect, and Modality: A Discoursepragmatic Analysis of Verbal Affixes in Korean from a Typological Perspective. Doctoral dissertation, University of California Los Angeles.

Lee, H. S. 1993. Cognitive Constraints on Expressing Newly Perceived Information, with reference to Epistemic Modal Suffixes in Korean. *Cognitive Linguistics* 4(2): 135-167.

Moon, C. H. 2014. *Hyenday Hankuke Conggyelemi -ney(yo)wa kwun(yo)* [The Sentence-ending Suffix *-ney* and *-kwun* in Korean]. *Language and Linguistics* 64: 83-110.

Park, J. Y. 1999. *Kwuke Yangtay Pemcwuuy Hwaklipkwa Emiuy Uymi Kiswul* [Categorization and Semantic Descriptions of Modal Endings in Korean]. *Journal of Korean Linguistics* 34: 199-225.

Park, M. J. 2003. The Meaning of Korean Prosodic Boundary Tones. Doctoral Dissertation, University of California Los Angeles.

Park, J. H. 2011. *Hankwukeeyse Cungkesengina Uyoysenguy Uymisengpunul Phohamhanun Mwunpeopyoso* [Grammatical Elements Containing Evidential or Mirative Components in Korean]. *Language & Information Society* 15: 1-25.

Pomerantz, A. 1986. Extreme Case Formulations: A Way of Legitimizing Claims. *Human Studies* 9(2-3): 219-229.

Sacks, H., Schegloff, E.A., & Jefferson, G. 1974. A Simplest Systematics for the Organization of Turn-taking for Conversation. *Language* 50: 696-735.

Schegloff, E. A. 1996. Confirming allusions: Toward an empirical account of action. *American Journal of Sociology* 102(1): 161-216.

Sohn, H. M. 1999. *The Korean Language.* Cambridge: Cambridge University Press.

Song, J. M. 2007. *Cungkeseng(Evidentiality)kwa Cwueceyyakuy Yuhyenglon - Hankuwke Mongkole, Thipeyselul Yeylo Tule* [Typology of Evidentiality and Subject Restriction: Based on Korean, Mongolian and Tibetan]. *Morphology* 9(1): 1-23.

Song, J. M. 2014. *Hankwuke 'Cungkeseng' Congkyelemi '-ney' - Cheng Kyeng Swukey Tayhan Taytap* [Evidential Suffix *-ney* in Korean: A Reply to Chung (2007, 2012)]. *Korean Journal of Linguistics* 39(4): 819-850.

Song, J. M. 2015. *Hankwuke Congkyelemi '-ney'uy Uymikinung* [Semantic Functions of the Korean Sentence-Terminal Suffix *-ney*]. *Journal of Korean Linguistics* 76: 123-159.

Strauss, S. 2005. Cognitive Realization Markers in Korean: A Discourse-pragmatic Study of the Sentence-ending Particles *-kwun*, *-ney*, and *-tela*. *Language Sciences* 27: 437-480.

Young, R. F. & Lee, J. 2004. Identifying units in interaction: Reactive tokens in Korean and English conversations. *Journal of Sociolinguistics* 8(3): 380-407.

Abbreviations

ACC	Accusative
ATTR(RL)	(Realis) Attributive
CIRCUM	Circumstantial
COMP	Complementizer
CONN	Connective
DECL	Declarative
DEF	Deferential particle
DISJ	Disjunctive
DM	Discourse marker
HON	Honorific
IE	Informal ending
INTERR	Interrogative
LOC	Locative
NOM	Nominative
PL	Plural
PST	Past suffix
QT	Quotative construction
RESUL	Resultative
RETRO	Retrospective
TOP	Topic marker
UNASSIM	Unassimilated

Poster Session Abstracts

Poster Session Abstracts

For this edition of Japanese/Korean Linguistics proceedings volume, presenters from both the talk and the poster sessions of the conference were invited to contribute a paper for their work. The abstracts by authors from the poster session appear below. The full papers are available on the volume's supplementary webpage at

https://cslipublications.stanford.edu/ja-ko-contents/JK25/

Stancetaking in Korean conversation: *maliya* construction to accomplish intersubjectivity

HYUNJUNG AN
University of Hawaii at Manoa

This study examined the cases of *maliya* (roughly translated as "What I am saying is that") used in indirect quotative constructions. The findings report that *maliya* portrays a speaker's epistemic, affiliative, and disaffiliative stances in different sequential contexts, attempting to accomplish intersubjectivity through negotiation between co-participants. The stance marked by *maliya* differs as to whether the words are quoted in the previous sequence or not, and whose words are quoted in the sequence.

What Can Save Adjuncts?

AKIHIKO ARANO
University of Connecticut

This paper investigates the additional scrambling effect in Japanese, i.e., the fact that long-distance scrambling of 'true adjuncts' improves when accompanied by scrambling of arguments. Taking as a starting point Boeckx and Sugisaki (1999), who argue adjuncts and arguments have to be clause-mate for this effect to arise, I show that the clause-mate condition does not hold when non-finite clauses are involved. I argue that the additional scrambling effect is best accounted for by Koizumi's (2000) vP-fronting approach.

Korean Wh-island Effects in Scrambling Constructions
JUYEON CHO
Seoul National University

In this paper, I investigate the *wh*-island constraints in Korean scrambling constructions. Based on where the *wh*-island effect occurs, I separate *wh*-PF-island and *wh*-LF-island. A grammatical judgement experiment was conducted and the results reveal the existence of island effect with *wh*-LF-island, but not with PF-island. While the speakers generally prefer the interpretation as a direct question, the results accords with Saito (1989) that *wh*-scrambling can be undone at LF.

Raising-to-Subject in Korean: Evidence from Honorific Agreement and NPI Licensing
JINSUN CHOE
Hankuk University of Foreign Studies

This study investigates a purported raising pattern in Korean, using subject honorification and licensing of negative polarity items (NPIs) as diagnostics. The results of a large-scale acceptability task show that participants accept raising sentences in Korean, contrary to reports in the literature, suggesting that Korean does indeed have subject-to-subject raising.

Projection Analysis of the Displacement of *un/nun*
HAN-BYUL CHUNG
University of Hawaii at Manoa / Seoul National University

While Korean contrastive marker '*un/nun*' canonically appears to the immediate right of a contrasted constituent, it may also be embedded within a contrasted constituent. Interestingly, such a displacement is only allowed with heads and arguments but not adjuncts. Based on this, I argue that the displacement occurs as contrastiveness marked by morphological markings may project, similar to how focus marked by phonological markings project in English information focus.

Discourse Effects of Biased Questions in Japanese
HITOMI HIRAYAMA
University of California, Santa Cruz
This paper explores discourse effects of some biased questions in Japanese: outer negation questions, questions with *no(da)* and questions formed by

the combinations of nai and *no(da)*. By characterizing the basic effects of outer negation questions and *no(da)* questions, I argue that the discourse effects of complex biased questions can be derived compositionally, focusing on (un)availability of ambiguous interpretations of negative morpheme nai in certain combinations reported by Ito and Oshima (2014).

Causatives and Inchoatives in Korean: A Unified Account

SUNWOO JEONG
Stanford University

This paper provides a unified semantics for the Korean causative and inchoative suffix *-i*. It argues that the suffix *-i* can sometimes signal causativization of the verb, but other times signal inchoativization of the verb, depending systematically on whether the event associated with the verb stem is standardly construed to be externally caused vs. spontaneously occurring. Building on Grimm's (2012) treatment of the number marking affix in Dagaare, the paper proposes that the affix *-i* signals that the event denoted by the verb is marked and non-canonical along the causal dimension.

A syntactic account of morphological causatives in Japanese and Korean

JINWOO JO
MAI HA VU
University of Delaware

In this paper, we give a purely syntactic analysis of productively formed morphological causatives in Japanese (*-(s)ase*) and Korean (*-Ci*). We propose that *(i) -(s)ase* and *-Ci* are morphological realizations of the head, Caus(e) (a la Pylkkänen, 2008), and that (ii) the similarities and differences between Japanese and Korean (i.e. negation, Binding Condition B, subject-oriented adverbials, and coordination) are due to Japanese *-(s)ase* selecting for TP, and Korean *-Ci* selecting for VoiceP.

Plural Forms in Yoron-Ryukyuan

NOBUKO KIBE
HAJIME OSHIMA
MASAHIRO YAMADA
National Institute for Japanese Language and Linguistics

In Yoron-Ryukyuan, some kinship and human nouns can take either one of the two distinct plural markers. One is -*taa* with no pitch rise; it yields the associative plural reading. The other is -[*taa* with a pitch rise ("["marks pitch rise); it gives non-associative additive plural reading. The split can be accounted for by assuming a noun class with respect to whether the host noun can be used as an address term or not.

Pronoun Interpretation with Referential and Quantificational Antecedents in SLA

EUN HEE KIM
University of Illinois at Urbana-Champaign

This study aims to examine how Korean-speaking learners of English interpret English pronouns with both referential and quantificational antecedents. Results show that they were inaccurate a) in rejecting a pronoun bound by a local referential antecedent and b) in accepting a pronoun bound by a non-local quantificational antecedent. Their non-nativelike performance seems to be attributed to their dispreference to allow a bound variable reading for an overt pronoun in Korean, suggesting a possible L1-transfer effect.

The Syntax of Path/Range PP Constructions in Japanese

RYOICHIRO KOBAYASHI
Aichi University of Technology/Sophia University

This paper investigates the syntax of from-to PPs in Japanese. Different syntactic tests show that two types of from-to PPs must be recognized. I claim that some NP-kara NP-made 'from NP to NP' (FNTN) form an inseparable constituent before they merge to larger structure. I propose a syntactic analysis of the complex PP and other FNTNs in Japanese. It is suggested that the complex PP has parallel structures that share some features with coordinate structure.

A Pragmatic Account of the Relative Readings in Korean Superlatives

SARAH HYEYEON LEE
University of Southern California

I provide novel data on the range of readings available in Korean adnominal superlatives and show that they can only be derived under the In-situ theory of superlative ambiguities (Farkas and Kiss 2000; Sharvit and Stateva 2002), which maintains that -est stays inside the DP. The Scope theory (Heim 1985;

Szabolcsi 1986), which maintains that *-est* stays inside the DP. The Scope theory (Heim 1985; Szabolcsi 1986), however, cannot derive the different readings available in Korean because Korean adnominal modifiers block *-est* movement for the virtue of being relative clauses (M.-J. Kim 2002).

Positioning the Expressions of Recommendation
TOMMY TSZ-MING LEE
University of Southern California
TONY TSZ-FUNG LAU
University of Edinburgh

This paper explores the semantic properties of the expressions of recommendation in Japanese, such as *ba ii* , *tara ii* and *to ii* . We argue that they are a subtype of possibility modals, but differ from the better recognized possibility modal expressions of permission, such as -temo ii, in terms of logical strength. The distinction mirrors an analogous split in necessity modals.

Branching, Kanji, and Accentuation in Sino-Japanese: From a Corpus-based Approach
CHIHKAI LIN
Tatung University

This paper examines accent patterns in Sino-Japanese trimoraic nouns by looking into the number of kanji and internal branching. The results suggest that LHH(H) is pervasive in A+BC with two kanji, and HLL is common in AB +C with two kanji. In three kanji, 80% of the corpus instances are in medial accent. This paper also discusses phonetic variants alternating between LHH(H) and HLL in the corpus.

The Syntax and Semantics of the Japanese Pseudo-Partitive Construction
AKITOSHI MAEDA
Kobe University
YUTO HIRAYAMA
Osaka University / JSPS

This paper argues against Watanabe (2006) that a measure phrase that occurs in the 'floating' position is base-generated in that position. Our claim is supported syntactically (there is a case where a measure phrase is associated with its host NP beyond the boundary of a syntactic island) and semantically (the interpretation of a measure phrase differ according to where it occurs). We further propose the semantic condition of the association of a measure phrase and its host NP. Our proposal will raise the possibility that the association of the two elements is a fully semantic matter.

The Influence of OCP-Place on Word Truncation: A study of Modern Japanese Abbreviation of Compound Loanword Nouns with Long Vowels

CHANGYUN MOON
University of Tsukuba / JSPS

This study discussed influence of OCP-Place on word truncation. We conducted an experiment focusing on the difference in place of articulation. The results are as follows. 1) Sequential labials were avoided more often than sequential dorsal and coronal gestures; 2) The more similar the sequential consonants are, the more likely it is avoided in the output forms; 3) The OCP effect can take place not only within a morpheme but also in the morpheme boundary.

Two Types of Reflexivization in Japanese

TOHRU NOGUCHI
Ochanomizu University

Reinhart and Siloni (2005) argued that reflexive verbs are derived either in the lexicon or in the syntax. This paper shows that reflexive verbs in Japanese can be derived either way: the prefix *zi-* reflexivizes verbs in the lexicon, while *ziko* and *zisin* do so by undergoing SELF movement in the syntax (cf. Reuland 2011). This supports Marelj and Reuland's (2016) general idea that the parameter must be reduced to the availability of syntactic clitics.

Acquisition of V-V and N-N Compounds in Japanese: From the Viewpoint of the Compounding Parameter

REIKO OKABE
Senshu University
MIWA ISOBE
Tokyo University of the Arts

The present study proposes that the availability of verb-verb compounds (VVs) depends on the positive setting of the Compounding Parameter (TCP), based on spontaneous speech data from three Japanese-speaking children.

Specifically, our corpus study elucidates that these children acquire noun-noun compounds (NNs) and VVs at around the same time and proposes that TCP also regulates the availability of VVs, as well as NNs and other complex predicates.

Expectation-Driven Facilitation in Japanese: Its Independence from Distance

HAJIME ONO & MAO SUGI
Tsuda University

We designed an experiment with Japanese interrogative sentences, and show that the expectation-driven facilitation and the locality-driven difficulty are independently observed even when both of the dependencies are simultaneously terminated by the single word (V+ka). In sum, we suggest that the parser handles a dependency with a syntactic wh-feature and that with lexical/semantic information separately, even when they were encoded in the same lexical item.

Semantic Specificity and Syntactic Realization of Japanese and Korean Ideophones

JI YEON PARK
Nagoya University/JSPS Research Fellow

This paper discusses that semantic specification can be applied to the explanation of the syntactic realization of the verbal and adverbial usages: (i) 'quasi-verbal', (ii) 'predicative-verbal', and (iii) 'deideophonized'. The classes of too-high and too-low semantic specificity reveal that (i) and (iii) prohibit verbalization. The 'quasi-verbal' class shows the strong semantic relationship between an ideophone and a host verb. The 'deideophonized' class shows a general information such as the degree and frequency of an event.

On Sentence-final Particle *Sa* in Hokkaido Japanese

SANAE TAMURA
Hokusei Gakuen University
TOSHIO MATSUURA
Hokusei Gakuen University
YOSHIHISA KISHIMOTO
Hokkaido University

Hokkaido Japanese has the sentence-final particle *sa*, which marks hearer-new information (Izutsu & Izutsu 2013) and does not easily attach to an utterance about the hearer (Matsuura & Kishimoto 2016). This paper presents new data about *sa* in directive speech acts and propose that *sa* in Hokkaido Japanese encodes instructions for the hearer, such that there is no need to induce an inference or decide to do any action based on the utterance.

Pseudogapping in Japanese

HIDEHARU TANAKA
Mie University
SHINTARO HAYASHI
Nanzan University

Developing Funakoshi's (2016) claim that pseudogapping is possible in Japanese, we address how different or similar Japanese pseudogapping and English pseudogapping are. We establish that while they are uniformly characterized as movement of the remnant (Move-R) out of VP ellipsis (e.g. Jay-aseelan 1990), Move-R is more restricted in English than in Japanese. We propose to derive this disparity by identifying English Move-R with overt QR (e.g. Johnson 2008) and Japanese Move-R with semantically non-vacuous scrambling.

The Social Meanings and Functions of the Korean Subject Honorific Suffix *-(u)si*

SANG-SEOK YOON
University of Iowa

This paper discusses that the use of *-(u)si* does not always appear following the honorific agreement rule in real conversations. In this study, I argue that the basic function of *-(u)si* is to express the speaker's affective stance of emotional attachment to the addressee in a ritualized way, and it is not a mere politeness marker, but it is used strategically to regulate honorific meaning in Korean conversations.

Index